THE COMPLETE BOOK *of* GREENHOUSE GARDENING

Henry T. Northen
•
Rebecca T. Northen

THE RONALD PRESS COMPANY · NEW YORK

Library of Congress Catalog Card Number: 56-10168

PRINTED IN THE UNITED STATES OF AMERICA

TO

Betty, Philip, and *Tommy*

Preface

Gardening in a greenhouse is a fascinating and engaging hobby, one which is an endless source of pleasure and satisfaction. It can be profitable, too. For those now gardening under glass we have many suggestions for extending your activities and increasing the kinds of plants you can grow throughout the year. For you who do not yet have a greenhouse we have added suggestions for selecting, building, and equipping a greenhouse. While you are waiting for your greenhouse, you will enjoy reading about the great variety of plants that can be grown under glass, and you will find that many of the methods described here may be adapted for growing plants successfully in the home.

Those of you who now own a greenhouse know what we mean when we say that greenhouse gardening is a fascinating and engaging hobby, one that increases in interest as time goes by. Very few, if any, greenhouse growers have lost interest in their hobby. Instead, their interest continually increases. They soon want to try techniques which at first they thought were only for professionals; then they want to try exotic specialty plants, and to have a try at controlling blooming time.

A book on the home greenhouse must therefore present more than the bare essentials. We have strived to make this book comprehensive enough to carry the home gardener along as his hobby develops, to introduce him to new possibilities, new ways of making the most of his space, and to enable him to grow the plants of his choice to perfection.

Progress is being made in greenhouse gardening. New and improved methods are continually being brought into use. We give you these methods in easily understood language.

We have tried to help you select compatible plants for your greenhouse by grouping together plants which grow under similar conditions. First we take up bench and pot plants which thrive in a greenhouse maintained at a night temperature of 50 degrees Fahrenheit. Then we cover kinds which like a night temperature of 60 degrees; these we take up by families. Culturing members of one or several of these famous families makes a wonderful hobby. The beginner may already be interested in one member of a family—for example, African violets—but later his interests might also encompass their relatives. The chapter that includes the African violets also discusses its many gorgeously beautiful relatives, most of which thrive under the same conditions. There are chapters on amaryllis, begonias, bromeliads, cacti and succulents, orchids, philodendrons, and their relatives. Each chapter on a hobby family includes easily understandable directions for growing, as well as interesting information about the plants. We have included not only the usual plants but also some unusual ones.

Selecting illustrations for the space available was a real problem. We had two things in mind. First, we felt it important to show all the necessary steps in the raising of a great variety of plants. These step-by-step photographs will enable the beginner to carry on the operations successfully, and they set this book apart from others. With few exceptions, the how-to-do-it pictures were taken by us, as we went through the stages of growing the plant. Secondly, we wanted to illustrate well-grown specimens of many kinds of plants.

Many of the flower pictures were furnished by friends, and we are grateful for their help. Our requests for illustrations and information met a hearty response. Among those who contributed pictures, information, or both, are: Aluminum Greenhouses, Inc., Antonelli Brothers, George J. Ball Seed Company, Bodger Seed Company, Boyce Thompson Institute, Bromeliad Society, H. M. Butterfield, Cornell University,

Ladislaus Cutak, *Flower Grower,* Mulford B. Foster, A. R. C. Haas, Scott E. Hazelton, *Horticulture,* Hozon Company, Alex Laurie, Lord and Burnham, Missouri Botanical Garden, National Greenhouse Company, New Mexico Agricultural Experiment Station, The New York Botanical Garden, Ohio State University, Pennsylvania State University, *Popular Gardening,* Kenneth Post, A. Earl Pritchard, Purdue University, John Roche, Vaughan's Seed Company, Vetterle and Reinelt Company, Waldor Greenhouses, and Romaine B. Ware. The photograph used for the frontispiece was furnished by Lord and Burnham. To these and others who helped in the preparation of this book we express our gratitude.

Henry T. Northen
Rebecca T. Northen

Laramie, Wyoming
July, 1956

Contents

THE COMPLETE BOOK
of
GREENHOUSE GARDENING

CHAPTER 1

GARDENING UNDER GLASS

SURELY THE ULTIMATE DESIRE of the true gardener is to be able to grow plants the year around. A greenhouse in his own back yard makes this possible. Just to be able to walk into a haven of warmth and color in midwinter, to smell the damp earth and mixed fragrances of flowers, to dig and pot and water and handle green growing things when it is cold and inhospitable outdoors—all this is enough reason for having a greenhouse. But there are many additional reasons, of both practical and esthetic significance, and the things you can do with a greenhouse are many and varied.

A greenhouse widens the scope of gardening, because in it you can control climate. You need no longer be limited in choice of plants to the hardy things or the seasonal varieties that can take the climate in your back yard. The artificial climate of a greenhouse gives you almost unlimited possibilities, for it can be planned to suit the needs of the plants you find appealing.

The control of environment in a greenhouse offers an opportunity to grow plants more nearly to perfection than in the outdoor garden or the home. Winds, heavy rains, hail, and pests make it difficult to raise perfect specimens outdoors. Even though the protected atmosphere of a home allows certain plants to be grown nicely, it is difficult to raise choice specimens of most kinds indoors, where there is little control of temperature, humidity, and light. Pest control is simpler in a greenhouse than it is outdoors because many pests can be excluded.

In a greenhouse you have an intimate relationship with plants, as you follow closely the germination of seeds, the development of roots on cuttings, the formation of flower buds. If you are a camera enthusiast, you will never lack fascinating subject material, for there is beauty in every part of a plant or flower.

If arranging flowers is one of your hobbies, your greenhouse will furnish you with a year-round supply of flowers and attractive foliage. You can also raise a nice selection of potted flowering and foliage plants to bring into your home for decoration. Friends cherish gifts of plants and flowers, especially when you have grown them yourself. Fascinating corsages can be made from your own flowers—kinds not seen in florist shops.

The greenhouse is a wonderful adjunct to the outdoor garden. In it you can start flowers and vegetables, to be set out in the garden when the danger of frost is over. You can grow varieties not readily available from the commercial growers in your locality. In addition to annuals, perennials, and vegetables, you can start evergreens and deciduous trees and shrubs and later plant them in the garden.

Greenhouse growing will be satisfying and interesting if you select varieties carefully. In later chapters we describe and give cultural directions for a great variety of plants. After studying these chapters, select the plants that appeal to you. Perhaps you will decide that you want chrysanthemums as the main feature of the autumn season. These may be followed, for winter and spring flowers, by snapdragons, carnations, stocks, calendulas, pansies, or other companionable plants. These are grown in much the same way that you grow plants in your outdoor garden. They are planted in soil contained in benches, watered as necessary, and grown with full sun and at a night temperature of 50 degrees Fahrenheit. These bench plants will reward you with bright flowers, and they require a minimum of attention and work.

Perhaps you are a specialist at heart and would enjoy centering your interest on the members of one plant family—begonias, orchids, bromeliads, cacti and succulents, or African violets and their relatives. There are many varieties of begonias which can be chosen to give a succession of bloom. Orchids can be a fascinating hobby. There are not only the familiar orchids seen in florist shops, but many others of great charm and beauty in a tremendous variety of shape and color. The members of the pineapple family are called *bromeliads*. Certain members of this exotic family have brilliantly colored and patterned leaves and unusual combinations of colors in the flowers. African violets are well known, but the family Gesneriaceae, to which they belong, also includes episcia, gloxinia, achimenes, the cape primrose, and such less known but beautiful kinds as chirita, columnea, and trichosporum. Certainly, a collection of these plants would be a wonderful hobby, as would, of course, a collection of members of the other families considered in this book.

Your enthusiasm for a hobby plant and its relatives may lead to a fine collection, to a breeding program, and to expert knowledge of the group. You may wish to join a society devoted to your specialty. Societies exist for fanciers of African violets, begonias, bromeliads, cacti and succulents, camellias, chrysanthemums, gloxinias, orchids, and primroses, to name only a few. In addition to greater knowledge about your hobby flowers, these societies will bring you new friends whom you will enjoy because of mutual interest.

Or you may desire more variety than that afforded by one group. Even a specialist usually finds affection to spare for other kinds of plants. A knowledge of the requirements of various varieties will enable you to select those which will grow well together. For example, cattleya orchids, begonias, African violets, gloxinias, certain ferns, and bromeliads grow well with a night temperature of 60 degrees. Individual differences in the matter of shade can be handled easily, so that they can be grown as companions in the same greenhouse. On the other hand, if you plan to maintain a night temperature of 50 degrees you shouldn't select these plants, but instead should perhaps raise carnations, snapdragons, stocks, primroses, cyclamen, geraniums, cymbidium orchids, and other plants with similar requirements.

The cost of a greenhouse and its maintenance is modest compared with the pleasure one gets from it. A small greenhouse will cost no more than a terrace or even an elaborate outdoor fireplace, but it will afford greater opportunity for activity and interest.

Of course, the greenhouse—like any structure—requires an outlay for upkeep, and heating a greenhouse will add to your fuel bills. The cost of fuel varies with the size of the greenhouse, the climate of your region, and the temperature at which the greenhouse is maintained. It costs about twice as much to keep a night temperature of 60 degrees as one of 50. The saving in fuel is due both to the lower night temperature and to the length of the heating season.

Most of us operate our greenhouses chiefly for fun, rather than for profit. But at times we may have a surplus of plants and flowers which are in demand. We have made our own greenhouse more than pay its way by selling surplus orchid blooms to local florists. Other small growers have found that gloxinias, begonias, African violets, cinerarias, cyclamen, and other plants are in demand and bring a good price. Although we prefer to deal with florists, others have found that supermarkets and dime stores are good outlets for those plants which they wish to sell. In any community there is a strong demand for plants to set out in gardens during the spring. If you are planning your greenhouse only for profit, study market conditions thoroughly to guide you in what to raise.

To obtain the greatest satisfaction from a greenhouse you should consider carefully its selection and building. Secure one that is durable and that requires a minimum of upkeep.

If you become familiar with the principles of greenhouse management, you will be able to raise plants successfully. Then you can select those plants which are good companions and which have special appeal, and you can grow an assortment of plants which will insure color and interest during all seasons of the year.

CHAPTER 2

SELECTING AND BUILDING YOUR GREENHOUSE

SELECTING AND BUILDING a greenhouse is truly an adventure. You will be more satisfied with the end result if you consider carefully the variety of greenhouses available before making a choice. Visit the greenhouses in your community. Talk with the owners and get their opinions of the kinds they have. Study the various types of greenhouse and learn how easy or how difficult they are to build. Look at the foundations, the walks, the arrangement and construction of the benches, and make notes about the desirable and undesirable features of each. In each greenhouse you visit, inspect the heating system and inquire about cost, operating expenses, reliability, and other features.

Write to greenhouse companies for literature. (A number of greenhouse companies advertise in *Flower Grower, Popular Gardening,* and other gardening magazines which are available at newsstands or at your library; from these ads you can secure addresses.) Greenhouse manufacturers are featuring small greenhouses of excellent design, which are more attractive, less expensive, and more serviceable than those available a few years ago. The modern aluminum greenhouses have many desirable features. They do not require painting and there is nothing to rust or rot. Of course, aluminum greenhouses are more expensive than wooden ones. If your budget is limited, a good wooden greenhouse will give you many years of satisfaction. There are also greenhouses that have a supporting structure of steel but sash bars of wood. These, too, are very satisfactory.

If wooden greenhouses are protected with paint they will last a lifetime. The woodwork should be given a primary coat at the factory, consisting of pure linseed oil with a small amount of white lead. As soon as the framework is erected, and before glazing, paint the framework inside and outside with a paint consisting of white lead, linseed oil, and zinc oxide. Apply another coat after the greenhouse has been glazed. Red lead paint is best for the first coat on steel, which should be hot-galvanized. White lead paint should be used for the second and third coats. The outside of a greenhouse should be repainted every other year, the inside every four or five years.

Types and styles

Several types and styles of greenhouse are available. You can select a breezeway type, a lean-to model, a free-standing even-span greenhouse, or an even-span greenhouse to be attached to a building. Even-span greenhouses are symmetrical, with the two sides of the roof equal in length from the ridge to the eaves. They are adaptable to almost any location and are preferable to uneven-span greenhouses for the home owner. An uneven-span greenhouse runs east and west and the side of the roof toward the south is wider than that facing north.

The greenhouse may have vertical sides or slanting ones, and the eaves may be curved or straight. Greenhouses with curved eaves are reminiscent of the old "conservatory" and appeal to many people, but are more expensive. The straight-eaved greenhouse is the usual type, and is more economical from the point of view of glass replacement. These various kinds of greenhouse are prefabricated. All the parts will come cut to fit, and you need only assemble them according to the directions furnished. All the fastenings are supplied, down to the last nut and bolt. Glass, putty if necessary, glass clips, and other items come with the order, as do foundation plans and assembly plans.

In certain types of wooden and aluminum greenhouses the panes of glass are overlapped about an eighth of an inch, and the edges of the glass rest on a bed of putty or some other

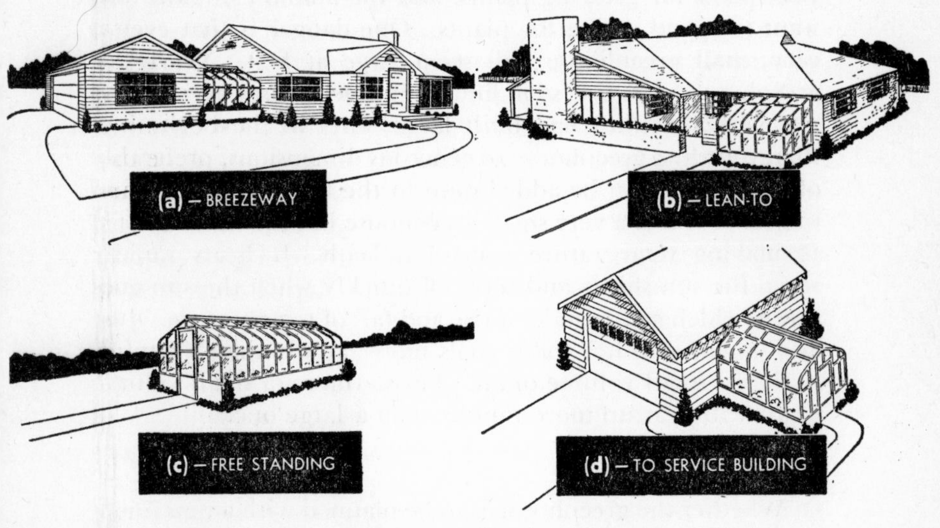

Different styles of greenhouse. (Aluminum Greenhouses, Inc.)

glazing compound. If the sash bars are made of aluminum, the glass is held securely in place by specially designed clips. These clips facilitate assembly and glass replacement. If the sash bars are made of wood, glazing nails are used to keep the glass in place, one directly below the lower edge of the glass on each side to keep the glass from sliding down, one on each side 2 inches from the lower end of the pane, and one on each side at about the middle.

The Orlyt aluminum greenhouses have large panes of glass, the edges of which rest in a rubber channel. The glass is held in place by pressure of an aluminum barcap fastened to the sash bars on the outside. No putty is necessary.

The greenhouse you select should have ample ventilation, preferably on both sides of the ridge. Side ventilators are also desirable. Ventilation may be made automatic by the installation of a thermostat which controls a motor that opens and closes the ventilator. This is a great convenience to anyone who is likely to be away during the day.

Obtain a greenhouse of a size that will fit your budget, your plans for growing plants, and the amount of time you want to spend caring for plants. One danger is that even a very small greenhouse will seem large at first. Nearly all greenhouse hobbyists soon find their greenhouses overflowing and wish that they had built larger ones in the beginning. Plan your first greenhouse of generous dimensions, preferably of a type that can be added onto in the future. In addition to lack of space, a very small greenhouse has the disadvantage of making temperature control difficult. It heats rapidly when the sun shines and cools off quickly when the sun goes down, which causes sudden rise and fall of temperature. Just as a spoonful of hot coffee cools more rapidly than a cupful, so does a small volume of air. Furthermore, a small volume of air will heat up more rapidly than a large one.

Location

Whether the greenhouse is to be planned with a new home or is to be built at an already existing residence, locate it where it will receive an abundance of light through the day. Ideally, the location should be such that the south, east, and west rays of the sun are not cut off. Don't build the greenhouse under or too close to trees, even small ones. Remember that the trees will grow large and that you will be using the greenhouse for many years.

It is best to have the floor of the greenhouse at ground level. If the floor is much below ground level drainage may be poor, and if rains are heavy the greenhouse may be flooded. If the floor of the greenhouse is several feet below ground level, the greenhouse may be too damp, and it may be difficult to heat it uniformly. Furthermore, nearby buildings, trees, and shrubs may shade it excessively.

If your home is on the south side of the street, you should not have any problem in locating the greenhouse in an open place in the back yard. If your residence is on the north side, place the greenhouse toward the very back of the yard, out of the winter shadow of the house. If you want an attached greenhouse, it is better to locate it on the south or east side of the residence than on the north or west side. The great benefit of a south exposure is that it affords more sun in the winter. A greenhouse on the east side should be placed to take advantage of the sun from the south in winter. In a greenhouse that receives sun for only half a day, shade-loving plants would thrive, but sun-loving plants might not do their best. A *small* greenhouse on the west side can become very hot in the summer and must often have heavier shade than is good for the plants. The point to keep in mind is to locate a greenhouse where it will receive the most hours of light each day, and plan to use seasonal shading on the glass when necessary.

If possible, locate the greenhouse where it will harmonize with the garden and architectural features. If you are planning to build a new home, have the architect incorporate the greenhouse in the plans. Supply him with the plans and the information that you have obtained from the greenhouse manufacturer, and insist that the greenhouse be situated where there is good light. In general, a greenhouse fabricated by a reliable company is better, and, of course, less expensive, than a custom-made one.

Foundations

As with any permanent building, a good foundation is important and determines to a large extent the durability of the structure. Generally you will have to construct the foundation for the greenhouse; that is, the foundation does not come with the greenhouse. But don't start until you receive detailed specifications from the greenhouse manufacturer. Never rely on the pictures which illustrate the manufacturer's advertisement, for these do not show such things as sill structure and bolts to fasten the framework to the sill.

Before you start on the foundation, lay out the walks and plan the footings for the benches. If you intend to use gravel under the benches, haul it to the proper place before the foundation goes up. Also plan the water supply. We will have more to say about paths, benches, and water later.

Many of the conventional greenhouses are supported by metal posts that rest on concrete footings. The posts and columns, not the walls, support this type of greenhouse. The footings should extend below the frost line, generally about 2½ feet below ground level in the northern states, and should be on solid ground. The walls may be of concrete, 4 inches thick and extending about 4 inches below ground level, or may be constructed of bricks, cut stone, concrete blocks, cinder blocks, or stuccoed tile, resting on a concrete footing.

Many of the hobby-size greenhouses do not have posts and columns for support. The weight rests on the foundation wall, which must therefore be sturdy. A greenhouse sill of special design is fastened to the top of the wall, and to this sill the greenhouse is secured. Concrete walls 8 inches thick and extending below frost level are strong and durable. If you prefer brick or concrete blocks, lay them on a base of poured concrete. If you plan to move from your residence in five years or so and do not want a permanent greenhouse, you can build the foundation of wood. However, for a permanent greenhouse, we do not recommend wood for constructing the foundation, because in a few years the posts will rot and the greenhouse will sag.

Walks

The walks may be of concrete, flagstone, or brick. The concrete may be colored if desired. Flagstones or bricks laid on a cement base and pointed up with mortar are attractive and serviceable. The width of the walk depends on a number of factors—the types of plants grown, the width of the greenhouse, the size and arrangement of the benches, and the owner's desires. Two feet is a good average width. The walks should be higher than the floor; this makes it easy to hose them clean without leaving puddles of water or mud to soil the shoes. Do not have a full concrete slab for the floor. The atmosphere in the greenhouse will be more moist if sand, soil, or gravel is used under the benches instead of concrete, which dries quickly after it is sprinkled.

Benches

The greenhouse company will suggest bench arrangements for the greenhouse you purchase; some companies sell prefabricated benches. Benches are built from 24 to 36 inches high. The usual height of benches in commercial greenhouses is 30 inches. In your own greenhouse you should consider a number of factors before deciding on the bench height. A bench which suits a short person may be uncomfortable for a tall one. The height of the greenhouse to the eaves should also be considered in deciding on the height of the benches, as should the kinds of plants which are to be grown. Some plants—snapdragons, roses and carnations, for example—need a lot of head room; African violets, gloxinias and plants of similar habit require only a small amount. If the benches are high and the roof low the former plants may touch the glass whereas the latter ones would not. You may wish to use stepped-up benches to display your plants better. The basic height might be two feet, with three shelves, one on each side of the bench and the third running down the middle. The two side shelves should be about 5 inches above the bench and the center one about 10 inches.

The supports for the bed of the bench may be constructed of concrete, angle iron, pipe, or wood. The pipe or wood should rest on concrete footings, or on bricks or concrete blocks.

The bench itself may be made of aluminum, wood, concrete, transite (an asbestos and concrete mixture), or heavily galvanized wire mesh (called *hardware cloth*) of half-inch mesh, or better still, of quarter-inch mesh. For wooden benches, pecky cypress and redwood are preferred because they outlast other woods many times over. If other kinds of wood are used, they should be treated with preservatives such as Cuprinol or Kopex. Do not use creosote. Creosote is injurious to plants. Many orchid growers prefer benches made of hardware cloth, which provides perfect drainage and few places for slugs and insects to breed. Such benches are also splendid fo other pot plants, such as African violets, gloxinias, cyclamen, and cineraria. If wood, aluminum, transite, or concrete is used, make sure that there is good drainage.

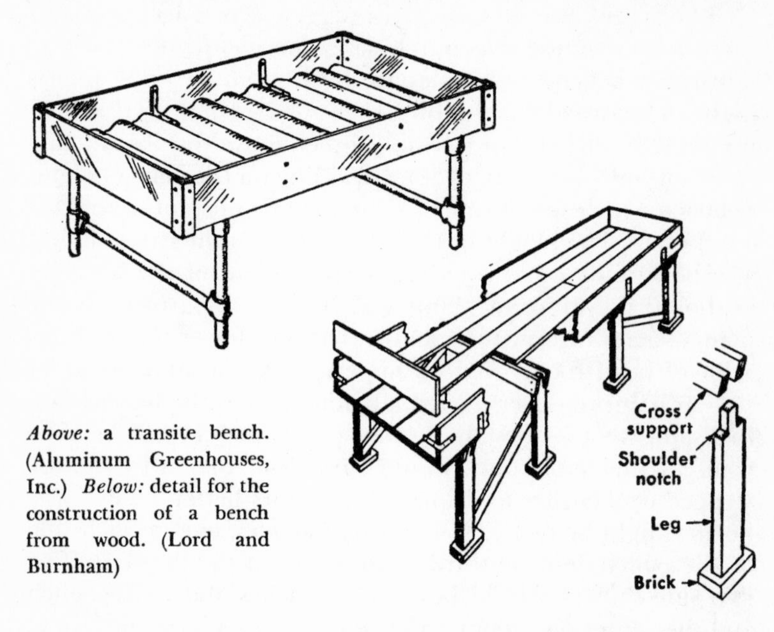

Above: a transite bench. (Aluminum Greenhouses, Inc.) *Below:* detail for the construction of a bench from wood. (Lord and Burnham)

Leave spaces between boards or pieces of transite, punch holes in the corrugated aluminum, or use molds for the concrete which leave holes in the finished piece. Even with such precautions for drainage it is wise to cover the bench with an inch of gravel to insure drainage. Potted plants are set on the gravel. When the bench is to be filled with soil, the gravel is laid down first. If you are going to raise plants in soil-filled benches, the benches should have sides 6 inches high.

If you plan to raise plants without soil (see p. 57), or if you plan to use a system for watering plants automatically (see p. 31), you will need to construct a waterproof bench, preferably with a V-shaped bottom (see pages 31 and 33).

Such a bench may be constructed of concrete, steel, or wood lined with vinyl plastic. Concrete and steel should be painted on the inside with horticultural asphalt to prevent possible injury to plants from toxic substances dissolved from the material of which the bench is constructed.

Heating

For your own safety, and for a dependable supply of heat, secure plans for a heating system from a reliable firm. The company from which you buy your greenhouse will probably design and sell a heating system for the greenhouse. Of course, you will have to tell them what kind of fuel is least expensive in your locality (*artificial* gas should never be used in a greenhouse; it is extremely poisonous to plant life), the temperature at which you are going to run the greenhouse, and the lowest temperatures expected in your locality. Your pocketbook probably will be a deciding factor, but the cheapest method is not always the most economical. For several years we used the least expensive method available, open-flame unvented natural gas heaters that cost about $20 each. Natural gas is inexpensive in our locality. The plants themselves seemed healthy, but during very cold weather when the ventilators were closed tight we noted injury to cattleya flowers from fumes resulting from incomplete combustion. Also, since these open-flame heaters did not have an automatic shut-off valve, the greenhouse became filled with gas when we accidentally put out the flame while watering. Fortunately, no explosion occurred and the natural gas did not injure our plants. Because of these dangers we replaced the unvented heaters with vented ones equipped with a pilot, an automatic shut-off valve, and a reliable thermostat. These heaters have been fairly satisfactory, and flowers have been of much better quality. There is still a danger with these heaters when the pilots are occasionally blown out in gusty weather. To guard against undue fall and rise of temperature we have an alarm which sounds a warning in the house when the temperature drops below the setting in cold weather or when the greenhouse becomes too hot in summer.

We are looking forward to the time when we will have hot water heat in our greenhouse. A hot-water system with gravity flow or forced flow is ideal, and when properly installed it is safe and furnishes a gentle heat. Furthermore, the

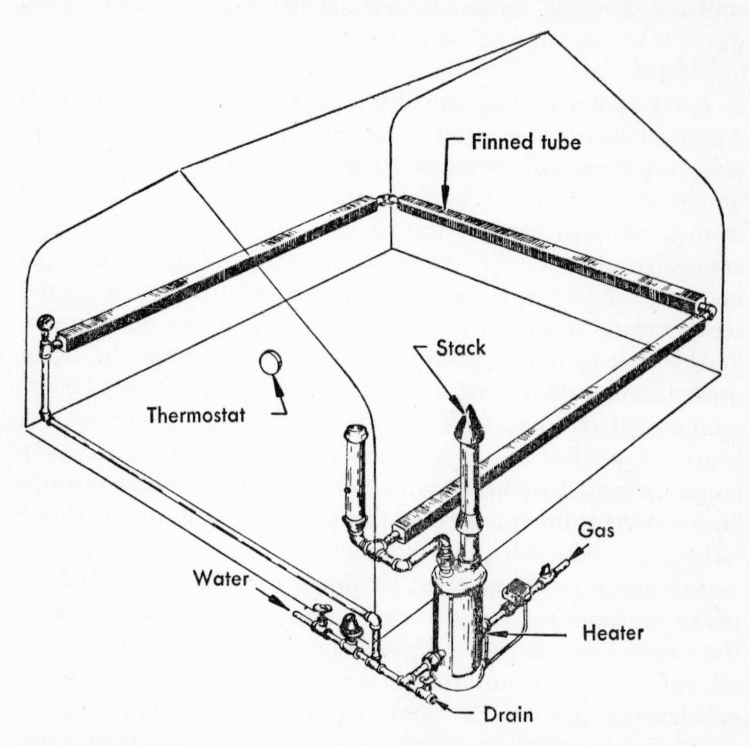

This automatic heating system uses a copper coil heater and finned tubes for radiators. The system includes all safety devices, such as relief valve and automatic pilot, to comply with strictest heating codes. (Aluminum Greenhouses, Inc.)

temperature in the greenhouse is quite uniform because the pipes remain warm for some time after the fire is out. The hot water is conducted from the boiler to the radiating surfaces, which may be two-inch wrought iron pipes or finned tubes. Finned tubes are better radiators than wrought iron pipes and one line of them is equal to about four lines of 2-inch hot-water pipe. For a small greenhouse, the radiating surfaces should be set at the sides of the greenhouse. The pipes or finned tubes should be 2 or 3 inches away from the wall and a similar distance above the floor. The flow of hot water through the radiating pipes can be accelerated by installing a circulator propellor, or a pump, in the system. If a circulator is used, less radiating surface will be needed. The fuel for the boiler may be coal, oil, bottled gas, or gas. A coal-burning boiler should never be set inside the greenhouse, nor should one using artificial gas, because the fumes from these fuels are detrimental to plant life. When coal or artificial gas is used, the heater should be in a structure separate from the greenhouse. Properly constructed and vented boilers using natural gas or oil may be placed in the greenhouse. Oil heaters should have a high flue or an induced-draft fan and vent pipe. A gas heater requires a vent pipe with a top only slightly higher than the greenhouse ridge. A heating specialist or the greenhouse manufacturer will help you determine the size of boiler, the amount of radiating surface needed, and the best placement of the boiler and the radiating surfaces.

Some owners of small greenhouses have found that an ordinary hot-water heater can be used instead of a boiler to heat the water. They connect either finned tube or ordinary pipe to the hot-water heater and install a water storage and expansion tank in the system. Unless you are thoroughly familiar with heating systems, you had better secure expert advice and assistance in installing such a system.

If your home has a hot-water heating system, a heating engineer can devise a means to attach the boiler to finned tube radiating surfaces in the greenhouse, provided, of course, that the boiler can carry the extra load, and he will plan it so that a thermostat controls a circulator pump. If you have a steam boiler of ample capacity, a heating specialist can plan a dual system which uses steam heat, as usual, for your residence, and circulating hot water for the greenhouse.

A hot-air heating system may be extended into the greenhouse if the greenhouse is close to the residence, not over 50 feet away at the most. Warm air supply and cold air return ducts are run from the furnace to the greenhouse. The burner controls must be rewired so the burner will go on if either the thermostat in the house or in the greenhouse calls for heat. The greenhouse thermostat not only controls the burner but is also wired to control motorized dampers in the ducts leading to the greenhouse or to control a blower fan located in the greenhouse. If motorized dampers are used to open and close the ducts leading to the greenhouse, it will be necessary also to install motorized dampers in the ducts leading to the residence. There are certain disadvantages to such a hot-air system which should be considered before it is decided upon. With hot air it is difficult to get uniform heat throughout the greenhouse, and the temperature is not likely to be even. The temperature will go up quickly as the hot air enters the greenhouse, and will drop quite suddenly when the flow is shut off. Furthermore, the air is likely to be dry, and this does not favor vigorous plant growth.

In regions in which winters are mild, electric heaters are often feasible. For example, a hobbyist in Birmingham, Alabama, uses electricity to maintain his 15 x 10-foot greenhouse at a night temperature of 50 degrees, and he reports that the electricity costs $30 a year. In regions in which winters are cold, electric heating is likely to be very expensive. In Burlington, Vermont, it costs about $150 a year to heat a greenhouse 9 feet square to a temperature of 60 degrees at night. Electric heaters equipped with thermostats and fans to circulate the heat are available. They require a separate electric line from the fuse box and should be installed by an electrician.

We have just seen that heating by electricity is expensive in cold localities. How about the cost of other fuels? The table on page 20 has been taken from a booklet on Orlyt Greenhouses, published by Lord and Burnham. The table was compiled from answers furnished to *Flower Grower* by owners of home greenhouses.

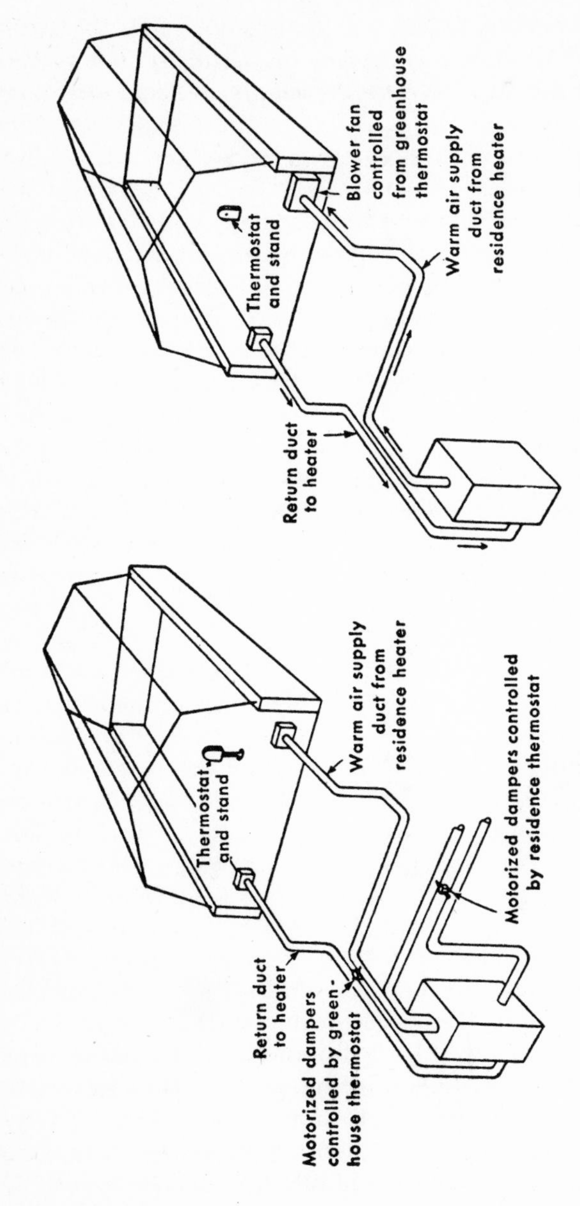

Hot air from the residence can be used to heat the greenhouse. The thermostat in the left greenhouse controls motorized dampers. The thermostat shown in the right sketch controls a blower fan. With both plans the thermostats also are wired to control the furnace. (Lord and Burnham)

City and State	*Size of Greenhouse*	*Annual Heating Cost:* Oil	Gas	Elec.	*Greenhouse Temp.* Cool	Warm
Birmingham, Ala.	10 x 15			$30	x	
Stephens, Ark.	15 x 24		$30			x
Trumbull, Conn.	10 x 21	$75				x
Westminster, Colo.	16 x 27		50			x
Winter Park, Fla.	8 x 15			50		x
Griffin, Ga.	16 x 26		40			x
Moline, Ill.	8 x 12		30			x
Mundelein, Ill.	10 x 18		30			x
Wilmette, Ill.	9 x 18	50				x
Indianapolis, Ind.	10 x 24	100				x
Loyal, Ky.	10 x 18		75			x
Farmington, Me.	13 x 16	80				x
Frederick, Md.	12 x 26	60				x
Springfield, Mass.	14 x 18	75			x	
Ann Arbor, Mich.	15 x 28	100				x
Kirkwood, Mo.	14 x 14		80			x
Plymouth, N. H.	13 x 16	60				x
Stratford, N. J.	10 x 11		100		x	
Westmont, N. J.	9 x 15	50			x	
Schenectady, N. Y.	10 x 20	80				x
Canton, O.	16 x 32		100			x
Minco, Okla.	11 x 30		70			x
Altoona, Pa.	9 x 11		25			x
Pittsburgh, Pa.	9 x 15		65			x
Parkesburg, Pa.	10 x 22	30			x	
Providence, R. I.	11 x 14	80				x
Memphis, Tenn.	8 x 16		30			x
Corpus Christi, Tex.	13 x 20		30			x
Burlington, Vt.	9 x 9			150		x
Eau Claire, Wis.	11 x 14	150				x

In general, it costs about twice as much to heat a greenhouse to a temperature of 60 degrees at night as it does to a level of 50 degrees. The saving in fuel is due partly to the difference in night temperature and partly to the shorter heating season necessary for "cool" crops.

If your greenhouse is 20 or more feet long, you may install a partition of glass to provide one area for warmth-loving plants and a different one for cool-loving plants. Naturally,

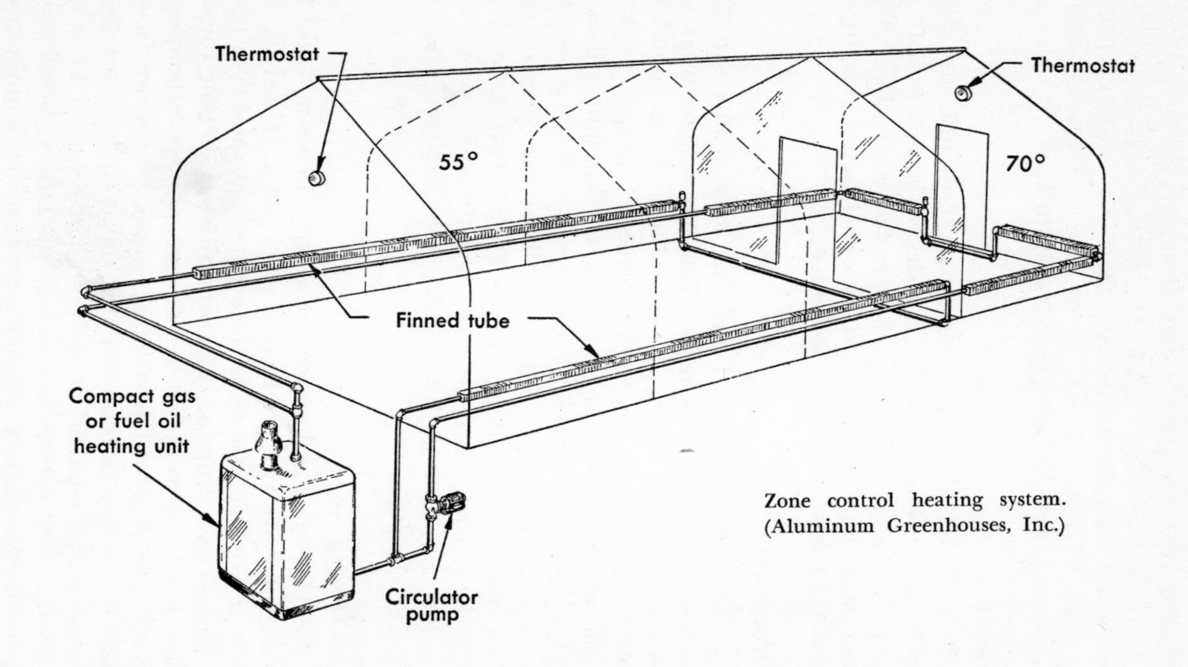

Zone control heating system. (Aluminum Greenhouses, Inc.)

the warm part will require more heat than the cool part and you should plan accordingly. An ideal arrangement would be to have one area maintained at a night temperature of 50° and the other at 60°. With this combination a great variety of plants can be grown successfully.

Water

You should pipe water into the greenhouse and locate faucets at convenient places. It is desirable to have both hot and cold water piped in, and a mixing faucet installed. Many plants do not thrive if watered with cold water. Ideally, the water used should be about 60 degrees.

Humidity

In dry regions you will find that most plants will grow better if you keep the air moist. You may wish to install mist sprayers under the bench, or a humidifier. Some humidifiers come equipped with automatic controls. When the humidity of the air drops below the set value, the humidifier goes on. Although a humidifier is a convenience, it is not a necessity. Many amateur owners, and practically all commercial greenhouse operators, get along without them. They keep the air moist by wetting down the walks and the ground under the benches, and at times by spraying water on the plants and between the pots.

Electricity

Electric lights and outlets are a convenience and will add to the pleasure you get from a greenhouse. Good lighting makes it possible to work in the evenings, or show your plants to friends who drop in. By artificially lengthening the days with electric lights the growth of some plants can be speeded up and the time of flowering of certain plants can be controlled. Electricity is needed for the automatic control of humidity and ventilation and may also be used for power spraying. Perhaps you will want to plug in a radio and listen to a football game or a symphony while working in the greenhouse.

The greenhouse at the top, an Everlite Aluminum Curved Eave Greenhouse, was erected on the roof of a high school. Installed in this house is a hot water heating system consisting of gas heater vented to the outside, fin tube radiators, thermostat, and so forth. The benches are of transite. (Aluminum Greenhouses, Inc.) *Below:* a free-standing aluminum Orlyt greenhouse. (Lord and Burnham)

The Everlite Curved Eave Lean-to above has been fitted neatly to the residence. (Aluminum Greenhouses, Inc.) *Below:* a good potting room with a supply of soil, fertilizers, tools, and other equipment facilitates greenhouse work. Oil drums of soil, sand, and leaf mold are set on dollies so they may be moved about easily. (Roche photo)

Above: cyclamen grows and flowers best at a night temperature of 50 degrees Fahrenheit The plants shown (from left) were grown at night temperatures of 50, 60, and 70 respectively. *Below:* didiscus flowers profusely at a 60-degree night temperature, but not at 50. (Kenneth Post and Cornell University.) *Center:* plants become tall and spindly when grown in weak light, and often do not flower. The gloxinia on the left was grown in deep shade, the one on the right with good light.

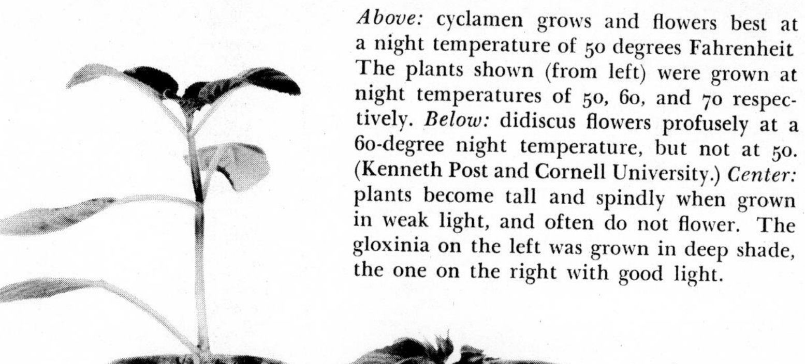

Lath frames, *above,* provide shade and are quite attractive. (Lord and Burnham) *Right:* a temperature alarm is almost indispensable. Here you see one set to ring an alarm when the temperature drops to 45 degrees or rises to 80. *Below:* used for orchid growing, this greenhouse is shaded with Alumalath, which is long-lasting and neat. Notice that the benches are constructed of hardware cloth. (Horto Corp.)

Minute seeds may be mixed with fine sand (*above, left*) to aid in getting an even distribution. After the seeds are sown, cover with a piece of glass. A cork was inserted into the drainage hole of the small pot in the center; the pot is filled with water, which moves into the surrounding soil. *Below, left:* covering marigold seeds, which were sown on soil, with vermiculite. An even stand of seedlings two weeks later is shown to the right.

Potbound plants benefit from periodic applications of fertilizer. A scant quarter-teaspoon of fertilizer (for a 4-inch pot) is added to the soil surface, keeping it away from the stem and foliage. The fertilizer is worked into the upper quarter-inch of soil with a wooden label, then the plant is watered.

Workroom

A heated workroom, connected to the greenhouse, preferably on the north side, will enable you to be comfortable and will permit you to pot, sow seeds, plant bulbs, make cuttings, and carry on other activities even when the outdoor temperature is below freezing. In the workroom you will want bins for the storage of soil, sand, peat, pots, and tools, as well as cupboards *with locks* for the storage of insecticides and fungicides. Certain cupboards may be reserved for the storage of seeds, tools, labels, and supplies.

You will certainly need a potting bench. The space under this bench may well be separated into compartments for the storage of soil and pots.

Those of us who do not have a workroom can do many of the jobs in the greenhouse by means of a portable potting table. The garage may be used for storage of soil, insecticides, and tools. The portable potting table is made somewhat wider than the walk, and rests across the walk on the edges of two benches. It should have the back and ends built up to keep soil from spilling out. A board across the front is also useful, although it may make potting a little more tiring. When potting, always have a receptacle nearby to receive old soil, dead leaves, and the like.

Cold frames

A *cold frame* is a useful adjunct to a greenhouse and has many uses. It is an excellent place to store hardy bulbs which are planted in the fall and to store potted roses and hydrangeas until it is time to bring them into the greenhouse. Certain plants, such as azaleas and cyclamen, grow better during the hot summer months in a shaded cold frame than they do in a greenhouse. A cold frame is a desirable intermediary between the greenhouse and the outdoor garden during late spring. Before plants are moved from the greenhouse to the garden they should be inured gradually to the outdoor environment by keeping the plants in a cold frame for about two weeks before planting them in the garden.

A cold frame consists of a frame and a cover. The frame may be constructed of wood, concrete, brick, cinder blocks, or concrete blocks. It may be 24 to 36 inches high on the north or west side and lower on the south or east side. Ideally, a cold frame would run from east to west. The length and width of the frame is best made to accommodate a standard sash, which is 3 by 6 feet. However, hotbed sashes—3 by 3 and 2 by 4 feet—are also available from certain manufacturers.

Many substitutes for glass are available as coverings for cold frames. Compared with glass, the light-transmitting capacity of some substitutes is relatively low. For plants that prefer full sun this is undesirable, but for shade-loving plants it is all right. The glass substitutes are easily fastened to light-weight sashes, which are convenient to handle. The substitutes are relatively short-lived as, of course, is glass unless it is carefully handled. With any type of covering, provide some means to anchor the sashes so they will not be blown off by strong winds. A rope extending over the sash from one end of the frame to the other and anchored at each end is suitable. Or the sashes may be fastened at the tall end with hinges and secured at the other end with hooks and eyes. With the latter construction, ventilation is provided by propping up the lower end. Sashes which are not hinged may be propped up at one end or they may be slid up or down to provide ventilation.

During very cold weather the cold frame may be protected with straw mats, wooden shutters, or similar materials to moderate the temperature.

Hotbeds

If a frame is heated we call it a *hotbed*. Hotbeds may be heated by manure or by electricity. A manure-heated hotbed is made by digging a pit 12 to 18 inches deep, walling it with planks, bricks, or cinder blocks, and setting the frame on the walls. The pit is filled with fresh horse manure to a depth of 12 to 18 inches and then the manure is covered with 4 inches of soil. For a time the hotbed will be too warm for

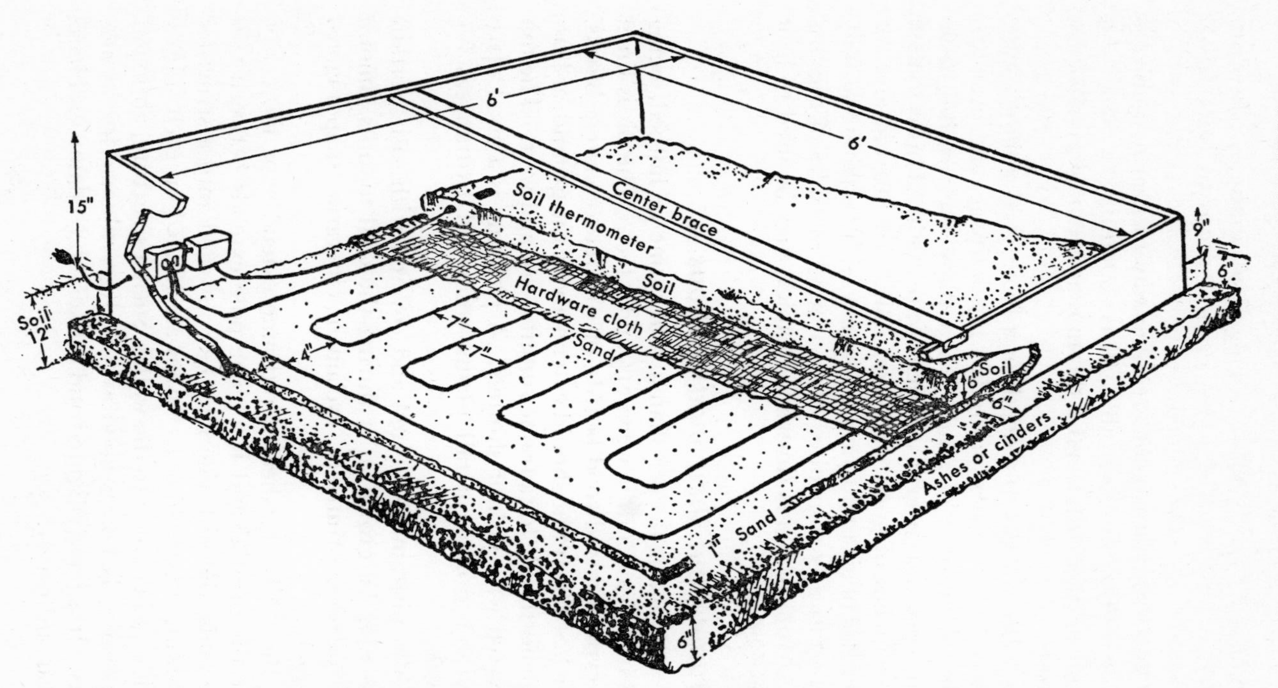

A hotbed is a useful adjunct to the greenhouse. (*Flower Grower*)

good plant growth. Before placing plants in the bed or planting seeds, wait until the temperature drops to the desired level.

A more convenient and reliable way to heat a hotbed is with an electric heating cable. Kits containing flexible lead-covered heating wires and a thermostat are now available at low cost.

Excavate the pit to a depth of a foot. Add a 6-inch layer of coarse gravel, ashes, or cinders for drainage, and over this put a 1-inch layer of sand. Then place the heating cable on this sand and cover it with hardware cloth. This is topped with 6 inches of good soil. For additional heating and for the control of air temperature you may wish to string a second, thermostatically controlled cable around the sides of the hotbed. Banks of lights (instead of cables) may be used to heat the hotbed.

Pitframes and their modifications

A *pitframe* is deeper than a cold frame or hotbed, being excavated to a depth beween 2½ and 4 feet. The pit is lined with cypress or redwood boards, or concrete, concrete blocks, or brick. The frame should extend above the ground, at least on the north side for a frame running east and west. The top is covered with sash or shutters. A pitframe is a good place for winter storage of tall plants—roses and hydrangeas for example.

If the pitframe is heated and covered with sash, certain plants may be grown in it during the cold months, among them pansies, primroses, cyclamen, cineraria, snapdragons, and stocks.

If the walls of a heated pitframe extend 2 or more feet above the ground and if a ridge pole extends between two gable ends, the pitframe may be converted into a structure resembling a greenhouse. Sashes are hinged on each side of the ridge and extend to the walls. Such a structure, although inexpensive, is not as good as a real greenhouse for raising plants. It is poorly lighted and is likely to be damp and hard to heat uniformly.

CHAPTER 3

MANAGING YOUR GREENHOUSE

YOU CAN RAISE fine plants in your greenhouse by furnishing them a balanced environment for their growth, development, and flowering. Your plants need water, a suitable relative humidity, air, minerals from the soil, the right amount of light, and a temperature suitable for the variety.

Watering plants

Even though all other environmental conditions are ideal, plants won't grow well without a sufficient supply of water. Without water in the soil, minerals cannot be absorbed and conducted throughout the plant. When water is lacking, food manufacture ceases. Without an adequate food supply, plants can't grow, flower, and fruit. Furthermore, water is directly necessary for growth. When water is lacking, cells do not divide and increase in size. When plants wilt, growth ceases. That plants should be watered before they wilt is evident. There are many plants that do not wilt when water is deficient, such as orchids, bromeliads, some geraniums, kalanchoë, the Christmas cactus, and others. These just cease to grow and to make food. During drought, part of the root system may die. If this happens, it may take some time for the plants to grow vigorously again after watering. Drought may also result in the development of slender woody stems which cannot conduct water quickly. Such hardened plants may not develop into specimens even though they are later given good care. For most plants, there should be no check in development, but instead they should be kept growing continuously.

Skill in watering is one of the requirements for successful plant culture. For most plants it is best to apply water directly into the pots or in the bench rather than to spray overhead. At each watering, give the plants sufficient water to moisten the soil from the top to the bottom, but be careful not to use such force as to wash away the soil. A water breaker attached to the end of the hose will lessen the force. After watering let the soil dry somewhat before watering again. Plants such as cinerarias, hydrangeas, and acalypha use large amounts of water and therefore require frequent waterings, whereas cattleya orchids and cyclamen use water sparingly and require less frequent applications. Plants do not thrive if the soil is kept wet continuously. Both water and air must be present in the soil if plants are to grow. If the soil is constantly saturated, there will not be enough air.

During the warmer months of the year many plants, but not all, may require water daily; but during cold, cloudy weather several days may elapse between waterings. There are a number of ways to tell whether or not plants need watering: by tapping the pots, by the color and feel of the soil, and by the weight of the pots. If you tap a pot and hear a dull sound, the soil is moist and the plant does not need watering. If you hear a dry ringing sound, water the plant. If the soil is dark it still has available moisture; if light in color, the soil

The water breaker and watering can are for watering, the mist nozzle for syringing. (*Popular Gardening*)

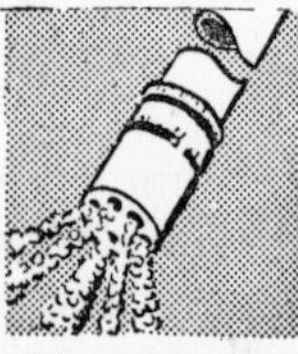
Water breaker

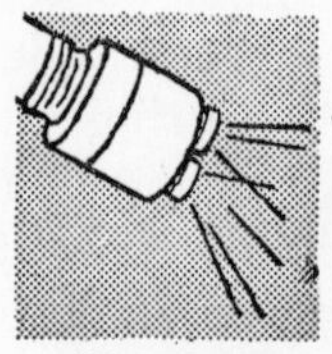
Mist nozzle

Watering can

is dry. Many growers lift a pot here and there and decide by weight whether or not the plants require watering.

Determining when to water bench plants is not so simple. You cannot rely entirely on the appearance of the upper layer of soil because during winter, when heat is on, the soil may dry from the bottom of the bench upward. To determine whether or not the soil is dry insert a clean trowel or bamboo cane in the soil. If they are hard to insert, make a grating sound, and come out clean and free of soil particles, the soil is dry and should be watered. Soil tensiometers may be used to determine when watering is necessary. A tensiometer consists of a porous clay cup, an air trap, and a vacuum gauge. It may be purchased from certain greenhouse companies. The porous clay cup of the tensiometer is inserted in the soil and then water is poured into the air trap until it is completely filled and free of air. As the soil dries out, water diffuses from the porous cup into the soil, generating a tension which registers on the gauge of the tensiometer. The gauge records the pull in inches of mercury. Plants usually need watering when the gauge records a tension of 1 inch.

Plants just potted or transplanted should always be watered thoroughly immediately after the job is done. Bulbs and tubers should also be given a good watering after they are planted. However, after this first watering you should keep the bulbs and tubers on the dry side until roots develop, after which water them as you would other actively growing plants. If unrooted bulbs or tubers are maintained in soggy soil, they may rot. Remember, too, that until roots develop the water in the soil is not readily absorbed.

You will have to water seeds and seedlings carefully, or you may wash them out of the soil. These may be watered with a can equipped with a fine rose (a nozzle with many small openings at the end), or you may place the flat or pot in a tray of water and let the soil take up water from below.

Some plants have alternating periods of activity and rest. The resting period is often during the winter, and at this stage of development the plants use less water than when they are actively growing. Soon after the turn of the year, poinsettias will enter their rest period. No matter how much you water the plants, the leaves will fall off. In the autumn tuberous begonias and gloxinias generally enter their rest period. You will notice a gradual dying and shriveling of the foliage. This is a sign they are entering their rest period, and water should be withheld. During the resting period several days, or even weeks or months, depending on the species, may elapse between waterings. When active growth begins again, the plants will require water more frequently.

If possible, use water which is the same temperature as that of the greenhouse. Very cold water may check the growth of some plants and may cause spotting of the foliage if splashed on the leaves; African violets, begonias, cape primroses, and gloxinias are especially sensitive to spotting by cold water.

Because many greenhouse plants make their best growth when the soil is neutral or slightly acid, it is best to use water which is not strongly alkaline. Continued use of alkaline water may make the soil too alkaline and the leaves may turn yellow, a result of the iron in the soil becoming insoluble and hence not available to the plants. If this happens to your plants, you may correct the iron deficiency by watering the plants every other week with a solution made up of one ounce of iron sulfate and two gallons of water. Rain water is ideal; some growers collect it and use it for watering their plants, but this is often not practical. Certain water conditioners (not the ordinary water softeners) are on the market which will correct the alkalinity of the tap water.

What to do about watering when one is away on vacation or business presents a real problem. Many greenhouse growers call on their neighbors for help during such times. Another possibility is use of an automatic system for watering the plants. In general, automatic systems are not so good as careful hand watering because, of course, they lack judgment. All the plants, large and small, newly potted and well-established, resting and nonresting, are furnished the same amount of water with an automatic system. In spite of this major disadvantage, you may want to install an automatic system.

The essential features of an automatic system for watering plants growing in soil in a bench are illustrated in the accompanying figure. The major features are a perfectly level, waterproof bench with a V bottom and a water tank in which the water level is controlled by a float valve, such as the inexpensive kind used for poultry watering. The tank may be located on the side or at the end of the bench, and is connected to the bottom of the bench with pipe or hose. The bench itself must be waterproof and may be made of concrete, metal, or wood lined with vinyl plastic. The inside of a metal or concrete bench should be painted with horticultural as-

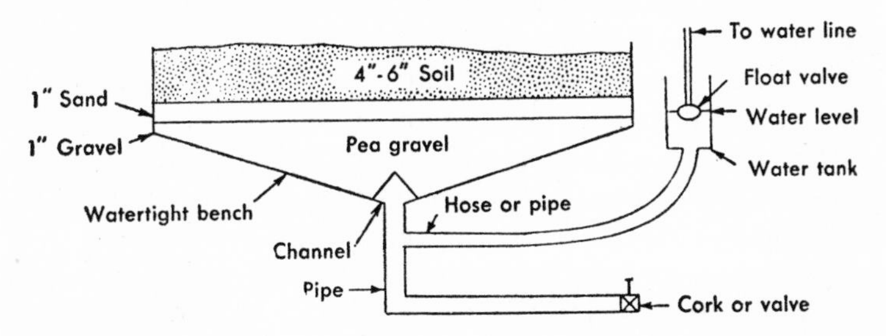

Cross section of bench for flowers to be grown by the constant-level subirrigation method. (From *Commercial Flower Forcing,* by A. Laurie and D. C. Kiplinger; the Blakiston Co.)

phalt to eliminate any toxic substances. A channel to conduct the water the length of the bench is placed in the center, at the bottom of the V. The channel may be made of angle iron or half-round tile. The bench is filled with pea gravel to a point 1 inch above where the V begins. The gravel is then covered with a 1-inch layer of sand, over which the soil is placed. All layers must be perfectly level. The whole bench should then be thoroughly watered from above. With this arrangement, the water level in the bench will be the same as the water level in the tank. The water level in the tank must be adjusted so that the water level is maintained in the lower half-inch of sand. If the water level in the bench is too high, the soil will be waterlogged, the roots will die from lack of air, and foul-smelling marsh gas may be produced. To locate the water level in the bench, place a 5- or 6-inch pot in the bench so that the bottom rests on the gravel. You will see the water height in the pot. Some adjustments may be necessary. If the soil is too dry, raise the water level slightly, but never let it reach the soil.

The bench should be equipped with a drainage pipe that can be opened and closed. By removing the cork or opening the valve, the water tank and the bench may be drained, after the float valve has been raised. Before fertilizing plants, drain the bench, then apply the fertilizer, and water it into the soil with a hose. Then close the drainage valve and start the float valve in action again. If salts accumulate on the surface of the soil, drain the bench and then, with the hose, apply about three gallons of water per square foot of bench area. Let drain and then start the system going again.

Pot plants may be watered automatically with a similar system. The system is the same as that described above, except that the sand layer is thicker and no soil is used. The pots should not have drainage material (broken pot or gravel) over the hole, or at most just one piece of broken pot should be placed over the hole. To establish the pots in the benches, they should be watered overhead thoroughly and then be plunged in the sand firmly to a depth of about 1/4 inch. The float should be adjusted to maintain the water level about 1 inch below the bottoms of the pots. During the first few weeks, keep a close watch on the plants. If some become dry, water overhead and then plunge the pots slightly deeper. If some are getting too much water, raise them slightly.

Electric controls can be used for the subirrigation of plants benched in soil. However, the installation is very complicated and quite expensive, and the results have not always been satisfactory. The items needed for this system are a soil tensiometer, time clock switch, solenoid valve, and a transformer. The necessary equipment with instructions for installation may be purchased from certain greenhouse companies. A solenoid valve is connected to the water line, which in turn is attached to the inlet in the bottom of a waterproof bench filled in the manner described on page

31. The porous clay cup of a soil tensiometer, which has electric contacts in the vacuum gauge, is placed in the soil. As the soil in the bench becomes drier, the hand on the gauge moves. When the soil dries to the set point, an electrical contact is made to the time clock switch which controls the solenoid valve. The time clock switch is set to admit water for 20-minute periods at 2-hour intervals as long as the contact remains in the vacuum gauge. That is, when contact is made in the gauge, the valve opens, permitting water to enter the bench very slowly for 20 minutes. Then the valve closes and remains closed for 2 hours, when it opens again if electrical contact is still made in the vacuum gauge. In the 2-hour interval, water moves upward in the soil by capillarity. This pattern continues until the soil is moist, when the controlling contact at the gauge is broken.

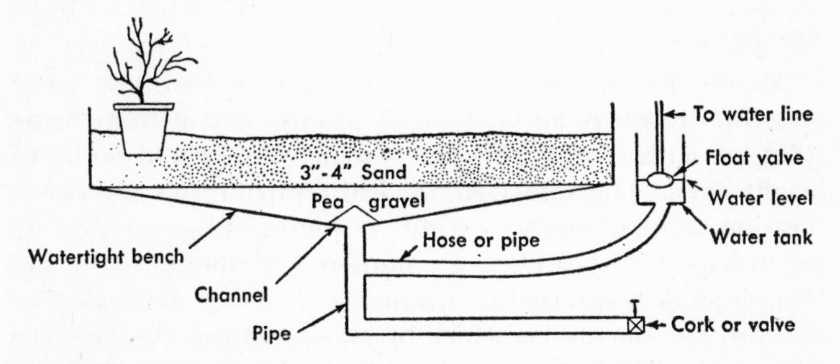

Cross section of bench for pot plants to be grown by the constant-level subirrigation method. (From *Commercial Flower Forcing*)

Gadgets are fine and have their place, but to grow plants to perfection nothing takes the place of human skill, care, and judgment. The raising of plants then becomes an art, an opportunity for one to develop his own skill.

Humidity

The amount of moisture in the air plays an important role in the growth of plants. Many plants grow poorly in the home because the air is too dry. When moved into a humid greenhouse these plants thrive. When the air is dry—that is, when the relative humidity is low—plants lose water rapidly through their foliage and stems. This loss of water as vapor we call *transpiration*. Transpiration is high when the air is dry, the temperature warm, the day bright, and when the air is moving. When the relative humidity is high, transpiration is decreased. Hence, try to keep the air humid in the greenhouse. The ideal relative humidity is between 50 and 70 per cent. (At higher relative humidities plants grow well, but there is greater danger of disease getting started.) You can increase the humidity by spraying water on the walks and under the benches. Mist nozzles may be attached to pipes installed under the benches, or perhaps you will want a motor-operated humidifier. The latter can cost from $50 to $150, depending on the make and capacity, and can be operated with automatic controls.

Syringing

Many plants, among them orchids, carnations, snapdragons, cyclamen, and chrysanthemums, benefit from being syringed with a mist of water during the hotter hours of bright days. The spray reduces leaf temperatures and transpiration. Furthermore, forceful syringing washes insects off the foliage. Red spider, a common greenhouse pest, can sometimes be controlled in this manner. There are a number of nozzles on the market which break water from the hose into a fine mist suitable for syringing. Syringing is not a substitute for watering. When syringing, wet the foliage but do not apply enough water to fill the pots or benches.

Plants just moved into flats or pots should be syringed until they become established, as should cuttings. Spraying with water at frequent intervals will keep the leaves from wilting too much. Syringing sometimes encourages buds to develop. For example, newly potted dormant roses will develop faster if the stems and dormant buds are sprayed with water.

Certain plants, such as ferns, gloxinias, African violets, and tuberous begonias may be injured if syringed with cold water. These plants should not be sprayed with water, or, if sprayed, the water should be at greenhouse temperature.

Ventilation

We are more comfortable in a well-ventilated room than in a stuffy, hot one. Opening the windows brings in fresh air and often lowers the temperature of the room. In a greenhouse in summer, the day temperatures become unbearably hot if the ventilators remain closed. Even in winter, the greenhouse needs some ventilation to furnish the plants fresh air.

Fresh air contains both oxygen and carbon dioxide, which are essential for plant development. Plants use oxygen much as we do, to combine with sugars, to oxidize them. As the sugar is oxidized, energy is released and made available for the plants' activities. Roots, stems, leaves, flowers, and fruits all require a continuous supply of oxygen.

The carbon dioxide in the air is used by the plant to make sugar. In the leaves and other green parts of the plant, the carbon dioxide of the air is combined with water during the day to form sugar and to release oxygen. Light furnishes the energy for the process.

The plant makes many substances from the sugar. Sugar is changed into starch, cellulose, and fats, and with the addition of nitrogen, sulfur, and phosphorous, into proteins. These substances are combined in various ways to form additional tissues, and thereby the plant grows. They are also used to form flowers, fruits, and seeds and to make hormones, vitamins, chlorophyll, and red, blue, and orange pigments. Hence we see that if our plants are to thrive they must make an abundance of food, and for this process carbon dioxide is essential.

A greenhouse should have ventilators on both sides of the ridge. Side ventilators at the eaves or below the benches are desirable but not absolutely essential. With ventilators on both sides of the ridge, drafts can be avoided. If you open the ventilators on the lee side on windy days, the plants will not be exposed to strong drafts. Of course, on quiet, hot days, you may wish to open all of the ventilators. During the summer in many regions the ventilators may be kept open both day and night. In winter it may be necessary to have them open only for a short time each day. Closing them before the temperature drops toward late afternoon will make for a more equable temperature and will reduce the fuel bill. In winter, ventilation is one way to minimize the incidence of disease. Without ventilation on a cloudy day the relative humidity may become excessive, thereby favoring the development of disease-causing organisms.

When the weather is changeable, the sun out one hour and behind the clouds the next, the temperature may fluctuate widely unless you open and close the ventilators with the vagaries of the weather. Many amateurs, especially those who are away from the greenhouse during most of the day, find automatic ventilation very desirable. Greenhouse companies sell motors which are attached to the ventilators and which are controlled by a thermostat. When the temperature in the greenhouse reaches the setting, the motor opens the ventilators. When the temperature drops below the setting the motor closes them.

During the summer you may have to screen the ventilators to keep out wasps, bees and other undesirable visitors, especially if your plants are in flower. Fasten ordinary window screen to the frame of the ventilator. When flowers are pollinated, their life is much reduced. For example, orchids may last several weeks if the blossoms are not pollinated, but only about a day if pollinated. By neglecting to screen the ventilators one summer, we lost many orchid flowers.

Light

Some plants—carnations, calendulas, snapdragons, and others—make their best growth and flower profusely with full sun. Others—African violets, gloxinias, philodendron, and begonias—prefer shade. Carnations and other sun plants make more food at high light intensity than in shade.

In African violets and other shade plants the amount of food made increases as the light intensity increases up to one-tenth to one-fifth full sunlight, or between 1000 and 2000 foot-candles. Higher light intensities do not increase the amount of food made or the rate of growth. As a matter of fact, higher light intensities may be detrimental, resulting in burning the foliage. Shade-loving plants, therefore, must have the light intensity reduced when grown in a greenhouse.

Even plants which do best in full sun out of doors will require shade in a greenhouse during the summer months. During summer the full glare of the sun would result in temperatures so high that the growth of the plants would be retarded, or the plants might even be killed by the heat. Furthermore, when the temperatures soar, insects thrive and become a serious menace. Hence, in most parts of the country, it is necessary to shade the greenhouse from early May to late September. Of course, regional differences in climate may make it necessary to have a longer or shorter shading period, or to shade at some other season.

Even though the greenhouse is shaded during the summer, the temperatures may still be too high for certain plants—cyclamen and azaleas, for example. These may be kept in a lath house or in a cold frame with lath shading, or, if hail is not a problem, in the garden.

As we have said before, the light requirement for different plants varies; some thrive with full sun, others in moderate shade, and still different species with heavier shade. The appearance of your plants and their behavior will indicate whether or not they are receiving the proper amount of light. If the plants are leggy, deep green, and flower sparingly, the light intensity is too low. If the foliage becomes a pronounced yellow green (or sometimes red) and is hard and small, the plants are getting too much light, as they also are if burned spots appear on the leaves.

You can raise both sun-loving and shade-loving plants in the same greenhouse by shading one part of the greenhouse and not the other. Also, you will find the shaded part a good place to keep cuttings until they are rooted and newly potted plants until they recover from the shock of transplanting.

There are a number of ways to shade a greenhouse: painting the glass or using roller blinds, fixed lath frames (of wood or aluminum), or cloth. We shade our greenhouse by painting the glass on the outside with Garland White Shading Compound, following the manufacturer's directions. If you find that the shading compound is too easily washed off by rains, you can add a small amount of linseed oil to the mixture. The shading compound may be sprayed on, or may be painted on using a calcimine brush fastened on to a long stick. Shading compound without linseed oil may be scrubbed off fairly easily in the autumn, using a stiff brush and plenty of water. If linseed oil has been added, the shading compound may have to be scraped off with a sharpened putty knife. We have tried painting the inside of the glass with various compounds, but none proved satisfactory. The condensation on the glass washed them off. Other growers prefer to paint the outside of the glass with a mixture of a pound of white lead thoroughly mixed in 5 quarts of gasoline. This can be applied with a brush or sprayed on the glass. The white lead chalks off gradually and can be brushed off easily.

Greenhouses that are shaded with roller blinds or fixed lath frames are neater in appearance than those that are painted. For certain shade-loving plants, African violets and gloxinias for example, roller blinds or fixed lath frames by themselves may not furnish ample shade. Often it is necessary to supplement such shading by tacking a layer of cheesecloth on the sash bars. The cheesecloth breaks any of the sun's rays which may penetrate. The roller blinds and lath shading can be obtained from greenhouse manufacturers.

In our own greenhouses we supplement the paint shading by tacking up cheesecloth on the inside of the greenhouse during the hottest months of the year. Furthermore, we use cheesecloth for spot shading, that is, to shade a group of plants which require additional shade.

If the winter days are dull in your locality, even shade-loving plants will grow best if the glass is left unshaded. It is important that the shade be removed gradually as winter approaches. If the plants are shaded one day and exposed to bright sun the next, the leaves may burn. On the other hand, if the shade is removed gradually the plants will become adapted to the brighter light and they will not be injured.

Many plants which can be grown without shade during the darker winter months will need shade when the days become brighter in late winter or early spring. Gradually increase the shade. For example, don't apply a heavy coat of shading compound all at once. Apply a thin coat, and later, when necessary, an additional one, with perhaps even a third one for the hottest part of the summer. In other words, never subject plants to a sudden change in environment, but instead provide a gradual change.

Temperature

The plants we grow in greenhouses have come from all parts of the world. Some have been introduced from tropical regions, others from temperate zones, different ones from cooler regions or high elevations. Plants from diverse climatic regions cannot all be grown at the same temperature. Both the day and night temperatures must be suitable for the variety. Night temperatures are especially critical. If they are too high or too low for the species the plants will not thrive and flower. African violets, tuberous begonias, cattleya orchids, and many foliage plants thrive and flower well when the night temperature is 60 degrees, but carnations, snapdragons, and stocks would not flourish at this night temperature. The latter make their best growth and flowers at a night temperature of 50 degrees. We are increasingly recognizing that night temperatures not only influence the growth of plants but also affect flowering. In later chapters, when only one temperature is given for culture we mean the night temperature. Stocks and cymbidiums flower well when the night temperature is 50 degrees, but only sparsely or not at all when the night temperature is 60 degrees.

Day temperatures are also significant. In general, they should run about 10 or 15 degrees higher than the night temperature. If the plants you want to grow are adaptable to a house maintained at 50 degrees at night, the ideal day temperature would be 60 or 65 degrees. If you raise those plants which do best at a night temperature of 60 degrees, plan to keep the day temperature 70 to 75 degrees. Of course, during the summer months the day temperatures are bound to exceed these limits. But do not become alarmed. The plants will do all right nevertheless. As previously mentioned, day temperatures can be somewhat moderated by shading, by proper ventilation, and by syringing.

If you will place thermometers in different parts of your greenhouse, you will probably find that the temperature is not uniform throughout. In one of our greenhouses we have the thermostat set for 60 degrees at night, an ideal night temperature for cattleya orchids. In one corner of the greenhouse, however, the night temperature is 55 degrees, and here we place cypripediums and other kinds that prefer cooler conditions. You may find similar variations in your own greenhouse. Often the temperature near the roof will be several degrees warmer than on the bench, and plants that need a bit more warmth can be hung or placed on shelves. Ideally, if you want to raise both warm and cool plants in any large number, the greenhouse should be partitioned as described in Chapter 2.

During winter, leaves which touch the glass may become frozen. Keep the plants away from the glass or tack up some glass substitute on the sides to keep the leaves away from the cold glass.

You are probably curious to learn why temperature control is so important in raising plants. Temperature affects many processes in a plant: food making, food using, growth, and flowering. As the day temperature increases, up to about 85 degrees, the rate of food manufacture also increases. But 85 degrees is not an ideal day temperature for most plants. As the temperature goes up, so also does the rate of the food-using process called *respiration*. In respiration, food and oxygen are used and carbon dioxide and water are formed, and energy for carrying on the manifold activities of a plant is released. At temperatures of 85 or 90 degrees the rate of respiration may be so great that there is little food left for growth and flower production. At a temperature of 70 degrees much more food is made than is used, and plants thrive. During the night, food manufacture does not go on, but respiration continues. If night temperatures are too high, too great an amount of food will be respired and little or none will be available for growth. Hence, we see the reason for keeping the night temperature about 10 degrees lower than the day. During the day we maintain a temperature which results in a favorable balance between food making and food using, and during the night a temperature that gives a balance between food using and growth.

Sanitation

If your greenhouse is kept clean, you will take greater pride in it and the plants will grow better. Remove dead leaves and shriveled flowers. Don't permit mosses and algae to cover the outside of pots. They may be washed off easily with water and a rag or brush. Remove weeds from under the benches and rake the surface occasionally. Such practices will cut down the population of slugs, insects, and disease organisms. A yearly scrubbing of the woodwork in the greenhouse, and painting about every four years, will make it more attractive and create better growing conditions. In many regions some plants, such as carnations, stocks, snapdragons and others, require all the light they can get during the winter months. Glass covered with dirt and the remains of shading markedly reduce the light intensity. Hence in the autumn a scrubbing of the glass is beneficial for these plants. A stiff brush fastened to a long handle and plenty of water can be used to clean the glass.

There is a great temptation to crowd too much into a small greenhouse. The plants get larger, we divide some and acquire others. We hesitate to throw things away. Finally, the greenhouse almost bulges. Overcrowding is common in most greenhouses, but it does not pay. It is far better to have fewer plants, given better care and space. Crowding allows the plants to shade each other, cutting down the amount of light per plant, and the plants become spindly and flower poorly. Crowding makes it very difficult to water properly. Some plants become waterlogged, others remain dry. Diseases and insect pests thrive where plants are crowded, and it is difficult to keep them under control because sprays do not adequately cover the plants.

Hail protection

Let the experiences of local people with similar greenhouses help you decide whether or not protection from hail is necessary. Small panels of glass seem to be more readily broken by hail than large ones. Greenhouses are protected from hail by fastening hardware cloth to a metal or wooden frame about 6 inches above the glass. Generally it is only necessary to protect the glass on the roof.

Keeping records

It would be wonderful if we could always remember when and how we did certain things, when certain plants flowered, and the number and quality of the flowers. But most of us are forgetful. When we have had remarkable success with a certain plant we try to think back about the culture we used, but too often the details are missing. If we had kept a daily diary, or even a weekly one, we might be able to duplicate in another year the conditions which resulted in such success.

You will find that it pays to keep records about the soil and the fertilizer program, the light intensity, and the temperature. Further, you will want to record the time seeds were sown, when cuttings were made, when the plants were pinched, and when they flowered. If you grow bulbs, keep records of when they were potted, where they were stored and for how long, as well as when they were brought into the greenhouse and when they flowered. If you keep records about when plants bloom with the cultural conditions you use, you will be better able to plan a desirable sequence of blooms.

If you have valuable plants that live for many years, such as African violets, amaryllis, camellias, hibiscus, gardenias, orchids, and others, you may want to keep a card for each plant. Record when the plant was purchased and from whom. On the card write the common and scientific names of the plant, the variety, and, if known, the pedigree. Record the native habitat of the plant and the conditions in its native home. Write down when the plant was potted or divided, the soil used, the fertilizer program. Record its flowering time, and the number of flowers produced and their quality. Such records will show up those plants which in spite of good care either do not flower or give poor flowers. It is well to dispose of these to make room for better plants.

CHAPTER 4

SOILS AND NUTRITION

WE HAVE SEEN that plants need light, air, water, and a proper temperature if they are to thrive. In addition, they require certain minerals, which we often call *plant food,* for their development and flowering. Plants secure the minerals from soil. If the soil is lacking in one or more nutrients the plants will not grow, even though all other conditions are favorable. But minerals alone are not enough. In addition to a proper ratio of minerals, a good soil should also be of good texture, hold plenty of water, be well aerated, and have the proper degree of acidity.

The type of soil needed for thrifty growth varies with the plant. Some grow best in a sandy soil, others in a loam soil, some only in soils rich in organic matter, and others in soils made up entirely of organic matter. Many plants flower well in fertile soils, but others may flower more profusely in less fertile soils. Some plants prefer acid soils, others alkaline ones, and so it goes. If we are going to raise a variety of plants we must have the ingredients to make several kinds of soil. Later in the book we will list mixtures suitable for individual kinds of plant.

Soil mixtures

To make the various mixtures you will need a supply of loam soil, manure, peat, leaf mold, sand, and, if possible, compost. If you plan to grow orchids you will need the matted roots of the royal fern, called *osmunda fiber* or *osmun-*

dine. You will find it convenient to have a supply of these ingredients in the potting shed. Here they will be available for use in cold or wet weather and they will be at a warm temperature. A compost of soil and manure by itself is suitable for many plants, and can be mixed with other ingredients for a great variety of plants.

You can make a compost pile by alternating layers of soil and manure. First pile soil, top soil or, better, sod, to a depth of 8 inches and then add 4 inches of fresh or rotted cow or horse manure; continue to alternate 8 inches of soil with 4 inches of manure until the pile is of the desired height, but don't make it over 4 feet high. Over each layer of soil sprinkle superphosphate at the rate of 5 pounds per 100 square feet. Make the top of the pile, which should be soil, concave to hold water. After a month or so, turn the pile by spading, and turn it again every two or three months. Compost made in the spring will be ready for potting plants the following spring. The compost will be in good condition for use in benches in about four months, and for some kinds of plants is used without the addition of other materials except for drainage. If you do not have compost you can get along very well by mixing loam (good topsoil) with well-rotted manure just prior to use, or perhaps you can purchase some compost from a local grower. For certain bench crops, place about 4 inches of soil in the bench and then add about 1 inch of well-rotted manure and superphosphate, about 5 pounds per 100 square feet. With either compost or soil it is desirable to add a 1-inch layer of fine cinders or Haydite. Mix the ingredients with a spade or fork. It is desirable, but not absolutely necessary, to have an inch of gravel between the bench and the soil to make certain that there is good drainage.

In later chapters you will notice that many plants grow best in soil high in organic matter. Generally, *leaf mold* or *peat moss* is mixed with soil for this purpose. Both leaf mold and peat moss increase the water-holding capacity and the aeration of the soil. Furthermore, they keep the soil open, prevent it from becoming packed, and tend to increase its acidity. As the peat moss and leaf mold decay, essential minerals are gradually made available to plants. Neither peat moss nor leaf mold is so rich in nitrogen, phosphorous, and potassium as is manure. You can purchase leaf mold by the sack, or you can make your own by gathering leaves and placing them in a crib. If they are dry, moisten them and place boards on top to compact the leaves. Maple leaves will generally be sufficiently decayed in a year's time; oak leaves will require two years.

Peat moss can be purchased at reasonable cost from many supply companies. It is soft, spongy, and brown-colored, retains moisture well, and has a fairly high nitrogen content—about 1 to 3 per cent—but it is low in phosphorous and potassium. Peat moss is an important ingredient of many soil mixtures, and in many instances it can take the place of leaf mold, which may be difficult to obtain. Many plants grow well in a mixture of one part peat moss to four or five of loam, or of a compost of soil and manure. Peat moss is also valuable for mulching plants which are growing in benches. A 1-inch mulch of peat moss over the soil makes for more vigorous growth of some bench crops. Many plants grow well in a half-and-half mixture of sand and peat, provided fertilizers are added at intervals. Usually we raise chrysanthemums in soil, but it has been found that they grow well in half sand and half peat. Superphosphate is added to the mixture, and fertilizers later. We mention this because perhaps good soil is not available in your locality.

Soil mixtures are most conveniently made on the potting bench. Supposing a mixture of two parts of loam, one part of well-rotted manure, and one part of peat moss is desired. If the soil has many rocks, bits of wood, and other debris in it, the soil should be passed through a half-inch mesh screen. It is generally necessary to screen both peat and manure, using a quarter-inch mesh screen. Make a flat pile of loam, say 6 inches high. Then add a 3-inch layer of manure, followed with a 3-inch layer of peat. Using a spade, start at one end of the pile and turn it over. Repeat twice. If the mixture is dry, dish the top of the pile and add water. In a day or two the mixture will be evenly moist throughout, and after turning once it is ready for use. For potting, soil should not be too wet or too dry. The soil should be damp enough to adhere to itself and not crumble when a handful is gently squeezed, but not so moist that it drips.

Soil acidity

Even though the soil is well supplied with air, water, and the essential minerals, plants will not thrive unless the *acidity* or *alkalinity* of the soil is suitable to their demands. Most plants thrive best in a neutral or slightly acid soil, but some, such as rhododendrons, azaleas, African violets, oranges, and orchids, prefer a more acid soil.

The *p*H *scale* is used to designate the degree of acidity or alkalinity of soil. A soil with a *p*H of 7 is neutral. Soils with *p*H values below 7 are acid, and the lower the figure the more acid the soil. A soil of *p*H 5 is more acid than one with a *p*H of 6. Because *p*H values are logarithms, a soil with a *p*H of 5 is ten times as acid as one with a *p*H of 6. Soils with *p*H values above 7 are alkaline and the higher the number, the more alkaline the soil. It is easy to determine the *p*H of soil. Various companies sell kits which measure *p*H. Generally, a colored solution of an indicator dye is made to flow through a soil sample. The color of the solution as it drains through is then compared to a standard chart from which the *p*H value is read. Another method is even simpler. All one needs is a spoon and a specially prepared paper. (The paper, with complete directions and *p*H preferences of various plants, sells for about a dollar.) A small amount of soil is placed in the bowl of a spoon close to the handle. Water is added to the front of the bowl and the spoon is then set on a level surface. The water will then flow into the soil. Next, a piece of the test paper is placed in the front of the bowl and the spoon is tilted so that the water from the soil runs on to the paper. The color of the paper is compared with colors printed on a chart, which also gives the *p*H value for each color.

Most plants thrive when the soil is in the range of about *p*H 6 to 7, for instance carnations, chrysanthemums, roses, calendulas, snapdragons, stocks, asters, clarkias, marigolds, pansies, and most primroses. Other plants grow best when the soil is more acid, in a range of *p*H 5 to *p*H 6, among them ageratum, amaryllis, begonia, cyclamen, fuchsia, gloxinia, lily, palm, and many orchids. Plants which prefer a very acid soil, *p*H 4 to *p*H 5, are azaleas, bromeliads, callas, camellias, and hydrangeas. If the soil in your region is too acid, the acidity may be diminished by the application of lime. The amount needed varies with the type of soil, the original *p*H of the soil, and the desired *p*H. Five pounds of limestone per 100 square feet of bench area will raise the *p*H of certain soils one unit, from *p*H 5 to 6, or from *p*H 6 to 7.

If soils are too alkaline, as they are in parts of the West, for the best growth of the plants being raised, the soil may be made neutral or acid by the addition of sulfur. One-half pound of sulfur per 100 square feet of bench will lower the *p*H about one unit, from *p*H 8 to 7, or *p*H 7 to 6.

While iron salts are usually present in the soil, they may be insoluble unless the soil is of the proper acidity. Iron sulfate (ferrous sulfate or copperas) may be used to acidify soils and, at the same time, to furnish plants with available iron. Even in some moderately acid soils there may not be enough iron in solution to meet the demands of certain plants. Azaleas, camellias, gardenias, and hydrangeas benefit from application of iron sulfate at a rate of 1 pound per 100 square feet of bench area, or from biweekly waterings with a solution containing one ounce of iron sulfate in two gallons of water. Pot plants are best furnished iron by watering them with a solution of iron sulfate. When peat moss and leaf mold decay, organic acids are produced and the soil becomes more acid. Alkaline soils can thus be made neutral or acid by the addition of organic matter, and neutral and slightly acid soils can be made more acid. A mixture of one part soil and one part peat moss will bring soil into the range of *p*H 5.5 to 6.5, which is ideal for gardenias, begonias, and gloxinias. Azaleas do well in peat moss alone, which has a *p*H of 4.5 to 5.5, provided they are given applications of fertilizer at intervals to make up for the lack of minerals in the peat.

Mineral nutrition of plants

Plants, like animals, need certain elements in their diet to make normal growth. If any one or two of these is deficient, growth veers from normal in some way. Iron is necessary to the formation of hemoglobin in human beings, and we know that an iron deficiency is one cause of anemia. A calcium or phosphorus deficiency results in poor teeth or poor bones. Plants show definite symptoms when some essential element is unavailable to them. An iron deficiency denies them one of the elements necessary in the formation of chlorophyll, so that the leaves become yellow, or *chlorotic.* When nitrogen is deficient, growth is stunted.

There are fifteen essential elements, some of which are necessary in large amounts, called *macronutrients,* and others in small amounts, called *micronutrients* or *trace elements.* The latter group is peculiar in that, while extremely small quantities are required for normal growth, concentrations over the beneficial amounts are injurious. The role of the trace elements was not suspected for a long time, partly because the quantities required by plants are so small, and partly because most soils contain them. By the use of a technique called, variously, *nutriculture, hydroponics,* or *water culture,* scientists were able to give plants arbitrary diets and watch their reactions. They learned what elements the plants used in growth, and how various concentrations affected them. They were able to chart the symptoms when some element was omitted from the diet, or present in too great an amount. With their knowledge and their chart of symptoms, they were able to diagnose ailments and prescribe a cure.

Plants obtain three of the fifteen essential elements from air and water: *oxygen, carbon,* and *hydrogen.* The rest they obtain from the soil as dissolved mineral salts; these are *nitrogen, phosphorus, potassium, calcium, magnesium, iron, sulfur,* and the trace elements, *manganese, boron, copper, zinc,* and *molybdenum.* Most soils have large reserves of calcium, magnesium, and sulfur so that usually these do not have to be added. Plants require large amounts of nitrogen, phosphorus, and potassium, and the soil reserves of these are limited. It is therefore often necessary to add fertilizers containing compounds of these three to soils. Manufacturers give symbols like 5-10-5, 4-12-4, and so on, on the labels; these signify the percentages of nitrogen (N), as the pure element, phosphorus (P), as P_2O_5, and potassium (K), as K_2O, respectively. Certain greenhouse plants may suffer from lack of iron. Except for iron, nitrogen, phosphorus, and potassium, the reserves of the other elements are generally great enough to meet the needs of the plants.

A deficiency of nitrogen results in stunted growth and a yellowing of the foliage, but the leaves do not fall off. When the supply of nitrogen is ample, the leaves have a good green color. An excessive amount of nitrogen encourages the development of leaves and stems at the expense of flowers, and makes a soft growth which is susceptible to disease. Nitrogen can be added to the soil in organic form or as certain salts. Dried blood and manure are rich in nitrogen. Sodium nitrate, calcium nitrate, ammonium sulfate, and ammonium nitrate are salts which furnish available nitrogen to plants.

When phosphorus is deficient the plants are stunted and the foliage is dark green. Phosphorus hastens the ripening of fruits and seeds. Bone meal and superphosphate are excellent sources of phosphorus. A moderate excess of phosphorus is not likely to injure most plants. However gardenias and azaleas are especially susceptible to an overdose of phosphorus. Too great amounts of phosphorus may make iron insoluble and not available to plants.

A deficiency of potassium is shown by dwarfness, and by the death of the tips and edges of the leaves. Wood ashes and potassium chloride are sources of potassium. Slight excesses of potassium are not injurious, but large overdoses may cause a yellowing of the foliage, wilting, and even death of the plant.

The symptoms exhibited by a deficiency of nitrogen, phosphorus, potassium, and other essential elements are summarized in this table:

KEY TO NUTRIENT DEFICIENT SYMPTOMS *

I. Effects general on whole plant or localized on older, lower leaves.

A. Effects usually general on whole plant, although often manifested by yellowing and dying of older leaves.

1. Foliage light green. Growth stunted, stalks slender, and few new breaks. Leaves small, lower ones lighter yellow than upper. Yellowing followed by a drying to a light brown color, usually little dropping. *Minus nitrogen.*
2. Foliage dark green. Retarded growth. Lower leaves sometimes yellow between veins but more often purplish, particularly on petiole. Leaves dropping early. *Minus phosphorus.*

B. Effects usually local on older, lower leaves.

1. Lower leaves mottled, usually with dead areas near tip and margins. Yellowing beginning at margin and continuing toward center. Margins later becoming brown and curving under, and older leaves drooping. *Minus potassium.*
2. Lower leaves yellow, with dead areas in late stages. Chlorosis (yellowing of leaves) between the veins, veins normal green. Leaf margins curling upward or downward or developing a puckering effect. Necrosis (dead areas) developing between the veins very suddenly, usually within 24 hours. *Minus magnesium.*

II. Effects localized on new leaves.

A. Terminal bud remaining alive.

1. Leaves chlorotic (yellowish) between the veins; veins remaining green.
   a. Necrotic spots (dead spots) usually absent. In extreme cases necrosis of margins and tip of leaf, sometimes extending inward, developing large areas. Only larger veins remaining green. *Minus iron.*
   NOTE: Certain cultural factors, such as high *p*H, overwatering, low temperature, and nematodes on roots, may cause identical symptoms. However, the symptoms are still probably of iron deficiency in the plant due to unavailability of iron caused by these factors.
   b. Necrotic spots usually present and scattered over the leaf surface. Checkered or finely netted effect produced by even the smallest veins remaining green. Poor bloom, both size and color. *Minus manganese.*
2. Leaves light green, veins lighter than adjoining interveinal

* Ohio Agricultural Experiment Station.

areas. Some necrotic spots. Little or no drying of older leaves. *Minus sulfur.*

B. Terminal bud usually dead.
   1. Necrosis at tips and margins of young leaves. Young leaves often definitely hooked at tip. Death of roots actually preceding all the above symptoms. *Minus calcium.*
   2. Breakdown at base of young leaves. Stems and petioles brittle. Death of roots, particularly the meristematic tips. *Minus boron.*

Feeding plants

For some time after plants are potted or moved into flats or benches they will not need fertilizer. After they have made extensive root growth they may be shifted into fresh soil. If they are to remain in the same size pots or in the bench for a long time they will need periodic applications of fertilizer. Soil in which plants have been grown for some time may be deficient in nitrogen, phosphorus, or potassium, or deficient in all three.

If nitrogen, phosphorus, and potassium are lacking you should use a complete fertilizer with a ratio of 5-10-5 or 4-12-4. The complete fertilizer may be applied dry or in solution. The usual dose of dry fertilizer for bench crops is two to four pounds per 100 square feet. A half teaspoon per 6-inch pot is about right for potted plants, proportionately less for plants growing in smaller pots and more for those in larger sizes. For both bench crops and plants in pots the dry fertilizer should be applied to the surface of moist soil, taking care to keep the fertilizer away from the stems and foliage. After applying the fertilizer, scratch it into the uppermost quarter inch of soil and then water thoroughly.

Complete fertilizers may be dissolved in water and applied to the bench or to the pots. We have found this a convenient way to apply them. If only a few plants need feeding, you can use a watering can. Dissolve the recommended amount of fertilizer in a gallon of water, and apply this solution to the pots or bench. The soil in the bench or pots should be moist before the solution is applied. Apply the same amount of solution as you would water. If many plants require feeding, an apparatus such as that illustrated in the accompanying figure will make the job easier. The fertilizer is dissolved in water in the bucket. As the water flows through the hose, the fertilizer is mixed with it.

A Hozon or similar gadget enables you to fertilize plants with a hose. The fertilizer solution is sucked from the bucket and mixed with water. (Courtesy Hozon Co.)

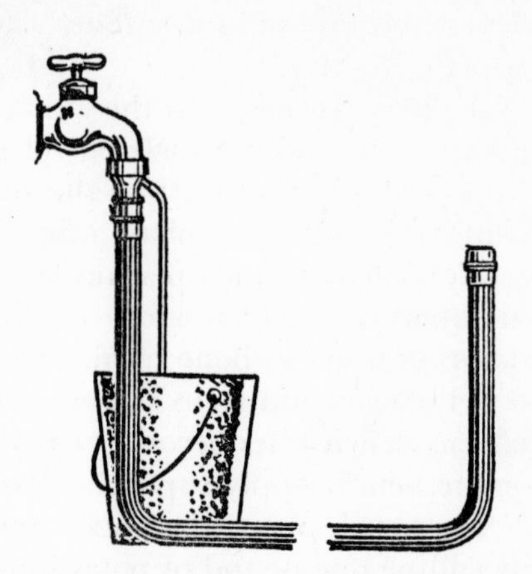

Although roots are the primary absorbing organs of a plant, minerals may be taken in through the leaves when the fertilizer solution is sprayed on the foliage. We refer to this method of supplying minerals as *foliar feeding*. A complete fertilizer may be sprayed on the foliage. One must be careful, though, to use a solution so diluted that the leaves will not be burned. Certain manufacturers have placed on the market fertilizers which, when made up according to directions furnished, are suitable for foliar feeding.

In many instances only one element need be added to the soil in which established plants are growing. For example, nitrogen may become deficient, but phosphorus and potassium may be abundant in the soil. Sodium nitrate and ammonium sulfate are good sources of nitrogen. Sodium nitrate is the preferred form for sweet peas, but for most other plants ammonium sulfate is desirable. The former tends to make the soil more alkaline, the latter to make it more acid. Ammonium sulfate and sodium nitrate are applied at a rate of one pound to 100 square feet of bench area. Nitrogen fertilizers are best applied to pot plants in liquid form. Dissolve one ounce of ammonium sulfate or sodium nitrate in two gallons of water, and water the plants with this solution, making sure that the soil is moist before the solution is added. In general, large established plants will benefit from applications of ammonium sulfate, once every two weeks, when growth is active.

To make certain that the soil used for pot plants has ample phosphorus, add a 5-inch pot of superphosphate per wheelbarrow of soil at the time the soil is prepared. For bench plants mix superphosphate into the soil prior to planting at a rate of five pounds per 100 square feet. The phosphorus in superphosphate is more readily available to plants than that contained in bone meal. Bone meal contains 3 to 4 per cent nitrogen and 20 to 25 per cent phosphoric acid. If phosphorus deficiencies become evident in plants growing in pots or the bench, apply superphosphate or a complete fertilizer.

For bench plants the potassium requirements may be met by adding one pound of potassium chloride or potassium sulfate to 100 square feet of bench space, or by using a complete fertilizer. The potassium needs of growing plants can be fulfilled by periodic applications of a solution of one ounce of potassium chloride dissolved in two gallons of water.

Azaleas, camellias, gardenias, hydrangeas, as well as other plants requiring high acidity, benefit from biweekly or monthly applications of iron sulfate, prepared by dissolving one ounce of iron sulfate in two gallons of water. Without periodic applications of iron sulfate, the leaves of the above plants may become yellowish.

There are a great many fertilizers, but we get along well with a complete fertilizer which we apply in liquid form, as well as bone meal, superphosphate, ammonium sulfate, and iron sulfate. We mix a 5-inch pot of superphosphate or bone meal per wheelbarrow of soil prior to use. For some plants we also add a 4-inch pot per wheelbarrow of 4-12-4 fertilizer. Certain plants—chrysanthemums, calendulas, gardenias, snapdragons, stocks, cinerarias, cyclamens, and others—receive biweekly or monthly applications of ammonium sulfate or

Above: some helpful tools. A spotting board, rear left, speeds up transplanting. A dibble and potting stick lean against the spotting board. Sieves, tampers, and furrow makers are other useful implements. *Below:* a potting stick, instead of two thumbs, may be used to firm soil when a plant is potted. (Roche photos)

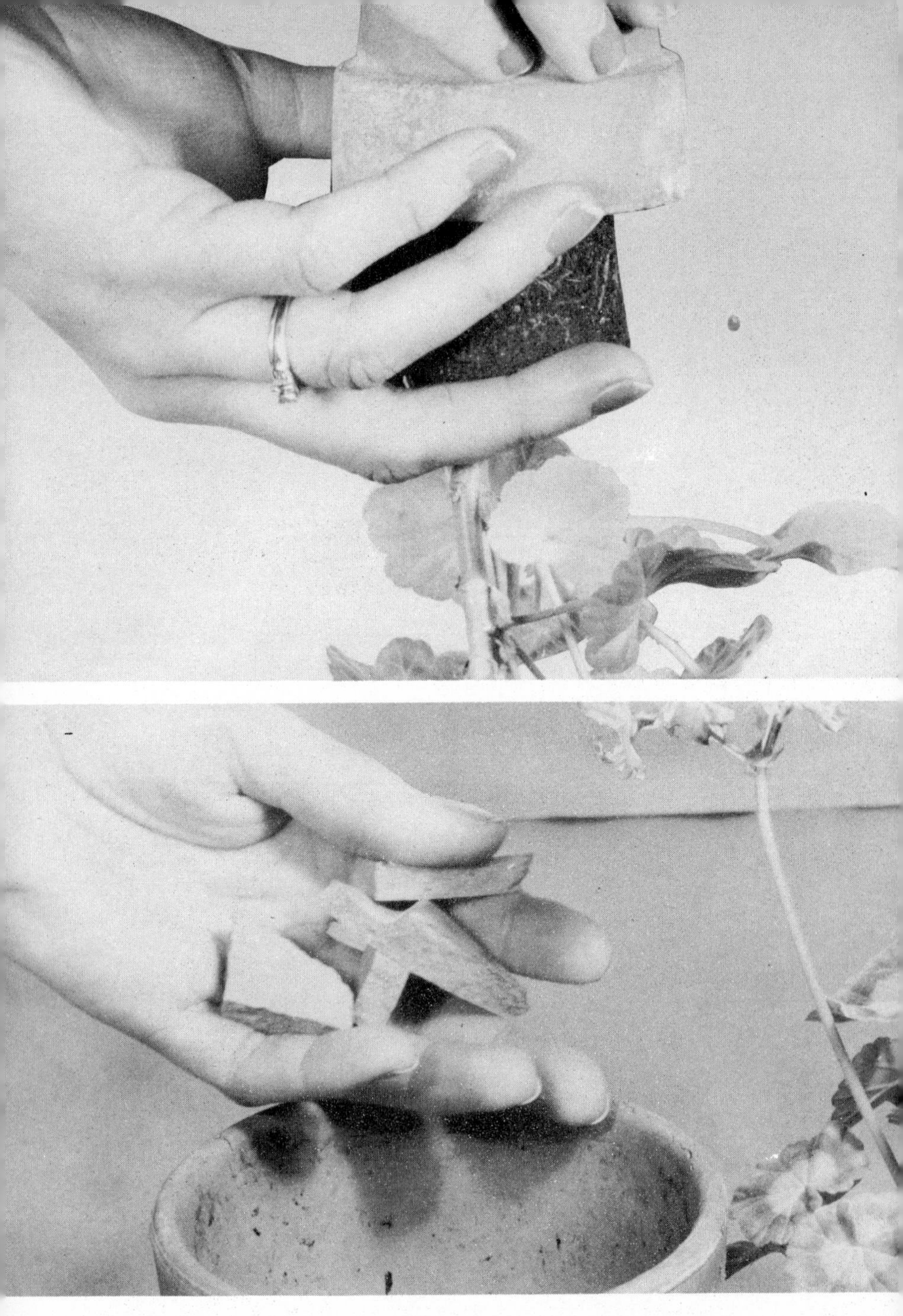

This page, above: a plant is removed from a pot by tapping the rim of the pot on the potting bench. *Below:* adding crock to a 4-inch pot. *Facing page, above:* in potting, cover crock with soil, place plant in position, and fill with soil. Then firm the soil with the thumbs (*below*).

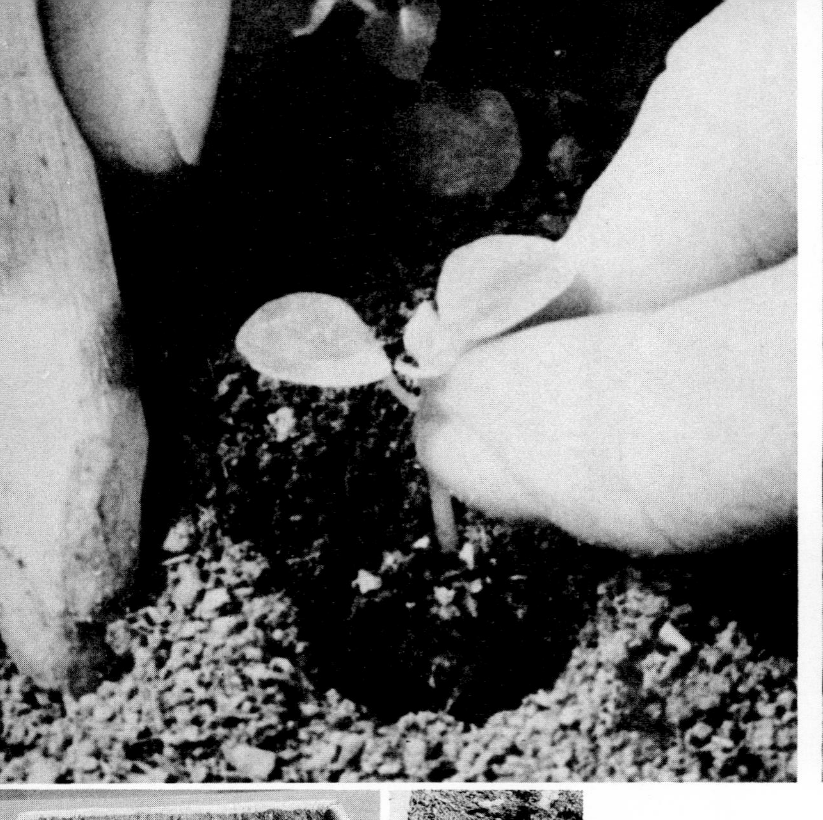

Pricking off. A flat is filled with soil, firmed, and marked for planting (*below, left*). *Below, right:* part of the flat after seedlings have been set in. In the larger pictures: the root system is inserted into the hole made with the dibble, then the soil is firmed.

Above: stem cuttings. A rooted cutting of the fiddle-leaf fig is shown at left. *Right:* a geranium cutting is rooted in a pot containing a mixture of equal parts loam, leaf mold, and sand. Rooting is hastened by inserting the cutting toward the side of the pot. *Below:* a case for the propagation of plants.

Above: rooting hormones hasten root formation in many plants. On the right are camellia cuttings that were dipped in a rooting hormone. Those at the left were not dipped. (Boyce Thompson Institute). *Center:* a leaf of the Beefsteak Begonia was placed on sand and anchored with wire: notice the young plant. *Left:* sansevieria is propagated by inserting leaf segments in sand.

Facing page: the petiole (leafstalk) an African violet is shortened (*botton* then placed in sand or vermiculite. time young plants will develop at the er of the petiole. The plants are separat and then potted. Gloxinia and certa begonias may be increased in like manne

The geranium cutting at the upper right was rooted in sand as at left. The lower figures show how rooted cuttings are potted. The cutting is held in position in a pot partly filled with soil and then more soil is added and firmed.

periodic applications of a complete fertilizer, at least until flower buds appear. If the foliage becomes yellow, and if we are sure it is not due to disease, improper watering, or too low a temperature, we apply iron sulfate. If we suspect that minerals other than nitrogen and iron are lacking, we use a complete fertilizer, omitting the ammonium sulfate for a time.

Excess of nutrients

Too much fertilizer may be more harmful than too little. When nutrients are in excess plants grow poorly, flower sparsely if at all, and may die. When plants are actively growing they can benefit from periodic applications of fertilizer, but when growth is slow, as it is during the winter months, plants won't benefit and can be injured. Don't make the mistake of believing that adding fertilizer will always speed growth. Growth may be slow because the days are short, as they are in the winter months, or because they are cloudy, or because the temperatures are not right for the species. Too much or too little water makes for poor growth, as does improper *p*H. Furthermore, plants may have inherent rest periods.

Periodic applications of fertilizer to soil in a bench may result in such an excess of salts in the soil that plants will not grow. The excess salts may be removed by *leaching* them out. Apply an abundance of water to the soil, at least one gallon per square foot, and let the surplus drain through the soil and out the drainage cracks. Repeat this procedure three times, at half-hour intervals. It is best to use warm water (65 to 75 degrees). Leaching takes out beneficial nutrients as well as harmful and useless ones. After leaching, add fertilizer to bring the soil to the proper nutritional level. If the soil in the bench is not changed at the end of one year, be sure to leach out the excess salts.

Soil sterilization

If plants are to thrive the soil must be free of such harmful agents as nematodes, pathogenic fungi, and insects. Perhaps you have had young seedlings topple over and die. They were attacked by a fungus which lives in the soil and causes a disease known as *damping-off*. Small roundworms known as nematodes attack the roots of many plants, producing galls on the roots and lowering the vitality of the plants. Cutworms and certain aphids may be present in the soil. Certain chemicals are now available which will kill the destructive organisms in the soil as well as weed seeds.

Methyl bromide gas is such a chemical. This gas is poisonous to man, and should be used carefully. If properly used, however, you need not fear it. One excellent preparation of methyl bromide is sold as Dowfume MC-2. You can purchase a complete kit which includes such items as the Dowfume, a plastic hose dispenser, and a sheet of polyethylene film. A 1-pound can is sufficient to sterilize a pile of soil 100 square feet in area and 1 foot deep. In using this chemical make a bed of the prepared soil outdoors. The pile of soil should be about 1 foot in depth, and the temperature at least 50 degrees, preferably higher. The chemical is relatively ineffective at lower temperatures. Make a frame about 4 inches above the soil to support the polyethylene film. Place a short length of pipe on the soil to hold the plastic tube in position. Then place the film on the supports, letting the edges of the film touch the ground. Seal the edges by heaping soil over them. The can of the soil fumigant is placed in the dispenser, and then a lever is pressed, which releases the gas through the plastic tube into the air between the soil and the polyethylene cover. Leave the cover over the soil for two days; then remove it. The soil can be used three or four days later.

Soil may be sterilized in a clean garbage can with Dowfume G, a chemical which is too dangerous to use indoors. In a convenient place outdoors add 2½ gallons of soil to the can and then a scant tablespoon of Dowfume G. Add another 2½ gallons of soil, over which place a scant tablespoon of Dowfume G. Continue in this manner until the can is full. Place moist newspaper over the soil, and then the lid. Seal around the edge with masking tape. Keep the can at a temperature above 50 degrees over night. Then remove the lid, outdoors. Do not use the soil until all of the odor has disappeared. This will require at least two days.

Formaldehyde dust can also be used to sterilize soil. Because formaldehyde has an unpleasant odor and is irritating to the eyes and mucous membranes, the soil should be treated outdoors. The soil may be treated in a can with a lid, or in a pile on a smooth surface. Add one ounce of a commercially prepared dust which contains 15 per cent formalin to each gallon of soil. Mix thoroughly, water the soil, and then put the lid on the can or cover the pile with wet newspapers or a tarpaulin. A day later remove the covering and stir the soil. When the formaldehyde odor has gone completely the soil is ready for use. This may require two or three weeks.

If only a small amount of sterilized soil is necessary the soil may be heated in an oven. Place moist soil in a shallow pan and insert a potato in the center. Place the pan in the oven. When the potato is cooked the soil will be free of harmful agents. An oven temperature of 200-250 degrees for 45 to 60 minutes will generally do the job.

Steam sterilization of greenhouse soil is ideal and is widely practiced by large commercial growers using special equipment. The soil is exposed to steam for about an hour and a half.

Nutriculture

Growing plants without soil can be an interesting hobby and a great deal of fun. But the interest has at times been almost ruined by grossly exaggerated claims and even misrepresentations. Plants will not grow bigger and better in water than in the best soil culture.

Growing plants without soil is called *nutriculture, hydroponics,* or *soilless culture.* The only fundamental difference between soil culture and nutriculture is the manner in which the nutrients are supplied. When plants are grown in soil, the minerals are furnished by the soil. In nutriculture they are furnished in a solution made of water and dissolved inorganic chemicals.

In soilless culture the nutrient solution may be prepared by adding the essential minerals to water. The minerals can be purchased ready-mixed under various trade names, and the amount specified in the directions should be added to a given unit of water. For those who wish to make their own culture solution, a formula is furnished at the end of this chapter. The ready-mixed or homemade culture solution should contain the essential minerals in the proper proportions, because the diet of the plants depends entirely on what is added to the water.

The three general methods which can be used for the soilless culture of plants are *liquid culture, sand culture,* and *gravel culture.*

In liquid culture the roots of plants grow in a culture solution held in a tank or other container. An ivy growing in a bottle of water is a kind of liquid culture. Some plants, tomato for example, may be supported above the surface of the solution by wire netting or by a board with holes drilled in it. A wire netting support can be made from chicken wire fashioned to form a shallow basket. The basket is filled with a layer of straw or excelsior, and the young plants are set in the basket just as you would put them in a flat. Their roots extend through the basket down into the culture solution held in a tank below. The level of the culture solution should be one inch below the basket. If desired, seed may be sown in the mulch of straw. If this is done, the mulch must be kept moist by watering with the culture solution until the roots of the seedlings extend into the tank. When the roots are several inches long they will absorb enough water and minerals, and need no longer be watered from the top. The scope of this method may range from one plant in a small tank to 100,000 in a large tank.

Plants make better growth in liquid culture when the solution and roots are periodically aerated. Air should be bubbled through the solution at intervals during each day. If this is not possible, the roots may be lifted out of the solution for brief intervals and replaced before they dry out, although this is a poor substitute for aeration of the solution.

There should always be a space left between the plant support and the surface of the solution to help aerate the solution.

As the roots develop in the culture solution, the composition of the solution changes, because some minerals are absorbed faster than others. Not only do the amounts of minerals change with time but so also do the proportions of one to another. To maintain the proper mineral environment for roots it is necessary to change the solution at weekly or biweekly intervals. The used solution is poured off and a fresh solution poured in.

The need for supports and the lack of natural aeration of roots are the major disadvantages of the liquid culture method. These disadvantages do not hold for the sand- and gravel-culture methods.

Practically all plants make excellent growth when cultured in sand contained in beds, pots, or other containers and irrigated periodically with a nutrient solution. The containers should be furnished with drainage so that the surplus nutrient solution will drain off and leave the sand well aerated. The plants can be started in the sand or transplanted to the sand from soil. The plants are irrigated at weekly intervals with a nutrient solution. Between such irrigations the plants are watered with tap water as necessary. At monthly intervals the accumulation of minerals should be flushed out by pouring a large volume of water over the sand and letting the water drain through.

Plants which thrive best in an acid soil may be grown in a mixture of half sand and half acid peat which is watered weekly with a culture solution. The sand-peat mixture is also an excellent medium for the growing of seedlings and rooting of cuttings. During seed germination and the rooting of cuttings water should be used, but after the seeds have germinated and the cuttings rooted, weekly applications of a culture solution are called for.

Silica gravel of 1/4- to 1/2-inch diameter and Haydite (grade B, 3/8 inch in diameter and some finer) are ideal aggregates for the gravel culture of plants. Plants may be grown in pots, boxes, or other containers filled with Haydite or silica gravel. The containers should be well drained. The plants are irrigated with a nutrient solution one to three times a day, depending on the crop and the weather. The irrigations must be frequent because the coarse aggregate retains only a small volume of the solution. The culture solution may be applied by surface irrigations, or, better, by subirrigation. Pots can also be subirrigated by dipping them in a bucket of nutrient solution.

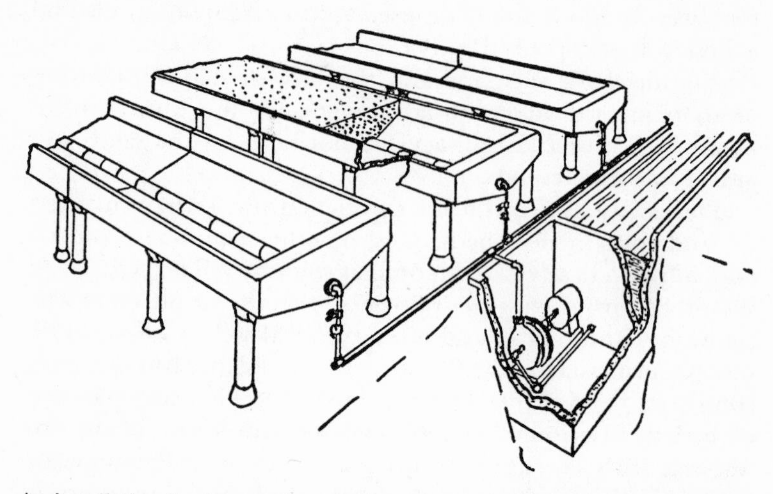

An installation for the gravel culture of plants. A half-round tile extends the length of the concrete bench, which has a V-shaped bottom. The nutrient solution is pumped from the reservoir into the bench once to four times a day. After each filling, the solution must drain back into the reservoir. (Purdue University Agricultural Experiment Station)

Gravel culture with subirrigation is an excellent technique for raising many greenhouse crops such as roses, carnations, chrysanthemums, snapdragons, gardenias, asters, and stocks. For large-scale production the plants are grown in watertight benches of concrete or steel which have been painted with horticultural asphalt emulsion. The bench is 6 inches deep at the edge and about 8 inches deep in the center. A V-shaped bottom is necessary for proper subirrigation and drainage. The bench should have a fall of one inch for each 100 feet in length. Half-round 4-inch drainage tile is run down the center of the bench to conduct the culture solution and drain it off. A reservoir for the storage of the nutrient solution is located under the bench. A centrifugal pump is installed to pump the solution from the reservoir into the bench. The reservoir should have a capacity of 40 per cent of the cubic feet in the bench.

The bench is filled with silica gravel, or, better, with Haydite, in which the plants are then placed. The nutrient solution is pumped into the beds one to four times a day, depending on weather and the crop. As soon as the solution reaches the surface of the gravel, it is allowed to drain out again, back into the reservoir. The solution can be used over and over again for about two months, provided it is tested and adjusted, as described later.

The nutrient solution used for subirrigation, sand culture, and liquid culture can be purchased ready-mixed or it can be mixed at home. The ready-mixed culture solution is prepared by adding the appropriate amount of a mixture of minerals to a certain amount of water; the manufacturers specify on the labels the amount to add to a certain quantity of water. Many mixtures of essential nutrients are on the market. Usually the mixture of salts that is used for liquid feeding is also suitable for a culture solution.

It is cheaper, but more bothersome, to mix the chemicals yourself. The following table shows the composition of the WP solution:

COMPOSITION OF THE WP FORMULA *

Chemicals	*Per 1000 gallons of water*
Potassium nitrate	5 lb. 13 oz.
Ammonium sulfate	1 lb.
Magnesium sulfate	4 lb. 8 oz.
Monocalcium phosphate	2 lb. 8 oz.
Calcium sulfate	2 lb. 8 oz.
Iron sulfate	4 oz.
Manganous sulfate	1 oz.

* Developed by Arnold Wagner and S. H. Poesch of the Horticulture Department at Ohio State University.

Another solution is that suggested by Dr. J. W. Shive. He gives the following formula for a nutrient solution which has been found suitable for many plants:

Superphosphate—2 teaspoonfuls—supplies calcium and phosphorus
Nitrate of soda—1 teaspoonful—supplies nitrogen
Epsom salt—2½ teaspoonfuls—supplies magnesium and sulphur
Muriate of potash—1 teaspoonful—supplies potassium

The amounts designated above should be dissolved in 5 gallons of water, but *do not* use any of the liquid containing the sediment which will settle to the bottom. Keep in a glass or crockery container. If fertilizer-grade chemicals and tap water are used, the trace elements needed by plants are likely to be furnished by impurities present in the chemicals and water. Iron may also be present as an impurity, but to be safe, add ½ teaspoonful of iron sulfate to 5 gallons of the solution.

Kits for testing nutrient solutions are available, or a soil testing kit can be used. On the basis of the test and if you are using the culture solution over and over again, enough salt of the deficient mineral should be added to bring the solution up to the original concentration of that mineral. The tests and additions should be made at biweekly intervals. It is usually necessary to add ferrous sulfate once a week at the rate of 4 ounces per 1000 gallons. It is wise to make *p*H tests twice a week. If the solution becomes too alkaline, it can be brought to the proper acidity by the addition of one-tenth normal hydrochloric acid. Add a few drops of acid, stir thoroughly, test for *p*H, and continue until the desired value is reached. If the solution becomes too acid, it can be brought back to the proper *pH* by the addition of one-tenth normal potassium hydroxide. Add this also in small quantities and check each time. If the *p*H is adjusted and deficient minerals added, the solution may be used for two months, after which it is discarded and a fresh solution used. If tests are not made and deficiencies are not corrected, it will be necessary to change the solution every week or two.

CHAPTER 5

GROWING PLANTS FROM SEED

GREENHOUSE PLANTS, like those in your garden, may be started in a number of ways—from seeds, bulbs, corms, tubers, and cuttings. Some favorites that are usually started from seed are aster, calendula, cineraria, cyclamen, marigold, pansy, primrose, schizanthus, snapdragon, and sweet pea. In addition, many that are familiarly started from leaf cuttings, such as begonia, gloxinia, streptocarpus, and African violet, may also be grown from seed.

When you make a cutting from a plant which you have seen in flower you know that the plant which develops will be identical. The characteristics of many plants that develop from seed cannot be known for certain until they flower. The plant-to-be is already established in the seed, as a fully formed embryo. Its growth habit and the color, size, and shape of the flowers are already determined by its inheritance. Good culture will allow its inherited characteristics to express themselves to the fullest degree, but no amount of care will produce desirable flowers from an embryo plant with poor inheritance. It is therefore important to buy seed only from experienced and reputable growers, who use the best stock as breeding plants. Some seed is produced by pure strains of plants, others by crossing pure strains to obtain a given type. Some seed you buy will be of mixed hybrid ancestry, and from it you will get a variety of colors. When you make a hybrid cross of your own, such as a cross between two varieties of African violet, the seed produced may give a wide variety of types. Some will resemble one or the other parent, some will be like various ancestors of the parents, and some will be new combinations of characteristics of the parents. From such a hybrid cross new varieties may spring.

The germination of seeds depends on their being planted at the proper depth and having the proper conditions of water, air, and temperature. Depth of planting is related to the size of seeds. Generally, seeds are planted at a depth of three or four times their diameter. However, very small seeds, such as those of begonias and gloxinias, and seeds which require light for germination, should not be covered, but instead they should be merely scattered over the soil surface.

Sowing seeds

You will probably want to start most seeds in flats, pots, or pans (shallow pots) filled with soil. A good general soil mixture consists of equal parts of finely screened soil, sand, and peat moss. This mixture or any other one should be moist, not too wet or dry, before it is used. Cover the drainage holes of the flat (or pot) with pieces of broken pot (called *crock*) or gravel, and then fill with soil, making certain that at least the uppermost layer consists of finely screened soil. With your hands, firm the soil around the edges, make smooth, and then, for many seeds, firm moderately with a board or block. Seeds of begonias, gloxinias, and other plants with tiny seeds germinate best when sown on a leveled but not firmed surface. The small roots cannot penetrate packed soil. The seeds may be sown broadcast or in rows. Small seeds may be mixed with fine sand and then scattered over the surface. After sowing, cover relatively large seeds with soil, sand, or, better, with vermiculite. Water by placing the pot or flat in a pan of water so that the water is taken up from below, or use a fine spray. Cover the pot or flat with a pane of glass to retard evaporation, and then, for most seeds, put a sheet of newspaper over the glass. Most seeds germinate well in darkness, but a few require light for germination, among them ranunculus, gloxinia, epilobium, lythrum, and veronica. Seed pots of the latter should not be covered with paper, but should be placed in a shaded part of the greenhouse.

In general, germination is rapid at a temperature about 10 degrees higher than that which is used for raising the crop. The temperature for quickest germination varies with the species. The table on pages 66 to 72 suggests the best temperature for the germination of seeds of many plants. The information is the most reliable now available. There may be some differences between varieties within a species, and with different conditions of germination the optimum temperature may be other than the one indicated in the table. If the indicated temperatures do not give good germination, try higher or lower ones. The lower figure in the column *Temperature to germinate* indicates minimum night temperature; the higher figure maximum day temperature. When only one figure is given, this indicates that a steady temperature should be maintained day and night. The table also shows whether the plants are annuals or perennials. Some of the plants classified as annuals may actually be perennials, but they are cultivated as annuals by florists. We remind you that the temperatures given are for the fastest germination. Seeds will germinate at lower temperatures, but the time may be prolonged. You should not hesitate to start certain seeds because you do not have a spot in the greenhouse where the temperature is in the indicated range. Seeds of many species germinate over a wide range of temperature. Most of us do not have places in the greenhouse where the temperature can be controlled precisely. However, we can place seed flats of those which germinate quickest at 65 to 70 degrees in a warm spot and those which prefer 55 degrees in a cool place in the greenhouse. Never let the soil become dry during the germination period. Avoid waterlogging the soil.

As soon as the seeds have sprouted, remove the paper cover, but leave the glass on for the first week or so. If moisture condenses on the glass, wipe it off, and prop up the end of the glass to allow air to circulate. If the atmosphere is too close

TEMPERATURE AND TIME FOR SEED GERMINATION *

Variety	*Annual or perennial*	*Temperature to germinate*	*Weeks to germinate*
Abutilon	P	68	2-3
Achillea ptarmica	P	68	1-2
Aconitum	P		
Needs light. For best results store seed in damp sand at a temperature of below 40 degrees Fahrenheit for six weeks and then sow.			
Acroclinium	A	68-96	2-3
Ageratum	A	68-86	3
Agrostemma	P	68	2-3
Alyssum	A	68	2-3
Alyssum	P	68-86	3-4
Amaranthus	A	68-86	3-4
Amaryllis	P	68-86	
Slow and uneven to germinate.			
Ampelopsis	P	68	
Slow			
Anchusa italica	P	68-86	3-4
Anemone coronaria	P	68	5-6
Slow and uneven to germinate.			
pulsatilla	P	68	5-6
Anthemis kelwayii	P	68	3-4
tinctoria	P	68	3-4
Antirrhinum	A	54	1-2
On hybrid varieties, it is found better results are obtained at 60-65 degrees Fahrenheit.			
Aquilegia	P	68-86	3-4
Slow to germinate.			
Arabis	P	68	3-4
Aralia	A	68	
Slow and uneven to germinate.			
Arctotis	A	68	2-3
Armeria	P	68	3-4
Asclepias tuberosa	P	68-86	3-4
Fresh seed needs chilling.			
Asparagus plumosus nanus and *sprengeri*	P	68-86	4-6
Cracking seed coat with a knife may increase and assist germination.			
Aster	A	68	2-3
Aster	P	68	2-3
Aubrietia	P	54	2-3

* Vaughan's Seed Company.

TEMPERATURE AND TIME FOR SEED GERMINATION (*Cont.*)

Variety	*Annual or perennial*	*Temperature to germinate*	*Weeks to germinate*
Balsam	A	68	3-4
Baptisia	P	68	
Slow and uneven to germinate.			
Begonia (Fibrous, Tuberous)	P	68	2-3
Needs light.			
Bellis perennis	P	68	1-2
Bell of Ireland	A	86	2-3
Bocconia	P	54-90	1-4
Needs light.			
Boltonia	P	68	2-3
Browallia	A	68	2-3
Cacalia	A	68	2-3
Calceolaria	A	68	2-3
Calendula	A	68-86	2-3
Campanula varieties	P	68-86	2-3
Campanula carpatica	P	68-86	2-3
lactiflora coerulea	P	55-90	2-3
medium	P	68-86	2-3
persicifolia	P	55-90	2-3
pyramidalis	P	68-90	2
Candytuft	A	68-86	1-2
Needs light.			
iberis	P	68	2-3
Canterbury Bells	A	68-86	2-3
Carnation	A & P	68	2-3
Catananche	P	68-86	2-4
Celosia	A	68-86	1-2
Centaurea	A & P	68-86	3-4
Cerastium	P	68	2-4
Cheiranthus	P	54	2-3
Chrysanthemum	A	68	2-4
Chrysanthemum	P	68	2-4
Cineraria	A	68	2-3
Clarkia	A	54-90	1-2
Cleome	A	54-90	1-2
Coleus	P	68-86	2-3
Coreopsis	P	68	2-3
Cosmos	A	68-86	1-2
klondyke	A	68-86	2-4
Cyclamen	P	68	3-4
Cynoglossum	A	68	2-3

TEMPERATURE AND TIME FOR SEED GERMINATION *(Cont.)*

Variety	*Annual or perennial*	*Temperature to germinate*	*Weeks to germinate*
Dahlborg Daisy	A	68	
Slow and uneven to germinate.			
Dahlia	A	68-86	2-3
Daisy shasta	P	68	2-3
Delphinium	P	54	3-4
Dianthus	A & P	68	2-3
Dicentra (Dielytra)	P		
For best results store seed in damp sand at a temperature below 40 degrees Fahrenheit for six weeks and then sow.			
Dictamnus	P		
Give same treatment as *Dicentra.*			
Didiscus	A	68	2-3
Dielytra	P		
See *Dicentra*			
Digitalis	P	68-86	2-3
Dimorphotheca	A	68	2-3
Doronicum	P	68	2-3
Dracaena	P	86	3-4
Dusty Miller	A	68-86	2-4
Echinops	P	68-86	1-4
Edelweiss	P	68-86	1-2
Euphorbia	A & P	68-86	2-3
Fern Spores	P	70-90	
Slow and uneven to germinate.			
Festuca	P	52-90	1-3
Needs light.			
Forget-Me-Not (Myosotis)	P	68	2-3
Freesia	P	54	4-6
Gaillardia	A & P	68	2-3
Gentiana	P	68	1-4
After freezing seed for at least ten days, raise temperature to 68 degrees Fahrenheit.			
Geranium	A & P	54-90	1-6
Slow and uneven to germinate.			
Gerbera	P	68	2-3
Geum	P	68-86	3-4
Gloxinia	P	68	
Needs light.			
Godetia	A	68	2-3
Gourds, ornamental	A	68-86	2-3
Gypsophila	A & P	68	2-3

Temperature and Time for Seed Germination (*Cont.*)

Variety	*Annual or perennial*	*Temperature to germinate*	*Weeks to germinate*
Helenium	P	68	1-2
Helianthemum	P	68-86	2-3
Helianthus	A	68-86	2-3
Heliopsis	P	68	1-2
Heliotrope	A	68-86	3-4
Helleborus	P		
For best results store seed in damp sand at a temperature below 40 degrees Fahrenheit for six weeks and then sow.			
Hemerocallis	P		
Give same treatment as *Helleborus.*			
Hesperis	P	68-86	3-4
Heuchera	P	69-86	2-3
Treating seed with Arasan or Spergon recommended.			
Hibiscus	P	68-86	
Slow and uneven to germinate.			
Hollyhock	P	68	2-3
Hunnemannia	A	68	2-3
Impatiens	A	68	2-4
Incarvillea	P	68	1-2
Ipomoea	A	68-86	1-3
Cracking seed coat with a knife may increase and assist germination.			
Iris	P	54	
For best results store seed in damp sand at a temperature of below 40 degrees Fahrenheit for six weeks and then sow.			
Jacaranda	A	86	2-4
Kalanchoë	P	68	1-2
Kenilworth Ivy	P	54	1-4
Slow and uneven to germinate.			
Lantana	P	68-86	6-7
Larkspur	A	54	3-4
Lathyrus latifolius	P	68-86	2-3
Lavandula	P	52-90	2-3
Leptosyne	A	68	2-3
Liatris	P	68-86	3-4
Lilies	P	68	3-5
Linaria	A	54	2-3
Linaria cymbalaria	P	54	1-4
Slow and uneven to germinate.			
Linum	P	54	3-4
Lobelia	A	68-86	2-3
Lobelia	P	68-86	3-4

TEMPERATURE AND TIME FOR SEED GERMINATION (*Cont.*)

Variety	*Annual or perennial*	*Temperature to germinate*	*Weeks to germinate*
Lunaria	P	68	2-3
Lupinus	A & P	68	2-3
Lychnis	P	68	3-4
Marigold	A	68-86	1-2
Matricaria	P	68-86	2-3
Mesembryanthemum	P	68	1-3
Mignonette	A	54	2-3
Mimosa	A	54-90	3-4
Mimulus	A	54	1-2
Nasturtium	A	68	1-2
Nasturtium, Double	A	68	2-3
Nemesia	A	55	2-3
Nepeta	P	68	2-3
Nierembergia	P	68-86	2-3
Oenothera	P	68-86	1-3
Pansy	A	55-90	2-3
Pentstemon	A	68-80	2-3
Pentstemon	P	68-86	
Slow and uneven to germinate.			
Petunia	A	68	1-2
Doubles and some F-1 Hybrids may need light and higher temperatures for better germination; if not successful, try 80-85 degrees Fahrenheit.			
Phlox	A	68	2-3
Phlox divaricata and *decussata*	P		
Needs over-winter freezing.			
Physalis	P	54-90	3-4
Physostegia	P	54-90	2-3
Platycodon	P	68-86	2-3
Polemonium	P	68-86	3-4
Poppy	A	55	1-2
nudicaule and *orientale*	P	54	1-2
Portulaca	A	68-86	2-3
Potentilla	A	68	1-3
Primula obconica	A	55-90	3-4
Needs light.			
chinese	A	68	3-4
chinese stellata	A	68	3-4
malacoides	A	68-86	2-3
sorts	P	68	3-6
Germination temperatures in this group will vary. Some may require lower temperatures.			

TEMPERATURE AND TIME FOR SEED GERMINATION (*Cont.*)

Variety	*Annual or perennial*	*Temperature to germinate*	*Weeks to germinate*
Pyrethrum	P	68-86	1-3
Some seeds do not completely form. At most 50% germination may be expected.			
Ranunculus	P	68	1-4
Rudbeckia	P	69-86	2-3
Saintpaulia	P	85	3-4
Salpiglossis	A	68-86	2
Salvia	A	68-86	2-3
Salvia	P	68-86	2-3
Sanvitalia	A	68	1-2
Saponaria	P	68	2-3
Saponaria	A	68	2-3
Scabiosa	A & P	68-86	2-3
Schizanthus	A	54	1-2
Shamrock	A	68	1-2
Sidalcea	P	68	2-3
Smilax	A	68-86	3-4
Solanum	A	68-86	2-3
Statice	A	68-86	2-3
Statice	P	68-86	2-4
Some seeds do not completely form. At most 50% germination may be expected.			
Stocks	A	54-90	2
Stokesia	P	68-86	4-6
Streptocarpus	A	68	2-3
Needs light.			
Sweet Peas	A	68	2
Thalictrum	P	68	4-6
Thermopsis	P	68-86	2-3
Thunbergia	A	68-86	2-3
Thymus	P	54-90	1-2
Needs light.			
Tigridia	A	68-86	
Slow and uneven to germinate.			
Tithonia	A	68-86	2-3
Torenia	A	68-86	2
Tritoma	P	68-86	3-4
Trollius	P		
Slow. For best results store seed in damp sand at a temperature below 40 degrees Fahrenheit for six weeks and then sow.			
Tunica saxifraga	P	68-86	1-2
Needs light.			

TEMPERATURE AND TIME FOR SEED GERMINATION (*Cont.*)

Variety	*Annual or perennial*	*Temperature to germinate*	*Weeks to germinate*
Valeriana	P	54-90	3-4
Venidium	A	68-86	4-6
Verbascum	P	86	
Slow to germinate.			
Verbena	A	68-86	3-4
Verbena	P	54-90	2-4
Veronica incana	P	54-90	2
Vinca	A	68	2-3
Viola	P	54-90	2-3
Some varieties may need light.			
Wallflower	P	68	2
Yucca	P	68	
Slow. Never high germination.			
Zinnia	A	68-86	1-2

the seedlings may damp off. Damping-off is a fungus disease that attacks the seedlings at the ground line, and the stem becomes rotted so that the seedling topples over. The disease thrives under wet conditions. As soon as the disease is noted, keep the soil on the dry side, remove the diseased plants and give more air. Watering with a fungicide, such as Wilson's Antidamp or Sunox, is helpful, and may be used as a preventive for seedlings known to be susceptible to damping-off. These fungicides are diluted with water and watered on the soil immediately after the seeds are sown. To control post-emergence damping-off, another application is made a week after the seeds germinate. If the soil is sterilized with heat or chemicals (see pages 55 to 57), and if the seeds are treated with Arasan, Ceresan, Semesan, Spergon, or other fungicide according to the directions given on the package, damping-off can be controlled.

If the seeds are sown on sphagnum moss they germinate promptly and damping-off is seldom a problem. Damping-off and seed decay do not occur in this medium. For this method, nearly fill a pot or flat with soil, then firm it. Place over the soil a half-inch layer of moist sphagnum moss, which has been passed through a quarter-inch screen. If you prefer, you can purchase sphagnum moss that comes already sifted. After watering (preferably with a nutrient solution) and firming the moss, sow the seeds on the sphagnum moss. Small seeds are left uncovered; large ones are covered with screened sphagnum moss. Then place a pane of glass over the container, followed by a sheet of paper. Seedlings grown with this method are easily removed with their roots intact.

Instead of sowing seeds on sphagnum moss you may prefer to sow them on vermiculite. Fill a container nearly full with soil, and then add a three-eighth-inch layer of vermiculite. Fine seeds are merely scattered over this surface; large ones are covered with a layer of vermiculite.

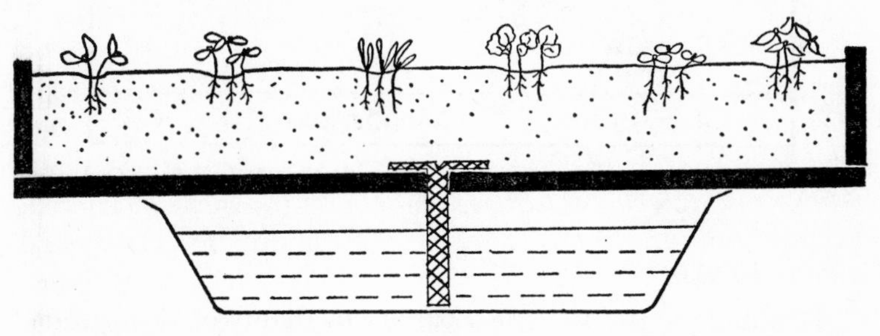

A subirrigated flat furnishes a uniform water supply with a minimum of attention. The wick, made of burlap or glass wool, flares out in the flat and extends into a pan of water on which the flat rests. (Redrawn from Cornell Extension Bulletin 579)

Surface watering of seed pots or flats requires constant attention. We can simplify the watering problem by using a subirrigated pot or flat, as illustrated in the accompanying figure. To prepare a subirrigated flat insert burlap or glass wool wicks in the drainage holes and let them flare out in the pot or flat. The free ends of the wicks extend below, into a vessel of water on which the flat rests.

Watering can also be simplified by sowing seeds on soil in a glass jar and then covering the jar with a sheet of polyethylene film. To prepare such a jar, place it on its side and put in it a layer of gravel, over which place a layer of moist soil. Firm the soil, plant the seeds, and water with a fine spray. Then cover the open end with a sheet of polyethylene film.

(George J. Ball Seed Co.)

Time to sow

If you are going to raise a variety of plants in your greenhouse you will probably want something in flower during all months of the year. Perhaps the fall chrysanthemums can be followed by carnations, snapdragons, calendulas, or some other flower crop. It will take some planning on your part to have plants of another kind ready to put in the bench when the plants which are through flowering have been removed. The following table will help you plan a year-round sequence of blooms. You will notice that the time of flowering is determined by the date on which the seeds are sown. For instance, if you sow seeds of snapdragons in March you can expect flowers from July on. A July sowing will enable you to cut the first flowers at Christmas, and one in November will give you flowers in March and later. Of course, various cultural practices, which we will discuss later, may modify the dates of flowering.

From seedling to mature plant

After the seedlings have made their first set of true leaves they are ready for transplanting; generally first into flats (transplant flats) and later into the bench or pots. (The first leaves to appear on certain seedlings are modified leaves, called *cotyledons.* These generally remain small and soon drop off. The true leaves appear somewhat later and will develop into full-sized ones.)

The general sequence for moving plants along may be diagrammed as follows:

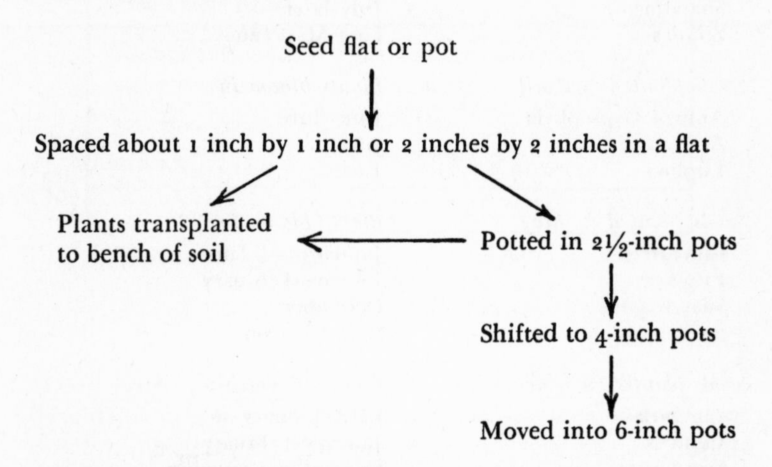

If the plants are to be grown in a bench they may be planted in the bench from the transplant flats or from 2½-inch pots.

FLOWERING SCHEDULE

Seeds planted in January	*Plants bloom in*
Begonias	August–December
Clarkia	April–May
Gloxinias	August–September
Petunias	April–June
Snapdragons	April–June
Stocks	May–June
Sweet peas	April–June

FLOWERING SCHEDULE (*Cont.*)

Seeds planted in February	*Plants bloom in*
Asters	June–July
Marigolds	May
Stocks	May–June
Sweet peas	April–June

Seeds planted in March	*Plants bloom in*
Asters	July
Gerbera	December and later
Primula obconica	December
Primula sinensis	April the following year
Snapdragons	July–later
Zinnias	Late May–June

Seeds planted in April	*Plants bloom in*
Annual Gypsophyla	June–July
Asters	July
Lupines	June

Seeds planted in May	*Plants bloom in*
Cinerarias	January and later
Lupines	January–February
Snapdragons	December
Sweet peas	September on

Seeds planted in June	*Plants bloom in*
Cinerarias	Early January on
Lupines	January–February
Sweet peas	September–December

Seeds planted in July	*Plants bloom in*
Calceolaria	April–May
Calendula	November
Pansies	November on
Primula obconica	April on
Primula sinensis	April on
Snapdragons	Christmas on
Stocks	January–February
Sweet peas	October–February

Seeds planted in August	*Plants bloom in*
Calceolaria	Late May
Calendula	December on

FLOWERING SCHEDULE (*Cont.*)

Seeds planted in August	*Plants bloom in*
Cineraria	February–March
Cyclamen	November–February of following year
Marigolds (winter flowering)	November–January
Nemesia	October–February
Pansies	December–March
Primula malacoides	March and later
Schizanthus	Late December
Snapdragons	February–April
Stocks	January–February
Seeds planted in September	*Plants bloom in*
Calendula	February–March
Cineraria	April–May
Larkspur	April–May
Lupines	January–February
Stocks	February
Sweet peas	December–March
Seeds planted in October	*Plants bloom in*
Calendula	March and later
Larkspur	Late May
Stocks	April on
Sweet peas	February–May
Seeds planted in November	*Plants bloom in*
Calendula	April–May
Larkspur	April–May
Snapdragons	March–June
Stocks	April–May
Sweet peas	March–May
Seeds planted in December	*Plants bloom in*
Calendula	April–May
Clarkia	May
Gloxinia	August
Godetia	June
Nemesia	May
Phlox	February and later
Salpiglossis	May–June
Scabiosa	June
Stocks	Late May
Sweet peas	March–May

Plants grown in pots are shifted to increasingly larger pots until they are in about 6-inch pots, when they should be large enough to flower. Generally the shift is made from 2½- to 4-inch pots and then to 6-inch ones. However, if space is no problem, plants may be shifted directly from 2½-inch into 6-inch pots. Of course, not all plants need be moved into 6-inch pots. A number of plants flower nicely in 4- or 5-inch ones.

Pricking off is a gardener's term for transplanting seedlings. The first step in this process is the preparation of a flat. Scatter gravel or crock over the bottom of the flat to furnish good drainage. Then fill the flat with a soil suitable for the plant. African violets, gloxinias, and tuberous begonias thrive in a mixture of three parts leaf mold, one part loam, and one part sand. Others will do well in good loam. We will have more to say about soil in subsequent chapters. Level the soil and firm it moderately.

Carefully remove the seedlings from the seed flats by lifting them up with a putty knife or similar tool. Avoid breaking roots. The seedlings are moved into the new flat with the help of a spotting board or with a dibble. A spotting board speeds up transplanting. This tool is used to make regularly spaced holes in the soil. Place the root system of a seedling in a hole, and then with your fingers firm the soil about the roots. The dibble technique is also suitable for pricking off seedlings. First, make rows in the soil at regular intervals. Then, with a dibble—a pointed stick—make a hole. Insert the root system, and then firm the soil by pressing with the dibble on the soil near the seedling. When the flat is planted, water it thoroughly. Shade the flat with newspaper or cloth stretched over wires above the plants for the first few days, until the seedlings have recovered from the shock of transplanting.

Seedlings from the seed flat may be moved into plant bands instead of into a transplant flat. Plant bands are square containers made of paper or wood veneer. Being square, they can be arranged without any waste space. When plants are removed from a flat there is always some injury to the root system, but plants may be removed from plant bands without injuring the roots. Arrange the plant bands in a flat or other container so that they rest against each other. Fill with soil. Tap the container to settle, firm the soil, then dibble the seedlings in, one to a band.

After the seedlings have made sufficient growth, they may be benched or potted. To remove plants from a flat, lift the flat and, holding it at an angle, tap one end of the flat on the potting bench. This will compact the soil and leave about an inch of space between one end of the flat and the soil. With a knife, cut through the soil between the first and second rows of plants; then cut between the plants in the first row and remove them.

For *potting and shifting* you will need several sizes of pot. Pots range in half-inch sizes from 2 to 7 inches, and in 1-inch sizes between 7 and 12 inches. There are also 14-, 16-, and 18-inch pots. The pot sizes are the inner diameters at the tops of the pots. With regard to depth of pot, we recognize standard pots, azalea pots, and seed pans. Standard pots are the usual ones. Azalea pots, sometimes called "three-fourths" pots, are only three-quarters as high as standard pots of the same size. They have a more attractive appearance and more stability than standard pots. They are preferable for ferns, azaleas, bulbs, and many other plants. Seed pans are earthenware trays usually 1 to 2 inches deep; they are useful for starting seeds.

Only clean pots should be used. If dirty pots are used the roots will stick to the inside of the pot, and they will be injured when the plant is removed from the pot. Old pots should be scrubbed with plain water and rinsed. If the pots are new soak them in water for about an hour, then allow the surface water to evaporate. The pores of the pot should be filled with water, but the surface should not be wet when the plant is set in.

Potting soil should be neither too wet nor too dry. If, after squeezing a handful of soil, you can see the impression of your fingers and several cracks in the soil, the soil is right for potting. On the other hand, if it won't hold its form it is too dry, and if it feels like a gob of mud it is too wet.

Plants from flats are generally potted in 2½- or 3-inch pots. The accompanying figures illustrate potting a plant. Add enough soil to the pot so that when the ball of the plant rests on the soil, the top of it will be about half an inch below the rim of the pot. Hold the plant in position with one hand and with the other fill the pot with soil. Then, with your thumbs, firm the soil. Tap the pot to settle the soil. Then water the plant and keep it in a shaded place for a few days.

In time it will be necessary to move the plants into larger pots. *Shifting* is the gardener's name for transferring potted plants to larger pots. An experienced grower can look at a plant and tell whether it needs shifting. If you are in doubt whether a plant is ready for shifting, knock it out of the pot and note the extent of the roots. If the roots form a fairly dense network around the soil, the plant needs shifting. If only a few roots are seen it is best to wait a while.

The removal of a plant from a pot is called *knocking out.* To knock a plant out of a pot, hold the pot by the rim with the thumb and little finger, and spread the other fingers over the surface of the soil. The stem of the plant should be between your first and second fingers. Hold the pot with the other hand and turn it upside down. Then rap the edge of the rim of the pot against the potting bench. Generally, only one sharp rap is needed to get the plant out of the pot. After the plant is removed, it is *shouldered;* that is, part of the surface soil is rubbed off so fresh soil may take its place in the larger pot in which it is to be placed.

Pots 4 inches in diameter and larger should be provided with crock or pebbles for good drainage. Place two or three pieces of crock (pieces of broken pot) over the drainage hole. Scoop enough soil into the pot so that when the ball of the plant is placed on it, the top will be about an inch below the rim of the new pot. With the ball in the center, scoop in enough soil to fill the pot somewhat above the rim. Then, with the thumbs of both hands, or with a potting stick, firm the soil. When potting into 4- and 6-inch pots, the soil can be firmed by pressure with the thumbs. For 8-inch and larger pots use a potting stick to tamp the soil. After the soil is firmed, tap the pot on the potting bench to settle the soil. Then water the plant thoroughly. When a plant is properly potted, there will be sufficient space between the rim of the pot and the soil to hold enough water to moisten the soil from top to bottom. This space varies from about half an inch for plants in 4-inch pots to an inch for those in 8-inch ones.

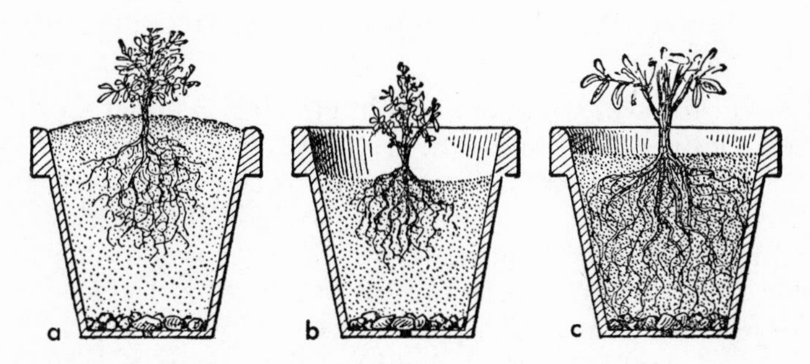

Examples of poor (*a* and *b*) and good (*c*) potting. In *a,* the pot is too full, with no space left for water. In *b,* the pot does not contain enough soil. (From *Propagation of Plants,* by M. G. Kains and L. M. McQuesten; Orange Judd Co.)

Wilting of newly potted plants may be reduced by syringing them several times a day and providing them with shade. After the first thorough watering keep the soil somewhat on the dry side until root action is good.

The techniques of sowing seed, transplanting, potting, and shifting which we have just described apply to plants which we grow in soil. Orchids and bromeliads require special techniques, described in Chapters 16 and 19.

CHAPTER 6

PROPAGATING PLANTS

THERE ARE CERTAIN advantages in growing plants from cuttings, bulbs, corms, and tubers. These methods, as well as others which do not make use of seeds, are collectively referred to as vegetative propagation. In cases in which plants will not come true from seeds, it is the only way to increase your stock of a particular variety. A stem or leaf cutting will reproduce the parent plant exactly, as will bulbs, corms, or tubers, and, of course, divisions. New varieties can be obtained by making hybrid crosses. When the seedlings flower, some may be mediocre, some average, and some superior. Among the best, there may be a few you will wish to perpetuate. Such strains often cannot be maintained by seed, but by vegetative propagation you can build up large numbers of plants of any given variety. Not only will plants grown from cuttings be exactly like the parents, but by this technique you can get larger plants in a shorter time.

If you will only try, you will find plant propagation very valuable and interesting. Fill a portion of a bench with sand or some other rooting medium and insert cuttings in it. This technique is an easy and dependable way to increase greenhouse plants, garden plants, and even trees and shrubs.

Cuttings

There are three major types of cuttings (sometimes called slips): *leaf* cuttings, *stem* cuttings, and *root* cuttings. Only a few plants, such as *Anemone japonica,* cottonwood, horseradish, oriental poppy, and raspberry, may be reproduced by root cuttings, but many kinds can be propagated by leaf and stem cuttings. Among the choice plants which can be increased by leaf cuttings are begonias, gloxinias, African violets, and kalanchoë. Practically all plants can be increased by stem cuttings.

If you plan to make many cuttings, it would pay you to set aside a portion of a bench just for propagation. Fill this part of the bench with the medium you will use for rooting cuttings. To reduce wilting and to furnish bottom heat you may wish to use a propagating box. The box should be about a foot high and it might well be furnished with a hotbed heating cable, especially if you keep your greenhouse at a night temperature of 60 degrees or below. A hotbed kit containing an electric cable, thermostat, and instructions may be purchased at seed stores or from mail-order houses. Put down a thin layer of sand on the bench, string out the cable, and then cover it with the rooting medium. The bottom heat given off by the cable hastens the rooting of many cuttings. After the cuttings are inserted in the case, a piece of glass or celloglass may be placed over the top.

Vermiculite, sand, peat, or a mixture of sand and peat are good rooting media, for they furnish the cuttings with ample oxygen as well as water. Cuttings of many plants root best at 70 degrees. In addition, a high humidity favors rooting.

Of course, a propagating bench is not absolutely necessary. Many gardeners merely fill a pot or flat with the appropriate rooting medium and keep it in a shaded spot. Other growers rig up an enclosure made of cellophane or polyethylene film around the container and the cuttings. Plastic plant domes or inexpensive glass or plastic bowls may also be placed over the cuttings to keep the air humid. We have found that an apple box with a glass cover serves very well. Cuttings of chrysanthemums and geraniums are often potted in a mixture of soil, sand, and well-rotted manure (or leaf mold). Here the cuttings take root and grow until they are large enough to require shifting.

Stem cuttings

Among the plants which are usually propagated by stem cuttings are carnations, chrysanthemums, geraniums, poinsettias, and gardenias. Before making the cuttings, examine the plants carefully and take cuttings only from desirable varieties and healthy plants. Never take cuttings from a diseased plant with the expectation that they will recover. You will merely be asking for trouble. The best stem cuttings are obtained from stems that are moderately hard, not soft and flabby. If the stem cracks as you bend it, it is about right. Cut off the top four or five inches of the stem, generally making the cut just below a joint. Remove the lower leaf or two and dip the basal end into a hormone powder, such as Rootone or Hormodin. Then insert the cutting in the rooting medium. Cuttings of a great variety of plants are best inserted in firmed sand, but those of other plants, for example carnations and geraniums, root well in sand that has not been firmed. With either a firmed or unfirmed rooting medium the sand should be moist before the cuttings are inserted. If the rooting medium is loose, simply push the basal end of the cutting into it. With a firmed medium, insert the cuttings in holes made with a dibble or in a groove made by drawing a knife through the packed medium. In either case, firm the sand after the cuttings are planted.

Vermiculite is being used more and more as a rooting medium. When using vermiculite, fill the bench, pot, or flat with it. Do not pack, but water thoroughly. Most cuttings can be pushed into the vermiculite. A hole or groove generally is not necessary.

Gardeners are experimenting with polyethylene film and sphagnum moss in the rooting of cuttings. The method seems to work very well. Spread out a strip of polyethylene film about 6 inches wide and a couple of feet long. Cover the top three inches of the sheet with moist sphagnum moss. Place the cuttings at intervals along the moss with their tops extending above the moss. Cover the basal parts of the cuttings with sphagnum, and then fold the lower three inches of the plastic over the sphagnum and basal parts of the cuttings. Start at one end and roll up the strip. It will now stand up, and it should be placed in a moist part of the greenhouse. Special kits containing sphagnum moss and polyethylene film treated with rooting hormones are now on the market. Polyethylene film is used for packaging carrots and other vegetables. These bags may be used, or you can get new ones at the dime store.

After the cuttings are inserted in the desired rooting medium, water them thoroughly. After-care consists of shading, syringing, and keeping the sand, vermiculite, or other medium moist but not wet. The cuttings should be provided with shade. If they are exposed to direct sunlight they lose water so rapidly that they shrivel. Frequent syringing of the foliage keeps them from wilting unduly.

Potting rooted cuttings

When the cuttings are rooted they should be potted without delay. The cuttings are ready for potting when the roots are between half an inch and an inch long. If they are allowed to remain in the rooting medium too long they become stunted, and may remain so even though they are subsequently given good care.

Cuttings are often potted in 2½-inch pots. Partially fill the pot with soil. Hold the plant so that the roots spread over the soil. Then fill the pot and firm the soil. Water the plants and place them in a shaded spot for a few days. From the 2½-inch pots they may be planted in the bench or shifted into larger pots, according to the method described in Chapter 4.

Air layerage

Philodendrons, the rubber plant, dieffenbachia, and dracaena may be propagated by air layerage, as illustrated in the accompanying illustration. A cut is made halfway through the stem, and the stem is slit up the middle for a distance of a couple of inches. The cut surface is then dusted with a rooting hormone, after which a small amount of sphagnum

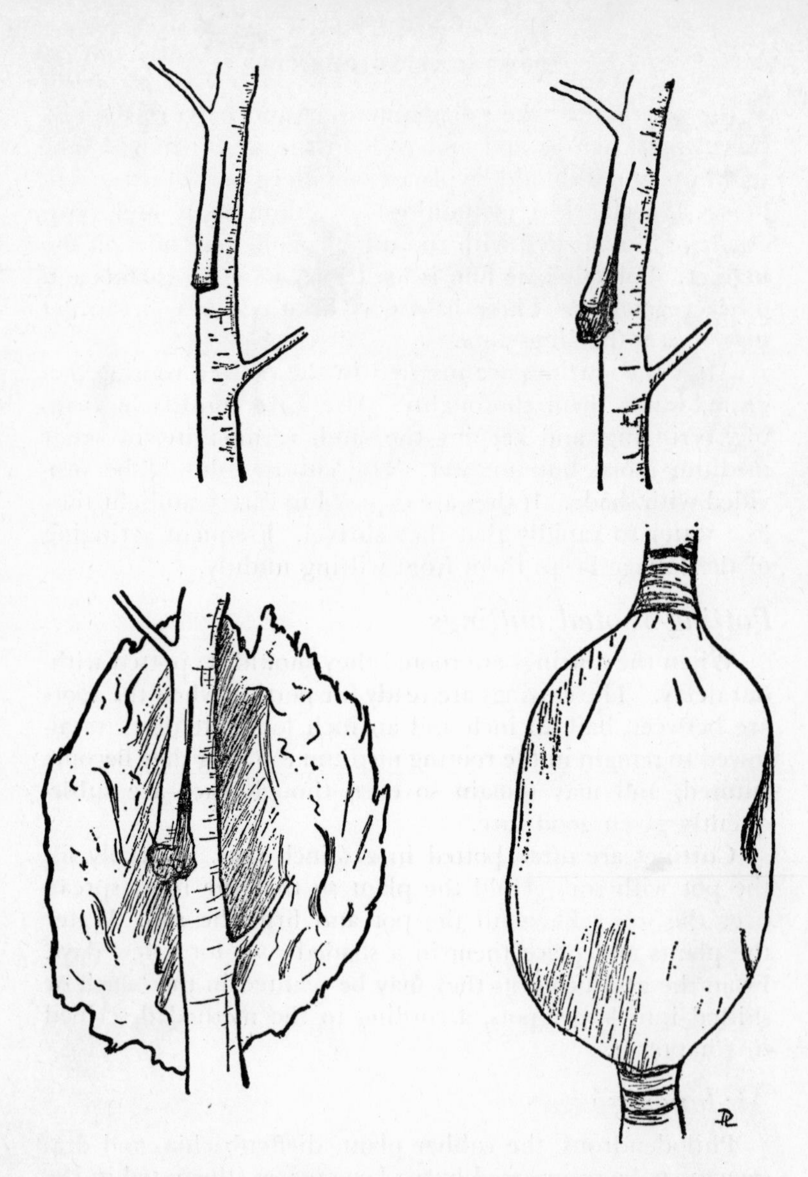

Steps in air layerage. The stem is cut about half-way through and then slit up the middle (*upper left*); moist sphagnum moss is inserted (*upper right*), sphagnum moss is wrapped around the area (*lower left*), and the sphagnum is covered with a sheet of polyethylene film. After roots form, the new plant will be potted.

Large chrysanthemums are grown by allowing only one flower to develop on a stem.

Below: pinching is used to promote branching and to time a crop. The left figure illustrates a soft pinch: only the very soft tip of the stem with immature leaves is removed. When several upper leaves and a considerable part of the stem is removed, the pinch is known as a hard pinch.

Left: a wire with a loop at the top is useful for staking many plants. Here you see the loop around a hyacinth stem. *Below:* wires running lengthwise and strings crosswise are used to support certain plants. This method provides good support for carnations, calendulas, chrysanthemums, snapdragons, stocks, and other plants.

Artificially shortening the days hastened flowering of kalanchoë, a short-day plant, shown in the top photograph. Left to right, short-day treatment started on July 15, August 1, August 15, and August 30 respectively; the plant at the extreme right had normal-day length. The plants were photographed on October 22. The day length may be shortened by covering plants with light-proof black sateen cloth (*below*). (Kenneth Post and Cornell University)

Below: Prolonging the day by turning on the lights just before sundown and letting them burn until 10 P.M. will prevent flowering of short-day plants and promote the flowering of long-day plants when the days are naturally short. Hundred-watt incandescent lamps, in reflectors, spaced 6 feet apart and 4 to 5 feet above the plants will do the job, as will 40- or 60-watt bulbs suspended 2 feet above the plants.

Above: cottony sacs of the woolly cactus scale. Parathion gives excellent control but is dangerous to use. (A. Earl Pritchard and California Agricultural Experiment Station) *Right:* leaf miner injury on chrysanthemum leaves. DDT gives good control. (Agricultural Research Service, United States Department of Agriculture)

Below: galls of the chrysanthemum gall midge on chrysanthemum leaves. The gall midge may be controlled with DDT or benzene hexachloride. *Left:* terminal growth of carnation, showing injury by the carnation leafroller. Pyrethrum dusts are reported to give effective control when a second application is made after a 30-minute interval. (A. Earl Pritchard of California Agricultural Experiment Station)

Webbing of two-spotted mite on chrysanthemum. (Agricultural Research Service, United States Department of Agriculture) *Below:* mealy bugs.

The wire and string method gives good support for carnations. *Above:* attaching the second tier of wires to the support at the end of the bench. The wires run lengthwise, strings crosswise. Later, another tier of wires will be run from top cross bar. *Below:* a close-up showing lengthwise wires and cross strings.

Aphids are sucking insects. They can be controlled with nicotine, pyrethrum, or rotenone.

Below: pressure fumigator in operation. (Pennsylvania State University Agricultural Extension Service, College of Agriculture)

How to grow carnations. Take cuttings from plants from December to February. Root the cuttings in sand. Pot the rooted cutting; when it is thoroughly established, pinch the young plant to promote branching. When flower buds appear, disbud the stems, removing all flower buds except the terminal one from each stem.

moss is inserted at the slit stem. Next, sphagnum moss is placed around the area, followed by a covering of polyethylene film. After roots form, the rooted top portion is separated and potted. The basal portion may be saved or thrown away. This technique may also be used for propagating trees and shrubs outdoors. The rooted twig is severed from the parent after leaf fall. In cold regions it is best to pot the new plant and carry it over the first winter in a cold frame or a greenhouse.

Leaf cuttings

You can increase your favorite gloxinias, African violets, Rex begonias, streptocarpus, and kalanchoë plants by leaf cuttings. Kalanchoë can be increased by placing a leaf flat on sand. New plants will develop from notches along the margin of the leaf. Sometimes young plants even develop on leaves which remain on the plant.

The Rex begonia is increased by removing a leaf, cutting through the main veins just below the point at which two large branch veins come together, and then placing the leaf flat on moist sand or on a half-and-half mixture of sand and peat which is in a box or other container. A few small pebbles may be placed on the leaf to keep it in contact with the sand, or staples made of wire may be used. The container should then be covered with a pane of glass and provided with shade. In time a young plant will develop at each cut. Another method of increasing Rex begonias is to cut the leaf into triangular pieces 2 inches across, making certain that each piece has a major vein. The pieces are inserted to a depth of half an inch in the rooting medium.

New plants develop at the base of leaf stalks (petioles) of African violets, *Begonia melior,* streptocarpus, and gloxinias. To propagate these plants, remove a mature leaf with its stalk from the base of the plant. Insert the leaf stalk in moist sand or vermiculite to a depth of 1 to 2 inches. If you do not have a propagating case, use a fish bowl, a large glass jar, a box covered with glass, or a terrarium as the container for the sand or vermiculite. Or you may fill a pot with vermiculite, insert the leaf stalk and then cover the pot with a jar. The moist atmosphere in such containers keeps the leaf from wilting and hastens the formation of new plants. In due time, one to several young plants will form at the base of the leaf stalk. These are removed to flats or small pots.

Time to start cuttings

Cuttings should be made at the appropriate season. June is a good time to propagate shrubs for outdoor use. The young shoots of lilac, forsythia, spirea, rose, eleagnus, clematis, and other shrubs are in the proper state of maturity in June. Cuttings of these shrubs root readily at this time. Cuttings of evergreens are best made in November.

The time for making leaf or stem cuttings of greenhouse plants will depend to some extent on the time you want the plants to flower and how large you want them to be when they flower.

The following table shows the time at which many commercial growers start cuttings of a variety of plants, and the time at which the plants flower. Of course, if the plants are to flower at the indicated times, they must be cultivated in a precise way. Methods of culture are given in subsequent chapters.

Plant	*Take cuttings*	*Flower*
Begonias, Rex	November	Plants in 4" pots by fall
Bouvardia	February–March	November–January
Carnations	December–February	Fall on
Chrysanthemums	May	October–December
Coleus	September	Large plants by spring
Fuchsia	March	June–July
Gardenia	December–February	December
Geraniums	August	May
Hydrangea	February	Following year
Lantana	August–September	May on
Philodendron	October	May–June for plants of fair size
Poinsettias	June–September	Christmas
Saintpaulia (African violet)	December–February	November on

Division of plants

Some greenhouse plants can be divided, among them orchids, African violets, aspidistra, and some ferns. The division of an orchid plant is described in Chapter 19. Large African violet plants generally have several crowns, each with its own tuft of leaves. These plants can be divided. Knock a plant out of the pot, loosen the soil ball, and separate the crowns with the least possible injury to the roots. Pot each piece separately.

Bulbs, corms, and tubers

Many desirable greenhouse plants are started from bulbs, corms, and tubers, among them daffodils, tulips, amaryllis, tuberous begonias, and gloxinias. We will have more to say about the propagation of these plants in subsequent chapters, but let us here consider the structure of bulbs, corms, and tubers. The *bulb* of a tulip or daffodil consists of fleshy scales surrounding immature leaves and flower parts. The bulbs of these plants which you receive in the fall should have the flower parts already formed in miniature. You may see the flower parts by slicing through a bulb vertically and examining it with a hand lens. You will see an immature flower surrounded by leaves in the center of the bulb. Because the flowers are already formed you need only give the bulbs the proper conditions for their development. Until the shoots of tulips and daffodils are two or three inches high the plants should be kept at a temperature of about 48 degrees. To meet this requirement place the potted bulbs in a room at 48 degrees, or place the pots in a cold frame and cover them with straw, or bury the pots in a trench and cover them with soil.

At a temperature of 48 degrees, the leaves, stems, and flower buds of tulips and daffodils elongate most rapidly and in proper balance with one another. Furthermore, root growth is most rapid at this temperature. When the shoots are 2 or 3 inches long and the roots well developed, the best temperature for growing the plants shifts from 48 degrees to 60 degrees. Hence when the shoots are 2 to 3 inches long, the pots can be moved into the greenhouse.

Flower buds are not present in bulbs of all plants. Inside the scaly leaves of a lily bulb a short stem bearing small leaves is present, but no flowers. In lilies the flowers form after the plant has made considerable growth.

Corms, such as those of the crocus and gladiolus, are often called bulbs, but from a structural standpoint a corm is very different from a bulb. In corms, the bulk of the tissue is fleshy stem tissue, whereas in bulbs it consists of fleshy scalelike leaves. Each ring that you see when you cut an onion or tulip bulb is a fleshy scalelike leaf. You will not see such modified leaves if you cut a section through a corm of gladiolus or crocus. A corm is solid, not scaly.

The tuberous begonia has a modified underground stem known as a *tuber,* which is a thickened stem and bears eyes. The entire tuber of a tuberous begonia is generally planted, but if you wish you can cut it into pieces, each with an eye, and plant the pieces separately.

CHAPTER 7

CONTROLLING SHAPE, SIZE, AND FLOWERING TIME

WE CAN CONTROL to some extent the shape of a plant and the time at which it will flower. We may want some plants to be bushy specimens, producing a multitude of blossoms; others we may want to grow to a single stem, bearing one large exhibition bloom. An understanding of where leaves, stems, and flowers are produced will enable you to control, at least to some extent, the shape, stature, and flowering of your plants.

The tip of the stem, both of the main and branch stems, is the region where new stem tissue, additional leaves, and flowers are formed. During the growing period the stem tips form leaves. Then, when conditions are just right they form flowers instead of leaves. Later in this chapter we will consider the conditions which bring about this remarkable change in behavior.

Pinching

If we remove the very tip of a stem, that stem cannot grow longer and no new leaves can form on it. If you will examine any stem you will notice that a lateral bud is present at every joint of the stem, just above the point at which each leaf is attached. These lateral buds, like the very tip of the stem, have the capacity to develop stem tissue and new leaves, and, under certain conditions, flowers. When the tip of the stem is present and producing leaves it forms a hormone that moves down the main stem and prevents these lateral buds from growing. When the stem tip is forming flowers, this hormone is no longer produced and the side buds grow into branches.

If we want the lateral buds to develop into branches before flowering time we simply remove the tip of the stem. Generally we remove the tip with our thumb and first finger, and hence call the process *pinching.* If we remove only the extreme tip we call such removal a soft pinch. If we remove a length of the stem with several leaves we call it a hard pinch. Never remove all the leaves from a plant when you pinch it, even though buds are present where leaves have fallen; but instead, leave enough foliage to support the plant. Remember the leaves are the foodmaking organs of the plant.

Suppose we want a bushy plant and that we now have a plant with just one stem. After we pinch the tip of the stem several lateral buds will develop into branches. When these are about 4 inches long we can remove the stem tip of each. Then several lateral buds on each branch will develop, and the resulting plant will be a bushy one.

With some plants we can delay flowering by pinching off the tip of the stem. Suppose the tip of a snapdragon stem is just about to produce flowers. If we let the plant alone it will flower in a short time. If we pinch off the stem tip, flowering will be delayed, because the lateral buds must first grow into branches bearing leaves before flowers can be produced. Only after the branches have reached a certain size will they produce flowers.

Hence we can delay the flowering of a plant and time the crop by removing the tip of the stem. If we pinch plants at a certain time we can have flowers on a predictable date. For example, if young snapdragon plants started from seed in July are pinched in August, they will flower at Christmas. On the other hand, unpinched snapdragon plants started from seed at the same time will flower in late October and early November.

Pinching standard chrysanthemums—those which are to bear just one large flower on a stem—on a certain date makes for higher quality flowers. After the plants are pinched, several branches will develop. One or two are allowed to develop; the others are removed. When side branches develop on the remaining stems, they are removed. Furthermore, the stems are disbudded. The date for pinching varies with the variety, as listed on page 137.

Disbudding

If only one flower develops on a stem it will be a large one. For instance, to secure large flowers of calendulas, carnations, and certain chrysanthemums, we remove all but one of the flower buds on each stem. The removal of unwanted flower buds is called *disbudding*. We will have more to say about disbudding when we discuss the culture of various greenhouse plants.

Plant supports

A number of greenhouse plants need support to keep their stems straight, and to enhance their beauty and symmetry. Furthermore, properly staked plants occupy less bench space than sprawling, unstaked ones. Don't wait until the stem becomes crooked and falls over before staking a plant. If you stake a plant before the need is apparent, the stem will be straight and the stake will be quite inconspicuous when the plant is in flower. Wooden, bamboo, or metal stakes made of #4 wire are suitable for pot plants. Sink the stake firmly in the pot. Fasten a piece of raffia or soft string to the stake, and after passing it around the stem tie it somewhat firmly to the stake, but not so tightly that it interferes with the growth of the stem. Hyacinths and some other plants may be supported with wire pushed into the soil and bent at the top to form a horizontal loop around the stem of the plant. Certain plants can be supported by an encircling string or wire attached at the proper height to three or more upright stakes.

Plants growing in benches may be supported by stakes. If the stakes are many feet tall they should be fastened at their tops to an overhead wire running the length of the bench, above the row. Wires running lengthwise some distance above the soil and between the rows of plants with crosswise strings at intervals furnish good support for carnations, pompon chrysanthemums, and snapdragons. A more detailed discussion of this method will be found on pages 131-32, 134.

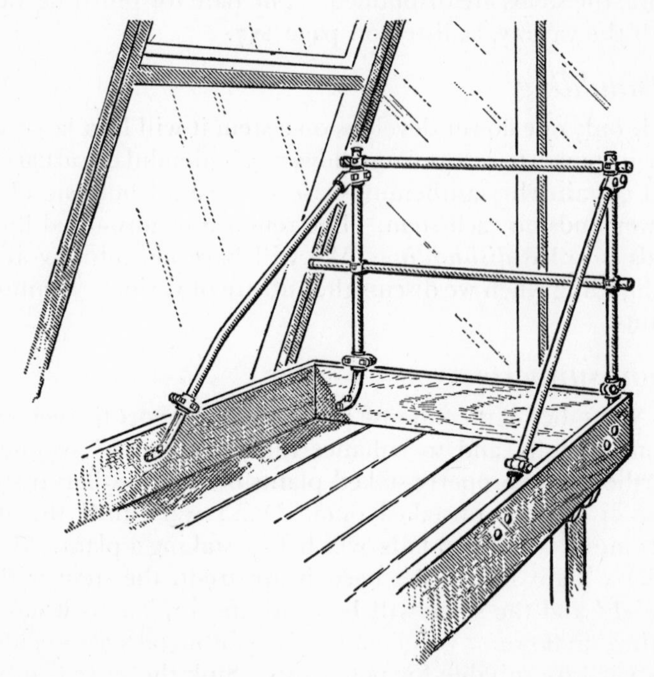

To support plants, wires will be run from this frame to a similar one at the other end of the bench. Strings, run crosswise, will then be tied to the wires. (Lord and Burnham)

Flowering

To get the greatest satisfaction from our greenhouses we want some plants in flower during all months of the year. When one kind is through flowering, we should have something else to take its place. We have seen that the time certain plants are started determines when they blossom, and we have noted that flowering of some kinds can be delayed by pinching. Furthermore, we know that some plants flower over a long period once they have reached a certain size, for example African violets, carnations, snapdragons, pansies, roses, sweetpeas, and calendulas.

Other plants flower only at certain seasons—chrysanthemums in the fall, poinsettias at Christmas, the China aster in the summer. Length of day and temperature markedly influence the season when these nonperpetual flowering plants bloom. These plants, as well as many others, will not flower unless the day length is within a certain range. We call chrysanthemums and poinsettias short-day plants; the China aster we call a long-day plant. Plants which flower when the days are either long or short are called day-neutral plants. The discussion which follows gives the general principles for the control of flowering. More detailed directions are given for certain plants when their culture is discussed in later chapters.

The short-day plants in general flower when the days are less than 13 hours long, that is, 13 hours of light and 11 hours of darkness each day. Among these are some species that will flower only when the day is less than 12 hours, and others for which 14 hours represents a short day. The long-day plants produce flower buds when the days are longer than 13 or 14 hours. It is possible to get earlier flowering of short- and long-day plants by giving them the day length they require to set flower buds. It is possible to delay their flowering by artificially imitating the day length that prevents flower bud formation.

Short-day plants. Short-day plants normally flower in autumn, winter, or early spring. Chrysanthemums, Christmas cactus, *Euphorbia fulgens,* kalanchoë, stevia, and poinsettia are typical short-day plants. They may be brought into flower earlier than usual by artifically shortening the day to the number of hours conducive to flower-bud formation. A framework of wood or wire should be constructed around the plants. Black sateen cloth that is light proof, or heavy black paper, is then arranged so that it can be conveniently drawn over the framework each afternoon and removed each morning. All light must be excluded, else the project will fail. The usual schedule is to cover the plants at 5 P.M. and uncover them at 7 A.M., thus giving them 10 hours of daylight, and 14 hours of darkness. (In the trade this is loosely called *shading*. You should not confuse this type of shading with lessening the light intensity by painting the glass or using cheesecloth).

Treatment must be started before the buds form, otherwise nothing is gained. It is well to know the normal time for bud formation, to be able to plan how long in advance to begin treatment. The periods of bud formation for some short-day plants are:

Plant	*Normal bud-formation period*
Chrysanthemum	August 15 to 25
Kalanchoë blossfeldiana	September 25 to October 5
Lady Mac begonia	October 10 to 20
Poinsettia	October 10 to 20
Stevia	September 20 to 27

The earlier in the season they are exposed to short days, the sooner they will flower. If the treatment is started so early that the flower buds form before the days become naturally short, the treatment must be continued until the flower buds are well developed. If the short days of fall coincide with your artificially shorted days, treatment may be discontinued.

Short-day treatment of chrysanthemums is widely practiced. Their flowers will be ready to cut 8 to 10 weeks after the beginning of the darkening period. Varieties of chrysanthemums which naturally flower in late October can be made to flower in September or even August by starting short-day treatment at the appropriate time. The days must be kept shortened until the flower buds of the spray types (pompons) show color and until those of the standards are the size of a nickel. When the buds are of this size they will complete their development with either long or short days. For kalanchoë, when the darkening period is begun July 20 and continued until September 20, the plants flower October 20. If they are shaded from August 15 to October 1, they flower early in December. Christmas begonias, such as Lady Mac and Melior, will flower in late November if they are grown with short days from September 1 until they bloom. The Christmas cactus flowers at Christmas if given short days beginning August 15. *Euphorbia fulgens* flowers in mid-December when given short days from September 20.

If you wish to delay the flowering of short-day plants, you act on the fact that they normally do not set flower buds when the days are long. You can postpone their flowering by artificially lengthening the days before, during, and after their normal bud-forming period. Then when you wish them to set flower buds, you simply discontinue the long-day treatment, and let them be exposed to the normally short days of the season. The artificial light used to augment the day hours need not be strong. Ordinary 40- or 60-watt incandescent bulbs in reflectors are placed 2 feet above the plants and 4 feet apart, or if you wish you can use 100-watt lamps spaced 6 feet apart and 4 or 5 feet above the plants. These are turned on at sunset, and turned off at 10 P.M., and serve to give the plants a day length of 14 hours or more.

By controlling the day length, chrysanthemums can be brought into flower during any month. For February flowering of chrysanthemums, the plants are given long days until December 1, when supplemental lighting is discontinued. Thereafter, the plants are exposed to the naturally short days and hence they produce flower buds. Flowering of other short-day plants can be controlled in the same way.

If you do not wish to delay the flowering of short-day plants during fall or winter, be careful not to prolong the days unintentionally by keeping the greenhouse light on in the evening.

Long-day plants. Long-day plants produce flower buds when the days are more than 13 or 14 hours long. In Miami, Florida, the days are more than 14 hours long (including civil twilight) from April 26 to August 15. (Civil twilight is the time after sunset or before sunrise during which, on clear days, there is enough light for ordinary outdoor occupations. It ends, or begins, when the sun is about 6° below the horizon.) In San Francisco the period of long days extends from April 11 to September 1; in Ithaca, New York, from April 1 to September 15. Many of the plants which flower in late spring and summer are long-day plants. Feverfew, scabiosa, rudbeckia, and the China aster are typical long-day plants. Long-day plants can be flowered in winter by supplementing the day length with artificial light. We refer to this lengthening of days as *lighting*.

You may want to light a portion of a bench in your greenhouse. Forty- or 60-watt bulbs in reflectors are suspended 2 feet above the plants and spaced 4 feet apart. The lights are turned on just before sunset, and turned off at 10 P.M. when the days are short, from fall to spring. You can control the lights manually, or install a time switch which will automatically turn the lights on and off. To keep the light restricted to the desired part of the bench, separate this area from the rest of the bench with pieces of black cloth hung vertically. Perhaps you have some plants which flower only when the days are short; these will not flower if they are exposed to the artificial lights being used on the neighboring plants.

Many plants, certain day-neutral ones as well as long-day plants, will flower earlier if they are grown in the area where the days are prolonged and in some instances they will be more floriferous. Among the plants which respond in this way are China aster, Boston yellow daisy, centauria, clarkia, feverfew, gardenia, lily, marigold, nasturtium, pansy, salpiglossis, and violet.

In general, plants should be well established before they are given additional light. Certain ones, the China aster for example, can be grown with long days from the seedling stage on. This plant can be flowered in March or April by sowing seeds in September and growing the plants with supplemental light until the flowers are cut. There are a few kinds which, although they can be flowered earlier with supplemental light, give low quality flowers borne on weak stems. For this reason do not light bouganvilleas, calendulas, carnations, cinerarias, snapdragons, and freezias.

Indeterminate or day-neutral plants. Plants such as carnations, African violets, snapdragons, roses, and tomatoes, which flower when the days are either short or long, are known as day-neutral plants. These plants flower almost continuously.

Temperature and flowering

Night temperatures markedly influence the initiation of flowers. If night temperatures are not appropriate for the individual variety, it does not flower. For a number of years we had cymbidium orchids in a greenhouse kept at a night temperature of 60 degrees. The plants were healthy and grew rapidly, but they did not flower. We moved them into our other greenhouse and kept the night temperature at 50 degrees. That fall they set flower buds and developed a profusion of blooms. For raising cymbidium plants to flowering size we recommend that they be grown at a night temperature of 60 degrees. When they are of flowering size they should be grown at 50 degrees. During winter, stocks flower profusely when the night temperature is 50 degrees, but do not flower at 60 degrees. Other plants which flower only when the night temperature is less than 60 degrees are greenhouse buddleia, calceolaria, cineraria, Martha Washington geranium, and wallflower.

The response of plants to length of day can be modified by temperature. At one temperature a plant may flower when the days are short, but at a different temperature it may flower when the days are long. Poinsettias are generally considered to be short-day plants, flowering at Christmas. Poinsettia plants exposed to night temperatures of 63 to 65 degrees are indeed short-day plants, but if they are grown at a night temperature of 55 degrees, they become long-day plants and at this cooler temperature will not flower during the short days of winter. If they are raised with a night temperature of 70 degrees, they do not flower at all. The flowering of Christmas cactus is also affected by both day length and temperature.

This plant flowers well with night temperatures of 60 to 65 degrees and short days. With night temperatures of 55 degrees, the Christmas cactus is a day-neutral plant, flowering when the days are either long or short. At night temperatures of 70 to 75 degrees, it does not flower under either long- or short-day conditions.

Length of day and dormancy

In the autumn we can look out our living-room window and see a cottonwood which is green on one side and golden on the other; one side bears leaves with the green of summer, the other leaves of autumnal color. The green side is near the street light, the gold away from the light. Where the days are artificially prolonged by the light, the leaves are active; where the light is too low to influence the branches, the branches are dormant.

One year we thought that we could get a head start by planting seeds of tuberous begonias in late fall instead of January or February, the recommended months. The seeds germinated promptly, but the seedlings did not grow appreciably until the following spring, when the days became longer than 12 hours. We know now that we could have kept those seedlings growing through the winter months by lengthening the days artificially until 10 P.M. When the days are 14 hours or more in length the seedlings grow, and flowering sized plants come into bloom. When the days are 12 hours or less, and the night temperature 60 degrees or above, growth ceases and mature plants stop flowering. During short days the tubers below the ground grow. Gloxinias seem to behave in a similar manner. Not only do gloxinia seedlings benefit when grown with supplemental light during the short days of winter, but so also do plants grown from tubers. If such plants are grown with supplemental light, they will make better growth and produce more and earlier flowers than those grown during short days.

We can keep orchid seedlings growing actively during the winter months by prolonging the days, thereby growing plants to flowering size in a shorter time.

You will find still other uses for the lighted area. Leaf cuttings of Lorraine and Elatior begonias remain healthy and root more quickly if they are grown with long days. Both stem and leaf cuttings of many plants respond in a similar manner if they are planted during the short days of December, January, and February.

CHAPTER 8

PLANT PESTS

PESTS WEAKEN PLANTS, deform and disfigure flowers, and spread disease organisms. It requires constant care to keep them under control. It is better to spray regularly, say at biweekly or monthly intervals, than to wait for the insect population to build up before control measures are taken. Pests can increase at an alarming rate when prevention is not practiced.

Good culture and cleanliness will help in controlling pests. Crowding of plants leads to a vicious circle of events. Crowding makes it difficult to reach plants with insecticides, and populations of insects build up. It also makes it difficult to water and fertilize plants, and the starved plants are more susceptible to many insects. If the greenhouse is continually too hot and dry you can expect an outbreak of red spiders as well as of certain other pests.

You will need a good sprayer and a duster, as well as insecticides for specific pests. A tank sprayer with a pump to build up a pressure great enough to break the spray into fine droplets is suitable for liquid sprays. If your greenhouse is very small you may find a hand sprayer adequate. When spraying or dusting, direct the insecticide to the tips of the shoots, the undersides of leaves, and at the junction between stem and leaves, where the insects congregate.

A large array of insecticides is available to use against specific pests. DDT, one of the first of the modern insecticides, is effective against thrips, flies, certain aphids, beetles, and scales. But it does not kill mites, springtails, slugs, and snails. When DDT is the only insecticide used, it often happens that large populations of mites and springtails build up, possibly because DDT kills off beneficial insects that prey upon them and would normally help keep them in check. It is good practice, therefore, to use a spray containing both DDT and some chemical effective against mites, such as rotenone. A mixture containing DDT and rotenone is sold under the trade name *Supercide*. Several years ago we kept insects under control with periodic applications of Supercide alternated with a Parathion spray. Parathion is remarkably effective against many insects. However, it is so deadly to man that we hesitate to recommend it. Some states even require one to get a permit before using it, and some professional extermination companies will not handle it. If you use Parathion you should wear old clothing, a plastic apron, rubber gloves, a swimming cap, goggles, and an approved gas mask. In addition, you should have available atropine tablets to be used as an antidote in case of emergency. Because of its extreme toxicity we have changed to Malathion, which is almost as effective but less poisonous to man. Although Malathion is much safer to use than Parathion it still requires the use of a gas mask and rubber gloves when applied in a greenhouse. With Supercide, Malathion, and Dimite, which is particularly effective against spider mites, we keep insects under control in our own greenhouses.

There are some growers who keep insects under control by spraying with nicotine sulfate every week or two whether or not any insects are evident. Rotenone and pyrethrum are effective insecticides of low toxicity to man. One or both of these insecticides will go a long way in controlling insects if used regularly, and they will not injure you if reasonable precautions are taken.

Each year new insecticides are put on the market. Some may be very effective and not injurious to plants; others may injure plants. Always try insecticides on a few plants before you spray all of them. Some growers have ruined their collections by using certain insecticides at improper dosages. A little later we will list some pests of greenhouse plants and suggest insecticides for the control of each kind.

Greenhouse pests may be controlled by fumigation as well as by spraying and dusting. If your greenhouse is attached to your home it may be dangerous to the occupants to use fumigation. If it is a separate structure distant from your home you may want to fumigate occasionally. Among the effective fumigants is Nicofume powder, which comes in cans. To use, you poke holes in the can and insert a lighted fuse, which ignites the powder and smokes up the greenhouse. Such fumigation gives good control of many insects. Many plants are not injured by nicotine, but some with delicate flowers may be harmed. Calculate the number of cans needed to fumigate your greenhouse and then follow the manufacturer's directions. The foliage should be dry when the plants are fumigated, and the humidity should be high. Wetting the walks will raise the humidity and aids in keeping the fumes in the lower part of the greenhouse. Late afternoon or early evening is a good time to fumigate. The following morning syringe the plants.

Calcium cyanide fumigation will control aphids, thrips, white flies, and certain scale insects. Think twice, though, before using this in your greenhouse. We have never used it and we do not intend to do so. In the presence of moisture, calcium cyanide liberates hydrocyanic gas, which is extremely poisonous to man as well as to insects. Calcium cyanide should be used at night, and when the atmosphere of the greenhouse and outdoors is quite dry. Dampen the walks and scatter the calcium cyanide, a grayish powder, along the walks. The gas is released so slowly that you will have time enough to sprinkle it before the concentration builds up to dangerous levels. The following morning ventilate the greenhouse, but do not stay in it until it is thoroughly aired. Some plants are severely injured by cyanide gas, among them violets, snapdragons, smilax, asparagus, sweet peas, and spirea. Don't fumigate these plants with cyanide.

Proprietary preparations of Parathion to be used as a fumigant are on the market. Parathion smoke is effective against many insects as well as against red spiders. Like the spray, Parathion fumigants are deadly to man. You should not use them if your greenhouse is attached to the house. Some kinds come in a canister equipped with a fuse. One canister or more, depending on the size of the greenhouse, is placed on the walks and the fuse lighted. Get out of the greenhouse immediately. Some kinds are ignited with a sparkler. We have tried the Parathion fumigants. They are effective in controlling many insects, but they are less effective than Parathion sprays, which have a longer residual action.

Insect enemies of greenhouse plants

Ants. These are annoying in the greenhouse, and the soil-dwelling ones may change the soil texture for the worse. Moreover, they transport aphids from one plant to another. At one time we were troubled with ants living in pots in which orchids were growing. Poison baits were somewhat effective in reducing the ant population. However, one spraying of the plants and pots with DDT eliminated these pests. Chlordane spray is also effective.

Aphids. You may know these ubiquitous insects as plant lice. They are small, plump-bodied, pale white or greenish to blackish insects with or without wings. Practically all greenhouse plants are vulnerable to their attack. Aphids may be controlled with Malathion, nicotine sulfate, pyrethrum, rotenone, or (for some kinds) DDT.

Beetles. Various kinds of beetles feed on greenhouse plants. Be alert for beetle damage on asters, hydrangeas, orchids, and roses. Beetles can be controlled with DDT or rotenone.

Chrysanthemum midge. This is a small fly which lays eggs inside the leaves of chrysanthemums. The eggs hatch into larvae and, concurrently, galls appear on the undersurfaces of the leaves. The galls extend out from the leaf about an eighth of an inch. Insecticides will not reach the larvae and hence will not kill them. However, the emerging flies are readily killed by DDT. Weekly spraying with this insecticide or with nicotine sulfate gives good control.

Cutworms. You may find cutworms feeding on the foliage of chrysanthemums. Scattering poison bait will usually control them. Spraying or dusting with DDT is also very effective, as is hand-picking at night with the aid of a flashlight.

Leafhoppers. Leafhoppers are wedge-shaped, slim, winged insects about 1/8 to 1/4 inch long. Asters, chrysanthemums, and lettuce are favorite food plants of leafhoppers. DDT or Malathion gives good control.

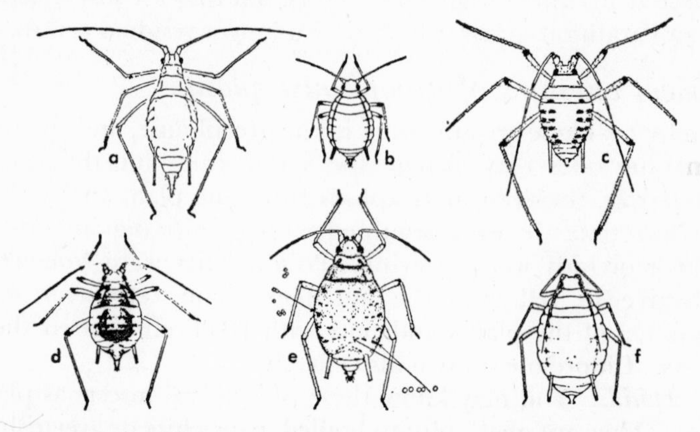

Species of aphid of most importance in the greenhouse. *a,* pea aphid; *b,* cotton or melon aphid; *c,* foxglove aphid; *d,* lily aphid; *e,* ornate aphid; *f,* green peach aphid. Each of these attacks a great variety of greenhouse plants. (A. Earl Pritchard and the California Agricultural Experiment Station)

Leaf miner. These are the larvae of minute flies which feed on the soft tissues inside leaves. They make characteristic tunnels in the infested parts. Leaf miners attack azaleas, chrysanthemums, carnations, cinerarias, and other plants. The larvae cannot be reached by sprays. Control consists of killing the adults with DDT before they begin to lay eggs. You should remove and burn infested leaves.

Leafrollers. Leafrollers are green or bronze caterpillars that bring about a rolling of the leaves. Aster, azalea, calceolaria, carnation, calendula, chrysanthemum, cineraria, geranium, rose, snapdragon, and sweet pea may become infested.

Spraying or dusting with DDT, pyrethrum, or Malathion gives good control.

Mealy bugs. Mealy bugs are troublesome pests of African violets, amaryllis, azaleas, begonias, cacti, chrysanthemums, gardenias, geraniums, kalanchoë, lantana, and poinsettias. Mealy bugs are generally oval in shape, about a quarter of an inch long; they have hairlike projections on the body, which is covered with a waxy white powder. Garden Volck, a miscible oil spray with nicotine sulfate added, is effective in controlling mealy bugs, as is a Malathion spray.

Scales. These are small insects that are covered with a flattened scale which is variously gray, orange, brown, or black in color. They move about after they are hatched, but they soon locate, insert their beaks into the plant tissue, and develop a covering scale. Scale insects are likely to attack cacti, ferns, orchids, palms, poinsettias, and succulents. DDT or Malathion will control many scale insects, and nicotine with soap is fairly effective.

Springtails. These are small, jumping insects which live in the soil and come to the surface when the plants are watered. The common springtail (Collembola, a relative of the silverfish) often increases after DDT has been used. It is not killed by DDT, while its predators apparently are. Malathion gives complete control, and lindane is effective.

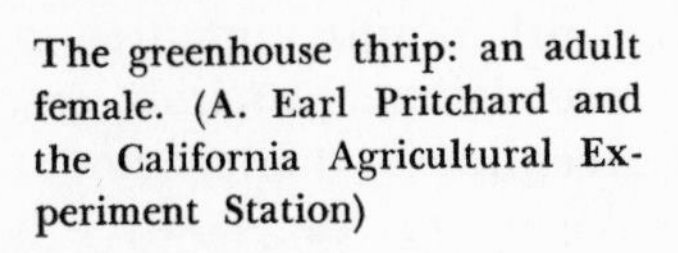

The greenhouse thrip: an adult female. (A. Earl Pritchard and the California Agricultural Experiment Station)

Thrips. Practically all greenhouse plants are subject to injury by thrips, among them African violet, aster, azalea, calceolaria, carnation, chrysanthemum, cineraria, cyclamen, geranium, gladiolus, hydrangea, orchid, primula, rose, snapdragon, and sweet pea. Thrips are minute, narrow, yellowish to brown or blackish insects that feed on both flowers and leaves. Petals of attacked flowers are often brown, and infected flowers may fail to open properly. On foliage, thrips produce a stippling and silvering by puncturing the surface and sucking out the juices. In addition to these symptoms, thrips leave small black dots of excrement scattered over the injured areas. Thrips are readily killed by DDT sprays or dusts. Malathion, nicotine sulfate, rotenone, or pyrethrum can also be used for control.

White fly. These tiny flies (about 1/25 inch long) have white powdery wings. They generally occur in large colonies and fly off in clouds when the plants are disturbed. They feed by sucking sap from the leaves, and can be very destructive. Calceolaria, calendula, cineraria, geranium, gerbera, lantana, pelargonium, tomato, and cucumber are especially susceptible to attack by white fly. DDT or Malathion gives excellent control.

Other greenhouse pests

Spider mites, sow bugs, millipedes, nematodes, slugs, and snails attack a great variety of greenhouse plants.

Spider mites. Spider mites are often called red spiders, and they are in the spider family. They have eight legs, as do true spiders, whereas insects have six legs. Red spiders are red to yellow in color and are no bigger than a pinhead. Some of them spin fine silky webs on the leaves. They feed by sucking, and produce a stippling and silvering of the leaf surface. Red spiders are serious pests of asters, azaleas, bouvardia, calceolaria, calla, carnations, chrysanthemums, cineraria, gardenias, gerbera, gladioli, hydrangeas, lantana, orchids, roses, and sweet peas. They thrive in greenhouses that are hot and dry. Keeping the temperature down and the relative humidity up will aid in keeping down the population of red spiders. Forceful syringing helps rid plants of both eggs and adults. Spraying with aramite, Dimite, ovotran, or Malathion is also effective. We have controlled certain kinds with Malathion, and others with Dimite, which seems to be remarkably effective.

Mites. Mites are sometimes called cyclamen mites; they are serious pests of African violets, begonias, cyclamen, kalanchoë, and snapdragons. The controls suggested for red spiders are effective against the cyclamen mite. Sodium selenate, deadly poisonous to man, is effective in controlling cyclamen mite on African violets and certain other plants. One gram of pure sodium selenate is added to 3 gallons of water. The plants are watered with this solution, adding just enough to wet the balls of soil. Never let the sodium selenate solution touch the foliage, never use it as a spray, and never get it in your mouth. Try it out on a few plants before treating the collection. The sodium selenate is absorbed from the soil by the roots and moved to the leaves. When the mites feed on the foliage they will be poisoned by the sodium selenate. Three waterings with sodium selenate at 3- to 4-week intervals will control some mites.

Sowbugs. Sowbugs are related to crabs, lobsters, and shrimp. They have seven pairs of legs, a hard, gray shell, and frequently they will roll into a ball when disturbed. They feed on organic matter and on stems and roots of plants. They can be controlled by spraying or dusting the area with DDT.

Millipedes. Like sowbugs, these are also related to the crustaceans. Ordinarily they feed on organic matter in the soil, but at times they eat the roots of plants. A spray of DDT or Malathion gives effective control.

Nematodes. Nematodes are minute roundworms that are abundant in some greenhouse soils. Some nematodes cause a serious disease known as root knot. The nematodes invade the feeding roots and cause galls to form on the roots. Infected plants are stunted and have difficulty in absorbing water and minerals. Among the plants that may be affected are African violets, gardenias, and roses. If nematodes are a problem in your greenhouse, you should sterilize the soil before use with steam, larvacide, Dowfume G, or DD fumigant. Remove and destroy badly infected plants.

Leaf blotch, or blight of begonias and chrysanthemums, is caused by nematodes which enter the leaves through the leaf

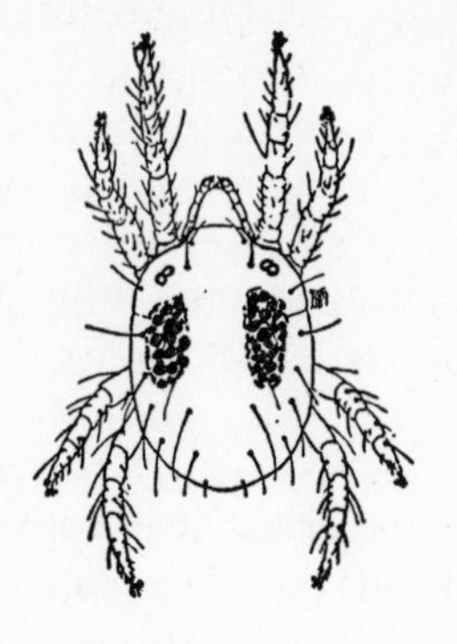

The two-spotted spider mite, which attacks carnations, cymbidium orchids, gardenias, hydrangeas, and roses.

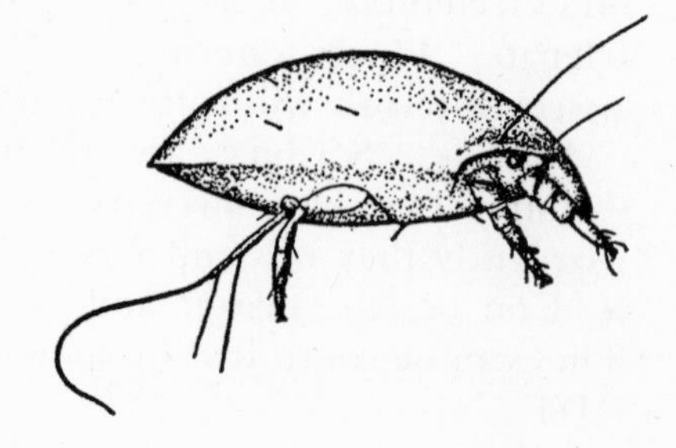

The cyclamen mite, a serious pest of African violets, gloxinias, fuchsias, azaleas, and fibrous begonias.

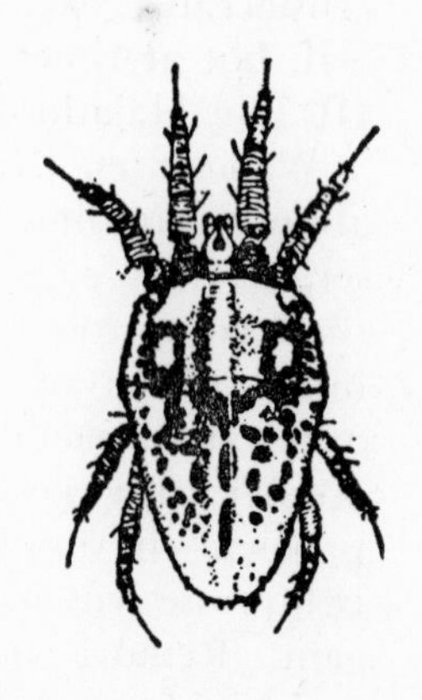

The privet mite, which attacks azaleas and fuchsias. (A. Earl Pritchard and the California Agricultural Experiment Station)

pores. The first symptoms on begonias are small brown spots with watersoaked edges. Later the spots merge to form large brownish blotches. Infected leaves of chrysanthemums exhibit brownish-black, wedge-shaped areas. Foliar nematodes are difficult to control. Some suggestions for control are: use sterilized soil; keep foliage dry; remove and destroy infected leaves; space plants so their leaves do not touch.

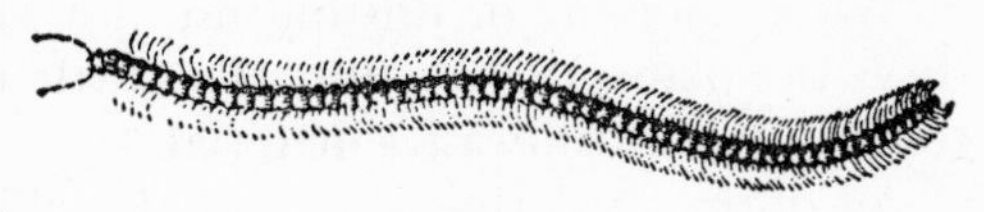

The slug, millipede, and sowbug may attack plants. (United States Department of Agriculture)

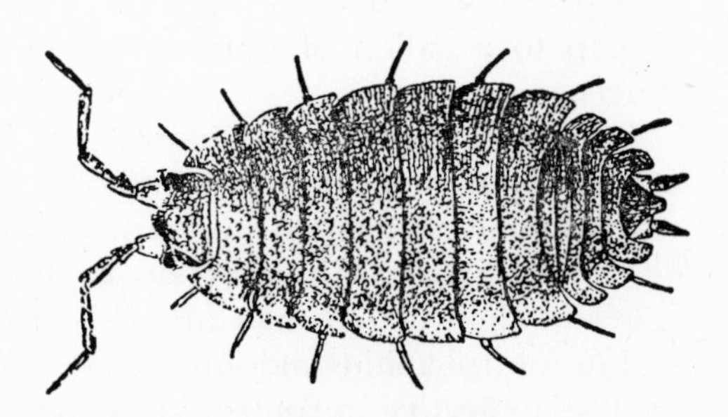

Slugs and snails. Slugs and snails are related to clams and oysters. The soft bodies of snails are protected by a shell, whereas the bodies of slugs are not protected. Slugs and snails usually hide during the day and feed at night. When abundant they may raise havoc with young plants. They can be controlled by scattering a bait containing metaldehyde and arsenate as the active ingredients. Plants can be dusted with a powder containing metaldehyde. Many slugs can be picked off by hand at night with the aid of a flashlight. Scattering lime under the benches will also aid in controlling these pests.

Chemical control of insects and other pests

Most chemicals used to control insects are poisonous in various degrees to man. All of them should be used with care, and the manufacturer's recommendations and precautions should be followed precisely. Some insecticides can be used safely on flowers but not on vegetables. For example, vegetables should not be sprayed with DDT or lead arsenate just before harvest. The residue left on them is harmful to human beings.

When spraying or dusting use just enough insecticide to cover the plants thoroughly. Too little may give inadequate control; too much wastes material.

Nicotine. Nicotine is one of the oldest and best known insecticides. It is usually sold in the form of nicotine sulfate containing 40 per cent nicotine. Nicotine sulfate is more effective when soap is added to the spray. A spray containing 4 teaspoons of 40 per cent nicotine sulfate and 1 to 2 ounces of soap to a gallon of water will control aphids and leaf miners.

Rotenone. Rotenone is one of the safest insecticides to use. It is poisonous to insects and cold-blooded animals, but nonpoisonous to man in quantities used to control insects. Rotenone mixtures kill insects by paralyzing them. They are slower in their action than nicotine mixtures. Rotenone is used to control aphids and some beetles and borers. It is also somewhat effective in controlling spider mites. Some manufacturers include rotenone with DDT in their products in order to furnish a spray which will kill more kinds of insect.

Pyrethrum. This insecticide is nonpoisonous to man. It kills insects by paralyzing them when the pyrethrum, in a spray or dust form, contacts their bodies. Pyrethrum is effective against cabbage worms, aphids, rose chafers, leafhoppers, and certain beetles.

DDT. This is the abbreviated name for dichloro-diphenyl-trichlorethane. It is poisonous to human beings, being about half as poisonous as lead arsenate. DDT is a deposit insecticide. It should be used with caution, and fruits and vegetables covered with a residue of DDT should not be eaten. The inhalation of excess amounts of DDT spray or dust should be avoided, and exposed parts of the body should be washed after using DDT. Insects die if they crawl over it or otherwise come in contact with it. DDT is effective against thrips, some aphids, leafhoppers, scales, rose chafers, mealy bugs, and rose slugs. Some plants are injured by DDT. Kalanchoë and camellia plants should never be sprayed with DDT. Cucurbits (cucumber, melon, squash) and tomatoes are injured by frequent sprayings.

Benzene hexachloride. This compound is sometimes referred to as BHC. It acts as a stomach poison, contact poison, and fumigant, depending on the insect. BHC is effective in controlling aphids and thrips and has been recommended for springtails. It is somewhat toxic to tomatoes, peas, beans, melons, and cucumbers. The odor of BHC makes it unsuitable for spraying these plants after the vegetables begin to form. BHC irritates human skin and eyes. It should not be inhaled, and any on the skin should be washed off as soon as possible. In general we cannot recommend this spray for greenhouse use.

Lindane. Lindane is a chemical related to benzene hexachloride. Lindane lacks the disagreeable odor of BHC and is less irritating. It appears that lindane is not injurious to most plants, and it is effective for aphid control.

Chlordane. Chlordane is the common name for a chlorinated hydrocarbon compound that is effective against wire worms in the soil, ants, grasshoppers, cutworms, springtails, and some leaf miners.

Dimite. This is the common name for Di (p-chlorophenyl) methyl carbinol. It kills only mites, not insects, and has a long residual action. It is poisonous to human beings and animals and must be used with care, following directions exactly.

Aramite. This is the common name for an organic sulfur compound (beta, chlorethyl beta-(p-tertiary butyl-phenoxy)-alphamethetyl sulfite) that is effective in controlling red spiders. It is relatively safe for warm-blooded animals. A spray made up of 1 ounce of the 15 per cent powder in 100 gallons of water is effective in controlling red spiders.

Ovotran. Ovotran, p-chlorobenzene sulfonate, is effective against red spiders. One-sixth of an ounce in 1 gallon of water is an effective control.

Parathion. Before using Parathion, make sure that you have a good gas mask (not just a piece of gauze), goggles to cover the eyes, rubber gloves, and special clothing to cover all parts of the body. Also consult your physician about obtaining a supply of 1/100-grain atropine tablets for emergency use. Symptoms of Parathion poisoning include nausea, blurred vision, abdominal cramps, convulsions, and tightness in the chest. In brief, Parathion is deadly poisonous and it has in several instances resulted in death. Parathion is the most effective insecticide against spider mites. It is also effective against thrips, aphids, beetles, and many other insects, but these can be more safely controlled with insecticides less poisonous to man. Because of its extreme toxicity to man and other warm-blooded animals, it cannot be recommended for use in the home greenhouse. If you should use it and any of the symptoms listed above occur call a doctor immediately.

Malathion. Because of the very poisonous nature of Parathion, scientists searched for another chemical that would be equally effective but less toxic to man. Malathion is proving to be effective against red spiders and many other insects. It is less dangerous to handle but, like all poisons, should be handled with caution.

Preparation of sprays

Before using any spray, read the manufacturer's directions and precautions carefully. If they are followed exactly, satisfactory control will usually be obtained.

The following table shows some concentrations of various insecticides which are frequently used:

Amounts of Insecticides To Use in Making Small Quantities of Sprays *

Insecticide and rate per 100 gallons of water		*Amount to use in:* [1] *1 gallon of water*	*2 gallons of water*	*3 gallons of water*	*5 gallons of water*	*10 gallons of water*	*Precautions*
DDT (50% wettable)	2 lb.	1 T.	2 T.	3 T.	5 T.	⅔ C. + 2 t.	Do not use on vegetables that are ready for harvest. Do not use more than two applications on cucurbits and tomatoes.
Lindane (25% gamma BHC)	1 lb.	1¼ t.	2½ t.	1 T. + 1 t.	2 T.	¼ C.	May burn tender leaf vegetables or give undesirable flavor to potatoes, carrots, and others.
Toxaphene (40% wettable)	4 lb.	5 t.	3 T. + 1 t.	5 T.	½ C.	1 C.	Same as for DDT.
Chlordane (40%)	2 lb.	2½ t.	5 t.	2 T. + 2 t.	4 T.	½ C.	Same as for DDT.
Parathion (15% wettable)	1 lb.	1¼ t.	2½ t.	4 t.	2 T. + ½ t.	⅓ C.	Do not inhale dust or spray mist or expose skin to excessive wetting.
DN-111	1¼ lb.	3½ t.	7 t.	3 T. + 1 t.	⅓ C. + 1½ t.	⅔ C. + 1 T.	Do not get spray in eyes.
Nicotine sulfate (40%)	1 pt.	1 t.	2 t.	1 T.	1 T. + 2 t.	3 T.	
Nicotine bentonite (14%)	3 lb.	2 t.	4 t.	2 T.	3. T + 1 t.	⅓ C. + 4 t.	
Rotenone (4¾%)	2 lb.	2½ t.	5 t.	7½ t.	¼ C.	½ C.	
Wettable sulfur [2]	8 lb.	2 T.	¼ C.	⅓ C. + 2 t.	10 T.	1⅓ C.	Do not use on cucurbits.
Cryolite (90+%)	4 lb.	1 T.	2 T.	3 T.	5 T.	10 T.	
Lead arsenate	2 lb.	1 T.	2 T.	3 T.	5 T.	10 T.	Do not use on vegetables that are ready for harvest.

1 Abbreviations and equivalents: C. = Cup; T. = level tablespoon; t. = level teaspoon. 1 Cup = 16 tablespoonfuls; 1 tablespoon = 3 teaspoonfuls.
2 Weight of wettable sulfur varies somewhat in commercial brands.
* From *New Mexico Agricultural Experiment Station Bulletin 361.*

CHAPTER 9

DISEASES OF GREENHOUSE PLANTS

PLANTS MAY SUFFER from unsuitable environmental conditions and from diseases caused by viruses, bacteria, and fungi. Ailments which result from poor culture are not contagious, so the sick plants need not be isolated. However, diseases caused by organisms are contagious. The viruses, bacteria, and fungi reproduce in the plants and the infective agents may be spread to other plants. Plants harboring harmful agents should be disposed of, or at least isolated from healthy plants. It will pay you to become familiar with certain diseases caused by viruses, bacteria, and fungi.

Virus diseases

Infectious agents so small that they cannot be seen with the ordinary microscope are known as *viruses*. These minute agents can be seen with the powerful electron microscope which gives magnification up to 100,000 times. Viruses are capable of reproducing themselves in the body of an appropriate host; there are many kinds. Some can infect only human beings, others cattle, others orchid plants, still different ones asters, and so forth.

Plant diseases known as *mosaics* are caused by several viruses. The leaves of infected plants are mottled with irregular light- and dark-green areas. Furthermore, the plants are dwarfed and often the flowers are streaked or splotched.

The mosaic disease is seen in beans, carnations, cinerarias, coleus, geraniums, gladioli, irises, lilies, daffodils, orchids, petunias, stocks, sweet peas, and other plants.

Diseases known as *yellows* are also caused by viruses. Aster yellows is one of the best known of this class. The first symptom of yellows is a slight yellowing along the veins; later the leaves become yellow throughout. The growth is spindly, the plants are dwarfed, and frequently they do not flower. If flowers develop, they are yellowish green, regardless of the normal color of the variety. Carnations and chrysanthemums are other plants which may have the yellows disease.

All virus diseases—mosaics, yellows, and others—are systemic; that is, they develop throughout the whole plant. Hence, the removal of parts of the plant, such as picking off mottled leaves or the stems bearing them, will not control the disease, and no external control has yet been found. To keep other plants from contracting a virus disease, ruthless elimination and burning of diseased plants is necessary. Most viruses are spread by aphids, thrips, or leafhoppers, which feed on infected plants and then on healthy ones. Control of insects will go a long way toward keeping your plants free of virus diseases. Plants harboring a virus should never be propagated, and only disease-free stock should be planted. Frequently weeds serve as reservoirs of plant viruses which are transmitted to greenhouse plants. Eliminating weeds in the greenhouse is a safeguard against some virus diseases.

Bacterial diseases

Bacteria are one-celled plants, extremely small, but visible with the ordinary microscope. Some of them are so small that fifty billion could be contained in a volume the size of a drop of water. Some bacteria have a spherical shape; others are rod-shaped or of spiral form. They reproduce rapidly by splitting in two. Some bacteria divide in two every 20 minutes. Starting with one bacterium and assuming a division every 20 minutes, the population would be astronomically large at the end of one day. The division does not usually proceed in such a regular manner, fortunately, being limited somewhat by a decreasing food supply and by poisonous substances produced by the bacteria themselves.

Certain species of bacteria cause plant disease. Usually a specific bacterium attacks a specific host, so that one which infects one kind of plant will not infect any other. There are a few, however, that are nonspecific, capable of infecting many kinds of plants, from carrots to orchids.

Many greenhouse plants are susceptible to the *bacterial leafspot* disease. Typically, the first symptom of bacterial leafspot is small, dark, circular spots on the leaves. The spots enlarge and frequently appear watersoaked. An ooze containing countless bacteria may appear on the leaves, and it is this ooze which may be carried to other plants by splashing water, insects, or contaminated hands. Begonia, carnation, dieffenbachia, geranium, gladiolus, ivy, various orchids, and others are a few of the susceptible plants. The species which causes leafspot on begonia will not cause leafspot on carnation or other hosts; for example, *Phytomonas begoniae* causes bacterial leafspot of begonia and *Phytomonas woodsii* infects carnations.

The bacterial leafspot may be controlled. First, isolate infected plants from healthy ones. Then remove and burn all infected leaves. If more than just a few plants are infected, spray with a good fungicide, such as Fermate or Zerlate. Certain sound cultural practices aid in disease prevention, such as giving the plants plenty of space so that there will be free air circulation, and watering early in the day so that the foliage and stems will be dry by nightfall.

Carnations are susceptible to the *bacterial wilt* disease. The most striking symptom is the sudden wilting of the plant or some of the branches, brought about by damage to the water-conducting system. Furthermore, the root systems of diseased plants are rotted. In this case it is best to remove all infected plants to check the spread of the disease, rather than to try to save any by cutting off infected parts. Only disease-free plants should be benched.

Soft rots of African violet, calla, cyclamen, hyacinth, iris, and orchid are caused by bacteria. In soft rot of African

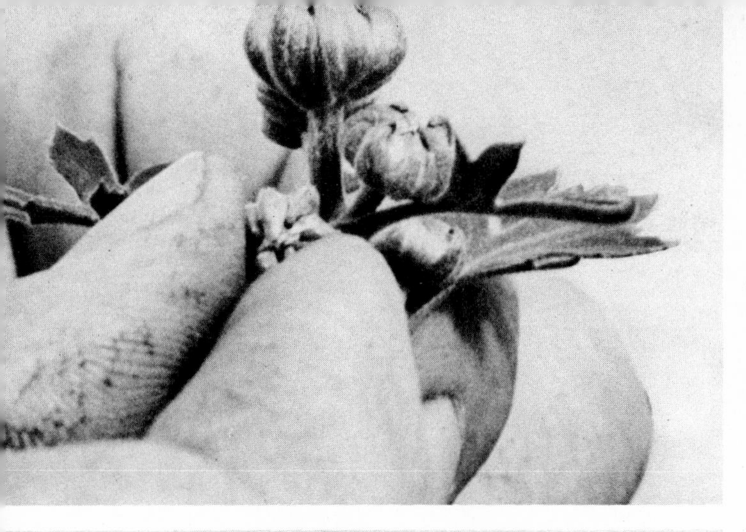

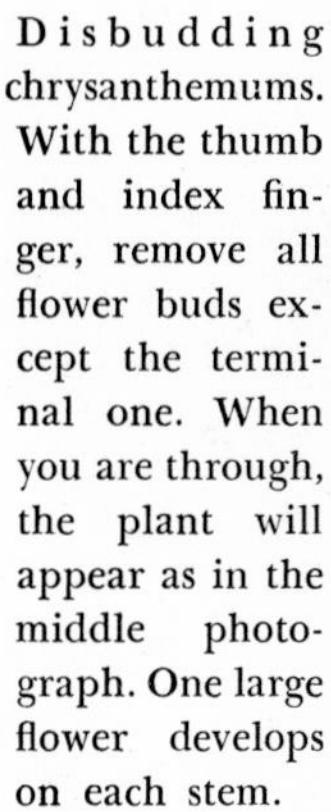

Disbudding chrysanthemums. With the thumb and index finger, remove all flower buds except the terminal one. When you are through, the plant will appear as in the middle photograph. One large flower develops on each stem.

Chrysanthemum cutting. One or two of the lower leaves are removed from the cutting; the cutting is then inserted into sand.

A rooted cutting, ready for potting or benching.

Pinching a snapdragon plan to induce branching.

Swiss giant pansies will reward you with elegant flowers on long stems.

There are many varieties of calendula, which produce large flowers on long stems. Pictured is Orange King. (Bodger photos)

Gerbera, the Transvaal Daisy, is a p
rennial that is well worth growi
(Bodger photo)

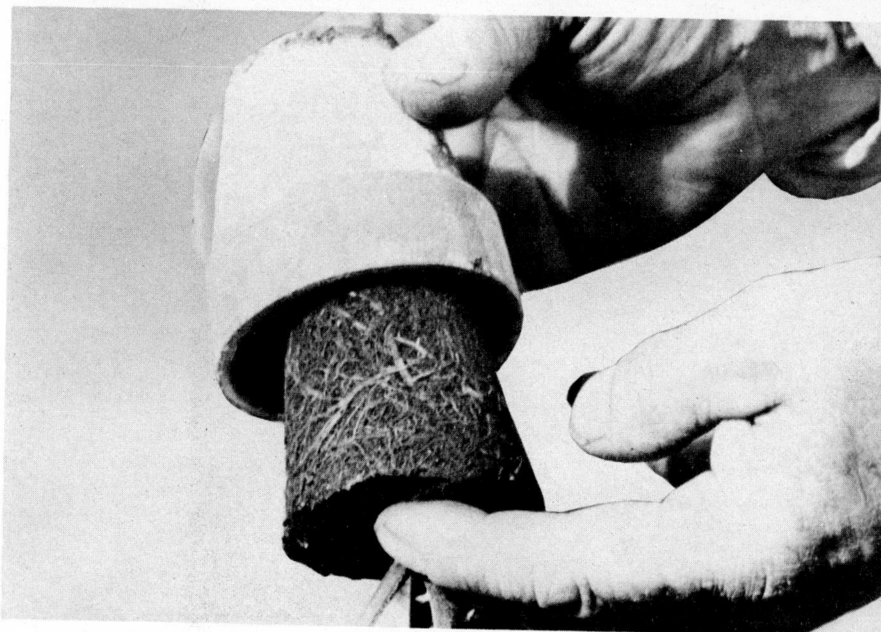

Stages in the culture of cinerarias. The seedlings in the flat are ready to be moved into 3-inch pots. When good root growth is evident, the plant is shifted into a 5-inch pot, in which it flowers. (Bodger photo)

Left: cyclamen seedlings removed from the seed flat and ready to be moved into a flat. *Above:* seedlings just moved into a flat. The corm should be at soil level, not buried. These seedlings will flower in about twelve months. *Below:* schizanthus is a fine pot plant, excellent for cutting. (Bodger photo)

violet and cyclamen the leaf stalks and flower stalks become soft and watery, with resulting wilting and death. Care in watering plants and the use of sterilized soil and pots are control measures. Infected calla plants rot at the soil surface and the leaves droop and die. You can avoid the disease by starting with disease-free tubers and by treating the tubers with New Improved Ceresan. Some hyacinth bulbs may be infected with soft rot. Infected bulbs do not produce flowers or if they do, the flowers open irregularly and rot at the top of the bulb. Again, plant only healthy bulbs.

Roses may have a disease known as *crown gall,* a disease characterized by the development of galls on the stems or roots. Diseased plants should be destroyed and new plants should be set out in sterilized soil.

Frequently bacteria are transmitted from diseased to healthy plants when plants are propagated, often when the presence of disease is not suspected. Sterilization of tools (dipping them in corrosive sublimate solution, 1 gram to 500 cc of water) between each cut is effective in preventing the spread of bacteria when propagating geraniums, irises, orchids, and other plants.

Fungus diseases

True *fungi* cause many diseases of greenhouse plants. These fungi have a cobweb-like body made up of many fine threads that penetrate the plant tissue. They reproduce by microscopic spores, formed on the plant surfaces, which are scattered by wind, insects, splashing water, and even by human hands.

Parasitic fungi injure plants by interfering with the conduction of food and water, by withdrawing nutritive substances for their own use, and by producing poisons which kill part or all of the plant. If the poisons are localized near the fungus, dead spots form on the leaves, stems, or flowers. In some diseases the poisons are carried from the point of infection to other parts of the plant where they kill the tissues.

Parasitic fungi enter plants in various ways. Frequently spores land on the leaves, and if moisture is present and other environmental conditions are favorable, the spores send out tubes which enter the leaf through open stomata (natural leaf pores). Insect punctures and wounds may allow some fungus parasites to gain entrance. Roots of plants may become infected through root hairs. Young seedlings often become infected at the crown, especially if the plants are crowded and kept too moist.

In most fungus diseases the body of the fungus (the thread-like *mycelium*) develops inside the plant (in the flowers, leaves, stems, or roots) so that it cannot be reached and killed by a fungicide sprayed on the surface. Spraying is generally a means for preventing infection or checking its spread rather than for curing a diseased plant. However, the coating left on the leaves kills any spores which subsequently light on the leaves, so if a plant is only slightly infected it can be saved. Hence you should spray plants with a fungicide as soon as the first symptoms of a fungus disease become evident. All diseased parts should be cut off and burned.

There is a notable exception to the rule that the body of a fungus is inside the plant tissue. The body of the one which causes *powdery mildew* remains on the outside of the plant parts; therefore a fungicide can come in contact with its body. This fungus sends absorbing organs into the plant, and these do not survive when the mycelium is killed. Plants infected with powdery mildew can be cured by dusting them with sulfur or by using a sulfur spray.

Preventive spraying with a fungicide is effective in controlling many plant diseases. Some frequently used fungicides are Bordeaux mixture, copper lime dust, wettable sulfur, dusting sulfur, organic mercury compounds of several types which are sold under such trade names as Semesan, Ceresan, Germisan, and synthetic organic iron fungicides such as Fermate.

Spraying and dusting are only parts of the control program. Many varieties of plant are naturally disease-resistant. These have been selected by seedmen and it is to your advantage to use them. For example, some varieties of chrysanthemum are resistant to the disease known as verticillium wilt. If you have had trouble with this disease, your best bet is to select resistant varieties.

Many diseases can be controlled by planting only those seeds, cuttings, bulbs, and corms which are free of disease. If a tulip bulb is infected with *Botrytis blight,* the resulting plant is sure to be infected and it will produce spores which will spread the disease. Similarly, carnation plants grown from cuttings taken from a plant suffering from fusarium yellows will harbor the disease and spread it to healthy plants. Seeds obtained from fields in which plants are diseased are likely to have some spores on them. When such seeds are planted, spores are also planted, and the plants become infected. To minimize seedborne diseases, secure seed from reliable dealers, and in some instances dust the seeds with a fungicide before planting them. Cuprocide, Ceresan, Arasan, Semesan, Spergon, and other fungicides are available for seed treatment. Directions for use are given on the label by the manufacturer. Small quantities of seed are frequently treated by adding a pinch of the fungicide to the seed packet and then shaking.

Remove infected leaves, flowers, and other parts as soon as noticed. Be careful not to transfer a disease to healthy plants when flowers are cut. Likewise, when making cuttings and dividing plants, sterilize knives, pruning shears, and the like, to make sure that the tools used do not carry a disease from diseased plants to healthy ones.

If seeds are planted in unsterilized soil, the seedlings may damp off, and they are particularly susceptible if they are crowded. The disease known as *damping-off* is caused by *Pythium debaryanum* and related fungi. These fungi are widely distributed in soil and practically all kinds of seedlings are vulnerable to their attack. Infected seedlings topple over suddenly, and the stems are seen to be watersoaked at the ground line. Sterilization of the soil will rid it of harmful fungi. Soil may be sterilized with heat or with methyl bromide (see pages 56-57). Good cultural practices will also reduce the losses from damping-off. The soil should be well aerated and the plants given ample room. Overwatering should be avoided, and treatment of seeds with a fungicide is desirable. Seeds started in vermiculite or sphagnum moss are less likely to damp off than those planted in unsterilized soil.

Mature plants are also more susceptible to infection when they are weak, poorly grown, and crowded. The ravages of disease may be reduced by paying attention to such cultural practices as careful preparation of the soil, proper watering, giving the plants ample light and space, keeping weeds down, and by purchasing top-quality seeds and plants.

In the table which follows some common diseases of greenhouse plants are listed. As you go through the table you will notice how the several control methods previously discussed are used to control diseases.

SOME COMMON DISEASES OF ORNAMENTAL PLANTS

Host	*Name of disease and fungus*	*Symptoms*	*Control*
African violet	Crown and rootrot *Phytophthora*	Glassiness and collapse of leaf-stalks.	Burn diseased plants.
	Rhizoctonia canker or stem rot *Rhizoctonia*	Petiole rots where it joins stem, but crown and roots healthy.	Remove diseased leaves and brush Fermate over cut surfaces.
	Rootrot and vascular wilt *Verticillium* and *Fusarium*	Wilting of plant, collapse of petioles, premature withering of flowers.	Burn diseased plants.
Amaryllis	Red Fire Disease *Stagonospora crini, S. curtisii*	Red streaks on leaves and flower stalk. Flower stalk deformed.	Cut off and burn diseased parts. Don't syringe plants. Secure healthy bulbs.
Aster	Wilt *Fusarium oxysporum*	Wilting and withering of foliage. Stems blackened at the base.	Use wilt resistant varieties. Do not plant in soil which harbors the fungus. Treat seed with Semesan or other fungicide.
	Rust *Coleosporium solidaginis*	Orange-red pustules on under side of leaves.	Spray with sulfodust, Bordeaux mixture, or Fermate.
Azalea	Flower spot *Ovulinia azaleae*	Pale or whitish spots on colored flowers and rust-colored spots on	Pick and destroy affected flowers. Spray with Phygon at rate of one

Some Common Diseases of Ornamental Plants (*Cont.*)

Host	*Name of disease and fungus*	*Symptoms*	*Control*
		white flowers. Spots enlarge, and infected flowers cling to shrubs. Disease spreads very rapidly.	lb. per 100 gallons when flower buds first show color. Spray three times a week thereafter.
Begonia	Crown and stem rot *Pythium* sp.	Crown and lower portion of stem watersoaked and soft.	Keep plants well spaced. Avoid overwatering.
Cacti	Bacterial spot or rot *Phytomonas cactivorum*	Rotted areas on shoots.	Water sparingly and keep water off shoots. Cut out infected parts and cover cut surface with fungicide.
Calendula	Leafspot *Cercospora calendulae*	Spots on leaves which later fuse.	Dust with sulfur or spray with copper oxide.
Calla lily	Bacterial soft rot *Erwinia aroideae*	Tuber and base of stem rotted.	Destroy infected plants. Use sterilized soil and healthy tubers.
	Phytophthora rot of tuber *Phytophthora richardiae*	Leaves streaked. Flowers brown and malformed.	Destroy infected plants. Use sterilized soil and healthy tubers.
Camellia	Flower blight *Sclerotinia camelliae*	Irregular brownish spots on petals. Eventually flowers become dull brown and drop.	Remove and destroy infected flowers. Pick up any fallen flowers and burn them.

Carnation	Fusarium wilt *Fusarium oxysporum*	Withering of the shoots and pale straw-yellow foliage.	Because fungus remains in soil indefinitely, it is necessary to sterilize soil or use fresh soil. Take cuttings only from healthy plants.
	Rust *Uromyces caryophyllinus*	Reddish brown pustules on leaves and stems.	Keep foliage dry so spores cannot germinate. Spray with Fermate or Bordeaux mixture. Use disease-free cuttings.
Chrysanthemum	Verticillium wilt *Verticillium dahliae*	Wilting of foliage. Plants stunted.	Plant disease-free stock. Select resistant varieties.
	Powdery mildew *Erysiphe cichoracearum*	Deformed leaves covered with a white powdery growth.	Dust with sulfur.
Cyclamen	Leafspot	Brown or black spots on foliage	Remove infected leaves and burn. Spray with Fermate or Zerlate.
	Soft rot	Leafstalks and flowering stems soft and watery.	Avoid overwatering. Use sterilized soil and pots.
Dahlia	Stem rot *Sclerotinia sclerotiorum*	Sudden wilting and dying of plants. Water-soaked areas at the base of the stem.	Remove and destroy diseased plants. Use well-drained soil. Wide spacing of plants.
	Storage rot Various species of *Botrytis*, *Fusarium*, and others.	Rotting of tubers during storage.	Because most tuber rots start in wounds made during digging, careful digging will reduce rot. Maintain a temperature of 40° F. in storage room.

Some Common Diseases of Ornamental Plants (*Cont.*)

Host	*Name of disease and fungus*	*Symptoms*	*Control*
Delphinium	Crown rot *Sclerotium delphinii*	Discoloration of lower leaves. Wilting of young shoots. Death and drying up of the plant. Roots are rotted and black or dark brown.	Remove all badly diseased plants. Drench surrounding soil with 1:2000 solution of corrosive sublimate.
Fuchsia	Gray mold	Rotting of buds.	Avoid wetting foliage and buds. Provide good ventilation. Cut off and burn infected parts.
Gardenia	Stem canker *Phomopsis gardeniae*	Stem near soil surface enlarged and cracked. Plants stunted.	Destroy infected plants. Avoid injury to plants. Use sterilized soil. Use disease-free cuttings.
Geranium	Blossom blight and leafspot *Botrytis cinerea*	Premature fading and drying of petals. Irregular brown, water-soaked spots on leaves which later become dry and wrinkled.	Prompt removal of infected flowers and leaves. Proper spacing and ventilation. Keep flowers and foliage dry.
Gladiolus	Yellows *Fusarium orthoceras*	Foliage becomes pale or yellow. Corm shows a brown rot and may rot in soil. Corms slightly infected survive, but disease increases during storage.	Use such resistant varieties as Alice Tiplady, Apricot glow, Dearborn, Hopi, Minuet, Picardy, and Souvenir. Eliminate diseased stock. Disinfect corms before planting with a 3-hour soak in one pint lysol to 25 gallons of water, or 6 to 8 hours immersion in 1:1000 mercuric chloride.

Hydrangea	Powdery mildew *Erysiphe polygoni*	White powdery growth develops on the leaves.	Dust with sulfur.
Iris	Leafspot *Didymellina macrospora*	Minute brown spots on the leaves, surrounded by watersoaked areas. Spots may fuse and the leaves may die.	Remove and burn infected leaves. Spray with Bordeaux mixture or Fermate.
Lily	Botrytis blight *Botrytis elliptica*	Circular orange or reddish-brown spots on the leaves.	Spray with Bordeaux mixture or dust with copper-lime
	Foot rot *Phytophthora cactorum*	Sudden wilting and death.	Plant only healthy bulbs secured from reliable source.
Narcissus	Basal rot *Fusarium bulbigenum*	Rotting of the bulbs begins at the base of the scales and spreads through the inside of the bulb.	Discard diseased bulbs. Dip bulbs in a solution of one lb. New Improved Ceresan to 25 gallons of water for 2 to 5 minutes.
Orchids	Leafspot *Rhizoctonia*	Black areas on leaves.	Don't syringe. Spray with Fermate or Zerlate.
	Soft rot *Erwinia carotovora*	Watersoaked areas on leaves followed by collapse of tissue with wrinkling of leaf surface.	Cut off infected leaves and destroy. "Paint" cut surface with Fermate.
	Bacterial leafspot *Phytomonas cattleyae*	Watersoaked spots on leaves.	Remove infected leaves and destroy.
	Anthracnose *Gleosporium* and *Colletotrichum*	Reddish brown circular or oval sunken spots on leaves which later become brown or gray.	Remove infected parts and destroy. Spray with Bordeaux mixture or Fermate.
	Petal blight *Botrytis*	Small spots on petals often with pink rings.	Cut off and destroy diseased flowers.

Some Common Diseases of Ornamental Plants (*Cont.*)

Host	*Name of disease and fungus*	*Symptoms*	*Control*
Pansy and violet	Anthracnose *Colletotrichum violaetricoloris*	Dead spots on leaves and flowers.	Remove infected leaves and flowers and burn.
Poinsettia	Stem rot *Rhizoctonia* sp.	Decay and blackening of lower portion of stem.	Root cuttings in sterilized sand. Pot in sterilized soil.
Rose	Black spot *Diplocarpon rosae*	Circular black spots on the leaves. Spots have a fringed margin. Leaves may become yellow and fall off prematurely.	Remove diseased leaves and burn. Dust with a sulfur-copper mixture at the first appearance of black spot on foliage. Repeat at weekly intervals.
	Brown canker *Diaporthe umbrina*	Purple to white cankers on the stems, which ultimately girdle the stem. Purple or purple with white spots on the leaves.	Plant disease-free plants. Prune out and destroy infected parts. Make cuts well below infected area and sterilize the pruning shears between cuts. Dust with sulfur.
Snapdragon	Rust *Puccinia antirrhini*	Reddish-brown, powdery pustules on the leaves, stems, and seed pods.	Purchase varieties resistant to rust. Spray young plants with Fermate or sulfur.
Stocks	Rootrot *Corticum vagum*	Plants yellow, dwarfed, and sometimes wilted. Roots decayed.	Bench healthy plants. Use sterilized soil.
Sweet pea	Black rootrot	Plants dwarfed, yellow, and	Plant seeds in disease-free soil.

	Thielavia basicola	sickly. Root system partially or completely destroyed.	Do not use same plot year after year. Treat seed with red copper oxide dust, Arasan, or Spergon.
	Rhizoctonia rootrot *Rhizoctonia solani*	As above.	As above.
	Anthracnose *Glomerella cingulata*	General wilting of affected parts at flowering time. White areas on leaves. Flower stalks wither before flowers develop.	Use disease-free seed. Pull and burn infected plants.
Sweet William	Fusarium wilt *Fusarium oxysporum*	New growth is yellowed, plants stunted. Leaves point downward instead of upward. Leaves turn yellow and become tinged with tan as they die.	Plant in new soil.
Tulip	Blight or fire *Botrytis tulipae*	Yellowish spots on leaves surrounded by darker, watersoaked area. Spots often enlarge, fuse, and turn whitish gray. Lesions also develop on flowers, flower stalks, and bulbs.	Plant disease-free bulbs. After plants are up, remove all infected plant parts. Spray with Fermate, 2 lbs. per 100 gallons of water, when plants are 4 inches high. Repeat at 7- to 10-day intervals.
Zinnia	Alternariosis *Alternaria zinniae*	Reddish-brown spots, sometimes with grayish-white centers, on leaves. Brown spots on flowers which enlarge. Cankers on stems. Wilting of plants.	Treat seed with mercuric chloride 1:1000, Semesan, or cuprocide. Remove infected plants. Spray with a fungicide.

CHAPTER 10

COMMON CUT FLOWERS

BY RAISING PLANTS in benches filled with soil to a depth of about 5 inches you can have an abundance of flowers at all seasons of the year, with a minimum of work. Raising plants in this way requires no more time than growing plants in the garden, and many favorite outdoor plants grow much better in a greenhouse, among them calendulas, candytufts, carnations, chrysanthemums, daisies, feverfew, marigolds, pansies, salpiglossis, scabiosas, snapdragons, stocks, and sweet peas.

You will have to give some thought to timing if you want flowers throughout the year. When one variety has finished flowering, you should have plants of some other kind to take its place. For example, after the chrysanthemums are through flowering, you can remove them from the bench and fill it with snapdragons or stocks, the seeds of which were sown in flats in June or July.

Carnations

For a generous supply of fragrant, beautiful flowers of good lasting quality from September through June you can depend on carnations, *Dianthus caryophyllus,* a member of the pink family (Caryophyllaceae). Their requirements are simple: plenty of light and fresh air, an even supply of water, and a night temperature of 50 degrees with a 10-degree rise during the day.

You can get a start by purchasing rooted cuttings in winter or early spring. There are white, pink, red, yellow, and novelty varieties from which you can select. When the cuttings arrive, pot them in 2½- or 3-inch pots or in wooden plant bands. Don't let the young plants become potbound and hard-stemmed; keep them moving along, shifting them into larger pots if necessary. When the plants are 6 or 8 inches tall and thoroughly established in their pots, pinch the plants to promote branching. In May they may be planted in the bench with a spacing of 8 by 8 inches. Fill the bench with a mixture of 2 parts loam and 1 of well-rotted manure to a depth of 5 inches. Then add 5 pounds of superphosphate for each 100 square feet and mix the ingredients thoroughly. The plants in the greenhouse need light shade only during the bright summer months. At other seasons they should have full sun. Give the plants ample water and syringe them frequently.

If you prefer, you can raise the plants outdoors from late spring, when the danger of frost is over, until August. Prepare an outdoor bed in late spring and plant the carnations 8 inches apart in rows 16 inches apart.

The plants grown outdoors should be moved into the greenhouse in early August. If the plants are kept on the dry side for 2 weeks before they are dug, they can be moved with less injury. Lift the plants from the outdoor bed, keeping as much soil around the roots as possible. Plant them in the bench at the same depth they were in the field. After planting give them a good watering. Then wait about 10 days before watering again. Until the plants are established, provide shade and syringe them frequently. When the plants are established give them full sun, which is essential for strong stems and quality flowers.

It will be necessary to install supports for the plants. A frame of pipes, which can be purchased from a greenhouse supply company, is installed at each end of the bench, or you can rig up a frame of your own design. Attach wires to the frames and run them lengthwise of the bench between the rows. Then tie cotton strings to the wires and extend them across the bench with one string between each two rows of plants. You will need two or three tiers of wires and strings, one above the other.

The plants will not require fertilizer for the first two months after benching. Then apply 4 pounds of 4-12-4 fertilizer for each 100-square-foot area of bench. Repeat in October, February, March, and April.

Plants benched in early August and not pinched after June 1 will begin to blossom in September. Plants pinched in early July will generally not flower until November or December. For quality flowers let only one flower bud develop on each stem. Remove the side buds as soon as they are large enough to handle. With good cultural conditions you will get a sequence of blooms, as lateral branches develop and flower, as many as 25 from each plant during the season.

You can purchase new cuttings each year, as many commercial growers do, or you can take cuttings from your flowering plants. Cuttings are best made from December to February. The vigorous side shoots that develop on the lower part of the stem make good cuttings. You can pull the cuttings from the parent plant or cut them off. Peel off the lower pair of leaves and insert the lower ¾ inch of the cutting in sand. With a bottom heat of 60 degrees, the cuttings will root in three or four weeks. Move the rooted cuttings into pots or plant bands and keep them actively growing. Pinch the plants in the manner described previously. In May the plants may be benched or planted outdoors when danger of frost is past. Because the old plants will still be flowering in May, you may not wish to remove them to make way for the young ones. That is why you may prefer to raise the young plants outdoors until August, when the old plants may be replaced with the young ones. It is desirable to replace the old soil in the bench with fresh soil each year. By so doing the incidence of disease is kept down. However, some growers use the same soil for two or three years.

If you wish to grow the year-old plants a second year and even a third year instead of starting with new ones annually, keep the plants actively growing throughout the year. Do not cut the plants back and do not keep them on the dry side during the summer. In other words, carnations are perennial and will flower during all months, year after year.

Carnations are easily raised from seed. Many of the resulting plants may be inferior, but there is always the possibility of obtaining a variety of exceptional merit. Seeds are sown in the spring. Pot the seedlings and grow them on as you would cuttings. You may wish to hybridize some plants and collect seed for growing. Remove the stamens before they shed their pollen from the flower selected as the female parent. When the stigma appears fuzzy, it is ready to receive the pollen from the male parent. The pollen can be transferred from the anthers of the male parent to the stigma of the female with a brush. After the petals wilt, remove them and slit the calyx down the sides so that water will not stand inside the calyx and cause the developing pod to rot. As soon as the seeds are ripe, which requires six to eight weeks, plant them.

Pests. Carnations are attacked by aphids, leafrollers, thrips, and red spiders; all of these can be controlled with a Malathion spray. They may become infected with such diseases as rust, bacterial leaf spot, alternaria leafspot, septoria leafspot, and *fairy-ring,* diseases which can be controlled with Fermate or Zerlate. Stem rot and bacterial wilt are other diseases. Stem rot can be controlled by reducing syringing, avoiding injury to the plants, and by using sterilized soil. To control bacterial wilt, propagate only from disease-free plants and discard infected plants at once.

Chrysanthemums

For beauty and fragrance in the greenhouse during autumn, chrysanthemums are hard to beat. They will reward you greatly for your efforts. People everywhere enjoy these magnificent plants. The Chinese have admired chrysanthemums for more than 2000 years, and the Japanese since at least 1186 A.D. The chrysanthemum is the national flower of Japan. Over many years countless beautiful varieties have been developed and their culture has been perfected. It is believed that the cultivated forms of chrysanthemum have been derived from *Chrysanthemum indicum,* which grows natively in China and Japan. The chrysanthemum is in the sunflower family (Compositae).

If you are just getting a start, purchase rooted cuttings for delivery in early May. Plants which are wilted upon arrival should be soaked in water for about an hour before potting or planting. Dip any cuttings which show fungal damage into a solution of 2 tablespoons of Fermate to a gallon of water.

The rooted cuttings may be planted directly in the bench or they may be potted in 2½-inch pots and then benched in June. The bench should be filled to a depth of 5 inches with a medium consisting of 3 parts soil and 1 of well-rotted manure, with the addition of 5 pounds of superphosphate for each 100 square feet of bench. Mix the ingredients thoroughly and then plant the cuttings or plants with a spacing of 8 by 8 inches or 8 inches by 10. Frequent syringing and temporary shade are beneficial until the plants become established.

After benching the plants, provide them with some means of support. The varieties bearing small flowers, sometimes called pompons, may be supported by wires running lengthwise and strings crosswise, in the manner described for carnations. The large flowered kinds, called standards, are grown with just one large flower to a stem, and they are too tall to be supported in this way. If you are raising just a few standards you can tie the plants to wooden stakes pushed into the soil. If you are growing quite a number it is more convenient to tie them to metal stakes or vertical strings which are held upright by wires running 3 to 5 feet above the bench. Fasten an upright pipe or 2 x 4 at each corner of the bench and fasten a crosspiece at a level of 5 feet above the soil. Run wires from the crosspiece at one end to the crosspiece at the other end, each directly above a row of plants. Metal stakes are pushed into the soil next to each plant and the upper end of each stake is tied to the overhead wire. Another method substitutes strings for the metal stakes. Run a set of wires just above soil level adjacent to the plants, in addition to those higher up. Beside each plant, tie a piece of string from the lower wire to the overhead wire. As the plants grow they can be fastened loosely to the vertical string with string or Twist-Ems.

Chrysanthemums require a great deal of water. Once the plants are established it is difficult to overwater them. Frequent syringings are beneficial. In cloudy regions shade is not necessary, but in hot, bright areas a light shading may be needed during the hot summer months. When the plants are established cover the soil with a 1-inch mulch of peat moss. About the time the flower buds develop, water with ammonium sulfate (1 ounce to 2 gallons of water) and continue at biweekly intervals until the buds show color.

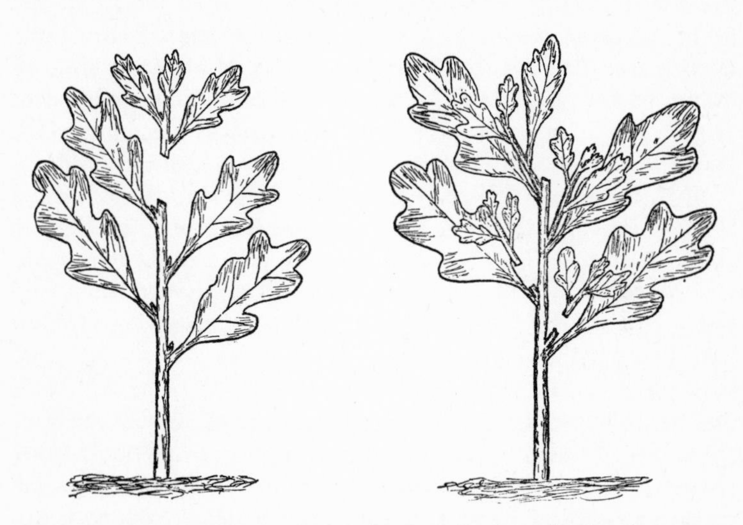

Left: pinching a standard. *Right:* after branches have developed, remove all but one to three of them. Two branches remain; the other two have been pinched off.

Pinching chrysanthemums on definite dates makes for better quality flowers and a more certain crop. You may wish to pinch the spray types more than once, although fine plants will develop with just one pinch. Standards, those with one large flower per stem, are pinched once. The date of making the last pinch, which may be the only one, for both spray and standard types varies with the variety. Catalogs published by chrysanthemum specialists list the date for the last pinch for each variety.

Culture of standards. By the proper selection of varieties you can have several types of standards in flower from October through December. The standards should be pinched on definite dates as shown in the following table.

After the standards are pinched, side shoots will develop. Remove all but one, two, or three of the side shoots. Commercial growers generally permit two of the shoots to grow. If you leave one shoot you will get one flower per plant; if two are left, two flowers will be obtained.

If side shoots begin to grow on the flowering stems, remove them, as well as any basal shoots that form. In time the top of the stem will form a cluster of flower buds, consisting of a central flower bud surrounded by other flower buds, generally smaller. As soon as the smaller buds are large enough to handle, they should be rolled off, using the thumb and index finger. Be careful not to break off the topmost large bud or there will be no flower at all. By removing the side shoots as they develop and by removing all but one flower bud from each stem we divert the energy of the branch to one flower, which becomes very large.

Generally, when varieties are pinched on the recommended dates a cluster of flower buds will form at the top of each stem. The dates work very well for most regions, but in certain areas it may be necessary to make the last pinch earlier or later. In Canada the pinching date should be about seven days earlier, and in the southern areas of the United States the pinch should be made a week later than the dates recommended. If the pinch is not made at the correct time a crown bud may form instead of a cluster of buds. You can easily recognize a crown bud. Only one flower bud, the crown bud, is formed at the top of the stem, instead of a number of flower buds. Below this solitary flower bud there will be a number of side shoots bearing leaves. The crown bud will develop into a flower, but with certain varieties it develops into a less choice flower. For most varieties, remove the crown bud if it forms and then remove all but one of the side shoots. The remaining side shoot will probably produce a cluster of flower buds at the top. The center one of the cluster should be retained, the others removed. It sometimes happens that the side shoot produces a crown bud. If so, remove the crown bud and let one of the branches develop as before.

DATES TO PINCH STANDARD VARIETIES AND TIME OF FLOWERING

Variety	*Color*	*Pinch*	*Flower*
Ambassador	Cream	July 15	Oct. 25
Amber Bright	Amber Bronze	July 15	Oct. 15
Anaconda	Coppery Red	July 20	Nov. 8
Betsy Ross	Ivory	July 15	Nov. 5
Bonaffon Deluxe	Golden	July 25	Nov. 20
Bronze Mistletoe	Buff Bronze	Aug. 5	Dec. 5
Bunbu	Lavender	July 20	Nov. 1
December White	White	Aug. 5	Dec. 5
Glitters	Red Orange	July 20	Oct. 28
Golden Mistletoe	Golden	Aug. 5	Dec. 5
Good News	Lemon	July 20	Nov. 1
Helen Frick	Rose	July 22	Nov. 20
Indianapolis Bronze	Buff Bronze	July 20	Nov. 5
Indianapolis Pink	Pink	July 20	Nov. 5
Indianapolis White	White	July 15	Nov. 5
J. W. Prince	Lavender	July 20	Nov. 5
Major Bowes	Dark Lavender	July 15	Oct. 15
Meteore	Lemon	Aug. 5	Dec. 5
Mrs. H. E. Kidder	Yellow	July 10	Oct. 20
Peggy Hoover	Pink	July 20	Nov. 10
Silver Sheen	White	July 10	Oct. 20
Smith's Late White	White	Aug. 10	Dec. 11
Yellow Ambassador	Light Lemon	July 15	Oct. 25

Culture of spray types. We are going to call the varieties which are generally grown with a number of stems, each bearing several to many flowers, *spray types.* There are a great many varieties which are excellent for growing in this way. Some bear single flowers, others anemone types, others decorative types, and different ones are true pompons. Sometimes all of these are called pompons, but strictly speaking the true pompons are characterized by small blooms, small leaves, and a dwarf habit.

After pinching the spray types, let several to many branches develop. Many commercial growers allow three or four stems to grow on each plant. If you wish many flowers, do not disbud the branches. If you want more open sprays with fewer, but larger, flowers, disbud the plants. As with standards, pinching of spray-type chrysanthemums on definite dates results in flowers of better quality. The date of the last pinch for many spray type chrysanthemums is given in the table on page 139.

Conditions necessary for setting of flower buds. Chrysanthemums need short days and a night temperature of 55 to 60 degrees to form flower buds. Under natural conditions flower buds form when the days become short in late summer. But they form only if the night temperature is 55 degrees or above. In most regions the night temperatures are naturally high enough in late summer for the setting of flower buds. If they are not above 55 degrees in your region, you should use artificial heat until the flower buds are visible, after which the night temperature may be allowed to drop to 50 degrees.

Controlling flowering. Chrysanthemums may be brought into flower during all months of the year by controlling the length of day. You can lengthen the day by artificial light. Install 100-watt lamps, spaced 4 feet apart and 2 feet above the plants. Turn them on at sundown and keep them on until 10 P.M. The day length can be shortened at will by covering the plants with light-proof black cloth from 5 P.M. to 7 A.M. the next day. The cloth is stretched over a frame built on the bench and it covers the top, sides, and ends of the frame. As we have previously mentioned, this practice of covering is sometimes called shading.

Young chrysanthemum plants are grown with long days, which promotes the development of leaves and stems. After the plants have made sufficient vegetative growth they are grown with short days, which favors flower bud formation.

DATES TO PINCH SPRAY TYPES AND TIME OF FLOWERING

Variety	*Color*	*Size and type of flower*	*Pinch*	*Flower*
Betty	Pink, Rose Center	Med. Decorative	July 10	Oct. 14
Cassandra	Orange Bronze	Med. Pompon	July 20	Nov. 5
Cordova	Cream	Med. Decorative	July 28	Nov. 30
Firebird	Red Bronze	Med. Decorative	July 15	Oct. 25
Freida	Light Lavender	Large Anemone	July 22	Nov. 15
Holiday	Crimson	Med. Single	Aug. 15	Dec. 10
Moonlight	Yellow	Med. Decorative	June 25	Oct. 1
Nuggets	Golden	Single Pompon	July 20	Nov. 5
Pink Dot	Pink	Med. Pompon	July 15	Oct. 25
Red Velvet	Crimson	Single Pompon	July 5	Oct. 10
Riviera	Luminous Pink	Med. Decorative	Aug. 10	Dec. 15
Rusticon	Rust Scarlet	Med. Pompon	July 25	Nov. 20
September Morn	White	Med. Single	June 25	Oct. 1
Shasta	White	Med. Anemone	July 22	Nov. 10
Silver Ball	White	Large Pompon	July 10	Oct. 15
Talmeda	White	Med. Pompon	Aug. 15	Jan. 5
Valencia	Orchid	Large Single	July 30	Nov. 28
White Doty	White	Large Pompon	July 20	Nov. 1
Yellow Cordova	Lemon	Med. Decorative	Aug. 5	Nov. 30
Yellow Doty	Buff	Large Pompon	July 20	Nov. 1
Yellow Nevada	Yellow	Med. Anemone	July 28	Nov. 20
Yuleflame	Yellow	Large Decorative	Aug. 15	Dec. 25

The plants may be raised in benches or in pots. Both spray and standard kinds can be grown for year-round flowering. Let us see how the variety *Shasta* may be flowered at any month of the year. This schedule can be used:

Plant Cuttings	*Light*	*Pinch*	*Black Cloth*	*Flower*
Jan. 5	Jan. 5–Mar. 9	Feb. 2	None	May 18
Feb. 16	Feb. 16–Apr. 9	Mar. 12	Apr. 9	June 18
Mar. 30	Mar. 30–May 11	Apr. 20	May 11	July 19
Apr. 27	None	May 18	June 8	Aug. 17
May 25	None	June 15	July 6	Sept. 10
June 22	None	July 13	Aug. 3	Oct. 12
Oct. 12	Oct. 12–Dec. 28	Nov. 2	None	Mar. 9
Nov. 23	Nov. 23–Feb. 16	Dec. 18	None	Apr. 27

A large number of other varieties can be grown with this schedule. Of the spray types the following can be raised in like manner: Encore, Madonna, Constellation, Barcarole,

Yellow Shasta, Rubicon, Chevron, Paragon, Pandora, Memorial, and Taffeta. Some standards which can be grown with the same schedule are Betsy Ross, Indianapolis White, Crystal Queen, Giant Betsy Ross, Monument, Indianapolis Yellow, Yellow Queen, Indianapolis Bronze, Indianapolis Pink, and Orchid Queen.

Plants started in January, February, March, October, and November need supplemental light to promote vegetative growth and to retard flowering until they have reached sufficient size. From the table it will be seen that plants started January 5 will need to have the electric lights turned on from sundown until 10 P.M. each day until March 9. The plants are pinched February 2. By March 9 the plants are large enough to produce good blooms. From then on they are not lighted. Because the days are naturally short it is not necessary to cover the plants with black cloth. Plants started from April 27 through June 22 do not need extra light because the days are naturally long enough to promote vegetative growth and to prevent flower buds from forming. But for early flowering it is necessary to shorten the days, beginning June 8 for those started on April 27. For these plants the black cloth should be drawn over the plants at 5 P.M. each day and removed at 7 A.M. the next. This covering may be discontinued when the flowers of the spray types show color and when the flower buds of the standards are the size of nickels. Remember that flower buds form when the days are naturally short or when they are artificially shortened, and when the night temperature is about 60 degrees. During the black-cloth period or period of naturally short days, keep the night temperature at 60 degrees.

Getting a start the second and subsequent years. Many commercial growers prefer to purchase cuttings each year. When they buy from a reliable dealer they are assured of disease-free cuttings. Perhaps you will also want to buy new cuttings each year.

However, you can carry your plants over and make cuttings of your favorite varieties. After the plants have finished flowering, select healthy plants of the varieties that you like.

Cut the plants back, remove them from the bench, and plant them in pots or deep flats. These plants are in a semi-dormant stage and should be kept in a cool place and on the dry side. They can be kept under a bench in a cool greenhouse, or if the region is not extremely cold, in a protected hotbed or cold frame. The cold frame should be well banked with leaves and protected with mats in extreme weather. In a very cold climate the cold frame will not give sufficient protection. Most greenhouse varieties of chrysanthemums are easily winter-killed. During the dormant period, water the plants occasionally, pinch them once or twice to prevent spindly growth, and keep pests under control.

Start the old plants into active growth in late March by placing the flats or pots on a greenhouse bench and giving them ample water. About a month later you can start to make cuttings. Late April is a good time to start making cuttings of the early-flowering varieties. Rooting may be hastened by dipping the ends of the cuttings in Rootone or Hormodin. The cuttings root well in sand. If the cuttings stay too long in the propagating bench, they will become stunted and will not develop into choice plants. As soon as the roots have formed, pot the plants in 2½-inch pots. If you prefer, you can root the cuttings in 2½-inch pots filled with a medium made up of equal parts of soil, sand, and well-rotted cow manure. Keep the young plants growing. Don't let them dry out or become potbound.

Another way to keep plants from one season to the next is to make cuttings immediately after the plants have flowered. Pot the rooted cuttings, keep them well watered, and give them supplemental light. Turn on the light just before sundown and keep it on until 10 P.M. Pinch the plants at intervals to stimulate branching.

Pests. Spider mites, aphids, thrips, Lygus bugs, chrysanthemum gall midge, leaf miners, and leaf rollers are principal pests. Malathion gives good control of all but chrysanthemum gall midge. However, Malathion may injure certain varieties. Better try it on a few plants before spraying all of them. Some growers use a combination spray of benzene hexachloride and aramite which controls all but the leaf rollers. Verticillium wilt, rust, leaf spot, and mildew are diseases to guard against.

Snapdragons

Snapdragons, *Antirrhinum majus* (of the family Scrophulariaceae), are among the finest flowering plants for the greenhouse maintained at a night temperature of 50 degrees with a rise of 10 or 15 degrees during the day. You can raise snapdragons in the same soil that you used for carnations, or you can use a mixture of two parts loam, one part leafmold or peat, and a half-part well-rotted manure, with the addition of superphosphate.

Many varieties of snapdragon have been developed for greenhouse culture; these should be selected instead of garden ones. Seeds should be sown thinly, in light soil, during June or July for a winter crop. Scatter the seeds over firmed soil and cover the seed pot or pan with a pane of glass, then with a piece of paper. Remove the glass and paper as soon as the seeds begin to germinate. When the seedlings are large enough to handle, move them into 2½-inch pots.

In August or September the plants may be pinched, leaving three sets of leaves. Generally a branch will develop above each leaf giving a plant with four to six branches. Plants pinched in August will flower in December, whereas unpinched plants from seed started the middle of July will flower in late October and early November. The plants may be benched during August, with a spacing of 8 by 8 inches. If at this time the benches are filled with chrysanthemums, you can shift the snapdragons from 2½-inch pots into 3- or 4-inch ones and delay benching until the chrysanthemums have finished flowering and have been removed from the bench. Snapdragons require supports of wires and strings, as recommended for carnations. The removal of the side shoots on the flowering branches usually does not result in better flowers although it does make a more attractive spike. However, do not remove all of the side shoots, otherwise the plants will be useless after they have produced their first flowers.

During late fall and winter, snapdragons do not respond to applications of fertilizer. During the spring, biweekly applications of ammonium sulfate (1 ounce in 2 gallons of water) are beneficial.

Plants pinched in August will generally flower by Christmas. The plants will produce additional flowers later in the season, but the second and third crops may have shorter stems than the first spikes. For better-quality flowers in May and June you may wish to sow seeds in January. When the plants are large enough, pinch them to three sets of leaves.

Raising snapdragons with a single stem. Most amateurs and many professional growers prefer to raise snapdragons in the manner suggested, that is, with several flowering branches to a plant. However, a recent trend among some commercial growers has been to raise snapdragons to a single stem. With this method the plants are not pinched. They are spaced 4 by 4 inches or 5 by 5 inches in the bench. After the flowers are cut, the plants may be disposed of or the plants may be thinned. If the latter method is followed, remove every other row and alternate plants in the remaining rows. The plants remaining will then be spaced 8 by 8 or 10 by 10 inches and will produce flowers at a later date.

Skillful growers obtain year-round flowering by sowing seeds at intervals. When the seedlings are large enough to handle, generally two to four weeks after sowing, they plant them directly in the bench. A brief schedule of when to sow, when to bench, and when the plants flower follows:

Sow	*Plant in bench*	*Flowers ready for cutting*
Jan. 7	Feb. 7	May 15–July 5
Mar. 3	Mar. 27	June 5–June 19
Apr. 14	May 5	June 23–July 7
May 12	June 2	July 14–July 28
June 9	June 26	Aug. 7–Aug. 11
July 7	July 21	Sept. 1–Sept. 15
July 21	Aug. 4	Oct. 27–Nov. 17
Aug. 18	Sept. 4	Dec. 11–Jan. 1
Sept. 1	Sept. 22	Jan. 1–Feb. 9
Sept. 29	Oct. 23	Mar. 12–Apr. 2
Nov. 10	Dec. 8	Apr. 4–May 4

This schedule (abbreviated from Vaughan's seed catalog) is only approximate. It fluctuates with varieties and with temperature. Seed catalogs list varieties which follow this schedule. On sunny days, the day temperature should be 55 to 60 degrees, with night temperatures of 52 degrees. On cloudy days the day temperatures should be 48 to 50 degrees and the night temperatures the same.

There are a great many varieties of snapdragon which have been developed for growing in the greenhouse. Some varieties flower in less time than others. You can select varieties of the following colors: white, light pink, rose pink, red, ivory, bronze, and lavender. Obtain a catalog from a seed company that caters to florists and make selections from it. The seed is quite expensive and, unless you have a large greenhouse, you may prefer to buy a package of a greenhouse mixture of varieties.

Pests. Aphids, cyclamen mites, leafrollers, red spiders, and sowbugs are pests that attack snapdragons. Snapdragons should not be exposed to cyanide, which causes fading of flower colors and interferes with their normal development. Uneven development of flower spikes, so-called *skips,* may result if the night temperature drops to 40 degrees following a cloudy day, provided the plants have been previously grown with a night temperature of 50 degrees. If the night temperature is continually maintained at 40 degrees during the night, *skips* does not develop; it does not develop when the days are bright. Rust is the most serious disease of snapdragons.

Stocks

Stock, *Mathiola incana* of the mustard family (Cruciferae), produces sturdy flower spikes 2 or 3 feet tall, bearing beautiful, fragrant flowers. Some plants bear single flowers, others double ones, which are more attractive. You cannot buy seeds all of which will develop into plants bearing double flowers. However, if you keep only the strong seedlings and discard the weak ones, nearly all of the plants will bear double flowers. When the seedlings have four leaves the young plants which will bear single flowers are noticeably weaker than those which will produce double flowers.

You can choose between varieties which produce only one stem and those which develop many branches. The former are called *nonbranching* or *column* stock, and they come in a variety of colors—white, rose, lilac, and yellow. There are many named varieties of the branching type, among them Antique Copper, Chamois, Elks Pride, and Appleblossom, to mention only a few.

Seeds of both types are generally sown in August for flowering in January. The branching types will continue to flower. For this reason they are often preferred by amateurs, even though the flower spikes are not so large as those of the column types.

After the flowers are cut from the nonbranching types the plants are discarded. For a sequence of flowers, successive sowings may be made every other month, beginning in August and continuing until February. Plants grown from seed sown in November will flower at Easter; those from seed started in February, during late May.

Sow the seed thinly and cover lightly with sand or soil. When the seedlings are large enough, move them into flats, from which they may be planted in the bench sometime in October from an August sowing. If chrysanthemums are still in the bench at this time, keep the stocks growing and plant them after the chrysanthemums are removed. The nonbranching stocks are planted close together, about 3 inches apart in rows 6 inches apart. A spacing of 6 by 8 inches is about right for the branching varieties. Remove the top of the stem of the branching types when the stem is 6 inches tall. This pinching will stimulate branching. To keep the stems straight, some means of support should be provided. The wire and string method is suitable.

A night temperature of 48 to 50 degrees in the greenhouse results in good growth and flowering. Stocks will produce an abundance of foliage when the night temperature is 60 degrees, but they will not flower at this temperature.

Plants started in August and benched in October will normally flower in January. However, they may be brought into flower in December by growing the plants with additional light or by keeping the young plants at a temperature of 40 degrees for two weeks before benching them. Additional light is provided by suspending 40- to 60-watt lamps in reflectors 2 feet above the plants. The lights should be 4 feet apart and turned on from sunset until 10 P.M. Lighting should begin about two weeks after the plants are benched. Early flowering can also be obtained by growing the young plants in a cold frame for about two weeks before they are benched. The ideal temperature for the cold frame is 40 degrees.

After the flowers are cut the leaves may wilt severely. To prevent wilting, immerse the stems deeply in water for 24 to 36 hours.

Aphids, thrips, and mites are pests that attack stocks. The wilt disease is characterized by a yellowing of the foliage, sudden wilting, and then death. Removal of diseased plants and the use of sterilized soil will help control this disease.

CHAPTER 11

UNUSUAL CUT FLOWERS

THE KINDS of cut flowers described in the preceding chapter are the staple flowers for all florists. However, you may wish a greater variety in your greenhouse. In this chapter we will consider briefly other plants that grow well in benches in a 50-degree greenhouse.

Aster

The China Aster, *Callistephus chinensis* of the Compositae family, is the common garden aster. Asters may be grown to perfection under glass, and they will make the greenhouse colorful from July through September if you grow early, mid-season, and late varieties. For flowers during the summer, sow seeds in April and move the plants into the bench in May, with a spacing of 8 by 8 inches. The soil recommended for chrysanthemums is good for asters also. The stems should be disbudded in order to obtain large flowers.

If you want asters in flower during the winter and spring months you must furnish the plants with long days by giving them supplemental light from sundown until 10 P.M. The Royal varieties are reliable for growing with supplemental lighting. Seed may be sown December 1 for flowering from April to June. After they have germinated (about December 10), give the seedlings additional light. The seedlings will be ready to plant in the bench about February 1. Continue lighting the plants until they are through flowering. Seeds of the Royal type may be started in August for flowering in March and April. When the days become short in late summer they should be prolonged in the manner just described.

Aster wilt is a serious disease. However, if you select wilt-resistant varieties you will not be troubled by it. A destructive virus disease, known as *aster yellows,* is spread by a leaf-hopper. The elimination of this insect with DDT will aid in control. Aphids, red spiders, thrips, and leafrollers are other pests.

Calendula

Calendula (*Calendula officinalis*) grows well in a greenhouse maintained at 45 to 50 degrees. Varieties which produce large flowers on long stems have been developed especially for greenhouse culture. Among the choice varieties are Gold, Lemon Queen, Orange King, and Masterpiece. Plants grown from seed sown in late July will begin to flower in October or November and produce flowers through the winter. For better-quality flowers, you can remove the first flower buds as they form, after which the plants will branch. Each branch will then flower in January. The branches should be disbudded to secure large flowers. After these flowers are cut you can get a second crop in April. The flowers of the second crop may be somewhat inferior to those of the first. For choice flowers from February to March it will pay you to sow seeds in October, and for flowers from April through June, in November.

The soil used for carnations, chrysanthemums, and other bench crops is suitable, as is a mixture of three parts loam and one part of well-rotted manure. The plants should be spaced 12 by 12 inches.

Candytuft

The giant hyacinth-flowered strains of candytuft (*Iberis amara*) are magnificent, growing to a height of 1½ feet and bearing large trusses of white bloom. For flowering in late

May, seed should be sown early in January. Move the seedlings into 2½-inch pots, and then, about the middle of February, plant them in the bench, spacing them 6 by 6 inches.

Clarkia

Clarkia elegans is excellent for cut flowers, in shades of white, rose, and salmon. However, there is a cultural peculiarity that must be observed. If it is planted in rich deep soil and watered frequently, clarkia produces an abundance of leaves, but few flowers. On the other hand, good flowering can be obtained by keeping the plants on the dry side or by raising them in flats, about 3 inches deep, filled with sandy soil. Seed should be sown in January for flowers during April and May. When benching, space the plants 8 by 10 inches.

Didiscus

Didiscus coeruleus, commonly called Blue Lace Flower, produces beautiful blue flowers on good stems. Because the plants are set back by transplanting, it is best to sow seeds in pots or directly in the bench. Leave one seedling in each pot, and bench when the roots fill the pot. If you sow the seeds directly in the bench, thin the plants so that they will be 6 inches apart in rows 12 inches apart. Seed sown in June will develop into plants flowering at Christmas; those sown in August will flower in March.

Gerbera

Gerbera Jamesonii, the Transvaal Daisy, bears daisy-like blooms of yellow, orange, red, pink, or white color. The plants are perennial. The clumps are best divided in June and then planted outdoors. Dig them in the fall before frost, and plant them in a greenhouse bench with a spacing of 12 by 12 inches. The plants prefer slightly alkaline soil. A mixture of three parts loam and one part manure is a good growing medium. If the loam is not naturally alkaline, add lime to it. *Gerbera* can also be grown from seed. Plants grown from seed sown in March will start to bloom in January and carry on until summer.

Gypsophila

You know *Gypsophila elegans* by the common name of Baby's Breath. The graceful lacelike sprays are useful in bouquets. In addition to white varieties, there are those which bear rose or crimson flowers. Seeds may be sown directly in the bench in rows 8 inches apart. You can have flowers in March by sowing seeds in January. If you sow seeds at monthly intervals you will have a succession of blooms.

Larkspur

You may enjoy this beautiful flower (*Delphinium ajacis*) in April and May by sowing seeds in September and benching the plants in December. The plants grow well in light soil which is neutral or slightly alkaline in reaction.

Lupine

Lupinus luteus is free-flowering and easy to grow. The graceful spikes of gaily colored pealike flowers are excellent for bouquets. Perhaps you will want some lupines for cutting after the chrysanthemums are through. Germination of lupine seeds may be hastened by chilling the seeds in a refrigerator for several days before sowing. Because lupines are difficult to transplant it is best to sow the seeds in 3-inch pots. Sow several seeds in each pot and later remove all seedlings but one. The plants are set 8 inches apart in the bench in November from seed sown in September. They will begin to flower in January. For flowers during May and June, sow seeds in January.

Mignonette

Mignonette, *Reseda odorata,* is noted for its sweet perfume. The Machet variety is the best for greenhouse culture. From seed sown in July you can have plants in flower at Christmas. Because Mignonette resents transplanting from seed flats, it is best to sow the seeds in 2½-inch pots. Sow a few in each

Fuchsia bears beautiful flowers from spring through summer. (Bodger photo)

Show Pelargonium, also called Martha Washington Geranium, produces many delightful flowers in the spring. *Above:* a plant one month after the top was pinched off. Plants should not be pinched after February 1. *Below:* plant in flower at Easter.

Potting an amaryllis bulb. Add drainage to the pot, then some soil. Mound the soil and place the bulb on the mound with the roots spreading. Fill the pot with soil and firm; one-third of the bulb should be in the soil. Keep the soil on the dry side until the shoot appears, then water more frequently.

Above: looking down at the flower cluster of Clivia. *Below:* Zephyranthes, the Zephyr lily.

Amaryllis in flower.

Top: anthuriums are noted for their attractive flowers and foliage. *Left:* many attractive foliage plants are in the Aroid family. Here are several varieties of Philodendron and Anthurium. The benches in the rear contain interesting Philodendron seedlings, many of which are quite distinctive. *Above:* Maranth-leaved Aglaonema (*Aglaonema marantifolium*) has decorative bright red fruit. The true flowers are clustered on a white spadix 2 inches long (2), below which is a greenish-white spathe. 3 shows a female flower magnified four times. (Addisonia and the New York Botanical Garden)

Spathiphyllum candidum in flower. Notice the white spathe, which is a modified leaf, and the spadix, which bears many flowers. *Right: Dieffenbachia picta,* Spotted Dumb Cane.

The beautifully colored, arrowhead leaves of caladiums make a beautiful display.

pot and later thin to one plant per pot. When the plants are of sufficient size, plant them 8 inches apart in the bench. The plants require staking.

Pansy

Few flowers have more character and appeal than pansies (*Viola tricolor hortensis*). Their texture, brilliance, arrangement of colors, shape, and fragrance have made them one of our favorite flowers. Some of the newer varieties are indeed elegant. You will be delighted with the Super Swiss Giants, which come in a number of colors that have been given such varietal names as Swiss Alpenglow (rich wine-red), Swiss Berna (dark violet blue), Swiss Blue, Swiss Coronation Gold, Swiss Raspberry Red, Swiss Pure White, and Swiss Rhinegold. These Swiss varieties bear round flowers of velvety texture and of large size, 3 or 4 inches across, on strong stems. The Maple Leaf varieties are also choice; the flowers are round, of heavy substance, and 4 or 5 inches across. They come in many attractive colors.

The seeds are best sown about the middle of July in a cold frame. If you do not have a cold frame, make a frame out of four boards 10 or 12 inches wide and place it over finely prepared soil. The soil must be finely raked, and then watered. A day or two after watering, sow the seeds in grooves 1/16 inch deep. The rows should be 3 inches apart. Cover the seeds with 1/16 inch of sand. Then cover the frame with boards, spaced so that there will be good ventilation. Pansy seeds require a temperature of less than 75 degrees for germination. Don't let the seed bed become dry. As soon as the seeds germinate, remove the boards and replace them with light muslin tacked to the top of the frame.

Four or five weeks after sowing, the seedlings will be ready for transplanting. They may be planted in a cold frame or in a raised bed in the garden. Space the plants 4 by 4 inches. In October the plants may be benched in the greenhouse, spacing them about 10 inches apart. If you raised the seedlings in a cold frame and have more than you need for planting in the greenhouse, you can winter the surplus in the cold frame. Before severe weather sets in, mulch the plants with straw or salt hay. Of course, you can move plants from this frame into the greenhouse at any time.

Pansies thrive when it is cool. They grow well in a medium of three parts soil and one of well-rotted manure. Do not let the plants become dry at any time. If you grow the plants with long days, furnished by turning on 60-watt lamps at sunset and off at 10 P.M., the plants will flower more profusely and the stems will be longer. Continued removal of old flowers is essential for good flowering.

Salpiglossis

The showy, velvety flowers of this easily grown plant (*Salpiglossis sinuata*) are fine for cutting. The deep colors of the petals—red, purple, blue, yellow, or brown—are attractively set off by the gold veins. Seeds are started in January for flowering in May. The plants are set 10 inches apart in the bench.

Sweet Pea

Perhaps you can find a place in your greenhouse for a few sweet peas (*Lathyrus odoratus*). You may wish to grow some in boxes at the end of the greenhouse or perhaps a few around the posts that support the greenhouse. Of course, you can raise them in a bench or in a ground bed. For flowers from December to March, sow seeds during September, either directly where the plants are to mature or in 3-inch pots or plant bands. From seeds sown in October you will get flowers from February through May. A soil consisting of three parts loam and one of well-rotted manure is suitable. If the loam is acid, mix lime with it because sweet peas prefer a slightly alkaline soil.

Sweet peas may be planted in double rows. Plant seeds or plants in a row, then 7 inches from this row plant another one. Leave about 2 feet and plant another double row. After the plants are established, thin them so that the remaining plants are 3 inches apart in the row. Strive to furnish the plants with good light and ventilation, a night temperature of 50 degrees, and moist soil. On cloudy days the day temperature should be kept at 55 degrees and on bright days at 60. When the plants are a foot tall, if the days are bright, the plants should be fertilized monthly with a complete fertilizer. Avoid feeding the plants during the dull weeks of winter. Do not allow the vines to be crowded by other plants, as this cuts out the light they need. Crowding is particularly bad in dull weather.

When the plants are a few inches high they will require support. Vertical strings tied between an overhead wire and one just above soil level are ideal for the plants to climb on. You will have to train the tendrils to the strings by hand at first.

Make sure that you select varieties which have been specially developed for greenhouse culture. These winter-flowering varieties flower much earlier than the garden varieties and they have a different habit of growth. The garden varieties form side shoots when they are young and during this period the plants appear to be checked in their growth. The winter flowering-varieties grow rapidly to a height of 2 feet or more and then flower, after which side shoots, bearing additional flowers, form. Among the choice varieties for greenhouse culture and their colors are: Apollo, salmon cerise; Ball Rose Improved, deep rose; Boon, salmon pink; Bridesmaid, silvery pink; Sequoia, golden salmon-rose; Harmony, lavender; Triumph, lilac mauve; Hope, white; Snow Queen, white; White Champion, white; Fiesta, orange cerise; Grenadier, scarlet; Ball Orange Improved, orange; and Treasure Island, golden orange.

The dropping-off of flower buds may be troublesome during the winter months. A lack or excess of water, improper temperature, and too much fertilizer during the cloudy winter months may be responsible. Various root rots can be troublesome. To control them, remove infected plants and use clean or sterilized soil. Among the pests of sweet peas are snails, red spiders, thrips, aphids, and cutworms.

Violet

The delightfully fragrant violet flowers make this plant (*Viola odorata*) a desirable one for the greenhouse. To get a start, purchase plants in September and plant them in a bench about 10 inches apart. The soil should be a mixture of four parts loam and one thoroughly rotted manure. The addition of 3 pounds of superphosphate and 1 pound of potassium chloride per 100 square feet of bench is desirable. Provide shade for the newly set plants and syringe them each day until they become established. After the middle of October, syringing should cease and the shade may be removed gradually. The runners which develop should be removed as they form. The runners will not produce flowers the first season. The runners can be rooted in sand and potted, if you desire to increase the stock. Throughout the growing season, water judiciously, provide the plants with good ventilation, a night temperature of 45 to 50 degrees, and a day temperature 10 degrees higher. Keep the benches free of weeds and remove yellowing and diseased leaves. A mulch of well-rotted horse manure in November is beneficial but not absolutely essential.

When the plants are through flowering, remove them from the bench and divide them. Runners may be rooted in sand. The divisions and rooted runners are planted in benches, preferably containing fresh soil. Keep the plants shaded after planting, throughout the summer. They will benefit from frequent syringings until October. If you wish, you can move the plants into a shaded part of the garden for carrying through the summer. In September put them back in the greenhouse.

Both single and double varieties of violets are available. Princess of Wales, Governor Herrick, and California are choice single varieties, and Lady Campbell, Farquhar, and Marie Louise are fine doubles.

Aphids and red spiders attack violets, as do such diseases as leafspot and rootrot. Keeping the plants healthy, use of disease-free soil, and removal of dead, dying, and spotted leaves will minimize disease.

Additional plants

In this chapter we have singled out a number of plants which you can grow in benches in a 50-degree greenhouse. Others which you might like to try, the time to sow seed, and the spacing are:

Plant	*Sow*	*Space*	*Flower*
Centaurea	January	8 x 8 inches	May
Cynoglossum amabile	September	12 x 12 inches	March–April
Erysimum perofskianum	January	6 x 6 inches	May–June
Feverfew (*Chrysanthemum parthenium*)	October	12 x 12 inches	May
Marigold (*Tagetes erecta*)	February	4 x 4 inches	May
Forget-me-not (*Myosotis sylvatica*)	March	10 x 10 inches	December on
Nemesia strumosa	August	8 x 8 inches	October–February
Statice (*Limonium suworowii*)	October	8 x 8 inches	February–May

CHAPTER 12

POT PLANTS

THERE ARE MANY plants of great beauty that can be raised in pots in a greenhouse maintained at 50 degrees during the night, among them are calceolaria, camellia, chrysanthemum, cineraria, cyclamen, fuchsia, geranium, primrose, rose, and schizanthus. You may wish to grow a variety of these, or you may want to specialize in one kind. Building up a collection of geraniums would be fascinating, as would the culture of camellias, fuchsias, and primroses.

Calceolaria

The favorite species of calceolaria is *Calceolaria hybrida,* a member of the snapdragon family (Scrophulariaceae). There are several fine strains of this species, Grandiflora, Multiflora Nana, and others. The plants bear showy slipper-shaped flowers, often attractively spotted or blotched, in shades of yellow, orange, red, and rose. The color schemes are gay and of great contrast.

Calceolarias are grown with a night temperature of 50 degrees and they do well in a soil mixture of equal parts of loam, leaf mold (or peat), well-rotted manure, and sand. They are started from seed sown in July or August. The above mixture, without the manure, is suitable for the seed pans. The seeds are very small and are best mixed with fine white sand, which is then scattered over the slightly firmed soil surface. The seeds should not be covered. After sowing, water from below, place a pane of glass over the pot, and keep it shaded. When the seedlings are large enough to handle, move them into flats, spacing them 2 inches apart. Before the seedlings crowd each other, pot them singly in 3-inch pots. Later, shift them into 5- or 6-inch pots, in which containers they will flower. To prevent the leaves from rotting, keep the plants well spaced so that the leaves of one plant do not overlap those of another. During the bright months, shade the plants, and maintain the night temperature as near 50 degrees as possible. At all times keep the plants actively growing. When the roots fill the pots, either large or small, water with dilute liquid manure water or commercial fertilizer at weekly intervals.

Calceolarias generally flower in April or May. However, they may be induced to flower earlier by giving the plants additional light from 5 to 10 P.M. Suspend one or more 100-watt lamps in reflectors 2 feet above the plants and space them 4 feet apart. If plants are given additional light from the middle of November on, they will flower in February. Plants lighted from December 20 on will flower in March.

There is a shrubby species of calceolaria, *C. integrifolia,* which is not so frequently grown in greenhouses. The seeds of this species are generally sown in March and raised in the same general way as *C. hybrida. Calceolaria integrifolia* can also be propagated from cuttings taken in August.

Thrips, aphids, greenfly, whitefly, and red spiders may attack calceolaria as well as such diseases as leafblight and graymold. The latter may be controlled by removing infected leaves and giving the plants adequate spacing.

Camellias

These beautiful shrubs, members of the tea family (Theaceae) and natives of China and Japan, deserve a place in the cool greenhouse. They have handsome, evergreen, glossy leaves and beautiful flowers of white, pink, or red color, and of formal double, semidouble, or peony form. By selecting different varieties, you can have camellias in flower from September to March. For the little care that they require you will be rewarded with flowers of exquisite form, generous size, and pleasing color. The flowers make choice corsages and are attractive when floated on water, lasting about a week.

Three species of camellia, *Camellia japonica, C. sasanqua,* and *C. reticulata,* are available for growing in the greenhouse. The most popular varieties belong to the species *C. japonica;* the flowers are white, pink, red, and variegated. *Camellia sasanqua* has a more straggly growth habit and flowers earlier than *C. japonica.* Certain varieties have pink flowers, others white ones. *Camellia reticulata* has a less compact growth form than *C. japonica.* Certain varieties of *C. reticulata* have wavy, rose-pink flowers, 5 to 7 inches in diameter.

There are, of course, numerous named varieties of camellias, and many new ones are introduced each year. Not all of the new kinds are superior to the old. Perhaps you should start with well-tried ones first and add novelties later. Among the favorite varieties, their color, shape, and flowering season are: Alba Plena, white, double, September to December; Elizabeth, white, double, December to March; Otome, pink, double, January to March; Pink Perfection, pink, double, November to April; Debutante, light pink, peony, October to January; Jarvis Red, red, semi-double, December to March; Prof. C. S. Sargent, red, peony, October to April; Prince Eugene Napoleon, red, double, December to February; Wm. S. Hastie, red, double, February to April; C. M. Hovey, red, double, December to March; Elegans, pink, semi-double. We have listed here just a few varieties. If you are interested in a more complete listing you may secure from the Agricultural Experiment Station and Extension Service, University of California, Berkeley, a pamphlet on "Camellia Culture" for a small charge.

Camellias should be shaded from bright sun during all months of the year. Under glass the buds, blooms, and occasionally the leaves will burn in bright sunshine. Camellia plants require an acid soil. A mixture of equal parts of soil and peat with some sand is suitable. A wise precaution against yellowing of foliage is to add a 2-inch potful of iron sulfate to each wheelbarrow of soil. From autumn until after flowering a night temperature between 40 and 45 degrees is ideal, with a day temperature of around 50 degrees. Camellias should be syringed when actively growing and when the flower buds are developing. Syringing the flower buds favors their development and syringing flowers during the night gives them better substance.

When the plants have finished flowering, a night temperature of 55 degrees is desirable because at this temperature vegetative growth is stimulated. Potting should be attended to after the plants have finished blooming and before new growth begins, generally in March or April. Small plants require potting each spring. Larger ones do not require annual potting, but only a top dressing of new soil. Large plants may need repotting every third year. Potting time is also the time to prune camellias, although they require very little pruning. You may wish to shorten very long branches and remove unwanted and weak ones. When the plants are developing new leaves they require a good supply of water and benefit from frequent syringing, which also increases the humidity. During the entire year a high humidity is beneficial. If not recently repotted, the plants should be fertilized periodically with cottonseed meal or a 15-30-15 fertilizer, using 1 ounce to 2 gallons of water. Specially prepared camellia fertilizers are available. Plants should be fertilized just before they begin their new growth and then at biweekly intervals until flowering time. If the new foliage is yellow, water the plants with a solution of 1 ounce of iron sulfate in 2 gallons of water.

From June to September the plants grow better if they are kept outdoors than if left in the greenhouse, although they may be maintained in the greenhouse all year. If they are kept in the greenhouse during summer, provide shade and good ventilation. Outdoors, they may be placed in a lath house, in a cloth house, or under large trees. The pots should be plunged in the soil. At no time during the summer should the soil become completely dry, because drought causes flower buds to fall off. However, bud drop may also be caused by low humidity, by high temperatures during winter, and by wide fluctuations of temperature. The roots should be kept moist, but avoid excess water as well as drought.

If two flower buds develop on a branch and if you want especially choice flowers, remove the weaker of the two buds when it is about the size of a pea.

Camellias may be started from seeds, by air layerage, from cuttings, and by grafting. Usually they are started from cuttings taken from the mature wood of the current season's growth. Cuttings are taken any time between August 15 and February 15. From one branch a number of cuttings can be made. The cuttings may be 3 to 6 inches long and have three or four nodes, or they may be shorter with just one node. If you prefer the latter, cut a branch into segments so that each piece has one leaf with a live bud at the top and 1½ inches of stem below the leaf. Treat the basal portions of the cuttings with Rootone or Hormodin and then insert the cuttings, about an inch and a half apart, in sand with all the leaves facing in the same direction. Bottom heat of 70 degrees hastens rooting, which normally takes two or three months. After the cuttings have rooted move them into 2½-inch pots. When the roots fill the pots, transfer the plants to 4-inch pots. Shift into larger pots when necessary. When plants are large enough to move into 8-inch containers or larger, wooden tubs are better than clay pots.

It requires four to seven years for camellias to flower if grown from seed. Young plants produce only a few flowers; those large enough to be in 14-inch tubs will produce about 150 flowers per plant. Flowers from seedlings may or may not be of excellent quality. Certain seedlings may produce inferior blooms. However, there is always the possibility that one or more seedlings will be outstanding. The chances of getting excellent plants from seed are increased if especially choice parents are used for seed production.

Some growers hasten seed germination by carefully nicking the seed coat. Seeds are sown about ½ inch deep in the soil previously mentioned. When the seedlings are 6 inches high they are moved into pots.

Red spiders, mealy bugs, aphids, and scale insects are pests to watch for. Several varieties of camellias are injured by DDT, therefore do not use this insecticide. A refined oil emulsion with the addition of nicotine sulfate is safe to use for controlling insects attacking camellias, as are benzene-hexachloride, lindane, and lead arsenate.

Flower blight is perhaps the most prevalent of the fungal diseases. Flower blight is evidenced by a discoloration of the flowers and may be controlled by gathering and destroying all diseased flowers. It also pays to remove the upper three inches of soil and replace it with fresh soil.

Chrysanthemum

Many varieties of chrysanthemum make excellent pot plants, and all kinds can be raised in pots if you so desire. In catalogs of chrysanthemums, such as the one issued by the Vaughan Seed Company, certain varieties are designated as pot plant varieties. There are many named varieties in this category, and they come in the following colors: white, yellow, bronze, orange, red, pink, and lavender. Moreover, there are varieties with large flowers, others with medium blooms, and different ones with small flowers. Varieties with the following flower shapes are available: single, anemone, decorative, pompon, incurved, and semi-incurved. Contrast in size and shape add variety to a collection.

By the proper selection of varieties, chrysanthemums can be had in flower from September to January. Some varieties flower in September, others in October, November, or December. Catalogs indicate flowering periods.

Except during the period flower buds are forming, chrysanthemums thrive in a 50-degree house. A night temperature of not less than 55 degrees, preferably 60 degrees, is necessary for the initiation of flower buds. In many regions the night temperature will be naturally about 55 degrees during late August and early September, when the early and midseason varieties form flower buds. For late-season varieties you may have to turn on the heat to raise the night temperature to 60 degrees during the natural bud-forming period. After the flower buds are well developed, the temperature may be lowered to 50 degrees.

In many localities no shade is necessary during the summer months. In hot regions with bright sun, a light shade will be necessary. A soil mixture consisting of three parts loam and one of well-rotted manure suits chrysanthemums. If the soil is heavy, add some sand to the mixture.

Chrysanthemums are started from cuttings, generally made in April, May, or June, and rooted in sand. You can make the cuttings yourself or purchase them. Many professional growers prefer to buy cuttings each spring. Cuttings produced by specialists are likely to be vigorous and free from insects, pests, and diseases.

Three uniform rooted cuttings may be potted in a 6-inch azalea pot. If you prefer, you can pot the cuttings singly in 2½-inch pots, later shifting them singly into 4-inch pots and then into 6-inch ones. Water thoroughly after potting and syringe the plants several times each day to reduce wilting. When the plants are well established and about 6 inches tall, pinch them to promote branching. Use a soft pinch, removing only the very soft tip of the stem. At least six leaves should be left on the plant after the first pinch. When the branches are about 4 inches long, pinch them to induce additional shoots to form. These in turn may be pinched after they have grown to a length of 3 or 4 inches. Plants should not be pinched too late in the season. Varieties which flower in early October should not be pinched later than August 15; those which flower late in October, not later than August 20. Varieties which flower during the first half of November should not be pinched after August 25; those flowering the last two weeks in November, not later than September 3; and those which flower in December, not later than September 13. The last pinching dates vary somewhat with the variety. The exact dates for the last pinching may be obtained from catalogs, such as the chrysanthemum catalog put out by Vaughan.

During the growing period, the plants benefit from being syringed several times each bright day. Never let the plants become starved. Move them into larger pots or feed them.

Well-established plants can be fed every two or three weeks with a dry fertilizer or a liquid one. A half-teaspoon of 4-12-4 dry fertilizer for a 6-inch pot is the correct amount. Add the dry fertilizer to the pots when the soil is moist and then water the plants.

The plants may be allowed to flower naturally, or you may disbud, or remove the center flower bud from each spray. If you desire a plant bearing a few large flowers, disbud each shoot by removing all flower buds except the terminal one from each branch. A plant with many small flowers can be developed by removing the center flower bud and permitting the side buds to develop.

You will have to be alert for the presence of these insects: aphids, red spiders, thrips, leafrollers, midges, cutworms, mealybugs, and leaf miners. Verticillium wilt, mildew, leaf or black spot, and yellows are diseases of chrysanthemums.

After flowering is through, retain sufficient healthy plants of the varieties you like, to furnish a supply of cuttings next year. These stock plants should be cut back and then moved into flats, a bench, or repotted. Place them in a cool part of the greenhouse, water as necessary, and keep free from insects and disease.

Cineraria

There are a number of good strains of cineraria, among them Cremers Prize, Multiflora Nana, Potsdam, Siter's Rainbow, and Grandiflora. The Multiflora Nana strain is preferred by florists. It has a very compact growth habit and flowers profusely. The flowers are blue, red, or pink in color. In some catalogs cineraria is listed as *Cineraria cruenta,* but its correct botanical name is *Senecio cruentus,* a member of the sunflower family (Compositae).

Cinerarias grow rapidly and thrive in a 50-degree house. They may be had in flower from January through April, by successive sowings in June, July, and September. The seeds are small and should be sown on fine soil. After sowing just barely cover the seed with sand or soil. When the seedlings are large enough to handle, transfer them to flats. From flats they can go into 3-inch pots and then into 5- or 6-inch ones. A mixture of three parts loam and one well-rotted cow manure is suitable. For the last potting, add a 3-inch pot of 4-12-4 fertilizer per wheelbarrow of soil. Cinerarias require frequent waterings. They should be fertilized every two or three weeks after they are established and until the flower buds just begin to show color, after which feeding should cease. Keep the plants well spaced. Be on the alert for attacks by aphids, red spiders, leafrollers, white flies, and thrips. When the plants are through flowering discard them.

Cuphea

Cuphea, variety Firefly, is a semidwarf, compact plant, about 12 inches high. The flowers are numerous, of a deep rosy scarlet, deepening to almost purple at the center. Cuphea plants started from seeds planted in January will produce flowers in May. A suitable compost is half loam and half leaf mold. Syringing on bright days is beneficial.

Cyclamen

Of the 20 species of cyclamen, only one, *Cyclamen persicum* (of the primrose family, Primulaceae), a native of Asia Minor, is generally grown in greenhouses. This species is noted for its distinctively shaped, attractively colored flowers and for its handsome marbled foliage. Few plants can surpass the cyclamen for display during the winter and spring months. There are many varieties from which you can select; some bear salmon flowers, others pink, red, white, or orange-vermillion.

The favored way to grow plants is from seed, best sown in August or September, although they may be sown as late as December. Sow the seeds individually 1/4 inch deep and 1 inch apart in a mixture of equal parts soil, sand, and peat or leaf mold. After sowing, water thoroughly and cover the pot or flat with a pane of glass, and a sheet of paper. At a temperature of 55 to 60 degrees, the seeds will germinate in four to eight weeks. After the seeds have germinated, continue to provide the seedlings with light shade. Allow the seedlings to develop two or three leaves and then transplant them to a flat containing a mixture of two parts soil, one part sand, one part peat, and one part well-rotted manure. Space the plants 2 or 3 inches apart and insert the seedlings so that the corm is at soil level. If you prefer, you can move the plants from the seed flat to 2½-inch pots. In the spring the plants may be moved from the flats or 2½-inch pots into their flowering container, generally a 5- or 6-inch pot, or they can be potted in a 4-inch pot. If the latter practice is followed, shift them into 5- or 6-inch pots in July or August. When potting, provide plenty of crock and keep the corm half in the soil and half out. After the plants are established in the pots apply liquid fertilizer every two or three weeks. Throughout the growing period the plants should be well watered. Don't let the plants wilt before watering.

During summer the plants should be kept as cool as possible by placing them under trees outdoors or in a well-ventilated and shaded cold frame. The shade, either lath or a double thickness of cheesecloth, should be supported well above the frame so that there is free circulation of air. Although it is preferable to keep the plants outdoors during the summer, you can maintain them in the greenhouse if you provide heavy shade and adequate spacing. Plants outdoors or in the greenhouse benefit from frequent syringings during summer.

In early September, bring the plants into the greenhouse. If the plants have been kept in the greenhouse during the summer, gradually reduce the shade, beginning in September. From September on, keep the night temperature at 50 degrees and allow the day temperature to go 10 degrees higher. Staging the plants on inverted pots from September on promotes good aeration and seems to encourage the setting of flower buds. Flowers which appear prior to October should be pulled off in order to encourage vigorous growth of the foliage. The time from seed sowing to profuse flowering is between fifteen and eighteen months.

It is possible to carry plants over for flowering the next and subsequent year, although commercial growers prefer not to do so. To carry the plants over, keep the plants on the dry side when flowering is through by watering them only at biweekly intervals. The drought will induce rest which should be maintained until August. Then remove the dead leaves, knock the plant out of the pot, reduce the ball of soil, and repot in a pot just slightly larger than the ball. Syringe the corms daily. In a few weeks growth will be active.

Cyclamen may also be increased by dividing the corm. After the plant has flowered remove the corm and cut it into sections, each with at least one leaf. Place the pieces in sand, where they will root. Then pot each piece. Plants started in this way will flower the following winter.

Leafspot and crown rot are two diseases of cyclamen. Leafspot is characterized by brown or black areas developing at the margins of the leaves and is controlled by pulling off infected foliage. If you see a white fungus growth at the base of the leaves, the plant has crown rot. This disease can be avoided by not burying the corms when potting and by not letting water stand in the crowns during the night.

Nematodes, red spiders, aphids, thrips, and mites are pests that attack cyclamen. Nematodes cause knots to form on the roots and you can avoid them by using sterilized soil and containers. Mites deform leaves and flowers and they must be kept under control. Thrips give the undersides of the foliage a scaly appearance and cause streaking of the flowers. Colored flowers have white streaks; white flowers, brown ones. Cyclamen plants may be injured by many of the newer insecticides. Rotenone is satisfactory for the control of aphids and thrips and it is also somewhat effective against red spiders. An azobenzene spray is effective against cyclamen mite on a preventative basis. Infested plants should be destroyed.

Felicia

Felicia amelloides, commonly called Blue Marguerite, is a free-flowering perennial plant that bears exquisite sky-blue, daisylike flowers that are fine for cutting. Plants are started from seed sown in January or from cuttings made in the spring. The plants flower the following winter. A compost

Every greenhouse gardener is his own decorator *(above)*.

The greenhouse is a blaze of color with the popular autumn crop of chrysanthemums. *(Popular Gardening)* *(Plate facing p. 167.)*

acing page: The greenhouse in inter is a hospitable haven of armth and color. (Lord & Burnham)

The tuberous begonia is a showy and satisfying hobby flower. (Photograph by Bea Slinger for *Flower Grower, The Home Garden Magazine)*

Photograph on following page: Lord & Burnham.

of equal parts soil and leaf mold is suitable. The plants should be pinched two or three times to produce a bushy habit. They require light shade only during the brighter months of the year.

Fuchsia

Fuchsia (*Fuchsia hybrida* of the evening primrose family, Onagraceae) is among the most ornamental of flowering plants. It begins flowering in the spring and continues through the summer. The flowers are pendulous, of a charming bell-like form, and attractively colored. The cultivated ones are hybrids, the parents of which are native to South America. There are nearly 2000 varieties; some bear single flowers, others double ones. Many varieties grow erect; but certain ones are trailing, and these can be grown in hanging baskets or other containers. A few varieties of trailing form and their descriptions are: Anna, magenta and red, double; Cascade, carmine and white, single; Falling Stars, red and scarlet, single; Marinka, all red, single; Muriel, lilac and scarlet, semi-double; San Mateo, violet and pink, double; Swingtime, red and white, double. Among the favorite erect varieties are California, orange and pink, single, tall; Cardinal, scarlet and red, single, tall; Don Peralta, burgundy, double, tall; Guinevere, lavender and rose, semi-double, medium height; Mazda, orange and pale orange, single, tall; Minuet, purple and red, single, medium height; Mrs. Desmond, rose-mauve and red, double, medium height; Patty Evans, pink and rose, double, tall; Treasure, violet-pink and rose, double, medium height; Violet Gem, violet and carmine, semi-double, medium height; Whitemost, white and pink, single, medium height. These, as well as other erect varieties, may be grown as bushy plants or treelike specimens, so-called standards.

You will have no difficulty in raising these splendid plants. They grow well in a 50-degree house. While actively growing they require plenty of moisture, a high humidity, and benefit from biweekly feedings with manure water or liquid fertilizer. From March 1 until fall they require light shade. You can keep them in a shaded, well-ventilated greenhouse during the summer; or plunge them outdoors under the shade of trees, or under lath roofing made by spacing laths ½ to ¾ inches apart. Fuchsias have a rest period after flowering, in November and December. During these months keep the plants on the dry side; give them just enough water to keep the wood plump. In January, bring the plants into active growth by watering more frequently and syringing.

Bushy specimens are obtained by pruning. Just as the buds become active, cut out the dead and weak wood, and cut the vigorous branches back. Trailing varieties are also pruned in the spring. The heads of standard fuchsias are shaped in the spring by cutting the main lateral branches, leaving each about 10 inches long.

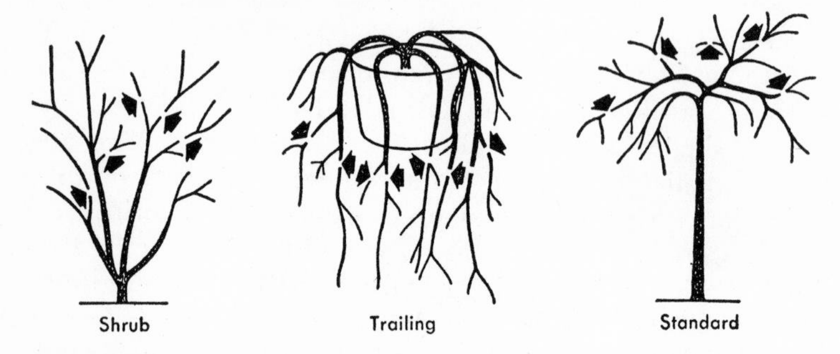

Pruning fuchsias. (H. M. Butterfield and the California Agricultural Experiment Station)

In the spring, knock a plant from its pot and remove as much soil as possible from the ball without tearing it apart. Repot in fresh soil. A suitable mixture consists of one part loam, one part leaf mold or peat moss, one part manure, and a little sand. Provide good drainage. Don't overwater after potting. Syringe frequently, preferably with water at the same temperature as that of the greenhouse. When the plants are in active growth water frequently; avoid letting the ball get dry. Feed the plants at intervals.

Fuchsias are readily propagated from cuttings made in February or March, or in September. The cuttings are rooted in sand or in a mixture of half sand and half vermiculite. When rooted pot off singly, generally in 2½-inch pots. Give further shifts as necessary. If you want bushy specimens, pinch the plants. Plants grown from cuttings started in the spring should be given a rest period during November and December; those started in September may be kept growing during the winter months.

The making of a standard, a tree-like fuchsia, starts with the cutting. Select a straight, stout, rooted cutting. Pot it, keep it growing, and stake it. If any side shoots appear, remove them. When the stem is of the desired height, pinch off the tip of the stem. Side growths will then develop near the top. After they have made sufficient growth, they should be pinched, the object being the production of a well-balanced head, on a stem about 4 feet tall.

Growing fuchsias from seed can be an exciting adventure. You can purchase superb mixtures resulting from crosses of a number of varieties. Such seed will probably produce new hybrid varieties as well as plants resembling the parents. Seeds may be sown in January; they germinate best at a temperature of 60 degrees. Seeds are sown in pots containing a mixture of equal parts of loam, peat moss, and fine leaf mold. Keep the seeds moist all the time; to let them dry out is fatal. Seed germination is sporadic; some seeds may germinate in ten days, others not for three or four months. When the seedlings have developed their second set of leaves they are potted in 2½-inch pots, best plunged in a flat of moist peat moss. The seedlings should be given shade. In about a month they can be moved into 4-inch pots and later, as needed, into 6-inch ones. After the seedlings have made sufficient growth—if you want bushy specimens—pinch off the top to promote the development of branches. Some of the seedlings may flower during the late summer and autumn months of the first year.

Fuchsias are remarkably free from disease. There are a number of insects which attack fuchsias, among them mealy bug, white fly, scale insects, aphids, thrips, and the cyclamen mite.

Genista

Two species of *Cytisus* (in the pea family, Leguminosae), *C. canariensis* and *C. racemoses,* are commonly called genista. Both are shrubs and produce yellow, pea-shaped flowers in the spring. They grow well in the 50-degree house and prefer a soil mixture of three parts loam and one part well-rotted manure. After they flower, cut the shoots back to within about 2 inches of their base and repot. At this time you can make cuttings, which root best with a bottom heat of 65 degrees. Cuttings may also be rooted in October. Pot the rooted cuttings in 3-inch pots and shift to larger pots as necessary. Regular pinching is necessary to produce compact plants. Genista benefits from being kept outdoors during the summer. Syringe the plants frequently and give them ample water.

Geraniums

Many greenhouse owners give geraniums front rank and take pleasure in building up a collection of these interesting and attractive plants. Certainly they have many varieties, classified in five groups, from which to select. The five groups of geraniums (all in the genus *Pelargonium* of the geranium family, Geraniaceae) are the zonal geraniums, the scented-leaved geraniums, the ivy-leaved geraniums, the show or fancy pelargoniums, and the succulent geraniums. All of the cultivated geraniums have come from South Africa.

The zonal geraniums (Pelargonium zonale). This group, the familiar geraniums, enjoys widespread popularity for greenhouse culture and for summer bedding. If you have had trouble raising geraniums in your home you will be delighted with how easy it is to raise them to perfection in a greenhouse. Certain varieties are distinguished for their abundance of beautiful flowers, others for their attractively marked and colored foliage, so charming that corsages can be made from them.

Among the choice varieties that are grown primarily for their flowers are: Alphonse Ricard, with vermillion flowers; Better Times, bearing cerise blooms; Fiat Queen and Madam

Landry, producing salmon-colored flowers; Madonna, a good white; Radio Red and Pride of Camden, with red blossoms. All of these are plants of normal stature.

Other varieties are dwarf, some attaining a height of only a few inches, yet flowering profusely. These dwarf zonal geraniums are fascinating and in a small space you can maintain a very interesting collection. Among the choice dwarf geraniums are Little Darling, with green leaves and pink flowers; Pigmy, bearing scarlet flowers; Alpha, a variety with golden leaves zoned with brown, and red flowers; and Black Vesuvius, with olive green leaves and huge flowers of a bright orange-scarlet. Other good dwarf varieties are Pixie, Madame Fournier, Bumble Bee, and Sleepy.

Certain varieties of zonal geraniums have beautifully colored foliage in shades of green, red, and yellow. Among the varieties with tricolored foliage and eye-catching leaf markings are Lady Cullen and Mrs. Pollock, with nicely lobed green leaves, edged yellow, and splashed brown and crimson. Skies of Italy has brilliantly colored maple-like leaves, and Mrs. Cox has leaves green in the center, then a zone of brown tinted with red, surrounded by a border of creamy white. Miss Burdett Coutts is another variety with beautiful foliage. The leaves are purple-zoned, green-centered, and cream-bordered.

Zonal geraniums are best grown in a 50-degree greenhouse, but can be grown in a 60-degree house. Except during the hottest summer months, when the glass should be shaded, they prefer an abundance of light. Although geraniums can withstand prolonged drought they grow better if watered regularly. However, avoid waterlogging the soil, which is harmful. Water thoroughly when the surface of the soil is beginning to get dry.

Geraniums are propagated from cuttings made in the fall, winter, and spring. The cutting should be about 4 inches long. Remove the lower leaf or two to facilitate inserting the cutting in sand or vermiculite, both of which are excellent rooting mediums. After insertion, water the cuttings thoroughly and from then on keep them somewhat on the dry side.

Some growers prefer to root the cuttings directly in 2½-inch pots filled with a mixture of equal parts of loam, leaf mold, and sand. The cuttings in pots or in a bench of sand or vermiculite should be shaded from the sun. They will root either in a 50-degree or 60-degree house.

After the cuttings have rooted they should go in 2½-inch pots. A mixture of three parts soil and one part well-rotted cow manure, with the addition of a 4-inch pot of superphosphate per wheelbarrow, is ideal. After the plants are established they should be pinched to induce branching. If you have allowed the plants to become very leggy with many leaves, remove the top three or four inches of the stem, a so-called *hard pinch*. The part removed may be rooted. If the plants are short, roll or pinch off the tip of the stem; in other words, use a *soft pinch*. When the roots become crowded the plants will need shifting into 4-inch pots, or into 5-inch ones if large specimens are wanted. If you want flowers during the winter months, do not overpot. Slightly pot-bound plants are more likely to flower than those which are in large pots. When the pots are well filled with roots, apply commercial fertilizer (about one-quarter teaspoon for a 5-inch pot) at about monthly intervals.

Raising geraniums from seed is an interesting venture. Of course, you must expect many mediocre plants for each superior one. Seed can be purchased or you can try hybridizing and collecting seed.

Geraniums may become infested with red spiders, mealy bugs, leafrollers, mites, and aphids. Malathion and DDT will not injure geraniums and will control insect pests. If the leafspot disease appears, remove the infected leaves and eliminate overhead syringing. Proper spacing of the plants and good ventilation are also helpful in controlling leafspot, as is the application of Fermate or Zerlate. *Crinkles,* a virus disease, causes translucent spots on the leaves. The only control is to dispose of the infected plants. Another disease is *blackleg,* which may be recognized by the blackening of the stem. This disease is most commonly seen in the propagating bench, although potted plants may be affected. Use fresh sand in the propagating bench or sterilize the old sand and dispose of infected plants. To avoid dieback or branch rot disease don't tear the flower stalk from the stem, because this leaves an open wound through which harmful fungi can gain entrance. Instead just pinch off the flower cluster, leaving 3 to 4 inches of the stalk. After it dies, the stalk naturally falls from the stem and a protective layer will form.

The scented-leaved geraniums. This group consists of a number of species with inconspicuous flowers and leaves which vary in shape according to the variety. The scented-leaved geraniums are grown chiefly for the fragrance which emanates when the leaves are rubbed lightly. Among the varieties are those with the fragrance of the rose, nutmeg, lemon, lime, strawberry, and mint. The culture of these interesting plants is the same as that of the zonal geraniums, with a night temperature preferably close to 50 degrees.

Ivy-leaved geraniums (Pelargonium peltatum). These geraniums are characterized by their trailing habit of growth, which makes them desirable for use in hanging baskets and window boxes. The leaves are glossy and green. There are many varieties of ivy-leaved geraniums: Charles Monselet, a red-flowered variety; Charles Turner, rose-pink; Comtesse Degrey, salmon; Giant Lavender; and many others. Their culture is the same as for the zonal geraniums.

Show pelargoniums (*Pelargonium domesticum*). These are also known as the Lady Washington Geraniums, Martha Washington Geraniums, Fancy Pelargoniums, and Pansy-flowered Geraniums. The show pelargoniums are not in continuous bloom. They generally flower in the spring, from Easter on. Like other geraniums, they are propagated from cuttings made in fall, winter, and spring. The favorite time is soon after the flowering season. After rooting, the cuttings are potted in 2½-inch pots and moved along into larger pots as is necessary. During the growing period pinching is desired to promote branching. Plants soft pinched for the last time in December will flower in March and April, those pinched in early February, in May and June. Pinching after February will prevent flowering.

The plants require rather heavy shade as well as syringing during the bright summer months. In the fall more light should be given and syringing stopped. Monthly applications of fertilizer are desirable. The plants do well with a night temperature of 50 degrees.

After flowering, the plants should be kept on the dry side until August or September. Then prune them into shape, leaving one or two nodes on each branch. Remove most of the old soil, trim the roots and repot. The plants should be shifted into larger pots in December.

Some favorite varieties are Azalea, Edith North, Springtime, Easter Greeting, Gardener's Joy, Marie Vogel, Salmon Springtime, and Pink Vogel.

Succulent geraniums. A few geraniums are strikingly different from those previously described. The Knotty Storksbill (*Pelargonium gibbosum*) has fleshy stems knotted at the joints. Another, the Cactus Geranium (*P. echinatum*), has stems armed with spines and lobed leaves covered with white hairs.

Grevillea

Grevillea robusta, commonly called Silk Oak, is raised for its attractive fernlike foliage. The plants are raised from seed sown in the spring. The seeds are large and flat. They seem to germinate better if placed point downward or sideways, instead of flat. Pot the seedlings in 2½-inch pots and move to larger ones as necessary. The plants require shade. Grevillea is best raised with a single stem; do not pinch the plants.

Primroses

Primroses (of the family Primulaceae) produce a grand display of flowers during the winter and early spring. Among the favorite species for greenhouse culture are *Primula malacoides, P. sinensis, P. obconica,* and *P. Kewensis. Primula malacoides* (the Baby Primrose), one of our favorite plants, bears myriads of flowers on slender stems, month after month. A number of superb varieties are now available with flowers of white, rose-pink, salmon-rose, lavender, pink, or red.

The Star or Stellata group of the Chinese Primrose (*Primula sinensis*) are graceful and very floriferous plants, that bloom over a long period. The flowers are long-lasting when cut, remaining fresh for many days. The color range includes white, pink, lavender, blue, and ruby. The Giant varieties of *Primula sinensis* are also worthy, and they come in colors of red, orange-red, pink, salmon, and blue.

Primula obconica, sometimes called Poison Primrose, bears huge heads of flowers on strong stems well above the foliage. The plants are compact and neat. Pink, rose, red, and crimson varieties are available. This species has one serious drawback: the foliage, when handled, causes a severe irritating rash on some individuals. Some persons are immune but others are susceptible. If you are sensitive and desire to raise this plant, you will have to wear rubber gloves when handling it, and keep it where it will not be readily handled by visitors.

Primula Kewensis is a strong-growing, floriferous species that bears beautiful yellow flowers. It is a hybrid resulting from a cross of the Buttercup Primrose with the Arabian Primrose.

All of the primroses mentioned require the same cultural conditions. Primroses are started from seed. Sow seeds of *Primula obconica, P. Kewensis,* and *P. sinensis* in April. Seeds of *Primula malacoides* are sown in June for Christmas flowering and in September for flowering at Easter and for Mother's Day. Seeds may be sown in 5-inch pots, using plenty of drainage material and fine soil. Firm the soil and scatter the seeds; then just barely cover them with fine sandy soil. Water by subirrigation or with a fine rose and then cover the pot with a pane of glass. It is essential that the soil be kept moist during the germination period. When the seedlings appear, provide more air by tilting the glass, and in a few days remove it completely. As soon as the seedlings are large enough to handle they should be moved into flats, spacing them an inch apart. A suitable soil mixture consists of two parts soil, one part sand, one part leaf mold, and one part well-rotted cow manure. When the plants begin to crowd each other, move them into 2½-inch pots. Before the plants become potbound shift them into 4- or 5-inch pots. When potting, keep the crown at soil level. Too-deep planting may induce a stem rot and too-shallow planting results in the plant's toppling over. During the bright months of summer the greenhouse should be shaded. In autumn the shade should be gradually reduced. If you prefer, you can keep the seedlings in a shaded, well-ventilated cold frame during the summer. Throughout the growing and flowering period, the ideal night temperature is 50 degrees.

Roses

The roses you see in flower shops have been raised in ground beds or raised benches. To grow long-stemmed roses to perfection requires considerable skill and, of equal importance, greenhouses of large size. However, certain varieties of rose grow well in a small greenhouse. Roses grown in pots make excellent greenhouse specimens. They can be raised at a night temperature of 50 degrees or at 60 degrees. Of course the plants will flower sooner in a 60-degree house than in a 50-degree one. You can raise a large variety, selecting from the Baby Ramblers, Hybrid Teas, Climbers, and Hybrid Perpetual Roses. Among the choice Baby Ramblers are Golden Salmon, Triomphe d'Orleans, Margo Koster, Ideal, and Gloire du Midi. Hybrid tea roses which do well in pots include Pernet, Talisman, Madame Herriot, E. G. Hill, President Hoover, Better Times, and Joanna Hill. A few choice climbers are Eugene Jacquet, Crimson Rambler, Rosary, and Dorothy Perkins. Choice perpetuals are Frau Karl Druschki, Magna Charta, and American Beauty.

In November, dig rose plants from your garden or purchase top-quality plants. Then plant them, without delay, in pots, using 6-, 7-, or 8-inch pots, according to the sizes of the plants. Roses grow well in a mixture of loam, three parts, and well-decayed cow manure, one part, and a 6-inch pot of bone meal per wheelbarrow of soil. As usual, provide good drainage. After potting, the climbers should be shaped on a wire form. Store the potted plants in a cold frame and protect them from winter injury by covering the canes with straw or leaves. In early January, bring the plants into the greenhouse and syringe them several times a day. Syringing promotes swelling and development of buds. Climbing roses should not be pruned, but others require pruning.

Commercial growers find a ready market for pot roses at Easter. The customers enjoy them as house plants and then plant them in the garden. A schedule to have roses in flower at Easter would be as follows: transfer the plants from the cold frame to the greenhouse on January 15, keep at a temperature of 45 to 48 degrees until February 15, then raise the temperature to 54 to 56 degrees, and in early March increase it to 60 degrees.

Roses prefer a high humidity, 60 to 70 per cent, and good ventilation. Water carefully, preferably with water at the same temperature as the greenhouse. Avoid both overwatering and dryness at roots. When actively growing, the plants respond to fertilizer.

In the spring you can plant the roses in your garden, or you can carry them over in pots to be raised in the greenhouse the next season. If you prefer the latter, and many growers do, plunge the pots in the garden in late spring. In the fall, repot the plants that need it, and top-dress the others with a mixture of half soil and half well-rotted manure. Early October is suitable for overhauling the plants. After they are overhauled, place them in a cold frame and cover with straw. Near the end of November you can bring some of the plants into the greenhouse. Others can remain in the cold frame until January.

Pruning of roses, except for the climbers, can be done before they are put in the cold frame or just after you bring them into the greenhouse. The climbers are pruned after flowering; cut out the old wood nearly entirely. This encourages a few strong shoots to develop near the base. These new shoots will be 6 to 10 feet long by fall.

Roses are increased by cuttings, generally taken in the spring. The best cuttings have three eyes on them, and they are best rooted with a bottom heat of 70 degrees. Cuttings root in one or two months. Pot the rooted cuttings in 2½-

inch pots and shift into larger pots as necessary. Roses are also propagated by grafting and budding.

Roses can also be grown from seed. However, the offspring will not be uniform; some may be excellent, others worthless. Before rose seeds will germinate, they must be exposed to a low temperature. Store the clean seeds in moist peat moss at a temperature of 41 degrees for four to six months, and then plant them.

If the roses become infected with mildew, dust them with sulfur. Aphids and red spider are troublesome pests that can be controlled with Malathion. Aramite and Ovotran may be used for red spiders.

Schizanthus

This plant, a member of the potato family (Solanaceae), is known as the Butterfly Flower or Poor Man's Orchid. Schizanthus grows 1 or 2 feet tall, has fern-like, light green leaves, and bears showy flowers in terminal clusters. The petals usually have streaks or spots of another color at the base. For handsome plants that will flower in April or May, sow seeds about 1/8 inch deep in August or September. For flowering in late spring and summer, sow seeds in January. The seeds germinate in a few days and the seedlings grow rapidly. The seedlings may be moved into flats, then into 3-inch pots, moving into larger pots as necessary. Or the seedlings may be moved from the seed pan directly into 2½-inch pots and later into larger ones. The plants grow well in a mixture of equal parts of loam and leaf mold with the addition of some well-rotted manure and superphosphate. The plants should be pinched once or twice to get a bushy habit. A night temperature of 50 degrees is ideal.

If you wish Schizanthus for cut flowers you can move them from the seed pan into flats, spacing the plants three inches apart. Do not pinch the plants; permit them to grow to a single stem. The plants will flower in the flat. Of course you can raise Schizanthus in benches; space them about 8 inches apart.

Schizanthus may be flowered early, from February on, by growing the plants with longer days. Just before sundown turn on the lights and let them burn until 10 P.M.

Streptosolen

Streptosolen Jamesonii, also a member of the potato family (Solanaceae), is a handsome evergreen shrub from Colombia. From January on, the plant produces clusters of attractive orange-red flowers. After flowering, cut the shrub back to promote bushiness, and then repot, using a compost of two parts loam and one of leaf mold. Established plants require plenty of water, occasional feeding, and a temperature of 50 degrees. The plants are easily propagated from cuttings made in the spring. Young plants should be pinched several times.

Swainsona

This shrub is a member of the pea family (Leguminosae) and a native of Australia. The favorite species is *Swainsona galegifolia,* which bears sprays of pea-shaped, red or white flowers, depending on the variety. The white variety is the one generally grown. Swainsona begins to flower in summer and continues well into winter. The plants do well in pots containing an even mixture of loam, peat, and manure. Swainsona may be started from seed sown in the spring or from cuttings taken in January. Pinch several times to get stocky plants. Plants may be kept growing for several years by cutting back and repotting when necessary. The plants flower better when they are potbound. During some years, only a top dressing of soil and manure will be necessary.

CHAPTER 13

THE AMARYLLIS FAMILY

THE AMARYLLIS FAMILY includes a number of choice plants, many of tropical origin, that grow well in pots in a greenhouse maintained at a night temperature of 60 degrees. Some are dainty while many have bold and showy flowers. Among the favorite kinds are *Amaryllis, Clivia, Eucharis* (Amazon Lily, Star-of-Bethlehem), *Haemanthus* (Blood Lily), *Polianthes* (Tuberose), *Sprekelia* (Aztec Lily), and *Zephyranthes* (Zephyr Flower, Fairy Lily).

Amaryllis—Hippeastrum vittatum

The modern varieties of amaryllis, with their open-faced flowers and broad, iridescent petals, are indeed spectacular. The flowers may be as much as 8 inches across, of white, salmon, deep red, or orange color. A large bulb usually produces two, sometimes three, flower spikes, each bearing three or four magnificent blooms.

Special temperature treatment that causes development of flowers within the bulb during the storage period has been perfected. When these are planted in November, the flower spikes begin growth immediately and flowers are open for Christmas. You can purchase these specially treated bulbs for delivery in early November, enjoy their early flowers, and then, after carrying them through the year, treat them yourself for flowering the following Christmas.

Treated bulbs are those which have been stored for four weeks at a temperature of 70 to 75 degrees. Plant the bulbs singly in standard 6- or 7-inch pots using a mixture of one part soil, one part sand, and one part rotted cow manure or peat moss or leaf mold. A tablespoon of bone meal should be added to that quantity of soil needed for a 6-inch pot. Cut off any roots which are dead, but do not remove or injure any living roots. These living roots will later branch and increase the root area. Plant the bulb so that one-third of it is in the soil and two-thirds above. After potting, water thoroughly, but thereafter, until the shoot appears, keep the soil somewhat dry. When the flowers are developing, watering should be more frequent. Sometimes the flowering shoot develops before the leaves and in some instances the plant flowers even before the leaves emerge from the bulb. During other years the same bulb may produce leaves and blossoms at the same time, making a more handsome plant. After the flowers shrivel, cut off the flowering stalk about 2 inches from the top of the bulb.

Because the food necessary for next year's growth is made when the plants are through flowering, keep them actively growing by giving them ample water, frequent syringings, and liquid fertilizer at three-week intervals. The plants should be given full light except during the hottest summer months.

If you want flowers at Christmas, select only the large bulbs (at least 8 inches in circumference) and treat them as follows. Cease watering them on August 15. On September 10 pull off the leaves if they are shriveled, or cut them off if green. Store the bulbs in the pots until October 13 at a temperature between 59 and 63 degrees. From October 13 to November 10 store the bulbs at a temperature between 70 and 75 degrees. On November 10, repot those that were not potted the previous year and just top dress those that were. Then water the bulbs. Keep them on the dry side until growth is active, after which water them regularly. We ourselves do not have a room in which the temperature can be controlled precisely. Nevertheless, we flower amaryllis near Christmas by withholding water after the recommended date and by cutting or pulling off the leaves on September 10. From September 10 to October 13 we keep the pots in the basement, where the temperature is about 60 degrees, and from October 13 to November 10 in a closet upstairs, where it runs about 70 degrees.

If you are not interested in early flowers, start drying off the bulbs in October (instead of August) by withholding water. Let the leaves wilt and shrivel. Then store the bulbs at 50 degrees. These bulbs may be started into active growth any time from January to March.

Amaryllis can be increased by offsets which will develop into plants exactly like the parents. By using them you can increase your favorite varieties. The offsets form at the base of the mother bulb. They should not be removed from the parent bulb until they are almost ready to separate of their own accord. Remove the offsets during the dormant period and pot them, taking care not to injure the roots.

If you raise amaryllis from seed, and this is not difficult, you can expect considerable variety among the offspring. Perhaps a few will be particularly outstanding. Seeds are best sown singly in 2-inch pots plunged in a flat of moist peat moss to keep them from drying out. Seeds germinate in about two weeks. When the roots crowd the pots, shift the plants into 3-inch pots, taking care not to injure the roots. From these pots the young plants may be shifted into 4- or 5-inch ones. With good culture, some of the plants will flower when they are two years old, others at three. During the entire period from seed-sowing to flowering, keep the plants in active growth. Do not dry them off during the autumn as with mature bulbs.

Clivia

Of the three species in this genus, all native of South Africa, *Clivia miniata* is the most popular. There are several varieties of this species; in addition there are choice hybrids resulting from crossings with the other two species, *Clivia nobilis* and *C. gardenii*. Clivias grow and flower without effort and are very satisfying plants. They have handsome,

Growing tuberous begonias from tubers. Plant the tubers in a shallow pot or in a flat containing a mixture of leaf mold and sand, or in peat. When the shoots are well developed, remove the plants and pot them.

Stages in the growth of tuberous begonias from seed. Sow the seeds on loose soil. The seedlings in the seed pan (*upper left*) are magnified here from their actual height of a quarter of an inch, and are ready to be moved into a flat or community pot. *Upper right:* plants ready to be moved from community pot to 2½-inch pots. When they have made good growth, remove the plants from the 2½-inch pots and shift into 4- or 5-inch ones (lower figures).

Erect varieties of tuberous begonias are grown in pots on the bench and pendant varieties in hanging pots. (Vetterle and Reinelt)

Facing page: An arrangement of tuberous begonias and ivy by Myra J. Brooks. (Roche photo)

Begonia. *Below:* Lady Mac in flower. *Above:* a young plant that developed from a leaf cutting. (Roche photos)

Bromeliads. *Upper left: Aechmea fulgens. Upper right: Billbergia vittata* (Brazil). *Lower left: Guzmania zahnii* (Panama). *Lower right: Neoregelia tristis* (Brazil). (Ladislaus Cutak photos)

evergreen, amaryllis-like leaves, about two feet long, and bear showy, lilylike flowers in shades of orange, yellow, and scarlet, at the summit of a stiff stem about 2 feet tall. The plants flower in the winter or spring.

A suitable compost is a mixture of fibrous loam, sand, and leaf mold. Established plants may be grown for several years in the same pots if they are fed with liquid manure or fertilizer during their growing period, which begins in February and continues until about November. When in active growth the plants should be kept well watered and at a night temperature of 60 to 65 degrees. In November and December, when they are resting, keep them on the dry side and in the cooler end of the 60-degree house. When the plants outgrow their containers, they should be repotted. This is best done in February. You can shift them into large pots or divide the plants and plant the divisions in smaller pots. It is difficult to divide plants without considerable injury to the thick fleshy roots. Hence, you may expect some retardation of growth after dividing. Clivias grow best and flower well under light shade. Provide them with shade except during the dark months of December, January, and February.

Clivias can be propagated from seed. Seedlings are moved from the seed pans into flats and then into pots, shifting them into larger pots as necessary. Keep the seedlings growing throughout the year.

Eucharis

The name *Eucharis* comes from the Greek word for *very graceful,* which describes these plants perfectly. They have handsome oval, evergreen leaves 8 to 12 inches long. The delightfully scented flowers are of purest white, borne on a cluster a foot tall. The plants flower freely. The blooms are attractive in bouquets and excellent for corsages.

Eucharis grandiflora, sometimes sold as *E. amazonica,* is native to Colombia and is the desired species for greenhouse culture. It is known as the Amazon Lily. The ideal night temperature is 65 degrees, but it will come along nicely at temperatures as low as 60 degrees. During the bright months of the year, usually from April to October, they require shade. In most localities they can stand full sun from fall to spring. The plant develops from a large bulb, some 2 or 3 inches in diameter, which should be planted in a 5-inch pot. The bulb should be set about half in the soil and half out. Use a soil made up of two parts loam, one part peat, and one part well-rotted cow manure. Bulbs are usually potted in May or June. Water sparingly after potting until growth begins, when ample water is called for. During the growing period the plants benefit from occasional feedings of liquid manure or fertilizer. After the leaves have developed fully move the plants to the cooler end of the 60-degree house, and keep them somewhat on the dry side for about one month, but don't let the leaves wilt. After keeping the plants on the dry side for a month, move them to a warmer part of the house and water freely. Flowers will soon appear, and, somewhat later, new leaves.

Shift the plants into larger pots as necessary. When they have become very large, it will be necessary to divide them, which is best done in May or June. Turn the plant out of the pot and wash the soil from the roots, taking care to avoid injuring them. Separate the offsets, pot them singly in 3-inch pots. Shift into larger pots as required. Water sparingly until growth begins, after which increase the frequency.

Red spiders, thrips, green fly, and mealy bugs are pests to look out for.

Haemanthus—Blood Lily

The genus *Haemanthus* includes about sixty species of bulbous plants from South Africa. *Haemanthus multiflorus, H. Katherinae,* and *H. coccineus* are the species most frequently grown. *Haemanthus multiflorus* has leaves 6 to 8 inches long and flowers borne at the top of a naked stem which is 1 to 3 feet high. The flower cluster is ball-shaped, about six inches in diameter, and bears thirty to one hundred blood-red flowers. This species generally flowers in the spring, usually before the leaves appear. *Haemanthus Katherinae* has three to five leaves about a foot long. The flowers are bright red and occur in a spherical cluster which is about 9 inches across. This species flowers in the spring after the foliage has developed. The leaves of *H. coccineus* are about 2 feet long and the flower stalk 6 to 10 inches high. The flowers are red and arranged in a spherical cluster at the top of the stem. Flowers generally appear in August or September, before the foliage comes out.

The bulbs of the species mentioned are about 2 to 3 inches across, or even up to 6 inches. They should be potted in a mixture of loam and peat. Let the neck of the bulb protrude from the soil. Haemanthus prefers a night temperature of 50 to 55 degrees. After potting, water the plants sparingly until they are in active growth, then more frequently. During the summer months, provide shade. When the plants of *H. multiflorus* and *H. coccineus* show signs of going to rest, gradually withhold water but don't let the soil become bone dry or allow the bulb to shrivel. *H. multiflorus* generally has a rest period during winter and *H. coccineus* during late spring and early summer. After the rest period is over start them into growth by applying water. *H. Katherinae* is nearly evergreen and does not need to be dried off. The bulbs do not need to be repotted every year; repotting every third year is usually sufficient. The plants flower much better when the roots are not disturbed. When the plants are potbound, they will benefit from biweekly applications of dilute fertilizer.

Polianthes–Tuberose

There are about twelve species in the genus *Polianthes.* Only one, *Polianthes tuberosa,* commonly called *tuberose,* is a favorite greenhouse plant. This species grows to a height of about 3 feet, has leaves 1 to 1½ feet long and bears sweetly scented, waxy-white flowers about 1½ to 2½ inches long.

The plants grow well with a night temperature of 55 to 60 degrees. The bulbs may be potted at intervals of three or four weeks from January on for flowers in April, May, and June. You may pot one bulb in a 4-inch pot or three or four in a 6-inch one. A mixture of three parts of loam and one of leaf mold is excellent. Water after potting and then keep the plants on the dry side until growth begins, after which they should be given ample water until they are through flowering. After the plants have flowered, the growths will gradually die down. Gradually withhold water during this period. After the growths have died down, rest the bulbs at a temperature of 55 to 60 degrees. Repot the bulbs the following year.

Sprekelia–Aztec Lily or Jacobean Lily

Sprekelia bulbs are planted in the spring for blossoms during the summer. The plant has narrow leaves about 1 foot long. One flower, about 4 inches across, develops at the top of a leafless stalk. The flowers are bright red in color and attractively shaped.

Zephyranthes–Zephyr Lily

The delicate Zephyr lilies have grasslike leaves, often appearing with the flowers. The flowers are borne singly on thin bare stems, 6 to 12 inches long. Among the species are *Z. candida,* which has white flowers, *Z. grandiflora,* with rosy flowers, and *Z. citrina,* a yellow-flowered species.

Zephyranthes grows best at a night temperature of 50 degrees. The bulbs are small, about an inch in diameter. Plant four or five bulbs, with the necks protruding, in a 6-inch pot containing a mixture of equal parts of loam and peat moss. During growth and flowering give the plants ample water. When the leaves begin to shrivel keep the bulbs on the dry side until growth is again active.

CHAPTER 14

EXOTIC FOLIAGE AND FLOWERING PLANTS

MANY OF OUR fine greenhouse plants are in the Arum family (technically known as Araceae, and often called aroids), which includes such exotic plants as alocasia, anthurium, calla lily, caladium, Chinese evergreen, dieffenbachia, nephthytis, philodendron, and pothos. For the past century, and today as well, plant explorers have searched the jungles of tropical America for new aroids to enhance the beauty of the greenhouse. And the plant breeders, too, are working to produce ever more beautiful forms. A majority of the aroids are confined to the tropics where they grow in damp forests, but a few are native to the United States, among them sweet flag, jack-in-the-pulpit, and skunk cabbage.

Certain aroids have beautiful foliage while the flowers, although interesting, are without beauty; these we use as foliage plants. Others—anthuriums, for example—have distinctive flower clusters of decorative value. The true flowers of all aroids are minute and inconspicuous. They are crowded on a finger-like spike, technically known as a *spadix,* which may be showy in some aroids. Below the spadix, there is a leaflike bract, known as a *spathe.* In certain species the spathe is colored and very attractive. The spathe and spadix of certain ones, such as anthuriums and calla lilies, are very decorative. We loosely refer to this attractive arrangement as a flower. Technically, of course, it is not a true flower, since the spathe is a leaf. When seed is desired, pollination is performed by rubbing the male (pollen-producing) flowers of one spadix over the female flowers of another when their pistils are receptive.

All the cultivated members of this family grow well in a greenhouse maintained at a night temperature of 60 to 65 degrees and, with the exception of the calla lily, they all prefer shade. Many plants of the arum family make good companions for the shaded 60-degree house, and they get along well with begonias, gesneriads, and orchids.

Aglaonema

The Chinese evergreen, *Aglaonema simplex,* is the most widely grown species of this genus. It grows to a height of 2 or 3 feet and bears oblong green leaves, about 10 inches long. A more compact species is *A. costatum,* which is about 8 inches tall and has foliage which is heart-shaped, green, and prominently marked with white patches. *A. Robelenii* (also known as *Schismatoglottis*) has handsome gray-green leaves, but it is especially noted for its clusters of shiny red berries. *A. marantifolium* is another species with beautiful fruits.

Aglaonemas thrive in soil composed of loam, leaf mold, rotted manure, and sand in equal parts. They do well in a 60-degree house. The plants are readily propagated by divisions and by cuttings rooted in sand.

Alocasia

The alocasias are gems among the foliage plants, with their beautiful forms and attractively colored leaves. Three species in which you may be interested are *Alocasia cuprea, A. lowii,* and *A. sanderiana.* In addition to these there are many hybrids. Among the best is *A. sedeni,* a hybrid of *lowii* and *cuprea. A. cuprea* has oval, nearly bronze leaves, rich purple below, and deeply indented veins. *A. lowii* is characterized by heart-shaped leaves, which are olive green above, purple below. The silvery bands along the veins add beauty to the leaves. The hybrid, *A. sedeni,* is vigorous with heart shaped leaves and beautiful vein markings. *A. sande-*

riana has deeply indented, arrow-shaped leaves with prominent veins that make a bold pattern against the dark green foliage with its metallic sheen.

The alocasias thrive in a mixture of half peat moss, one-fourth leaf mold, and one-fourth loam or sand. With this compost, occasional feedings with a liquid fertilizer should be given to established plants, especially during the active growing season, which begins in March and extends to early winter. They can also be grown in a mixture of sphagnum moss and small pieces of charcoal; with this mixture regular applications of liquid fertilizer are necessary. Alocasias like ample moisture, a humid atmosphere, a shaded location, and do best with a night temperature of 65 to 70 degrees. Hence, select a warm spot in the 60-degree house for them.

The plants may be propagated from suckers or cuttings of the rhizome which should be inserted in small pots containing an equal mixture of peat moss and sand. Plunging the pots into a propagating box with bottom heat of 75 degrees is beneficial. Alocasias may also be grown from seed.

Anthurium

In this genus, native of tropical America, there are about six hundred species. It is a genus that could well appeal to a collector and hybridizer. Some members are noted for their handsome, velvety foliage and others for their attractive flower clusters. The most conspicuous part of the flower cluster is the large, shiny, brightly colored modified leaf (spathe) below or around the fingerlike spadix that bears many inconspicuous flowers. The spadix with its surrounding spathe is beautiful, and lasts extraordinarily well, up to five weeks after it is cut and three months or so on the plant. A well-grown specimen is continually flowering. The flowers are prized for use in exotic arrangements and for corsages.

Anthurium andreanum and *A. scherzerianum* are the species generally grown for their flowers. *Anthurium andreanum* has a yellowish-white spadix, and a heart-shaped orange-red spathe, 4 to 6 inches long. The leaves are heart-shaped, green, and about 12 inches long and 6 inches wide.

Anthurium scherzerianum, called the Flamingo Flower, is the most popular species. The spadix is coiled and yellow. The spathe is red, yellow, rose, or white depending on the particular horticultural variety.

Anthurium crystallinum and *A. veitchii* are grown for their beautiful foliage. Both species have large velvety leaves but rather unattractive flowers. The leaves of *A. crystallinum* are somewhat heart-shaped, 14 inches long, 10 inches wide, green with white stripes above, pale rose-pink below. The spathe of the flower is narrow and green.

Anthurium veitchii is perhaps the best-known foliage plant of the group. The drooping leaves are oblong and very large, about 3 feet long and 10 inches wide, of metallic green color, with showy veins. The spathe of the flower is about 3 inches long and greenish-white in color.

All of the anthuriums grow well with a night temperature of 60 to 65 degrees and benefit from frequent syringings. They require shade, but during December, January, and February only a very light shade is needed. They do well in a mixture of one part chopped sphagnum moss, one part chopped osmunda fiber (preferably old fiber previously used for orchids), and one part rotted cow manure. Another suitable mixture consists of equal parts of peat moss, leaf mold, and coarse sand, to which can be added a small quantity of well-rotted manure and charcoal. They can also be grown in osmunda fiber without other ingredients, a medium which we prefer. We fill the pot about one-third full with crock to provide good drainage. Then we add some fiber. The plant is then inserted and fiber is packed around the roots. If grown in osmunda fiber the plants should be fertilized periodically. Whatever the compost, plants require repotting every two or three years. This is best done in January. Established plants should be furnished a uniform supply of water. Keep the soil or fiber moist but not wet. If the soil is continually soggy the roots will die.

The roots of anthurium have a tendency to extend above pot level. Therefore, in the interval between potting it is desirable to build up the compost around the stem to catch the roots. A fresh top dressing each year is also beneficial.

If a plant becomes too leggy, you can cut off the top, root it in sand, and give it a fresh start in a new pot. The old stock will send up new shoots which may be removed and potted in small pots or they may be permitted to develop on the plant.

Anthuriums can be increased by dividing the crown and by removing suckers. The suckers are inserted in small pots containing a mixture of peat, chopped sphagnum, and sand, in equal parts. In this medium they root rapidly if the pots are plunged in a propagating bed maintained at a temperature of 75 to 80 degrees, with bottom heat. Anthuriums may also be started from seeds sown on a mixture of peat and sphagnum. After sowing, cover the seeds lightly with chopped sphagnum. Seeds germinate best at a temperature of 80 degrees, at which temperature they germinate in about eight days. About six or seven weeks after sowing, the seedlings will be ready for transplanting into a flat. When the seedlings are six to eight months old, they can go into 3-inch pots, from which they can be shifted into larger pots. Well-grown plants will flower when they are three years old.

In their native shaded habitats of tropical America, anthuriums are pollinated by insects which are lacking in our greenhouses. If you wish the plants to set seed you will have to pollinate the flowers by hand. Many minute flowers bearing stamens and many bearing pistils occur along the spadix. You can recognize the stamen-bearing flowers by the powdery pollen which they liberate, and the pistil-bearing flowers by their sticky secretion and spicy fragrance. To perform pollination it is necessary to use two spadixes because on any one spadix the pistils mature before the stamens. Rub a spadix which has the anthers tipped with pollen against a spadix whose pistils are receptive, as evidenced by the minute drops of transparent fluid that the pistils exude. This procedure should be repeated once a day for several days. Two or three weeks after pollination the spadix will turn a dark green and increase in size. It will continue to increase in length and width. The seeds mature in four to nine months, depending upon the variety. When the seeds are ripe the berry which encloses them will change color and become so loose that it is easily removed. Remove the seeds from the berry and plant them right away. The seeds lose their viability in a relatively short time.

Caladium

There are about sixty species in this genus, but only two have contributed materially to the fancy-leaved caladiums of today, *Caladium bicolor* and *C. picturatum*. The fancy-leaved caladiums are beautiful foliage plants with arrow-shaped leaves that are richly colored and attractively marked. They are at their peak of beauty during the summer.

Rhizomes may be purchased for delivery from January on. Plant the rhizomes from January through spring in 3- or 4-inch pots. Pot them so that the rhizome is about an inch below the surface of the soil. Or, if you prefer, start the rhizomes in a flat of sphagnum moss, and then, after the roots have developed, move them into pots. Caladiums thrive when potted in soil composed of equal parts of loam, peat, rotted manure, and sand. When the plants in 4-inch pots have made sufficient growth, shift them into 6-inch pots, a size which will carry the plants through the season. During the rooting period, the plants should be watered sparingly, but once they are established the soil should be kept moist. Caladiums need shade, high humidity, and a night temperature of 65 degrees. They benefit from periodic applications of liquid manure or a liquid fertilizer.

The leaves generally begin to dry up in October. At this time gradually decrease the waterings. In about one month's time the leaves will be completely dried and the plants ready for storage. The pots are laid on their sides under the bench in a 60-degree house. During the dormant period withhold water. Instead of storing the rhizomes in pots, you can remove them from the pots, shake them free of soil, cut off the dried leaves, and store the rhizomes in sand at a temperature of 60 degrees. Caladiums can be increased by dividing the rhizome, and from seeds. The seeds germinate readily and the seedlings are easy to grow. The first five or six leaves of a seedling are generally green; the later ones are colored.

There are many named varieties of caladiums, among them Candidum, which has white leaves and green veins; John Peel and Crimson Wave, both with red leaves; Avalon Pink and Pink Cloud, with pink leaves; and Mrs. Arno Nehrling, Vivian Lee, and Fascination, all with varicolored leaves.

Calla Lily

The white calla (*Zantedeschia aethiopica*), the yellow calla (*Zantedeschia elliottiana*), and the pink calla (*Zantedeschia rehmannii*) are favorite greenhouse plants, each producing about six long-lasting flowers during the season. Callas grow well with a night temperature of 60 to 65 degrees when potted in a mixture of half loam and half peat moss. Pot the tubers so that there is an inch or two of soil above them. Until growth begins, water sparingly; then ample water should be given until the rest period begins. During their period of active growth, callas benefit from biweekly applications of manure water or a solution of ammonium sulfate.

Tubers of the white calla are planted in August or September. The plants should be watered sparingly until growth begins, then copious waterings are called for until June, when watering should be stopped. The pots should then be placed on their sides under the bench. In August the tubers are repotted and started into growth.

In contrast to the white calla, which flowers during the winter, the pink and yellow callas flower in the summer. They should be potted from January to April. When flowering is through withhold water and place the pots on their sides. Repot the tubers at the beginning of the year.

Dieffenbachia

This plant is also known as Dumb Cane because, according to legend, if you put a piece of the stem under your tongue it will render you speechless for three days. Dieffenbachias are handsome foliage plants that come from the rain forests of

Central and South America. The stem is somewhat succulent and bears at its top a cluster of large dark green leaves that are variously mottled or striped with white, yellow, or greenish-brown.

The plants grow well at a temperature of 60 to 65 degrees when potted in a mixture of equal parts of sand, loam, and leaf mold, with the addition of some rotted manure. If a plant becomes too leggy, you can cut off the top, retaining a considerable piece of the stem, and root it in moist sand. Thick roots will develop in about two weeks and the new plant may be potted. The remaining part of the stem may be cut into pieces about 2 inches long, each with one or more eyes. Plant the segments horizontally in a mixture of sand and peat. Each piece will develop roots and a shoot. Pot the cutting with its shoot in a 5-inch pot.

There are about a dozen species of dieffenbachia, four of which, *Dieffenbachia bowmannii, D. picta, D. sequine,* and *D. splendens,* are usually cultivated.

Nephthytis

There are about a half dozen species in this genus, but only one, *Nephthytis afzelii,* is frequently cultivated. This species has arrow-shaped leaves borne on a slender creeping stem. The plants prefer shade and a warm moist atmosphere. They grow well when potted in a mixture of equal parts of sand, loam, and leaf mold with the addition of some rotted manure and bone meal.

Philodendron

The philodendrons are often grown in greenhouses for their ornamental foliage, and they are in demand as foliage plants for the home. Their beautiful leaves and ability to thrive in the home make them deservedly popular. The genus includes about 250 species, but only a few are commonly grown and readily available. With the increased interest in this genus in recent years new varieties have been introduced and others have been developed by hybridization.

If you have known philodendrons only as house plants, you

will be surprised at their greater size when grown in ample rich soil in a greenhouse. For example, *Philodendron cordatum* has leaves about 3 inches long when grown in a 4-inch pot in the house. If it is planted in a bench of rich soil in the greenhouse, the leaves may be 16 inches long and the plant may attain a height of 20 feet or more if given support.

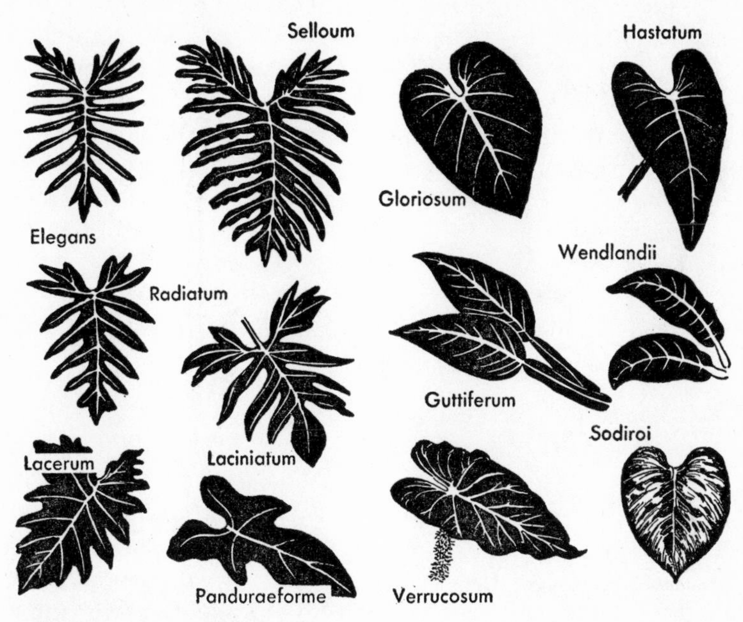

Philodendrons. (Ladislaus Cutak and the Missouri Botanical Garden)

Most species are climbers, but a few are self-heading plants. In their homes in tropical America the climbers use trees for support. The name *Philodendron* comes from the Greek words meaning *tree-loving*. The nonclimbers generally grow mounted on trees; we say they are epiphytes. However, there are some nonclimbers that grow on the ground.

Among the climbing types are such favorite species as *Philodendron cordatum, P. dubium, P. hastatum, P. panduraeforme, P. sodiroi,* and *P. pertusum*. *Philodendron pertusum,* more correctly *Monstera deliciosa,* is a *cut leaf* species, with large leaves looking as if portions of the leaves had been cut out. *P. sodiroi* has beautiful silvery leaves with darker green areas. *Philodendron panduraeforme* has green fiddle-

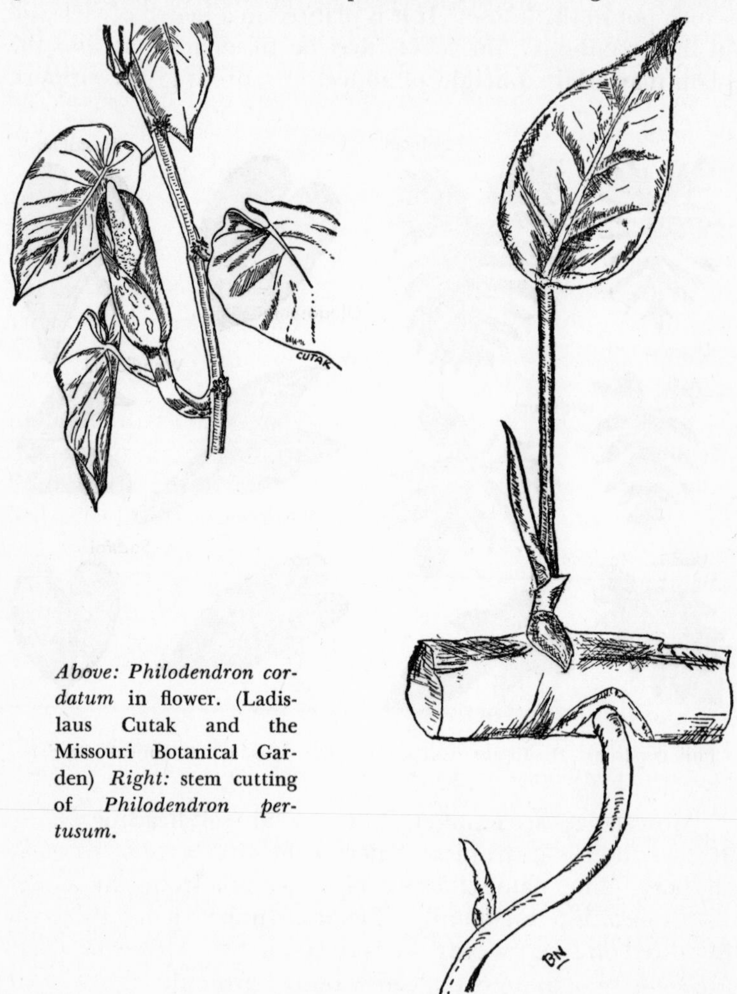

Above: Philodendron cordatum in flower. (Ladislaus Cutak and the Missouri Botanical Garden) *Right:* stem cutting of *Philodendron pertusum.*

shaped leaves; *P. hastatum,* dark green arrow-shaped leaves; *P. dubium,* green, deeply lobed leaves; and *P. cordatum* bright-green heart-shaped foliage. All of the climbing species require support. Totem poles made of fern fiber, or of wire frames stuffed and covered with sphagnum, are ideal for this purpose. Roots are produced along the stems of the climbing species; these attach themselves to or can be trained onto the totem pole. More artistic supports can be devised according to your own ingenuity. An unusual piece of driftwood can be used, plain or with sphagnum moss tucked into hollow places.

The rosette or nonclimbing species (also called self-heading philodendrons) do not require a pole. Some of the rosette types, such as *P. speciosa* and *P. eichleri,* are too large for the small greenhouse, but *P. wendlandii* and *P. undulatum* keep within bounds. *P. wendlandii* is a nice compact plant with oblong leaves about 2 feet long. *P. undulatum* has heart-shaped leaves which form a wavy cup.

Both the climbing and rosette types prefer acid soil, occasional feedings, ample water, high humidity, shade, and a temperature between 60 and 65 degrees. A suitable compost for philodendrons consists of equal parts of sand, loam, leaf mold, and osmunda fiber. Osmunda fiber is beneficial but not absolutely required. The plants will grow well if it is omitted from the mixture. Good drainage should be provided so that the plants may be watered freely without danger of waterlogging the soil.

The climbing types are readily propagated from stem cuttings planted in sand or in a mixture of sand and peat. They root quickly when the bottom temperature is 70 to 75 degrees. If your plants become too tall, cut off the top part of the stem and lay it on a mixture of moist sand and peat, or cut the stem into segments, each with at least one joint, and lay these on sand. Then cover the stem or segments with moist peat. In a short time a new shoot with roots will appear at each joint. Remove the stem and cut it so that each piece has a young plant. Pot each piece. Of course all species may be started from seed. Seeds germinate well when planted on sphagnum moss. Move the seedlings from the seed pans into 2½-inch pots. The seedlings grow well in peat moss, provided they are given liquid fertilizer every two weeks.

Pothos

These are handsome climbing plants from the East Indies and Malaya whose heart-shaped leaves resemble *Philodendron cordatum* but are much thicker. They require the same general treatment as philodendrons. Two species are generally grown, *Pothos nitens* and *Pothos aureus*. The leaves of the former are rich, shiny green, whereas *P. aureus* has leaves splotched with creamy white or yellow markings. Both species thrive in houses, as well as in the greenhouse, and are therefore in good demand.

Spathiphyllum

The spathiphyllum, like certain anthuriums, has attractive flowers as well as handsome leaves. A well-grown plant also bears beautiful red berries. Spathiphyllums can be grown in osmunda fiber or in a mixture half loam and half leaf mold. The plants grow well with moderate shade, an even supply of moisture, and a humid atmosphere.

CHAPTER 15

BEGONIAS

THE GREAT VARIETY of remarkably beautiful plants in the genus *Begonia* makes it a fascinating one for collectors. The genus was named after Michel Begon, a French patron of botany. The genus *Begonia* is the only one of horticultural value in the family Begoniaceae. The other genera in the family, *Symbegonia, Begoniella,* and *Hillebrandia,* have not found favor as greenhouse plants. Some begonias are raised primarily for their exotic foliage, others because they bear myriads of beautifully colored small flowers, different ones because they produce large, elegantly formed blooms. There are over 400 species in the genus *Begonia* and thousands of varieties which have been developed by hybridizers. Because of the multitude of kinds it is difficult to classify begonias. For our purposes we will consider four groups: the tuberous begonias; the winter-blooming begonias, also known as the Gloire de Lorraine series; the foliage begonias (rex begonias), usually rhizomatous; and the fibrous-rooted begonias.

Tuberous begonias

The perfect form, large size, and crispness of the flowers of tuberous begonias have a compelling beauty. The flowers vary in size from 3 inches to 8 inches in diameter. Some varieties bear single flowers, but more popular are those with double flowers, some of which resemble the rose, the carnation, or the camellia. The flowers come in many colors, apricot, scarlet, pink, white, rose, and yellow. Two kinds of flower, male and female, are produced on each plant, the male or staminate flower being flanked by two less attractive female or pistillate flowers. The male flowers are large and showy, and in double varieties most of the stamens have been transformed into petals. However in the latter part of the season many petals revert to stamens, bearing pollen. It is then that you can collect pollen from the male flowers and transfer it to stigmas of female flowers to produce seed.

You may wish to start some tuberous begonias in your greenhouse for bedding outdoors. Others you will wish to raise as pot plants for flowers in the greenhouse from June through October. Tuberous begonias will flower in the winter if they are grown with more than fourteen hours of light each day. Days are easily prolonged by turning on electric lights at sundown and letting them stay lighted until about 10 P.M. Tuberous begonias make good cut flowers, lasting five to six days when floated on water in a container. When cutting the flowers take only half the stem. The remaining half will dry up and then fall off, leaving no open wound for the entrance of fungi.

In addition to upright forms of tuberous begonias, there are beautiful pendant ones that are profusely floriferous. These should be raised in hanging baskets, or, better, in pots which stand on pedestals. Some of the pendulous varieties have stems 4 or 5 feet long and one plant may produce as many as 400 flowers.

Tuberous begonias are readily started from tubers, usually planted from January to March. As with other plants, select varieties with care, always remembering that the color of the flowers, their potential size and conformation are inherent in the plant and cannot be changed even with the most careful culture.

Do not plant the tubers until pink growth buds appear on the concave surface of the tuber. The appearance of the buds indicates that the rest period of the tuber is over. If the tubers are planted and watered for a considerable time before growth is active, they may rot. Tubers which have been stored at 40 or 50 degrees during the fall months may be moved to a warm dark place to encourage sprouting. When the sprouts are evident, plant the tubers with a spacing of about 2 inches in a shallow pot or flat containing a mixture of leaf mold and sand. If you do not have any leaf mold you can start the tubers in peat, which is not so desirable as leaf mold. They should be completely covered, leaving only the tips of the sprouts showing. Then water the tubers. Keep the growing medium moist, not wet, and maintain the tubers at a temperature of 60 to 65 degrees at night with a 10-degree rise during the day. When the shoots are well developed and the root system is extensive, about four or five weeks after the tubers were planted, move the plants into 5-, 6-, or 8-inch pots, depending on their size. Pot moderately firmly, not hard. A suitable potting mixture consists of two parts leaf mold, one of rotted cow manure, and one of sandy loam, with a small amount of bone meal added. Another excellent mixture consists of three parts leaf mold, one part peat, one part cow manure, and one part sand. After potting, water the plant. Then wait until the soil shows dryness before watering again. Throughout the growing season, avoid overwatering, which may bring about a rotting of the tuber.

Upright varieties of tuberous begonias are best grown with one main stem. If more than one shoot develops from a tuber remove the weaker ones and permit the strongest one to remain.

Hanging basket varieties of tuberous begonias are best grown with several shoots from each tuber. For best results one should use large tubers, as they will have more shoots than smaller ones. If only one or two shoots develop, pinch off the top of the stem when flower buds begin to form. Pendant types should be grown in large containers, 8 inches in diameter for small tubers, 10 inches for large ones. Shallow pots are ideal. Wire baskets lined with sphagnum moss and then filled with soil can be used, but the plants will not grow to the same degree of perfection as those raised in pots.

Tuberous begonias do not thrive in full sun. When the days become bright in the spring it will be necessary to shade the greenhouse. They do well for us in a greenhouse with a light intensity of about 2000 foot candles, which is about one-fifth full sunlight. Too heavy shade produces abundant leggy growth but few flowers; too much light results in dwarf plants with thick, shiny, curled leaves and burned flowers. You should seek the happy medium, not too little light, not too much. When actively growing, tuberous begonias benefit from monthly feedings of liquid fertilizer, either fish emulsion or commercial fertilizer. Staking is usually necessary. When danger of frost is over you may wish to move some of your plants to shaded parts of the garden. The plants may be knocked out of their pots and planted in humus soil about 1 foot apart, or the pots may be plunged in the garden. If the days are not extremely hot during summer in your locality, tuberous begonias will flower nicely in the greenhouse. On the other hand, if the summers are hot, the plants will do better in a lath house or in the garden than in a greenhouse during the summer months.

Plants started from tubers will generally begin to flower in June. When the first crop of blossoms on a tuberous begonia is over, a second crop may be obtained by resting the plant for three weeks. Keep the soil on the dry side during this period. When new shoots appear near the base of the stem, cut the old stem back. Permit two or three of the strongest shoots to remain and remove the rest. Then give the plant fertilizer. During autumn, when the second flowering is over and the foliage shows signs of dying, withhold water gradually, but not by any means suddenly, to induce dormancy. When the stem has dried, remove it. The tubers which have been growing in pots should then be stored in the pots at a temperature of 40 to 50 degrees. Lay the pots on their sides so that you will not be tempted to water them. Those planted in soil in the garden may be dug after the first light frost. Remove the stem when it can be pulled off easily and shake the soil from the roots. Then store the tubers in dry peat or sand at a temperature of 40 to 50 degrees.

Tuberous begonias start readily from stem cuttings. If you wish to increase a favorite variety, make stem cuttings of it. Sometimes several shoots grow from one tuber of an erect variety. The erect varieties are best grown with just one shoot. Hence, when the extra ones are sufficiently large they can be cut off next to the tuber and used for cuttings. Pot the cuttings in a mixture of sand and peat and then plunge the pots to their rims in peat contained in a box or propagating frame. Cover with glass and, if possible, use bottom heat of about 70 degrees. With this technique, the cuttings will root rapidly and flower the first summer.

Tuberous begonias may be grown from seed. The seeds of all begonias are minute; in one ounce there are about one million seeds. Plants grown from seed sown in January, or better in February, will flower during the summer and fall, generally later than those started from tubers. The seedlings will yield fine tubers by November. The next season's plants will be superb. Prepare a seed bed by adding drainage to a seed pan or flat and cover this with a 1-inch layer of well-decayed, moist leaf mold. Then add a thin layer of finely screened moist leaf mold, level it, but do not press it down. The surface must be spongy so that when the seeds germinate the roots can easily penetrate the soil. Place the pans in shallow water to subirrigate them. When the surface is moist, sow the seeds thinly. Seeds may be sown directly or they may be mixed with fine sand in a salt shaker from which the seeds are distributed over the surface of the soil. Cover the pan with a pane of glass and keep it in a shaded place at a night temperature of 65 to 70 degrees. Light is necessary for seed germination, which occurs in two or three weeks. During germination keep the surface of the soil moist. Even a slight drying of the surface is fatal to young plants. If you keep the surface overly wet, however, damping-off may be troublesome.

When the largest leaves are about the size of a dime transplant the seedlings into flats or pans containing two parts of leaf mold, one of sandy loam, and one of well-rotted cow manure. When the plants begin to crowd each other, pot them singly in 2½- or 3-inch pots. Later shift them into 4- or 5-inch ones, in which containers the plants will flower.

Throughout the growing period, shade the plants from bright sun and keep them in a moist atmosphere. After flowering is finished, withhold water gradually, then lay the pots on their sides and store at 40 to 50 degrees until January or February, when the tubers may be shaken free of soil and started. The tubers will be good for several years, but will make the best plants in their second year.

Begonias grow well and flower nicely when proper conditions are maintained. When the environment is not right they may drop their flower buds. During the summer months, when the temperature soars above 90 degrees, buds and flowers may drop off. When the days become cooler toward autumn the buds will develop properly. Poor drainage, very dry air, and overwatering may also cause bud drop.

Tuberous begonias are susceptible to powdery mildew. If the plants are dusted with sulfur at the beginning of plant growth and at biweekly intervals up to flowering time, this disease will not be a problem. Red spiders and thrips may be troublesome at times. These may be controlled with Malathion.

Winter-blooming begonias—Gloire de Lorraine series

These begonias, with their compact masses of flowers, add beauty to the greenhouse during the winter months, when it is most appreciated. The winter-blooming begonias originated in 1891, when Lemoine in France flowered a hybrid of *Begonia socotrana,* a bulbous species, and *B. dregei,* a semi-bulbous species. This hybrid was called Begonia Gloire de Lorraine. Since then additional hybrids have been developed, among them Lady Mac, Glory of Cincinnati, Melior, and Marjorie Gibbs.

The winter-blooming begonias are increased by leaf cuttings made from December to March. Cut the leaf stalk close to the stem, shorten the leaf stalk to about 1½ inches, and insert it in a mixture of one-third peat and two-thirds sand. Plant the cuttings so that they do not touch each other and in such a manner that the leaf blade is not in contact with the rooting medium. Cuttings should be kept in a moist place, in a propagating frame, or in a box covered with glass. Use bottom heat of 70 degrees. The cuttings will root better and more quickly if the days are prolonged by turning on electric lights at sundown and letting them remain on until 10 P.M.

When a young plant is evident on a cutting, pot the cutting in a 2½-inch pot in a mixture containing considerable sand and leaf mold or peat moss. You need not separate the young plant from the leaf stalk. The pots should be plunged in moist peat. In June the plants will be ready to shift into 4-inch pots, and by September into 6- or 7-inch ones. A good growing mixture consists of three parts soil, two parts manure, one part peat, and one part sand with a 4-inch pot of bone meal or superphosphate per wheelbarrow of soil. Watering with a solution of fertilizer at biweekly intervals promotes vigorous growth. A solution made up of one ounce of 15-30-15 fertilizer in 3 gallons of water is ideal. Pinching is necessary to get stocky plants. Even so, it will be necessary to stake the plants. The plants cannot tolerate bright sun, so during the bright months of the year shade the plants. This group of begonias thrives with a night temperature between 58 and 60 degrees.

The foliage begonias

Begonia rex is a noble species which has been the principal parent in the development of many begonias with ornamental foliage, the rex begonias. The rex begonias do flower, but their real beauty lies in the brilliant, iridescent coloring of the leaves, characterized by pink, bronze, crimson, or silver tones overlying the green, and the fascinating shapes.

Rex begonias may be started from seed or from leaf cuttings. Several seedmen sell seeds of hybrids, from which many different kinds can be expected. Seed may be sown on a fine mixture of equal parts of sand and peat moss. Best results are obtained by sowing in the spring. The seed should be scattered thinly so that the resulting seedlings can grow to a height of an inch or two without crowding. The seedlings are potted in 2-inch pots, later shifted into 3-inch ones, and then into larger ones when necessary.

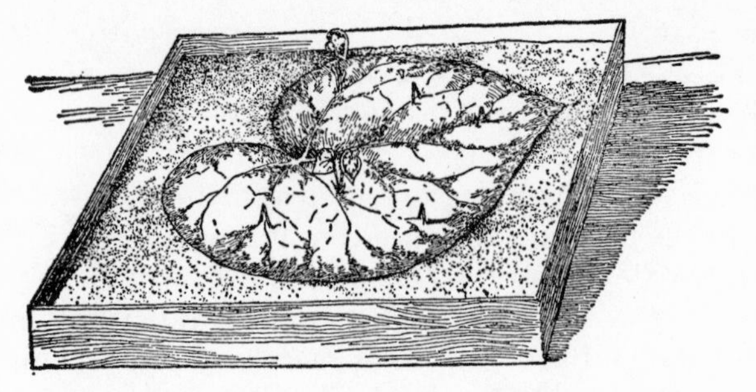

Propagating rex begonia from a leaf laid on sand (*above*). (From *Propagation of Plants,* Kains and McQuesten). Rex begonias may also be increased by inserting pieces of a leaf into a mixture of sand and peat.

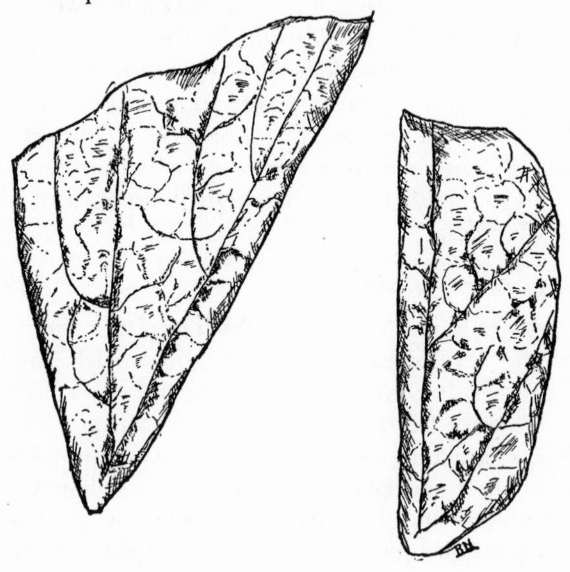

Choice varieties are increased by leaf cuttings. One of the easiest ways is to remove a large and well-matured leaf (retaining the leaf stalk). Cut through the principal veins on the undersurface and insert the leaf stalk in sand, letting the lower surface of the leaf rest on the moist sand. It can be kept in contact with the sand by placing a few pebbles on it.

A small tuber, which in time will form a new plant, develops near each cut place. The small plants are separated from the leaf and potted singly. Another method is to cut the leaf into triangular pieces, each with V-shaped main veins, and to insert each piece vertically in a mixture of sand and peat.

A suitable compost for growing rex begonias consists of two parts loam, one part leaf mold, one part well-rotted cow manure, and one part sand. The plants should not be exposed to bright sun, but instead they should be grown in a shaded greenhouse. They grow well with a night temperature of 60 degrees. Rex begonias are frequently grown in pots, but they may be grown in benches or pockets of soil. Some choice varieties are Magnifica, Marie Louise, Louise Closson, Crimson Glow, Pacific Sunset, Dawn, Our Indian, Calico, Lavender Glow, Black Star, Autumn, and Emerald.

Fibrous-rooted begonias

There are many varieties of fibrous-rooted begonias, a good number of which are classified as *Begonia semperflorens*. It is convenient to divide the fibrous-rooted begonias into three classes, based on the height of the plants—dwarf varieties, 6 to 8 inches high; plants of medium height, 9 to 11 inches high; and tall varieties, with heights of 12 inches or more. A few choice dwarf varieties are Pink Pearl, Red Pearl, Ball Red, Ball White, and Fire Sea. Some of medium height are Carmen, Indian Maid, Luminosa, Prima Donna, Scandinavia Pink, Scandinavia Red, and White Pearl. Tall varieties include Christmas Cheer Red, Ile de France, and Masterpiece. The fibrous-rooted begonias are useful pot plants for flowering during winter in the greenhouse. They are also good bedding plants.

The fibrous-rooted begonias are generally started from seed sown in the fall or early winter for good-sized flowering plants in May or June. For winter flowering, seeds are sown in spring. The plants will flower most of the winter if the seed pods are picked off. These begonias are also easily propagated from stem cuttings. Cuttings made in the spring will yield fine plants for late winter and spring flowering. A mixture of equal parts of loam and leaf mold or peat moss suits them. They grow well at a night temperature of 55 to 60 degrees. Like other begonias, the fibrous-rooted ones should be shaded from the direct rays of the sun.

Pests and diseases of begonias

Red spiders, mites, thrips, aphids, white flies, and mealy bugs are some of the pests which may attack begonias. The semituberous and fibrous-rooted varieties are occasionally attacked by nematodes. Brown spots surrounded by water-soaked margins on the leaves are symptoms of this pest. The nematodes feed on the inner tissues of the leaves but emerge when moisture is present and move from one place to another. Syringing plants hastens the spread of nematodes. Control of nematodes involves use of soil free of the pests, adequate spacing of plants, and removal and burning of infected leaves.

A wilt disease, verticillium wilt, may attack winter-blooming varieties. Use of disease-free soil and burning of diseased plants are control measures. Roots of seedlings are subject to black root rot, caused by the fungus *Thielaviopsis basicola.* Damping-off fungi may also attack seedlings. Raising seedlings in sterilized soil will prevent such injury. Harmful bacteria, fungi, and nematodes in the soil may be killed by adding .5 cc of Chloropicrin (commercial Larvicide) per gallon of screened soil. Treat the soil in a closed metal container. After treatment, allow the soil to stand outdoors for a week and then air it on the potting bench for one or two weeks before using it. Soil may also be sterilized by pouring boiling water through it.

Stem rot, caused by *Pythium intermedium* and by *P. ultimum,* is characterized by soft watersoaked lesions extending lengthwise on the stem. To control this disease, use sterile soil and avoid excessive humidity. Begonia blight, caused by the fungus *Botrytis cinerea,* may be serious at times. Diseased areas on the leaves or stem turn black, and then a brownish-gray mold becomes evident. To control begonia blight gather and destroy all plant parts that are affected. More ventilation and a lower humidity will reduce the incidence of this disease. Bacterial leaf spot (caused by *Xanthomonas begoniae*) may appear on tuberous begonias and fibrous begonias. This disease may be controlled by removing affected plant parts, decreasing the humidity, and by giving the plants more space and better ventilation.

Spotted wilt is a destructive virus disease of begonias. The virus is spread from one plant to another by thrips. Control consists of eliminating thrips and removing and burning all diseased plants.

CHAPTER 16

BROMELIADS

IF YOU LIKE the unusual, you will find fascination in the bromeliads, for this group includes beautiful and bizarre plants. The bromeliads are in the family Bromeliaceae, the pineapple family, which includes about 40 genera and 900 species. The family is mostly tropical American, with a few species reaching into sub-tropical Florida. Some species are grown for their flowers, which often exhibit unique color combinations. Others are noted primarily for their distinctive, often brilliantly colored, leaves. In many species the bases of the leaves are arranged to form a "cup" or "vase" which will hold water. You can actually use certain ones as living vases.

Interest in this group of plants is consistently increasing and many are in strong demand as house plants, for which they are indeed suitable.

Many of the choice bromeliads are epiphytes (grow on trees), but others are terrestrial in habit, often growing on rocks. Most bromeliads can endure drought and neglect. You can delay potting them and forget to water them, yet they will survive. However, they do respond to good culture.

Some of the interesting genera of bromeliads are *Aechmea, Billbergia, Cryptanthus, Guzmania, Neoregelia, Nidularium, Tillandsia,* and *Vriesia,* all of which grow well under the same general cultural conditions. They grow vigorously and flower with a night temperature of 60 degrees, and with half shade except during the darkest months. Too much sun will burn the foliage.

Fresh osmunda fiber is ideal for a potting medium, especially for *Vriesia, Guzmania,* and some *Tillandsia*. Fill the pot about one-third full of pieces of broken pot. Hold the plant in position and firm osmunda fiber around the roots. While we prefer osmunda fiber for all kinds, certain growers use a potting medium of equal parts of sand and leaf mold, or a mixture of one-fourth sand and three-fourths peat for certain bromeliads, for example, *Aechmea* and *Billbergia*. Bromeliads may also be grown in pots, or in osmunda fiber wrapped around slabs, driftwood, or some other support. These must be watered more frequently than those in pots. Certain species of *Tillandsia* seem to thrive better when grown in this manner than when grown in pots.

In all bromeliads the parent plant eventually dies, about a year after flowering. In the meantime, however, one or more side shoots develop. When they are about 4 inches high they can be cut off, cutting them cleanly as close to the base as possible. If the offshoot has roots, pot it using osmunda fiber. Some growers fill the pot two-thirds full of a mixture of equal parts of sand, peat moss, and osmunda fiber and then top this with a layer of osmunda fiber. The tightly packed osmunda fiber furnishes good support for the offshoot. If the offshoot lacks roots, insert the base of it in a mixture of equal parts of sand and sphagnum moss. When the offshoot is rooted, pot it. A number of cryptanthus species produce many suckers which naturally fall off. These are easily rooted in sand. Offshoots generally attain flowering size in one or two years. Instead of separating offshoots you can culture the whole clump either in the old pot or in a new, larger one. Bromeliads should not be overpotted; they grow well in small pots. Newly potted plants should be kept somewhat on the dry side until root action begins.

During the winter months the plants are not active, and they should be kept slightly on the dry side. When they are making their growth they should be given ample water and a biweekly application of a dilute complete liquid fertilizer. During the latter period they also benefit from syringing and their "cups" may be kept filled with water.

Bromeliads may be raised from seed. If you want your plants to produce seed, you will probably have to pollinate the flowers by hand. In their native homes bromeliads are pollinated by hummingbirds, night moths, and certain ants and bees, pollinating agents which may be lacking in our greenhouses. Seeds are viable for only a short time, between three and five months. Secure fresh seeds and plant them right away. The seeds of some bromeliads are dry and

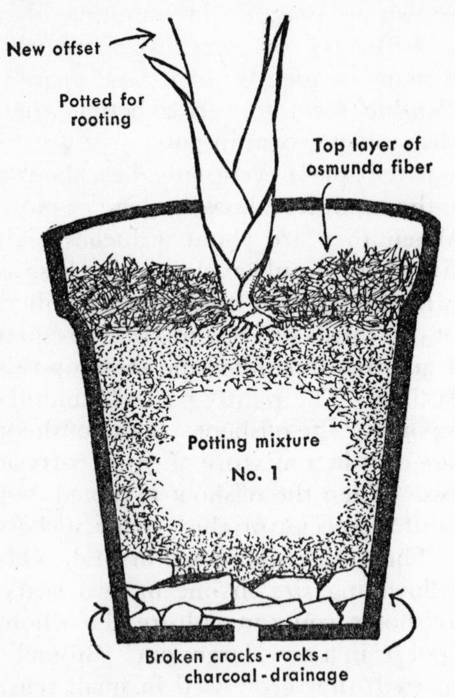

Potting an offshoot. The upper layer of osmunda fiber holds the offshoot securely. The remainder of the pot is filled with an even mixture of sand, peat moss, and osmunda fiber (mixture no. 1). (Mulford B. Foster and the Bromeliad Society *Cultural Handbook*)

have feathery or winged appendages, for example those of *Tillandsia* and *Vriesia.* The seeds of *Billbergia, Aechmea,* and certain others are encased in a gelatinous substance, which should be washed from the seeds before they are planted. The dry seeds with appendages do not require cleaning. Seeds are best sown in pots furnished with drainage and filled with a mixture of peat moss and finely chopped sphagnum moss. Don't cover the seeds, because they need light for germination. After sowing, keep the pots in a moist, shaded place where the temperature is about 75 degrees. Another way is to sow the seeds on a chunk of peat about 8 inches long and 4 inches wide. The piece of peat should be cooked about two hours and then be placed in a glass or plastic container which has a small volume of water in the bottom. When the peat is cool, sow the seeds. Then cover the container with a piece of glass. The time for germination varies considerably with the species. Seeds of *Aechmea* germinate in about a week; those of *Vriesia* require three or four weeks. When the seedlings are about half an inch high they may be watered weekly with a dilute fertilizer solution.

When the seedlings are large enough, transplant them to flats containing a one-to-one mixture of peat and sphagnum, or pots of osmunda fiber (for details as to the use of osmunda fiber see pages 244-246). Keep the seedlings in a moist, shaded place and feed them with liquid fertilizer. When they are eight to twelve months old, the seedlings can be moved into 2½- or 3-inch pots, using osmunda fiber. Later they can be shifted into 4-inch pots. Well-grown seedlings flower when they are three or four years old.

Bromeliads are remarkably free of pests and diseases. However, seedlings may damp-off. Wilson's Anti-Damp or a dilute solution of Fermate and good cultural conditions will minimize the loss from this disease. Two scale insects (*Gymnaspis aechmeae* and *Diaspis bromeliae*) may attack bromeliads. Malathion is used for control. Seedlings may be attacked by thrips, which can be controlled with Malathion or with a rotenone spray.

Aechmea

There are about sixty species in this genus but only three are generally grown in choice greenhouse collections—*Aechmea marmorata, A. fulgens,* and *A. fasciata. Aechmea marmorata* is distinguished by its artistic form, which has led to the common name Grecian Vase for this species. It holds a considerable amount of water and can actually be used as a vase. The pink and blue flowers generally appear in May.

The leaves are stiff, recurved, mottled, and arranged in a vase-like form.

Aechmea fulgens produces large numbers of flowers characterized by blue-tipped petals surrounded by rich red sepals. The pale green leaves spread from a basal rosette. This is a strong-growing species which produces many side shoots.

The leaves of *Aechmea fasciata* (sometimes called *Billbergia rhodocyanea*) are beautifully marbled with silver-gray crosslines, and they radiate from the urn-shaped rosette. The flower stalk is about a foot tall and bears several erect, attractive, pale red bracts as well as attractive sky-blue flowers, with petals about three-quarters of an inch long.

Billbergia

These plants are closely related to aechmeas, and they should be included in every choice collection of bromeliads. They are named for F. B. Billberg, a Swedish botanist. The flower cluster rises from the center of a rosette of long leaves whose clasping bases are arranged to hold water. The colored bracts of the flower cluster are usually very showy and the flowers are interesting and beautiful.

Billbergia nutans, a favorite species, has handsome linear leaves, 1 to 2 feet long. The flowers have green petals edged with blue, and attractive, long, golden stamens. The conspicuous red bracts of the flower cluster complete the color harmony. A more unusual and beautiful plant is *Billbergia vittata.*

Cryptanthus

The name *Cryptanthus* comes from the Greek and means *hidden flower.* The flowers are not especially decorative and are borne on a stalkless, dense head somewhat hidden in the cluster of leaves. However, these plants have superb and distinctive foliage. The low, flat plants have their leaves crowded in a rosette, recurved and spreading, with bizarre markings.

There are about a dozen tree-perching species, native to South America. Two of the favorite species are *Cryptanthus*

Bromeliads. *Upper left: Tillandsia Butzii* (Mexico). *Upper right:* removal of an offshoot from a bromeliad growing in osmunda fiber. *Lower left:* a hybrid Vriesia *(Vriesia Mariae)*. *Lower right: Vriesia splendens* (French Guiana). (Ladislaus Cutak photo)

Above: two ways to make leaf cuttings of gloxinia. *Left:* a somewhat triangular piece of the leaf blade was inserted vertically in sand. Notice the small tuber that developed at the base. *Right,* a half-inch of the petiole (leaf stalk) was inserted into sand. Notice the tuber at the base. *Below:* Episcias have handsome foliage. They are readily propagated from stem cuttings.

Facing page: Achimenes is easy to grow and will make a fine display through the summer and into fall. (Antonelli Brothers)

Gloxinia seedlings ready for potting. The larger ones will go into 4-inch pots, the smaller into 2½-inch pots.

A seedling in flower during late summer.

bivittatus and *C. zonatus. Cryptanthus bivittatus* has a rosette of leaves with undulating margins. The leaves are striped with bars of brownish green and rose. The horizontal, spreading leaves of *Cryptanthus zonatus* have markings somewhat like those of a pheasant feather. The leaves are crinkled and marked with transverse bands of white, green, and brown. It is indeed a distinctive plant.

Guzmania

This is a group of about seventy-five tropical American species, some of which are choice foliage plants. The flowers are borne on nearly stalkless clusters among the foliage. *Guzmania zahnii* is a favorite species. It has recurving leaves a foot or two long which are artfully arranged in a rosette. The lengthwise pencilings of bronze and red on the leaves add interest to the foliage.

Neoregelia

There is quite a mix-up of names in this group of bromeliads. In some catalogs you may find what we are going to call *Neoregelia* going by the name of *Aregelia* or *Nidularium.* The members of the genus have the leaves arranged in a rosette, and the flower cluster is a dense head borne among the inner leaves of the rosette.

Neoregelia marmorata, N. tristis, and *N. spectabilis* are attractive species. The charm of *N. marmorata* lies in its delightfully mottled foliage. The six to twelve symmetrical leaves of the rosette are marbled with red. The pale violet flowers are produced in the center of the rosette. The red spot at the tip of each leaf of *N. spectabilis* has given this species the common name of Painted Finger Nail. The leaves are about a foot long, undulated along the margins, and barred on the back with narrow bands of silvery hairs.

Tillandsia

Tillandsia is a large genus of epiphytes; nearly all are native to tropical America, but a few enter the United States. One of them, Spanish moss, is a familiar sight throughout the southeastern United States. Spanish moss has long stringlike stems and threadlike leaves. It is not commonly grown in greenhouses, but other species with large leaves and beautiful flowers make choice greenhouse specimens, for example *Tillandsia fasciculata,* and *T. lindeniana. Tillandsia fasciculata* has leaves about a foot long originating from a stem about two feet high. The flower cluster has greenish bracts tinged with red and beautiful blue flowers.

The leaves of *T. lindeniana* form a rosette and they are about a foot long. The flower cluster is large, with showy carmine bracts and large bluish-purple flowers, making a decorative color scheme.

Vriesia

In this genus, native to tropical America, there are several striking species which deserve greater popularity. *Vriesia carinata,* often known as the Painted Feather, develops a rosette of shiny grass-green leaves out of which there emerges a feather-shaped flower cluster, bearing bracts that are scarlet at the base and yellowish at the tip, and flowers of a yellowish-hue. The flower cluster lasts extremely long, up to six months.

Vriesia hieroglyphica is noted for its handsome foliage and beautiful yellow flowers. The leaves are arranged in a rosette, and they are banded dark green above and brown-purple below. This species adds beauty to any greenhouse, even when it is not in flower. Another interesting species with banded foliage is *Vriesia splendens,* sometimes called Flaming Sword. The flower spike bears red bracts and yellow flowers. *Vriesia duvalliana* is a striking plant that is easily grown.

CHAPTER 17

FERNS

FERNS COULD BE a hobby by themselves; there are hundreds of kinds from which to select. However, many of us are content to have a few ferns to use as background for other plants and to use for greens in making arrangements. Ferns are raised for their lovely leaves, which we call fronds. They are flowerless plants, reproducing by spores instead of seeds.

A clue to the culture of ferns can be obtained by considering where we find them growing in nature. Many inhabit shady places where they grow in humusy soil. A number of the more usual ferns that are raised in greenhouses come from tropical or subtropical regions. These ferns grow well in a greenhouse maintained at a night temperature of 60 degrees, potted in a mixture of four parts loam, four parts leaf mold, two parts sand, and two parts of rotted manure. Spring is a good time to repot ferns. Provide good drainage and make the soil moderately firm.

The greenhouse should be shaded from early spring to late autumn, and in bright regions during the winter as well. Ferns like a humid atmosphere and ample water at the roots. Never let the soil become completely dry; also avoid waterlogging the soil.

All ferns can be grown from spores which at certain seasons develop on the undersurfaces of the leaves. When the spores are shed on moist ground, each spore develops into a little, flat, green, heart-shaped structure called a *prothallium*. On the undersurface of the prothallium sperms and eggs develop.

If a fern plant is to develop, at least one egg must be fertilized by a sperm. Water is necessary to enable the sperms to swim to the eggs and fertilize them. When an egg is fertilized, it remains attached to the prothallium and is nourished by it while it develops into a young fern plant. It takes about six months from the time the spore germinates until the young fern plant attached to the prothallium is ready for an independent life. By that time its roots are long enough to furnish it with water and nutrients, and its leaves are large enough to make its own food.

Growing your own ferns from spores is a delightful experience. Fill a pot with soil to within a half inch of the top, and over this put a layer of crushed flower pot (with the powdery bits screened out). It is best to sterilize the prepared pots by pouring boiling water through them. Pieces of fern leaf on which the spore cases are ready to open can be laid flat on the moist surface, and the spores will be shed onto the broken bits of pot. You may want to collect the spores beforehand by placing the leaves in a paper bag and storing in a dry place. The powder shed from the leaves is the spores and may be dusted onto the pots. Spores can also be purchased from seed companies. After the spores are sown, cover the pot with a pane of glass and put it in a saucer of water to insure its being kept damp. After a few weeks the surface will be covered with tiny heart-shaped prothallia, and in a few more weeks the little fern plants will make an appearance from under their edges. Lift a prothallium and you will see that the fern plant attached to it is in the process of forming its first roots and leaves. The young fern plants can be transplanted, still attached to the prothallia, first to a flat, and later to individual pots. Keep the young ferns in a shaded spot.

An intriguing experiment would be to try your hand at making hybrid ferns by sowing spores from two species (preferably of the same genus) on the same pot. If they produce sperms and eggs at the same time and are compatible, you may have some very interesting results.

Ferns can also be increased by dividing the clump or rootstock. Spring is the best time to divide plants. Pot the divi-

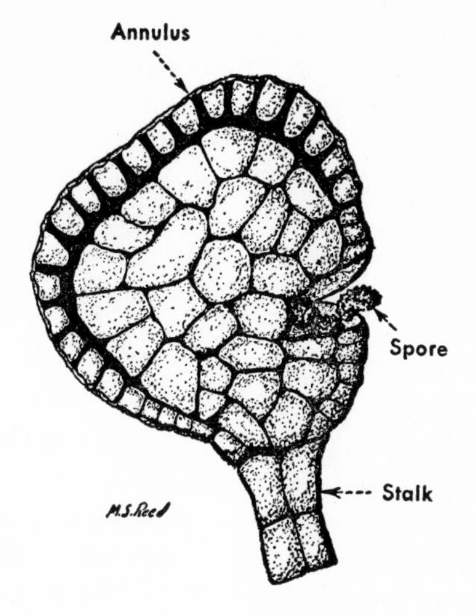

Spore cases containing spores develop on the undersurfaces of fern leaves. Here you see a spore case that is discharging spores.

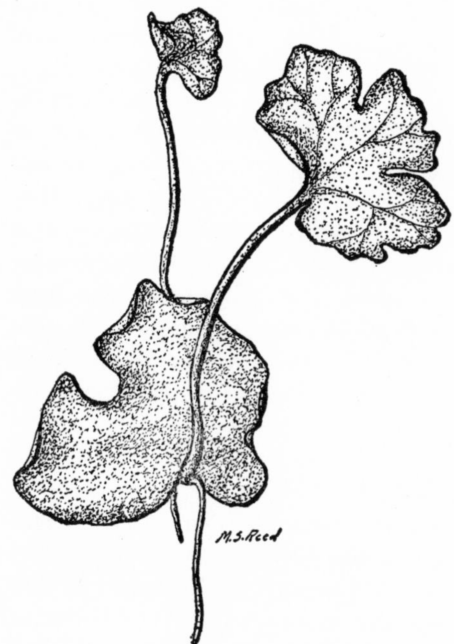

A spore develops into the heart-shaped prothalium, from which sperm and egg cells develop. The fertilized egg then develops into the beautiful fern plant. Here is a young fern plant still attached to the heart-shaped structure. In time the heart-shaped plant will shrivel and die, but the fern that developed from the fertilized egg will continue to grow. This fern is ready to be planted in a flat.

sions in pots just slightly larger than the clump. Avoid over-potting and keep the crown level with the surface of the soil.

The Boston fern, as well as some others, can be increased by runners. This fern produces many runners when grown in a bench. Ferns benched in early summer will produce many runners by fall. Separate the runners from the stock plants and pot the runners, one to each 2½-inch pot. Move them into larger pots as needed.

Bird's-nest fern (*Asplenium nidus-avis*)

This fern (found in tropical Asia) does not have divided fronds. The leaves are wavy-margined, light green in color with black veins, and they are about 2 feet long on an old plant, smaller and more attractive on a young plant. They radiate from a short central core of stem. Do not water in the crown, for this may induce a rotting of the leaves. The birds-nest fern is generally started from spores.

Boston fern (*Nephrolepis exaltata* var. *bostoniensis*)

There are a great many varieties of the Boston fern, whose native home is the West Indies. Some grow to large size, others are dwarf forms. Certain varieties have the leaves divided just once, others have fronds so divided that they are mosslike in appearance. Among the large forms are *piersonii, whitmanii,* and *rooseveltii. Scottii,* Dwarf Boston, and *wagnerii* are dwarf varieties. As previously mentioned, Boston ferns are readily propagated from runners. They do not respond well to division.

Creton brake fern (*Pteris cretica*)

You will find many uses for these small attractive ferns, native to Australia. The fronds are about a foot long. Among the fine varieties are Ribbon Brake, Riverton Brake, May's Brake, Wilson Brake, and Wimsett Brake. The brake ferns are generally started from spores sown in the spring.

Holly fern (Cyrtomium falcatum)

As the name suggests, the holly fern has firm glossy leaflets (pinnae) which are holly-like in general appearance. There are several good varieties, among them *Rochefordianum,* which grows to a height of about 1½ feet, and *Compactum,* a smaller variety. The holly fern is a good choice for the cool greenhouse, since it prefers a night temperature of 45 to 50 degrees.

Maidenhair fern (Adiantum)

Two species of *Adiantum, A. cuneatum* var. *croweanum* and *A. farleyense,* both native to South America, are wonderful ferns, perhaps the most graceful and attractive of all. They are useful in making corsages and flower arrangements as well as for lending beauty to groupings of plants in the greenhouse. Like most other greenhouse ferns the maidenhair prefer a night temperature of 60 degrees and a humid atmosphere. The plants are propagated by division of the crowns and by spores. The divisions should be fairly large and potted in 3- or 4-inch pots. Spores may be sown at any time of the year, but preferably in the spring. A temperature of 65 to 70 degrees brings about rapid germination of the spores. The young plants are grown in community pots or flats with a spacing of 1 inch by 1 inch. Later, about eight months from sowing time, the plants are potted in small pots, and when sufficient growth has been made into larger pots. Don't let the plants become potbound.

Staghorn fern (Platycerium bifurcatum)

The upright grayish-green fronds of this decorative and long-lived fern somewhat resemble in shape the horns of the European reindeer. The staghorn fern is best grown on a chunk of osmunda fiber wired on a board which is hung in the greenhouse. Even a small plant is decorative and eye-catching, and a large specimen is a true showpiece.

Selaginella

Selaginellas are not true ferns, but are allies of ferns. Like the ferns, selaginellas reproduce by spores. The spores are formed in cones borne at the tips of the branches. *Selaginella emmiliana* is a compact plant about 6 inches tall, whose branches are clothed with tiny leaves. Another good species, somewhat dwarf and more compact, is *S. kraussiana browni,* which resembles a cushion of bright green moss. They thrive in quite moist places and, if they overflow a pot, will spread rapidly in the soil of the bench. Small rooted clumps can be broken off from the main plant and be potted separately. The familiar "resurrection" plant sold in novelty shops is *S. lepidophylla.*

CHAPTER 18

GESNERIADS

THIS FAMILY is hard to beat. The cultivated members have not only remarkably beautiful flowers but also handsome foliage. The family (technically called Gesneriaceae) includes eighty-four genera and about five hundred species distributed in the tropics and subtropics of both hemispheres. However, only a few are in cultivation, among them achimenes, African violet, episcia, gesneria, gloxinia, and streptocarpus. All of these are worthy inhabitants of any greenhouse. They are good companions for each other, thriving with a night temperature of 60 degrees, and with diffused light, not full sun, and a high humidity. All of the gesneriads grow well in soil that is rich in leaf mold or peat moss.

Achimenes

If you are raising African violets and gloxinias you may wish to include these less well-known relatives which are native to tropical America. Achimenes, popularly called Cupid's Bower or Magic Flower, furnish a grand display of velvety, petunia-shaped flowers throughout the summer and autumn at little expense. The flowers are upwards of 2 inches across. The cultivated achimenes are for the most part hybrids derived from *Achimenes gloxiniaeflora, A. longiflora,* and *A. patens,* which bear white flowers, and *A. picta* and *A. coccinea,* with scarlet flowers. There are many named varieties in shades of red, rose, orange, blue, purple, and white.

You can obtain a succession of bloom by starting tubers at intervals from February until the end of May. The plants flower eight to ten weeks after planting. The tubers resemble miniature pine cones. Plant the tubers about half an inch deep; six or seven in a 5-inch pot or nine or ten in a 6-inch one, keeping varieties separate. Instead of potting the tubers directly in the pots in which they will flower, you can start them in flats filled with a mixture of sand and peat moss. When the plants are about 2 inches high, move six uniform plants into a 6-inch pot. Achimenes may be grown in baskets as well as in pots. For this culture, line a wire basket with wet sphagnum moss. Insert plants so that the shoots extend out through the sides. Then fill the basket with soil and plant a few plants on the surface. Achimenes grow well in a mixture of equal parts of loam, leaf mold (or peat), and sand, with the addition of one cup of superphosphate to every bushel of the mixture. Water should be applied sparingly until the tubers begin to grow, after which the soil should be kept moist and never be allowed to dry out. Achimenes thrive in subdued light and are injured by full sun. The night temperature should be 60 to 65 degrees. When the roots fill the pots, give biweekly applications of liquid fertilizer. Keep thrips, red spiders, and aphids under control.

After flowering is through and the plants show signs of resting, allow them to dry off gradually. The rest period may come on quite suddenly, and the entire plant may turn brown within a week. When the foliage is withered, remove the tubers from the pots, shake off the soil, and store the tubers in sand at a temperature of 45 to 50 degrees. In addition to growing from tubers, Achimenes may be propagated readily from stem cuttings or leaf cuttings taken in the spring, or from seeds.

African violets—Saintpaulia

African violets are native to Tanganyika in Africa, where they are found growing in pockets of humusy soil, in crevices of limestone and gneiss rock, always in shaded habitats. The technical name for them is *Saintpaulia ionantha. Saintpaulia* commemorates the family name of the discoverer of this fine genus. The genus was named after Baron Walter von St. Paul-Illaire, whose son discovered it in Africa. The species name *ionantha* is from the Greek meaning *with flowers like a violet*. Actually, of course, African violets are no kin of the violets. African violets are in the family Gesneriaceae, violets in the Violaceae.

African violets are indeed choice plants with their well-proportioned form, attractive foliage, beautiful flowers, and extended blooming period. Some varieties bloom continually, others periodically. Through hybridizing and the selection of mutations we now have hundreds of varieties of diverse types of foliage and of flower colors, and many new ones are introduced each year. The color range includes white, near blues, purples, pinks, and bluish reds. Most varieties have single flowers, but certain ones have double flowers. Among the attractive varieties are Blue Boy, Pink Beauty, White Lady, Red Bicolor, Dupont Lavender-Pink, Mentor Boy, Red Headed Girl, Blue Girl, Ruffles, Amazon Pink, Neptune, Plum Pink, and Orchid Beauty. We suggest that you obtain catalogs for descriptions of these and hundreds of other varieties, including the new varieties as they are developed.

The enchantment of African violets lures a grower to an increasingly large collection. Many fanciers started their African violet collections in their homes, but soon found that the home could not accommodate all of their plants, so they built a greenhouse.

It is certainly easier to grow African violets to perfection in a greenhouse than in a home. In a greenhouse, the light, the humidity, and the temperature may be adjusted to meet the needs of the plants much better than they can be controlled in the home. The ideal night temperature is 60 to 65 degrees. The day temperature should be 10 degrees higher, although higher seasonal temperatures will do no harm. A relative humidity of 60 to 70 per cent suits African violets. Damping down of walks and benches during the day will keep the humidity up, as will a humidifier.

African violets grow and flower well with a light intensity about one-tenth to one-fifth that of full sunlight; in other words, with light intensities between 1000 and 2000 foot candles. You can tell whether your plants are getting the proper amount of light by their appearance. If the petioles are long, the foliage dark green, and the flowers scarce, the plants are not getting sufficient light. On the other hand, if the leaves are small and with a yellowish cast or are burned, the light intensity is too high. If most of the winter days are cloudy in your locality you may not need any shade on the greenhouse from December to February. In February shade the glass lightly, and as the days become brighter toward spring apply heavier shade. Beginning in October or November, depending on the locality, the shade may be gradually reduced.

African violets do not thrive in soil that is either waterlogged or bone dry. Water thoroughly and then let the surface become dry before watering again. When cold water is used it is best to apply water directly to the pots and to avoid wetting the leaves. When cold water is splashed on the leaves, yellowish or whitish spots, rings, or streaks develop on the foliage. This trouble does not develop when water at the temperature of the leaves or slightly higher is splashed on the foliage. Moreover, the plants grow better when the water is warmed to the room temperature.

African violets are easily propagated from leaf cuttings. Cut through the leaf stalk close to the crown. Then shorten the leaf stalk to about an inch and a half, dip in a rooting hormone, and insert the leaf stalk in sand or vermiculite. Keep the cuttings in a moist place, preferably with bottom heat of 65-70 degrees, and keep them carefully watered. In about four to eight weeks, the new plants, which form at the base of the leaf stalk, will have grown well above the rooting medium. The leaf, with the attached plants, may then be removed, and the young plants may be separated from it and potted in 2½-inch pots. A suitable potting soil is made up of equal parts of soil, sand, manure, and leaf mold; peat can be substituted for the manure. Another satisfactory mixture consists of two parts loam, two parts leaf mold, one part sand, and one part manure, to which may be added some bone meal and broken charcoal. Still another mixture consists of one part loam, one part sand or vermiculite or both, and two parts leaf mold mixed with sedge peat. After the plants have become fully established in 2½-inch pots, they may be shifted to 4- or 5-inch pots, in which containers they will flower. It takes about nine months from the time the cuttings are made until the plants flower; for example, plants propagated in April will flower in 4-inch pots at Christmas.

Large plants should be potted annually. If you wish multiple-crown plants you shift the plants into larger pots. However, an exhibition plant is a one-crown plant. When growing a plant for show, remove young shoots as they develop on the crown. Large plants can be divided at potting time. To do this, let the soil become slightly dry and then knock the plant out of the pot. Break up the root ball, shake the soil from the roots and separate the crowns, keeping as many roots as possible on each. Pot each division.

African violets can be increased by offsets which develop from the main stem. When the larger leaves of an offset are 2 or 3 inches long, cut off the offset near the main stem. The offset is treated as a stem cutting. Root it in a mixture of sand and peat, contained in a pot.

African violets can also be grown from seed. Growing plants to maturity from seed requires about the same time as growing them from cuttings. Usually the plants grown from cuttings are exactly like the parents, but you can expect a variety of types in a group raised from hybrid seed. Some may be outstanding. There is suspense when you raise plants from seed. The seed is very small and it is best sown by first mixing it with a small amount of very fine sand. The mixture may be placed in a salt shaker to aid in scattering the seed over the surface of the soil. A mixture of equal parts of sand, loam, and peat, slightly firmed in a pot is suitable. After sowing, water the pot from below, cover with glass, and then with a piece of newspaper. The seeds will germinate in about three weeks if kept at a temperature of 60 to 65 degrees. When the seedlings are about half an inch high they may be transplanted to flats and later to pots.

You might wish to try your hand at hybridizing African violets and growing plants from the resulting seed. About two weeks after pollination, a small seed pod will begin to form and will ripen in about six to nine months. You may wish to cross one variety of *Saintpaulia ionantha* with a different variety, or if you are more adventurous you may try crossing a variety of *Saintpaulia ionantha* with a different species of *Saintpaulia.* As yet few, if any, crosses between species are on the market.

Saintpaulia species

Some species you may wish to add to your collection and to use in breeding work are *Saintpaulia amaniensis, S. diplotricha, S. Grotei, S. magungensis,* and *S. tongwensis.*

Saintpaulia amaniensis. This species, a close relative of *S. Grotei,* grows trailing on the ground. The leaves are oval in shape with petioles about 3½ inches long. The flowers are about an inch across, of violet-blue color.

Saintpaulia diplotricha. This species resembles *Saintpaulia ionantha* but has both long and short hairs on the leaves, whereas in *S. ionantha* they are of uniform length. Moreover, *S. diplotricha* has long and curved seed pods; *S. ionantha* has short ones. The flowers are violet in color and about 1¼ inches across. The leaves are pale green on the upper surface and nearly white underneath.

Saintpaulia Grotei. This has a long creeping stem bearing glossy, almost-round leaves, pale green above, whitish below. The flowers are pale blue-violet in color. *S. Grotei* can be trained as an ivy or philodendron can. Climbing house plants which flower are quite rare, which gives this species a special charm.

Saintpaulia magungensis. This species resembles *S. Grotei,* but the leaves are smaller and have shorter petioles. The flowers are a darker blue-violet.

Saintpaulia tongwensis. This species resembles *S. ionantha* but has elliptical, shiny, nonquilted leaves. The seed capsules of *S. tongwensis* are densely hairy, and longer than those of *S. ionantha.*

Pests and diseases

Mealy bugs, thrips, mites, and nematodes may attack African violets. Light sprayings with nicotine or Volck will help hold mealy bugs in check, or—if your collection is not large—you may dab the bugs with a swab dipped in alcohol. Be careful to keep the alcohol off the foliage. Thrips may injure the foliage and disfigure flowers. They may also pollinate flowers, which results in a quick dropping of the petals. Light dusting or spraying with DDT gives good control of these pests.

The commonest, most destructive, and most difficult pest to eliminate is the cyclamen mite (*Tarsonemus pallidus*), a pest so small that you need a hand lens to see it, but the damage is very obvious. The plants are dwarfed and the leaves become yellowish and covered with dense white hairs. Opening flowers are malformed and buds do not open. If the infestation is severe the entire crown may be destroyed. Mites may be controlled by frequent sprayings with NNOR, a rotenone spray, by applying sodium selenate to the soil, or by spraying with Malathion.

Springtails can be very annoying. These small, greyish insects can be seen jumping over the surface of the soil. These can be controlled with chlordane.

One of the worst afflictions of African violets is *root knot,* caused by tiny parasitic worms called *nematodes.* The worms invade the roots and cause pulpy enlargements, called *nodules,* to form on the roots. After invasion, absorption of water is interfered with and the foliage begins to droop and appears dull. The best control consists of using only sterilized soil and disposing of plants which are infected.

African violets are susceptible to a few fungus diseases, among them gray mold (*Botrytis*), bud rot, crown rot, and mildew. Plants that are chilled, overwatered, not properly ventilated, and given inadequate light are especially susceptible. Proper attention to good cultural conditions will minimize the incidence of disease. Never crowd plants. Give each one sufficient room for its proper development. Spraying with Fermate or light dusting with sulfur is also helpful.

Chirita

The lavender chirita (*Chirita lavendulacea*), a native of tropical or subtropical Asia, is a choice erect greenhouse plant about 2 feet high. The tubular flowers are delicate lavender in color, except the throat and the outside of the tube, which are white. The flowers are about 1½ inches long and are produced during the winter months.

Chirita is of easy cultivation and prefers a soil rich in humus. They should be given ample water and be grown in shade. A night temperature of 60 degrees is suitable. Plants are propagated from seed or by stem or leaf cuttings.

Columnea

The scarlet columnea (*Columnea gloriosa*), a native of Costa Rica, bears beautiful scarlet flowers, 2 or 3 inches long, during the summer months. The plant grows to a height of about 2 feet and bears fleshy leaves of a reddish hue. In nature it grows pendant on trunks of trees. Columnea is successfully cultivated in hanging baskets or in pots placed on pedestals. However, it may be grown erect by staking the stems. It grows well in the soil suggested for African violets and with the same environmental conditions.

Episcia

These less well-known gesneriads, natives of the American tropics, are choice and attractive plants. Most varieties bear trumpet-shaped, brilliant scarlet flowers, and all of them have graceful forms and beautiful foliage. Unlike African violets, Episcia has a limited flowering season. Their popularity is increasing as they become better known. The genus offers many opportunities for hybridization and selection. We can expect superior varieties in the future.

Episcias like a night temperature of 60 to 65 degrees, good light but not full sun, a high humidity, a soil mixture of equal parts of fibrous loam, peat, leaf mold, and sand, and biweekly feedings of fertilizer. The water used should be at the same temperature as the greenhouse. Episcias can be propagated from leaf cuttings and stem cuttings. Because leaf cuttings root slowly, stem cuttings are generally preferred. Stem cuttings inserted in a mixture of peat moss and sand or vermiculite will root in two to four weeks.

A number of species grow well in a greenhouse, among them *Episcia fulgida, E. coccinea, E. cupreata, E. chontalensis,* and *E. tesselata*. *Episcia fulgida* is a handsome creeping plant with oval-shaped, copper-colored leaves with green veins. The flowers are bright red. *E. coccinea* has dark metallic green leaves, is free-flowering, and bears scarlet flowers. *E. cupreata* is suitable for pot or basket culture. The blooms are scarlet and the foliage is a striking coppery hue. *E. chontalensis* has darkish green leaves, each with a narrow silver-colored center vein, and bears light blue blossoms. Unlike the species previously mentioned, *E. tesselata* has an upright habit of growth instead of a trailing one. The leaves are purplish brown and glossy and the flowers are yellow. Plants grow to a height of about two feet.

Gloxinia

Gloxinia (botanically, *Sinningia speciosa*), native to Brazil, is a superb greenhouse plant which bears large, velvet-textured, tubular flowers with colors ranging from blue to purple, from pink to carmine, and white. Some varieties have solid colors, others are bicolored, and some are beautifully spotted. The velvety sheen of the foliage is also handsome. Gloxinias will reward you splendidly for the effort expended.

The easiest way to start a collection is to purchase dormant tubers, available from about December on. Store the tubers in dry peat at a temperature of 50 degrees until the buds begin to develop. Some tubers start growing before others. At intervals, examine the tubers and plant those which show signs of growth. If tubers have become considerably shriveled during storage, pot them even though they do not show new growth. However, be careful not to overwater them. By starting the tubers at intervals you will get a succession of blooms. Tubers which are about 1½ inches across are planted in 5-inch pots, larger ones in 6-, 7-, or 8-inch pots, depending on their size. Small tubers of seedlings may be potted in 3-inch pots and later shifted into 5-inch ones. Prepare the pot by placing crushed charcoal, pebbles, or pieces of broken pot in the bottom for drainage. Nearly fill the pot with soil, firm moderately, and then place the tuber on the surface. Then add more soil and firm it moderately so that the top of the tuber is level with the surface of the soil. You can also start tubers in flats containing a mixture of equal parts of peat moss and sand which is kept damp. When the shoots are an inch or two tall, remove the plants from the flat and pot them. Gloxinias do well in soil which is rich in organic matter. A mixture of one-third loam, one-third leaf mold, one-sixth peat, and one-sixth sand, plus a 4-inch potful of bonemeal to a bushel of soil, suits them, or you may use a mixture of two parts soil, one part sand, one part well-rotted manure, one part leaf mold, and one part peat. Another good mixture consists of equal parts of loam, peat, and sand.

After the tubers are potted, water thoroughly, but thereafter water sparingly until active root growth begins. If the soil is kept continually wet before roots are present to absorb the water, the tuber may rot. Throughout the growing period, water carefully. Use water which is at the same temperature as the greenhouse, or slightly above. Avoid wetting the foliage with cold water. If cold water is splashed on the leaves, they are likely to become spotted. At each watering, water thoroughly; then don't water again until there are signs of dryness at the surface, for gloxinias do not thrive in waterlogged soil. They grow best when the air is humid. If you do not have a humidifier, you should wet the walks and the ground under the benches several times on bright days. After the plants are well established, biweekly applications of a dilute liquid fertilizer promote sturdy growth.

The plants should be raised in a shaded part of a greenhouse maintained at 60 degrees during the night. The day temperature should be about 10 degrees warmer. The appearance of your plants will tell you whether they are getting the correct amount of light. If burned spots appear and the leaves become yellowish, apply more shade. If the plants become leggy or spindly, give them more light.

The largest tubers will flower about four months after they are planted, the smaller ones later. By planting tubers at intervals you can have plants in flower from spring through summer and fall. We used to believe that the plants should be dried off after their first flowering, but now we know that many will bloom a second time if regular watering is continued. If only a few leaves turn yellow and die after the first blossoming, continue to water the plants as before. Soon you will notice new leaves, and within a few weeks a number of flower buds. These will give you a second display. Don't try to get a third flowering. After the second flowering, when the leaves begin to die, gradually withhold water to induce dormancy. Finally cease watering. The tubers may be allowed to remain in the pots. Lay the pots on their sides under the greenhouse bench. If storage space is limited, you can remove the dormant tubers from the pots, shake them free of soil, and store the tubers in dry peat. The tubers should be given a rest period of at least two months. Beginning in January, make periodic examinations and repot those which are beginning to grow. Remove the plant from the old pot, shake off the soil, and pot the tuber in fresh soil.

If all of the leaves become yellow and die after the plants have flowered the first time, cease watering immediately. Let the tubers become dormant and store in the manner just described.

If you wish to increase a choice plant, you may do so by leaf cuttings. Cuttings always come true. Remove a medium-size, healthy leaf by cutting through the leaf stalk close to the main stem. Insert the stalk of the leaf in sand, vermiculite, or peat moss. Keep the cuttings in a moist atmosphere and continue to water until the parent leaf dies. In time, a tuber will develop at the base of the leaf cutting. When the parent leaf turns yellow and dies, the tuber that has formed is ready for potting. Leaves rooted in June will have tubers 1½ inches across by November. Gloxinias can also be increased by cuttings made from the blade of a leaf. The leaf segment is placed vertically in sand. In time a tuber forms near the midrib.

Gloxinias are readily grown from seed. If you plant high quality hybrid seed, you have a thrill awaiting you. From such seed a great variety of plants may be obtained. Perhaps no two will be exactly alike; an occasional one may be very outstanding. The suspense of waiting for the seedlings to flower can be exciting. Many growers prefer to sow seeds in February, but you may, if you wish, plant them at any time. Plants grown from seed sown in November will flower in May and June; those from seed sown in February, during the summer months.

A finely screened peaty soil should be used; a mixture of equal parts of loam, sand, and peat is satisfactory. Another good way is to place a thin layer of vermiculite over soil such as that used for potting the older plants. Water well before sowing the seed. The seeds are tiny—about 600,000 seeds to an ounce—and they are best sown by first mixing them with fine sand. This mixture is then placed in a salt shaker and distributed over the soil. The seeds should not be covered, either with soil or vermiculite. Cover the pot with a pane of glass, over which lay a piece of newspaper. Water as needed, using subirrigation or a misty spray. If the seed pots are maintained at a temperature of 70 degrees, seedlings will appear in about two weeks. Germination is slower at lower temperatures.

Remove the newspaper as soon as the seedlings appear and give the plants good light, but never direct sun. Prop up the glass on one side to provide for air circulation and to prevent too great humidity, which might result in damping-off. Remove the glass before the seedlings touch it. During the seedling stage you can water from below or with a fine spray, using water at room temperature.

The seedlings grow rapidly at first, and then growth almost ceases. The slow growth of the top coincides with the development of a small tuber below the surface of the soil. If the plants are not crowded in the seed pot, you can let them remain there until they are an inch or so high, when they can be moved into 2½-inch pots. If they are crowded when smaller, move them into flats or large shallow pots and space the young plants about 2 inches apart in rows with 2 inches between. Later, these can be potted. As the plants become larger, shift them into 4-inch pots, a size suitable for their first flowering.

Even more thrilling than raising plants from purchased seed is the adventure you can have by hybridizing your own best plants, collecting seed, and sowing it. Select the parents carefully, considering color, marking, size, and substance, with the idea of combining the best traits of one with the best of the other. With a match stick or brush secure pollen from one parent and transfer the pollen to the stigma of the other. The best time to do this is when the flowers have been open about five days, at which time the stigma will be sticky and receptive. If pollination is successful, the petals will fall off the seed parent in a day or two, and shortly thereafter the seed pod will begin to enlarge. In six to eight weeks the seed pod will be fully formed and the seeds ripe. Remove the seed pod and place it upside down in a dish. As the pod dries, the seeds will be liberated. The seeds may be planted in about a week, or you can save them for later plantings. Seeds remain viable for at least three years.

Thrips, mealybugs, aphids, and the cyclamen mite are some pests that attack gloxinias.

Streptocarpus

Streptocarpus, also known as the cape primrose, flowers profusely and through many months of the year. There are many species, among them *Streptocarpus Dunnii,* a rose-flowered kind; *S. Wendlandii,* which bears violet-blue flowers;

S. Galpinii, with mauve flowers; and *S. luteus,* a yellow-flowered species. Except for *S. luteus,* the species mentioned develop only one large leaf. The species add interest to a collection, but they are not so beautiful as the hybrids, which have many leaves and bear flowers from 2 to 5 inches across. The flowers of the hybrids are often fringed and crested, and the color range is quite complete—with pink in all its shades, reds, blues, and whites with dark blotches. Well-grown plants are always admired.

The cape primrose is generally started from seed. By successive sowings from October to March, some plants will be in flower the year round. Plants grown from seed sown in January will begin to flower in August. The seeds are small and are sown in the same manner as those of African violets and gloxinias, using a planting mixture of equal parts of loam, leaf mold, peat moss and sand, which should also be used for the subsequent transplanting and potting. As soon as the seedlings are large enough to handle they should be transplanted into flats or pans with a spacing of about 2 inches. When the plants begin to crowd each other, move them singly into pots. Cape primroses should be grown in shade, not in bright sun, and they should not be allowed to dry out during their growing and flowering periods. In a greenhouse maintained at a night temperature of 60 degrees, they should be kept at the cooler end, especially when they approach flowering size. If you wish to grow the plants a second year, keep the plants slightly on the dry side (but not absolutely dry) from December until March. Then knock them out of the pots, remove some of the old soil, and repot in fresh soil. Plants with many crowns can be divided prior to potting.

Trichosporum

The genus *Trichosporum* is a large one of over fifty species, natives of the Malayan region and India. One choice species is *Trichosporum pulchrum,* an epiphyte with trailing or pendant stems about 2 feet long, bearing deep green, fleshy leaves. The flowers are scarlet externally and variegated with yellow markings within, and they are about 2½ inches long. *Trichosporum* flowers in the spring.

Trichosporum grows well in hanging baskets lined with sphagnum moss and filled with a mixture of sand, leaf mold, and loam. Osmunda fiber is also suitable. They grow best where the night temperature is 65 degrees with a 10-degree rise during the day. Like other gesneriads, they prefer shade. They are propagated from stem cuttings.

CHAPTER 19

ORCHIDS

ORCHIDS ARE an amazing family of plants. They range all over the world, from cool mountain forests at high elevations to low coastal areas where the climate is warm; from dry cliff tops to damp stream banks. Among the 20,000 species the plant sizes run from some taller than a man to plants only an inch high, of many forms and habits of growth. The flowers show an almost incredible variety of size, shape, and color. The familiar *Cattleya* now comes in many hues, from red-violet to yellow and bronze. It is also sharing its place as a favorite corsage flower with the waxy *Cymbidium,* which comes in many colors, from green to pink and yellow; the lovely white or pink *Phalaenopsis;* and the ladyslipper or *Cypripedium,* whose spots or stripes enhance a green, brown, or yellow background. In addition to these, known to the corsage-buying public, there are hundreds of kinds which make a spectacular show in a collection, which are beautiful in their own right, and which are all the more fascinating for being so different from each other as well as different from the familiar types.

Orchids are not difficult to grow. Although their needs vary according to their habits and the climate in their native habitat, their requirements are not hard to learn. As far as temperature is concerned, they are divided into three main groups. Those that come from the cooler places in the tropics need cool temperatures in cultivation and belong to what we call the *cool* group; those that come from areas of moderate temperatures require temperatures a little warmer and make up the *intermediate* group; and kinds that come from still warmer regions belong in the *warm* group. It is the night temperatures that are critical, so that the basic temperatures for each group are given as night temperatures. The cool orchids do best with a night temperature of 50 degrees, the intermediate kinds with a night temperature of 55-60 degrees, and the warm group with nights of 60-65 degrees. Each group offers a wide choice of lovely orchids, but it happens that the largest number of popularly grown kinds come in the intermediate range. In any one group some kinds will need more or less water, or more or less light, but if they are compatible regarding temperature, these other needs can be met individually.

Orchids are related to lilies and iris. In fact, they are the culmination of the lily line of descent, and are the most highly specialized plants of this line. As different as orchids are in appearance one from another, they are all built on the same basic flower pattern. The three outer flower parts are the sepals. Within the sepals are the three petals, one of which has been so transformed in shape and coloring that it is given another name, the lip or *labellum*. Within the lip, or standing above it, is found the *column*, the hallmark of the orchids. It is formed by the fusion of the reproductive parts. The column is a fleshy, more or less club-shaped structure, which bears the anther at its tip. Below the anther, and separated from it by a little partition, is the *stigma*, a sunken area containing a sticky fluid. The column is continuous with the ovary, which forms the "stem" of the flower and which develops into the seed pod.

Only a few of the favorite greenhouse orchids are found growing on the ground in soil, among them paphiopedilum or ladyslipper (usually called cypripedium). Most of the greenhouse orchids grow natively perched on trees, where their roots ramify through organic matter accumulated in the crotches, or cracks in the bark, and extend out to cling to the branch or to hang free in the air. These orchids are not parasites, for their roots do not penetrate the branches. They are no more parasitic than the birds and monkeys who make their home in the trees. The tree-perching plants are called *epiphytes*.

The tree-dwelling habit assures the plants good air circulation and good light. Some kinds prefer the higher branches where the light is brighter; some live on the lower branches and have more shade. All have better light than they would if they lived on the ground, although the light is modified by the moving leaves of branches above them. In greenhouses these orchids need plenty of air circulation and good light. They cannot take full sun during our seasons of warm weather and long days, however, so the light must be lessened from spring through fall by painting the glass with shading compound or by using lath strips or roller blinds. Winter sun is less strong and the temperatures are cooler, so that in many regions the orchids can have full sun. Even in winter the locality dictates the amount of light that can be given orchids, for in areas with bright sun some shade may still be necessary. We will give details about shade along with the general culture of various kinds of orchids later in this chapter.

You do not need to have branches for the orchids to perch on. Fortunately, they can be grown in ordinary flower pots, using osmunda fiber for a potting medium instead of soil. A few kinds can be grown in soil containing a large amount of organic matter. Practically all kinds grow well when potted in osmunda fiber (also called *osmundine*). We have grown diverse kinds of orchids in this material, which is a fern root, and all have grown well. Sometimes people are afraid of unfamiliar things, and you may feel this way about osmunda fiber. Don't give it another thought. Purchase a bale or sack of it. You will soon find that it is your favorite potting material.

Most epiphytic orchids grow where rainfall is abundant throughout the year; nevertheless, they are subjected to periodic drought. They do not have access to a continual supply of water as do plants growing in the ground. During a rain and for a short time thereafter, water is available to the roots. But from then until it rains again, little water is available.

We know that cacti, sedums, and other succulents can get along for a long time without water. During drought the plants use the water stored in the stems or leaves, or in both. Epiphytic orchids, like certain desert plants, also store water to be used in the interval between rains. Most of them have swollen stems called *pseudobulbs,* in which water is stored; many have thick leathery leaves which also store water. Although in nature they may be subjected to drying for only a few hours or days at a time, practically all of the epiphytic orchids can survive very long periods of drought. You cannot easily kill them by withholding water, but you can kill them by continually overwatering them. In nature the roots are well aerated and they must be kept so when raised in pots. If the potting medium is kept continually wet, the roots will not get enough oxygen and they will die. Mature orchid plants, growing in pots, should be watered only when the osmundine approaches dryness. For healthy plants, the potting medium must not be kept saturated with water.

Structure of orchid plants

There are two general types of growth habit in orchids. The one you most often meet is called *sympodial,* in which new and complete growths are made each year from a ground stem or rhizome. The other is called *monopodial;* in this case the plant does not have a rhizome. New growth is made from the top of the plant by the addition of new leaves year after year. We shall discuss the sympodial type here. Because cattleya is most widely grown, we shall use it as an example.

The rhizome grows just at the surface of the potting medium. The upright stems arise at intervals from the rhizome, produced in successive years. In a cattleya the stems are thickened, and are called pseudobulbs. New growth comes from the base of the pseudobulb made the previous year. A bud at the base of the older growth swells and grows out horizontally for an inch or so and then curves upward. The horizontal part becomes an extension of the rhizome, while the upward-growing part produces the stem, leaf, and flowers. Each growth produces its own set of roots, and older roots branch from year to year.

When the developing growth is 4 to 6 inches tall, the true leaf emerges from the thin sheathing leaves, and as it grows and expands, within it can be seen a sheath, a closed green envelope. The flower buds develop from the tip of the pseudobulb, grow up within the sheath, and as they reach the top of the sheath break out through it. The stems and buds grow larger and the flowers begin to open in two or three weeks.

The growing end of the plant is called the *lead* or *lead growth.* Sometimes two buds break from the base of the mature growth, giving the plant two leads. Occasionally a bud on an older part will also grow into a new lead. A plant with two or three leads gives that many more flowers.

Getting a start

For your first plants we suggest that you purchase a few mature plants, or seedlings ready to flower. From these you can become familiar with the growth and culture of orchids. If you tell the dealer that you want plants recently potted but fully established you will not need to pot them for about two years.

At a smaller expense per plant you can buy seedlings in 2½-inch pots which will flower in about three years. Or you can purchase still younger (and still less expensive) seedlings in what are called community pots. A community pot of the type we have in mind will be a 3-inch pot containing about ten seedlings which are ready to move singly into 2½-inch pots. Seedlings at these two stages are more economical than older seedlings; in fact, are probably the best buy for the amateur.

When you become familiar with orchids, you may wish to sow seeds and raise the seedlings to maturity. It requires five to seven years to get flowering-size plants from seeds. Occasionally an experienced grower offers seed for sale. Until you have rather fine plants to use as parents it would pay you to buy seed rather than make your own crosses.

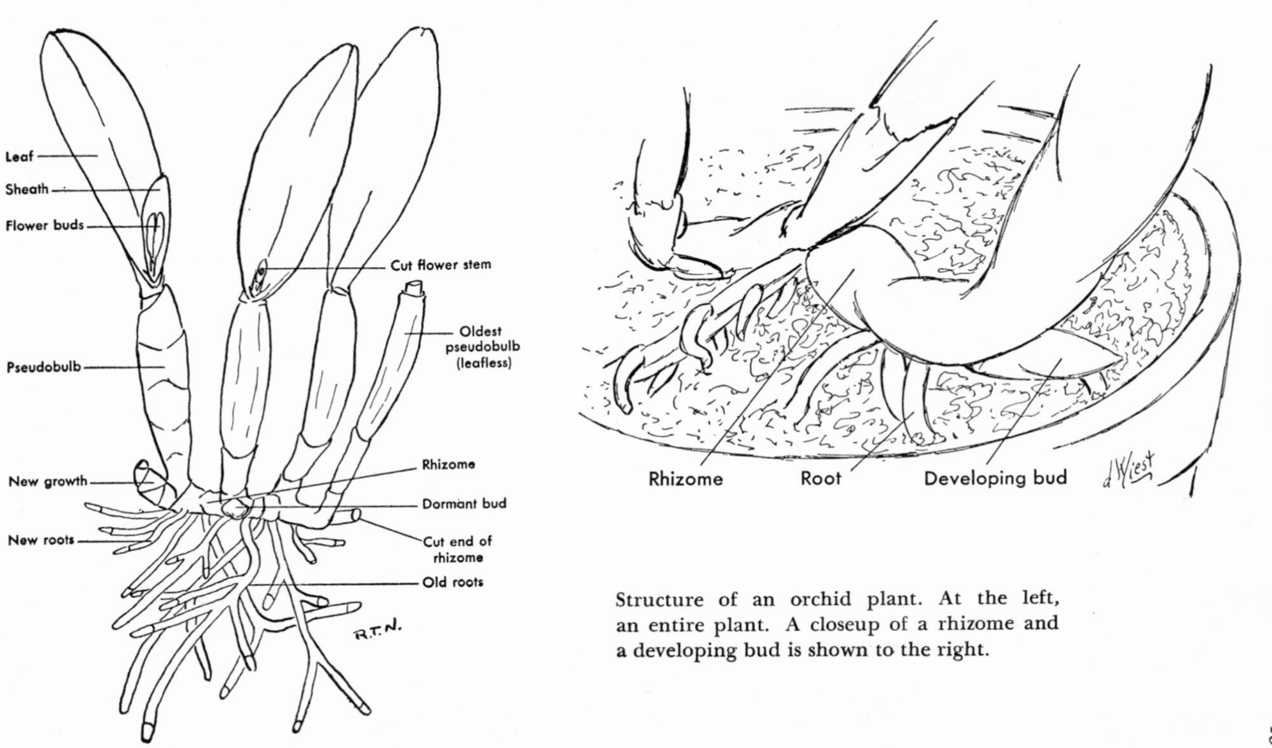

Structure of an orchid plant. At the left, an entire plant. A closeup of a rhizome and a developing bud is shown to the right.

Potting orchids

The process of potting is much the same for all kinds of orchids, so that, although cattleyas are again used to illustrate, the methods described are applicable to most others. Moving seedlings from community pots into 2½-inch pots or shifting seedlings from 2½-inch pots into 4-inch ones is quite easily and speedily performed.

Moving plants from community pots into 2½-inch pots. Use soft brown osmundine. To prepare the fiber for potting, soak the large pieces of fiber in water, remove, and then wring out as much water as possible. With a hatchet, cut pieces of the fiber about an inch thick and two inches long. Prepare the 2½-inch pot by adding several pieces of crock to the pot and then some moist fiber. Soak the pot of small seedlings in water for a while to loosen the roots from the sides of the pot. Then knock or pry the osmunda ball from the pot. Separate the seedlings carefully, keeping some fiber around the roots if possible.

Take two pieces of chopped fiber and place one on each side of the roots of the young plant, with the plant at its original level in the fiber. Insert the plant and fiber in the 2½-inch pot. Then, with your fingers, squeeze the ball toward the center of the pot and add additional pieces of fiber between the ball and the side of the pot. Continue with this procedure around the pot. A small potting stick will help insert the additional pieces of fiber. When you are through, the fiber should be quite firm, the surface fairly smooth, and there should be about ⅜ inch between the rim and the surface of the fiber. For several months after potting, care for the plants in the manner described for community pots. As they grow larger, gradually increase the amount of light and ventilation.

Shifting from 2½-inch to 4-inch pots. Use either soft or wiry fiber. Enlarge the drainage hole of a 4-inch pot by knocking in the edges of the hole, and then add several pieces of crock. Place some fiber over the crock. Soak the plant in water to loosen its roots and then knock it out of the pot.

Remove the old crock and some of the old fiber from the center of the ball without disturbing that fiber which is surrounded by roots. Replace the old core fiber with fresh osmundine. Insert the ball in the 4-inch pot, leaving as much distance between the front of the plant and the pot as you can. Often the front of the seedling will be near the center of the pot. With your fingers, insert fresh fiber between the ball and the side of the pot. Then insert additional pieces, using a potting stick. When you are through, the fiber should be more firm than in the 2½-inch pot. From the 4-inch size on, the plants must be potted hard. Orchids do not thrive when they are loosely potted, and the larger plants especially need to be potted firmly.

Potting mature plants. Mature orchids need not be repotted frequently; potting every other year, or even every three years, is sufficient. Potting a mature plant is quite an operation and must be done at the proper time. Do not pot a plant that is entering a rest period, generally in late fall or early winter. If you pot it at this time the roots are likely to rot. Orchids should be potted just when the new roots begin to form. Don't wait until the new roots are a quarter or a half an inch long, because then, since they are so brittle, they are easily broken off.

Soak the pot in water for a time before knocking the plant from the pot. After the plant is removed separate the old, decayed fiber from the back part of the ball. Generally, the fiber in the front part of the ball will be in good condition, and frequently the roots in this fiber will be healthy. Do not disturb this part of the ball. Remove the crock held in the bottom of the ball, and then work upward from the bottom and remove most of the old fiber in the center of the ball.

After removing the old fiber, examine the plant. If the plant has just one straight, unbranched rhizome and more than four pseudobulbs, cut off the old pseudobulbs, leaving the group of four or five front ones intact. The old pseudobulbs may be potted separately. If the rhizome forks so that there are two or more leads, the plant may be divided, or it may be potted as a unit after removing the old pseudobulbs.

If you prefer to divide the plant, cut the rhizome with pruning shears so that each part will have four healthy pseudobulbs.

Before proceeding further, fill in the empty spaces with fresh fiber. You are now ready to pot the plant or the divisions. The new pot should be of such a size that it will give room for two years' growth.

To prepare the new pot enlarge the drainage hole. Then fill the lower third of the pot with crock, over which place some fresh fiber. Soak pieces of osmundine in water and wring out the excess. With a hatchet, chop the large chunks into strips and then chop each strip into pieces 1½ inches long. Place the plant in the pot with the older end close to the rim and with the rhizome about half an inch below the rim. As we said before, the front bulb should be far enough from the rim to accommodate two new growths.

Fill the space between the ball and the pot with fiber until the distance from the fiber to the top of the ball is about an inch and a half. This space will be filled with solid pieces of fiber. Insert these pieces vertically against the old ball, starting at the front and working backwards on each side. It is best to start at the front. If you start at the back the ball will move forward and insufficient space will remain for the new growths. Many pieces can be inserted by hand, always pushing the previously inserted pieces toward the ball to make way for the new piece. Finally you will need to use a potting stick to insert additional pieces between the side of the pot and the fiber which is in place. The fiber must be hard when you are through. It takes a lot of fiber to pot a plant in a 6-inch pot. If the plant is properly potted the rhizome will be at the surface and there will be about half an inch from the rim of the pot to the fiber. This is the space that is filled with water each time that the plant is watered.

Don't forget to label each newly potted plant. Also, tie the pseudobulbs to a stake.

Care of newly potted plants. Keep the newly potted mature plants and older seedlings on the dry side until good root action is evident. If the fiber of newly potted plants is

eptocarpus, the Cape Primrose, is a magnificent plant. (Antonelli Brothers)

Potting an orchid seedling from a community pot into a 2½-inch pot. Here, seedlings are removed from a community pot.

Place one piece of fiber on each side of the roots, and then insert into a 2½-inch pot.

Add additional fiber until the fiber is firm.

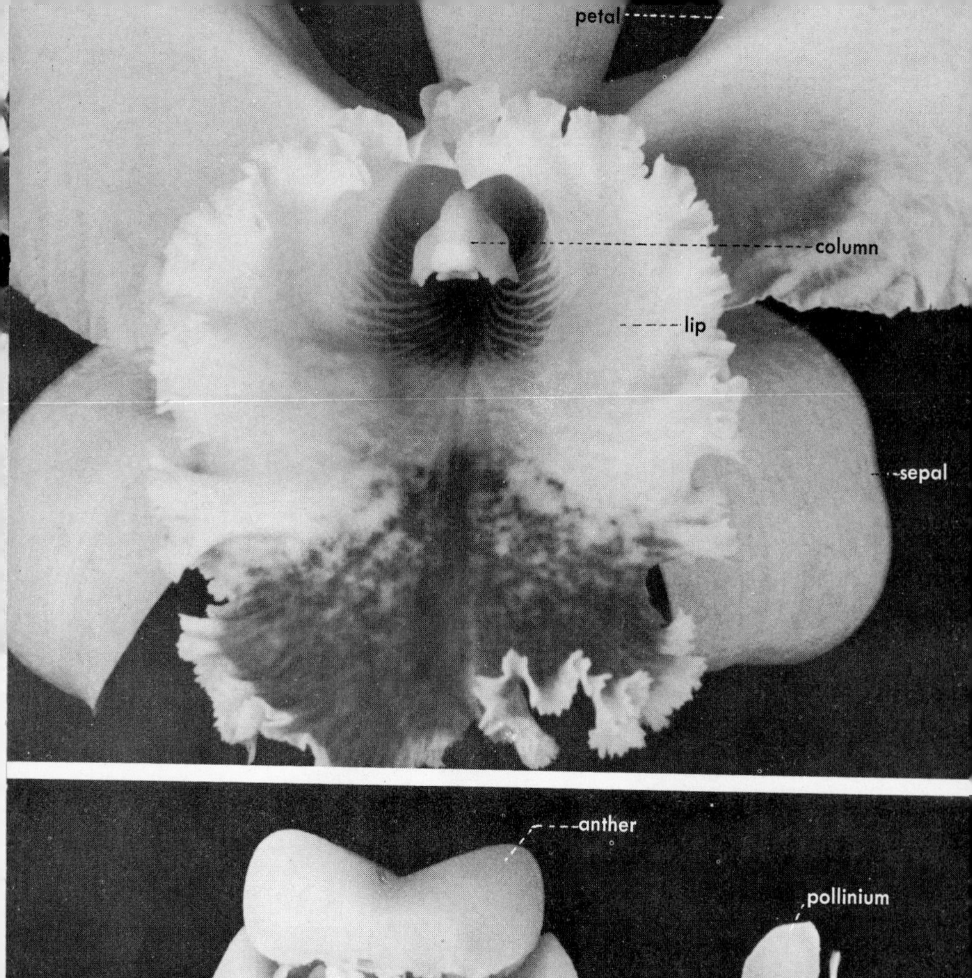

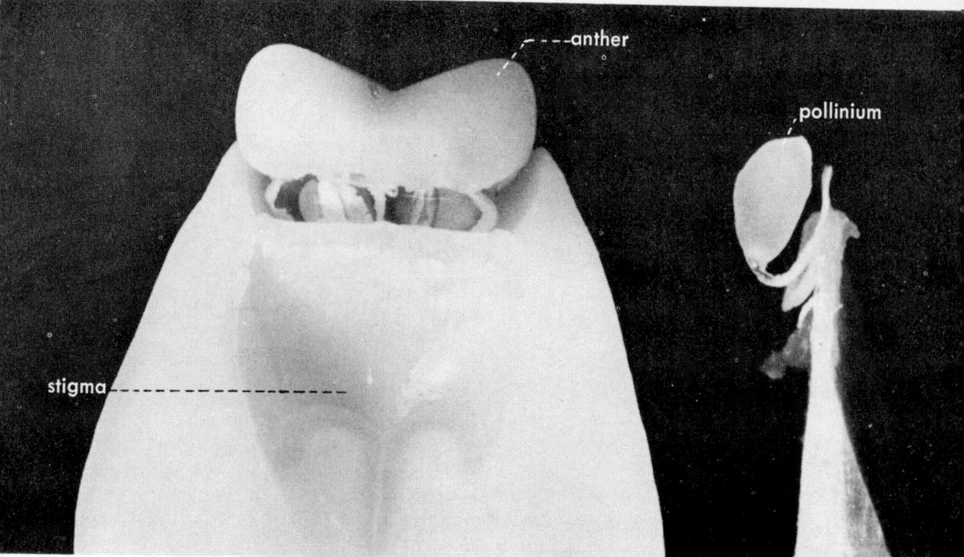

A closeup of a cattleya flower. Notice the large lip (labellum) that surrounds the column, the two other petals, and the three narrower sepals. *Below:* details of a column. The hinged structure at the top is the anther; it contains four pollen masses, called *pollinia.* The sunken area below the anther is the stigma. A pollinium is stuck to a sharpened matchstick at the right.

Above: Cymbidium. Cool, bright conditions and free air circulation favor the development of flower spikes. *Below:* the flower of a paphiopedilum (usually called *cypripedium*) is distinctive and lasts a long time. The lip is pouch-shaped and the two other petals extend laterally from the center of the flower. The large banner is the dorsal sepal. The structure behind the lip is formed by the fusion of the lateral sepals. *Left: Dendrobium densiflorum* bears a profusion of yellow flowers. This species does well with a night temperature of 50 degrees.

kept wet the old roots will rot and the plants will be set back, but if they are kept dry they will soon send out branch roots. No watering is necessary for at least the first two weeks. However, during this period give the foliage (not the fiber) a frequent mist of water, and shade the plants. As root growth commences and continues, waterings can be more frequent.

Importing plants and planting imports

At one time a large number of wild cattleya orchid plants were imported. However, since the technique of growing plants from seed has been perfected, the importation of cattleyas has diminished. In building up your collection of the ordinary cattleyas we recommend that you purchase cultivated plants instead of those from the jungle, for they will be of better quality than the wild plants.

In addition to cattleyas there are other kinds of orchids, some of which bear myriads of small, beautiful blooms, and others which are noted for their interesting foliage. These species are worth importing. We have had pleasure in building up a collection of orchids from Panama. These plants add interest to our collection. A word of caution is in order. Make certain that the dealer is thoroughly reliable. A number of growers have been disappointed with plants bought from unscrupulous dealers or through so-called "special" or "bargain" offers.

Before you may import orchid plants (or any other kind) you must obtain a permit from the United States Department of Agriculture, Hoboken, New Jersey. This permit is free and insures that your plants will be properly inspected and fumigated at the port of entry. With the permit you will receive some tags. Two of these tags are sent to the dealer from whom you are buying the plants. You should specify how the plants are to be shipped. For small packages of not too great weight air mail is very satisfactory, although quite expensive. Its advantages are that it is quick, and that the plants are not held up while arrangements are made to collect the duty. Instead the duty is collected by the delivery man at your door.

Imported plants usually arrive in excellent condition and should be potted quickly in osmunda fiber. Some leaves will turn brown and fall off, due to the shock of shipping and fumigation. After potting, stake each plant securely. If the plant lacks roots, firm fiber on each side of the rhizome and then anchor the rhizome to the fiber with large wire staples.

The fiber is kept on the dry side until new roots develop. During this period the plants should be syringed frequently and kept in a shaded part of the greenhouse.

Breeding orchids

Occasionally bees will pollinate orchid flowers in the greenhouse during summer. However, in breeding no one should rely on chance crosses made by insects, but instead should pollinate the flowers by hand. As in all breeding work, the parent plants should be carefully selected.

Remove the anther from the tip of the column of the male parent. With a match, pencil, or needle remove the masses of pollen grains, called *pollinia,* from the anther and then transfer them to the stigma of the column of the female parent. The anther of this column should be removed. In about nine months to a year's time the pod will be mature. Just as it starts to open, cut it off and let it dry for a few days in a glass covered with waxed paper. Then shake out the powdery seed into a clean glass, cover with waxed paper, and store in the refrigerator.

Growing orchids from seeds

Sowing seeds. Orchid seeds will not develop into seedlings if they are scattered on moist soil. The seeds are very tiny. In one pod there may be nearly a million. Very little if any food is stored in the seeds. Hence, the food necessary for their germination must come from an external source. In nature some seeds light where organic matter is present. Fungi are always present in organic matter and they change some of it into sugar, which can then be used by the orchid seeds. Orchid growers need not rely on fungi to produce this sugar. The seed is sown on a growing medium made of an agar jelly and containing sugar, water, and certain minerals. A mixture of the necessary ingredients is sold under the name of Bacto Orchid Agar by the Difco Laboratories. Thirty-seven grams of this Orchid Agar is added to a liter of distilled water (your local druggist has distilled water, and he will help you measure the ingredients). The mixture is then boiled until the Orchid Agar is dissolved. Flasks or bottles are then filled with the solution to a depth of 1 inch. The medium should be poured through a funnel into the containers. None of the medium should be splashed on the neck or sides of the flask or bottle. The flasks or bottles are then stoppered with cotton plugs about 2 inches long. Roll a strip of cotton into a plug 2 inches long. The flasks or bottles containing the Orchid Agar are then sterilized in a pressure cooker at 15 pounds pressure for 15 minutes.

When the gel has set and is cool, the seeds may be sown. First the seeds must be disinfected with a solution of calcium hypochlorite. To prepare this solution, add 10 grams of calcium hypochlorite to 140 cubic centimeters of distilled water. Shake the solution thoroughly and then filter it. Add a small amount of the clear solution to a vial. Add some seeds to the vial, stopper it, and then shake for 15 minutes. In the meantime you should have a medicine dropper immersed in another portion of the calcium hypochlorite solution. Suck the solution into the dropper. The whole dropper must be sterilized, inside and out. With the sterile dropper, suck up some of the solution in which the seeds are suspended. Remove the cotton from a flask and squirt five or six drops of the solution containing the seeds onto the agar surface. Replace the plug and then rotate the flask to distribute the seeds uniformly over the surface. Extra precautions may be necessary to prevent contamination, such as burning the outermost part of the cotton stopper before removing it and exposing the cotton and neck of the flask to a flame before replacing the stopper.

Cover the cotton and neck of the flask with aluminum foil or waxed paper. Then place the flasks in a box provided with extra shade. Move the box into the greenhouse.

Moving seedlings from flasks to pots

Six to twelve months after sowing, the seedlings will have leaves and roots and the seedlings may then be grown in osmunda fiber. Seedlings may be removed from the flask by removing the stopper and adding water. Swirl the water around and pour it into a dish. Many of the seedlings will be washed out in this way. Stubborn ones may be removed with a knife.

There are several ways to transplant seedlings. You can add crock to a 4-inch pot and then fill it with finely chopped moist osmunda fiber. Holes may be poked in this fiber with a pointed stick. Insert the roots in the hole and then firm the fiber around the roots. A 4-inch pot will accommodate twenty-five to fifty seedlings. The pot containing many seedlings is called a community pot. The sandwich technique, illustrated in accompanying photographs, is an excellent way to transplant the seedlings. We suggest that you try this method first.

The seedlings should be kept in a warm, humid, shaded place. We have found that a box covered with glass and cheesecloth is an excellent place to keep seedlings. If the box is tightly constructed, drill holes in the side to provide good ventilation. Seedlings should be kept moist. Never let them dry out.

Second transplanting

In six months to a year the seedlings will be ready for transplanting. Soak the community pot in water and then knock the ball from the pot. Separate the seedlings carefully, avoiding injury to the roots.

The seedlings are now ready for their second community pots. Five to ten seedlings may be planted in a 3-inch pot, ten or fifteen in a 4-inch one. Fill the pot about half way with crock, over which place some fiber. Cut chunks of fiber with a hatchet. Place one piece on one side of a seedling and another piece on the opposite side. Then place the seedling in the pot. Repeat with a second seedling and place it next to the first one. Repeat until the pot is full. If the fiber is not firm add additional fiber around the sides.

The seedlings in second community pots should be handled as were the younger ones. Give them shade, humidity, and ample water.

In about six months the seedlings may be removed from the second community pots. The larger seedlings may be potted in 2½-inch pots, using the method described on page 244. The smaller ones are best planted again in community pots.

Pests

A number of pests attack orchids, among them scales, mealy bugs, thrips, aphids, weevils, and the cattleya fly. Orchids are attacked by several species of scale insects which vary from white to dark brown, depending on the species. DDT and Malathion give good control of scale insects. Only rarely are orchids attacked by mealy bugs, which are readily controlled with DDT. Thrips often feed on flowers and ruin their beauty; certain kinds attack leaves and may raise havoc with seedlings. Thrips are controlled with DDT, rotenone, or Malathion. On occasion aphids attack orchids, and it has been demonstrated that they spread serious virus diseases. Aphids are easily killed with nicotine sulfate or Malathion, and some species with DDT. The favorite host of the cattleya fly is cattleya, but the flies will also infest laelia, brassavola, and epidendrum. This pest is rarely seen since the advent of DDT, and a regular spray program that includes DDT will eliminate it if it occurs.

Bees may be troublesome in the greenhouse during the warm months of the year. They do not feed on orchid plants but they bring about pollination, which results in a quick wilting and fading of blooms. It pays to screen ventilators to keep them out of the greenhouse.

Mites attack all types of orchids, feeding on blooms as well as on foliage. Some kinds are red in color and are called red spiders. Mites are difficult to control once they become established. Frequent sprayings with Dimite or Malathion, however, will keep them in check, as will forceful syringing with water. Aramite also gives good control.

A collection of orchids may be very valuable. Don't risk your whole collection by using an unfamiliar insecticide, a household spray, or an insecticide that has not been tried on a variety of orchids. If you wish to use a new insecticide not proven for orchids, try it on a few plants before you apply it to all.

Slugs and snails can cause much damage, especially to root tips, flowers, and young seedlings. Various poisons are on the market, the most effective of which have metaldehyde as the active ingredient.

Always follow the directions exactly. Poisons that kill pests can also damage plants if used in too strong concentrations or under the wrong conditions.

Cattleyas

The best known of the orchids are the cattleyas, named after William Cattley. Cattleyas grow well with a night temperature between 55 and 60 degrees with a 10-degree rise during the day. They like a humid atmosphere (an average of around 50 per cent relative humidity) and benefit from syringings on bright days. The air should be fresh. In summer the ventilators may be kept open night and day. Even in winter, the ventilators should be opened a little on bright days when weather permits.

In regions with dull winter days no shade will be necessary from early winter until February. After February a light shade is needed. Later in the spring the shade should be increased to cut down the heat from the sun during warmer weather. Beginning in autumn, reduce the shade gradually. In areas with bright winter sun, for instance in Florida, southern California, and in many western states, some shade is necessary even during the winter months. For our own greenhouse we put on a light coat of white shading in early March and often another coat toward May. During the summer months we supplement this shading with a layer of cheesecloth tacked up inside the greenhouse. In October the cheesecloth is removed. We do not scrub off the white shade. Rain and snow partially wash it off, leaving a speckled coating that suffices through our bright winter. The next spring we paint over the weathered shading. When the paint is very uneven and streaked, we scrape or brush off the old, and start with a fresh coat. In terms of foot-candles, cattleyas should have between 2000 and 3000 foot-candles of light if possible. This may have to be lessened a bit in very hot weather and can be increased in cooler weather.

You can tell from the appearance of the plants whether or not they are getting the right amount of light. If grown with too much shade the plants are dark green, the leaves and pseudobulbs are soft, and flowering is poor. If light intensity is extremely bright, the leaves become yellow and sometimes burned. At the right intensity the leaves will be a healthy bright green sometimes tinged with purple, the growth sturdy, and the plants will flower well.

Cattleyas cannot remain healthy if the osmunda fiber is kept soaking wet. If the fiber is waterlogged for a considerable period the roots die, the new leads are weak, and no flowers are produced. To avoid these troubles water the plant thoroughly and then wait until the fiber is almost dry before watering again. We say *almost dry* advisedly. If you let the fiber get bone dry, you may have difficulty getting it moist again. A plant in a 6-inch pot may require water every five days during spring and summer, whereas in the winter months, when the plants are more or less dormant and temperatures cooler, waterings may be half so frequent. These intervals cannot be followed rigorously, however. The firmness of potting, the light intensity, the humidity, and the size of the plant markedly affect the rate of drying of the fiber. A schedule applicable to one region may not be the best for another locality.

Cattleyas grow well in osmunda fiber even without periodic applications of fertilizer. However, there is some evidence that they grow better if fed at biweekly intervals with a weak solution of fertilizer. Special orchid fertilizers are sold, and they should be made up according to the manufacturer's directions. If you use a general fertilizer instead of an orchid one, use it half-strength.

Kinds of cattleyas

As with other plants, man has developed, through crossing and selection, varieties of cattleyas which are superior to the species in vigor of the plants, in flower production, and in the color, size, and texture of the flowers. We now have hybrids with a variety of flower color. Some are orchid-colored, others peach, rose, red, white, or yellow.

In developing these hybrids, the breeder has crossed different species of cattleyas and has crossed cattleyas with other genera, such as laelia, and brassavola. The hybrid resulting from a cross of cattleya with laelia is called laeliocattleya (abbreviated Lc), that produced when crossed with brassavola is called brassocattleya (Bc). A laeliocattleya may be crossed with a brassocattleya to produce a hybrid known as a brassolaeliocattleya (Blc.). We illustrate these crosses with the following pedigree:

Cattleya mendelii *Laelia purpurata*	*Laeliocattleya* *Canhamiana*	*Brassolaeliocattleya* *Mount Everest*
Brassavola digbyana *Cattleya dowiana*	*Brassocattleya* *Mrs. Leeman*	

The hybrid Brassolaeliocattleya Mount Everest resulted from a cross of *Laeliocattleya Canhamiana* (itself a hybrid of *Cattleya mendelii* with *Laelia purpurata)* with Brassocattleya Mrs. Leeman, a hybrid of *Brassavola digbyana* and *Cattleya dowiana*. All plants of this cross are called Blc. Mount Everest. You know from experience with other plants that not all of the plants resulting from a cross are the same. Some may be very inferior, only a few superior. The same is true of orchids. All members of an orchid cross go by the same name; in this example both the good ones and the poor ones are called Blc. Mount Everest.

There are now thousands of hybrids, differing in flower color, in shape and size of flower, and in blooming season. By the proper selection of varieties you can have cattleyas in flower during all months of the year. Catalogs produced for orchid specialists list many varieties and give the flower color and season of bloom. We suggest that you write for catalogs and make selections from them. Many fine orchid growers advertise in the *American Orchid Society Bulletin,* a magazine published by the American Orchid Society, Inc. Another good orchid magazine is the *Orchid Digest,* published by the Orchid Digest Corporation.

Many species of cattleya have contributed to the hybrids of today, and these are inexpensive and interesting plants to grow. Some of the more familiar species of cattleyas, their flowering season, and the color of the flowers are indicated in the accompanying table.

Species	*Flower color and size*	*When they flower*
Cattleya bowringiana	Five to twenty 3-inch flowers of rosy purple to a stem	Oct.–Nov.
Cattleya skinneri	Similar to *C. bowringiana* but a smaller plant	Spring
Cattleya bicolor	Four- to 5-inch flowers, waxy, green-brown	Summer
Cattleya labiata	Five- to 7-inch flowers, rosy lavender, deep lip	Oct.–Nov.
Cattleya mendelii	Five- to 6-inch flowers, pale blush with amethyst lip	May–June
Cattleya mossiae	Five- to 7-inch flowers, rosy lavender, lip veined with purple	April–May
Cattleya percivaliana	Four- to 5-inch flowers, rosy lavender with rich lip	Dec.–Jan.
Cattleya trianaei	Five- to 7-inch flowers, light pinkish lavender, purple lip	Dec.–Jan.
Cattleya gigas	Six- to 8-inch flowers, rosy lavender, magenta lip with yellow eyes	June–July

Cymbidiums

Cymbidiums have grasslike foliage arising from a spherical or egg-shaped pseudobulb. From the base of the pseudobulb new growths arise in spring or fall, and flowering spikes in the fall. Flowering spikes can be distinguished from vegetative growths by their more pointed, closed appearance.

The flowering spikes are formed from early September until November, the exact time depending on variety and environmental conditions. Earliest varieties will have flowers open in late November or early December, late-flowering ones not until April. The flowers last a long time, often four to six weeks. They are excellent for corsages and arrangements.

Cymbidiums are not so reliable in flowering as are cattleyas. If grown too warm and shaded they produce abundant vegetative growth, but few or no flowers. In order to flower cymbidiums, they are best raised in a cool, bright greenhouse. Night temperatures of 45 to 50 degrees from fall through winter, and summer nights of under 60 result in good growth and flower production. They require bright light, but not full sun, for flowering. Light shade is necessary from spring through summer and into fall to prevent burning and yellowing of the foliage. In many regions cymbidiums may be kept outdoors during the summer, provided with light shade using lath or one or more thicknesses of cheesecloth. After the new pseudobulbs have developed, the plants must have bright light, good air circulation, and a cool temperature if flower spikes are to develop. Especially must these requirements be fulfilled in the months of August and September. During these months only enough shade to prevent the burning of the leaves should be supplied. In fall and winter in many localities the plants may be grown with full sun except when the plants are in flower. Flowering plants may be grouped together and given light shade, which increases the life of the flowers and maintains a more attractive color.

Cymbidiums should be given ample water. At no time let the rooting medium become completely dry. They are heavy feeders and should be given dilute liquid fertilizer every other week during their period of active growth.

Cymbidiums can generally remain in the same pot for two years, after which they should be repotted and, in some instances, divided. They are best repotted just after they have finished flowering. Plants in 8-inch pots or smaller sizes may be shifted into larger pots without disturbing the root ball and without dividing the plant.

Plants which have outgrown 12-inch pots or tubs are probably in need of division, having many leafless back bulbs. Divide the plant by cutting through the rhizome between clumps of three to six pseudobulbs, then gently work the divisions apart, taking care to avoid excessive injury to the roots. Divisions should be moved into pots of suitable size. From some of the divisions leafless back bulbs may be removed and inserted in damp sphagnum moss. They may give rise to new growths from dormant buds. When the back bulbs have a new shoot developing (2 or 3 inches tall) they should be potted. New roots will come from the new shoot when it is about 4 inches tall.

As a potting medium we prefer pieces of moist osmunda fiber which have been lightly sprinkled with well-rotted cow manure. We pack the fiber as we do for cattleyas. Some composts are quite elaborate and one is a mixture of leaf mold, wood shavings, bone meal, soil, and hoof and horn meal. Cymbidiums also grow well in straight peat moss. Plants grown in peat moss should be fertilized at three- or four-week intervals with a 20-20-20 water-soluble fertilizer, using 1 ounce per gallon.

Hybrid cymbidiums are far superior to the species, excelling them in size, color, substance, and longevity of flower. In general, the fine hybrids are your best bet. A number of species have contributed to the hybrids, among them *Cymbidium insigne, C. grandiflorum, C. lowianum,* and *C. tracyanum.*

Epidendrum

Epidendrums grow easily and flower profusely under the same conditions and with the same care as cattleyas. There are hundreds of species, some little-known and rare in cultivation and others among the most popular of orchids. The few we can mention here are entirely different from each other in flower character and add delightful variety to any group of plants.

Epidendrum O'Brianianum hybrids are called reed-type plants because the stem is slender rather than pseudobulbous. The hybrids are more popular than the old fashioned tall

E. O'Brianianum itself because the plants are shorter and the flowers come in many colors—yellow, peach, orange, and red. The large, globe-shaped cluster holds fifteen to thirty small flowers, each with a little fringed lip. They flower at almost any time of the year.

Epidendrum atropurpureum has heavy pseudobulbs and bears long sprays of very fragrant flowers. They are 2 to 3 inches across, purplish-brown with a rose lip, and flower in the spring. *E. cochleatum,* also spring-flowering, holds the shell-shaped, green- and purple-striped lip uppermost while the yellow-green sepals and petals hang downward. *E. fragrans* has flowers shaped something like those of *E. cochleatum* but they are red and white. The plants are much smaller, with little, round pseudobulbs that spread rapidly, giving masses of flowers in late summer. *E. prismatocarpum,* a plant of cattleya proportions, gives a tall cluster of small waxy flowers. They are greenish-white, speckled with purple, and have a sharply pointed pink lip. It flowers in early summer.

Dendrobium

Some dendrobiums like warm temperatures, others cool. The genus has many types, which have rather different habits. However, we shall discuss two types that are lovely and which should do well for you. If your greenhouse has a night temperature of 60 to 65 degrees, *Dendrobium phalaenopsis* and its hybrids will grow beautifully with a bit more shade than cattleyas. If the night temperature is 50 degrees, *Dendrobium nobile, D. thyrsiflorum,* and *D. densiflorum,* all remarkably beautiful dendrobiums, will thrive with more light than cattleyas.

Dendrobiums are watered in the same way as cattleyas, and are potted in the same manner, except that they grow well in small pots without frequent repottings. They benefit from an application of fertilizer every two weeks.

Laelia

Laelias grow well with cattleyas—requiring the same environmental conditions, potting, and watering. Among the choice laelias are *Laelia anceps, L. autumnalis, L. cinnebarina, L. purpurata,* and *L. tenebrosa.*

As we mentioned before, laelias cross readily with cattleyas to produce hybrids known as laeliocattleyas, some of which are superb plants, and a number of which have brightly colored flowers. *Laelia tenebrosa* and *L. cinnebarina* have contributed to the development of laeliocattleyas with attractive yellow flowers.

Odontoglossum

Certain species of odontoglossum, for example *O. crispum,* come from subalpine regions where the nights are always cool, and must be grown in a cool climate or with air conditioning, so are not generally recommended. Other species require a night temperature between 55 and 60 degrees and these grow well with cattleyas. Among the attractive species of this latter group are *Odontoglossum grande;* large, bold yellow and brown flowers; *O. schlieperianum;* a smaller version of *O. grande; O. bictoniense;* pert green and brown flowers; and *O. pulchellum;* charming waxy white flowers, called the "lily-of-the-valley" orchid.

Odontoglossums are potted in osmundine, using the same technique as for cattleyas. They are watered a bit more frequently than cattleyas during their growing season, but are treated like cattleyas while inactive.

Oncidiums

Oncidiums are beautiful orchids that are easily grown. The flowers are not large, but they are produced in abundance. A small plant in a 4-inch pot may produce a flower spray 5 feet long, bearing hundreds of gay flowers well distributed, generally in shades of yellow and brown. Oncidiums flower consistently with nights of 55-60 degrees. By the careful selection of varieties they may be had in flower during all months. Oncidiums are good companions for cattleyas, thriving with the same conditions of watering, humidity, shade, and potting. Use osmundine for the potting medium.

Here are some beautiful species you may wish to grow:

Species	*When flower*	*Description*
O. ampliatum	March–May	Yellow flowers spotted red
O. macranthum	Spring and summer	Petals golden, streaked with red at base, lip purple-brown with white crest
O. ornithorhynchum	Autumn and winter	Rosy purple flowers
O. papilio	Variable	Sepals and petals brown with bands of yellow, lip yellow with brown band
O. splendidum	Spring	Sepals and petals yellow-green with brown bands, lip yellow
O. varicosum	Winter and spring	Sepals and petals yellow with brownish blotches, lip bright yellow

Paphiopedilum

Paphiopedilum is the correct name for plants that are frequently called *Cypripedium.* The flowers are excellent for corsages and as cut flowers, lasting four to six weeks after cutting. The plants are not very floriferous. Generally each growth produces only one flower.

Certain species with plain green foliage, for example *Paphiopedilum insigne, P. fairieanum,* and *P. spicerianum,* as well as their hybrids with plain green leaves, grow best with a night temperature of 50 to 55 degrees. We grow them successfully in a cattleya house by providing them with extra shade and by keeping them at the cooler end of the greenhouse. Other species, those with mottled foliage such as *P. lawrenceanum, P. villosum, P. callosum,* and *P. barbatum,* require a warmer night temperature of about 60 degrees. Hybrids between the plain and mottled-leaved species do well at night temperatures of 55-60, and some even at 65 degrees.

From March or April to early November paphiopedilums grow well with a light intensity of 1000 to 2000 foot-candles.

In cloudy regions they may not need any shade during winter months.

Paphiopedilums grow well when potted with osmundine, a medium which we prefer. However, certain growers have their own composts and may sell you some compost along with plants. Recently it has been found that they grow well in peat moss. Fertilize the plants growing in peat moss with a 20-20-20 water-soluble fertilizer, using an ounce per gallon at monthly intervals. They are best repotted soon after they have flowered. Winter-flowering varieties are repotted in spring, summer-flowering ones in early autumn. Plants do not require annual repotting; once every second year is sufficient. Plants can be divided at potting time. Don't divide the plant into many small pieces. If you do, they will be set back and it may take several years until the small divisions come into flower. We generally pot them into large pots without dividing them until they have a very large number of growths. Then we divide each plant into two or three large clumps, being careful to avoid injuring the roots.

Paphiopedilums lack pseudobulbs. You will recall that the pseudobulbs are enlarged stems which store water. Because paphiopedilums lack such structures they should not be subjected to drought. Keep the fiber moist, never permitting it to become completely dry. Syringe the foliage once a day but let it dry off before night.

There are now available many fine hybrids, many of which surpass the species in the size, conformation, and color of the flowers. The best hybrids are very expensive, less choice ones are more moderately priced, and the species are quite inexpensive. Some species which you might like are:

Species	*Temperature required*	*Flowering time*	*Flower color*
P. barbatum	55–60	Summer	Dorsal sepal white with purple veins. Petals brownish green at base, purple at tip. Lip deep brownish purple.

Species	*Temperature required*	*Flowering time*	*Flower color*
P. callosum	55–60	Spring	Dorsal sepal white with veins green at base, purple above. Petals pale green tinted rose at apex. Lip brownish purple.
P. fairieanum	50–55	Fall	Dorsal sepal greenish white with violet markings. Petals green striated with violet. Lip white at base, green at apex.
P. insigne	50–55	Fall-winter	Dorsal sepal apple green at base and center, upper part white, marked with purple brown spots. Petals pale yellow-green veined brown-purple. Lip yellowish green, brown shaded.
P. lawrenceanum	55–60	Spring-summer	Dorsal sepal white with deep purple veins. Petals green with purple tips and blackish warts along the margin. Lip purple, brown tinged above, green beneath.
P. spicerianum	50–55	Fall-winter	Dorsal sepal white with a crimson-purple band down the center, and a large green basal blotch speckled with red. Petals green, dotted, and suffused with brown. Lip violet, pale-green margined.
P. villosum	55–60	Winter	Dorsal sepal green, the base and center marked with purple-brown. Petals yellow-brown, midvein brown-purple. Lip brownish yellow.

Phalaenopsis

No orchid can surpass phalaenopsis in beauty of form. The flowers are white or rose-colored and are attractively displayed on long sprays. Phalaenopsis is unusual in that a flowering stem which has produced one crop of flowers may produce additional flowers at a later time. Therefore, don't cut off completely an old flowering stalk: cut it just below the first flowering node.

Phalaenopsis needs a warmer greenhouse than any of the orchids previously discussed. They must have a night temperature of 65 degrees if they are to thrive. We have a greenhouse maintained at a night temperature of 55 to 60 degrees. A great variety of orchids thrive in this greenhouse, cattleyas, epidendrums, some dendrobiums, laelias, certain odontoglossums, many oncidiums, certain paphiopedilums, as well as many less well-known orchids. But phalaenopsis does not thrive here. The night temperature is too low for them. We have, however, grown and flowered phalaenopsis splendidly in a glass case in the living room, where the night temperature is higher than in the greenhouse. In this case the night temperature is about 65 degrees, and the air in the case is humid. From fall to spring the case is next to a south window. In late spring and summer it is next to a west window.

Phalaenopsis are best grown in osmunda fiber packed firmly, but not so hard as for cattleya. They may be grown in pots or in baskets. They benefit from syringings and applications of a dilute fertilizer solution. They need more shade than cattleyas.

Many fine hybrids are now available. Three species which have contributed to the hybrids are *Phalaenopsis amabilis, P. schilleriana,* and *P. stuartiana.* These species are well worth growing.

CHAPTER 20

POINSETTIAS AND THEIR RELATIVES

OF THE 250 genera and 4000 species in the Euphorbiaceae family those that are familiar to us are poinsettia, codiaeum (garden croton), euphorbia, and acalypha, most of which thrive in a well-lighted greenhouse kept at 60 to 65 degrees. In addition there are a number of species which are succulent and cactuslike in appearance; these we will consider in a later chapter. Most members of this family have a milky juice, which in some species is poisonous. Valuable products come from certain members of this family; among the commercially important members are the *Hevea* rubber tree, the castor plant, and the *cassava.*

Acalypha

One of the most attractive acalyphas is *A. hispida,* known as the Red-hot Cattail or Chenille Plant, a plant with green leaves which bears striking pendant tassels of red flowers. Other species of *Acalypha* are grown chiefly for their attractive foliage—among them *A. godseffiana,* with green leaves, spotted white; *A. macafeeana,* a plant with red leaves blotched with deeper red; *A. musiaca,* whose foliage is bronzy-green variegated with shades of red.

The acalyphas do well in a greenhouse kept at 60 to 65 degrees. A mixture of three parts loam with one of well-rotted cow manure is suitable for potting. They are easily propagated from stem cuttings. For excellent winter-flowering specimens of *Acalypha hispida,* the most interesting species, cuttings should be made in the summer. The flower spikes become 8 to 10 inches long as the plant increases in size. Be on the alert for mealy bugs, scales, and red spiders.

Croton

The decorative crotons, grown for their beautiful foliage, are in the genus *Codiaeum,* a group of six species native to Malaya and the Pacific Islands. There are over a hundred horticultural varieties of the species *C. variegatum pictum,* varying in leaf shape and foliage color, which ranges from almost white to light and deep yellow, orange, pink, and red, often in charming combinations. The flowers of crotons are small and inconspicuous.

The crotons do best with a high night temperature, about 70 degrees. During the brighter months of the year, light shade is necessary because bright light will burn the leaves. They do well with a high humidity. The plants are easily propagated by cuttings taken from October to June and by air layerage. Cuttings may be rooted in sand with bottom heat of about 80 degrees. The potting mixture should consist of equal parts of sand, loam, and leaf mold with the addition of some cow manure (one-sixth) and bone meal. During the period of active growth they should be well-watered. When they are resting, keep the plants on the dry side. Red spiders and mealy bugs are the most common pests.

Euphorbia

Three species of *Euphorbia* make good greenhouse plants, *Euphorbia fulgens,* the scarlet plume; *E. splendens,* crown of thorns; and *E. pulcherrima,* the poinsettia. The genus is a very large one with more than 1000 species. The flowers of all members lack petals and sepals and they would not be showy if it were not for the highly colored bracts. The bracts, modified leaves, of the poinsettia are conspicuous, the flowers hardly noticeable. Similarly, the bracts are the beautiful part of the flower cluster of the scarlet plume and crown of thorns. All of the euphorbias have a milky sap, and in certain species the juice is poisonous.

Scarlet Plume (*Euphorbia fulgens*). This is a tropical shrub, native to Mexico, with slender drooping branches. The leaves are long-petioled, bright green, and lance-shaped. The bracts of the flowers are orange-scarlet and most attractive. The flowers are borne on long clusters that are suitable for cutting. After cutting the spray, sear the cut end to stop the flow of the sap. The flowers last about three weeks after cutting.

The scarlet plume grows well with good light, a night temperature of 60 to 65 degrees, and when potted in a mixture of four parts loam and one of well-rotted manure. Periodic feedings are desirable. The plants are readily propagated from cuttings taken after April. The cuttings should have about three nodes and be inserted in a mixture of half sand and half peat with a bottom heat of 65 to 70 degrees. The plants should be pinched in order to secure bushy specimens.

The normal flowering season is December and January, but the plants may be flowered earlier by shading them with black cloth from 5 P.M. to 7 A.M. If shading is started July 15, the plants will flower in September; if started August 15, in late October; if started in September, in mid-December. In all cases the shading period should continue until the flower buds are well developed.

After flowering, plants which are not covered with black cloth should be kept on the dry side until April, when they should be repotted and brought into active growth. When sufficient new growth has been made, cuttings can be taken. Plants which have been shaded with black cloth may be kept growing. They will produce a second, short-stemmed crop of flowers in March or April.

Crown of Thorns (*Euphorbia splendens*). This plant blooms throughout the year, but most profusely in the winter. It is a shrub armed with spines. The leaves are few in number and clustered at the tips of the branches. The scarlet bracts, which look like petals but are not, furnish the color. Plants may be propagated by cuttings and grown under the same conditions as the scarlet plume.

Poinsettia (Euphorbia pulcherrima). The true flowers of poinsettia are small, greenish-yellow, and not especially attractive. The beauty lies in the brilliant bracts below the cluster of flowers. The species is native to Mexico and it was named for Joel R. Poinsett, a Charleston, South Carolina, physician. Poinsettias are not only excellent pot plants for the Christmas season but they are also good cut flowers. The flowers last well after cutting, at least ten days.

Poinsettias, like the scarlet plume and crown-of-thorns, are sun-loving plants and do not form their colored bracts well if shaded during autumn. During the summer months, good ventilation is desirable. Throughout the growing period avoid letting the temperature drop below 60 degrees. Also, keep the plants out of drafts and don't let the soil become either dry or waterlogged. Low temperatures, drafts, waterlogging, and drought cause the leaves to fall, which detracts from the beauty of the plants. A mixture of three parts soil, one part well-rotted manure, and one part sand with the addition of a 4-inch potful of superphosphate per bushel is an excellent potting medium.

After the plants have flowered, stop watering them and lay the plants on their sides under the bench, preferably where the temperature is 50 to 55 degrees. In April, cut the plants back so that each branch is about 8 inches long, then repot. Place the plants on the bench where the temperature is 60 to 65 degrees and encourage active growth by syringing them frequently and by watering the plants. After growth is active, water with a solution of 1 ounce of ammonium sulfate to 2 gallons of water. When the new growths are 8 to 12 inches long, the terminal 4 to 6 inches may be cut off and rooted. Cuttings are best made in the morning, and they should be kept in water for an hour to prevent excessive bleeding. The cut need not be made at a node. Just one cut is needed, the one made when the cutting is removed from the plant. You can take cuttings from the plants throughout the summer.

After the last cuttings are made, as late as September, the stock plants are grown on at 60 degrees until they flower. Plants grown from late cuttings will flower at the same time as those started earlier. Of course, the earlier the cutting is taken, the larger the plant at flowering time. At all times leave at least two leaves on each cut stem of the stock plant to make food for the new growths. The thicker the cutting, the larger the flower; avoid taking cuttings from spindly growths. One or two basal leaves may be removed from each cutting to facilitate insertion into the rooting medium.

Cuttings are best inserted into a mixture of one part of peat to two of sand, contained in 2½- or 3-inch pots. Firm the mixture in the pot, poke a hole with a dibble, insert the cutting, firm the medium, and then water. Cuttings may also be rooted in sand, contained in a bench. The sand should be firmed, and then the cuttings dibbled in, spacing them 3 inches apart in rows 5 inches apart. After inserting the cuttings, firm the sand about them, and water. Cuttings in pots or in a bench should be syringed three or four times each day for the first ten days. The cuttings require shade, which should be some distance above them. Don't place paper or cheesecloth directly on the cuttings. Cuttings root in about three weeks.

Commercial growers often do not carry over stock plants, but prefer to purchase them each year. When the stock plants arrive, usually in early April, they are potted, and as the growths come on, cuttings are made. One stock plant will yield thirty-five to sixty cuttings.

After the cuttings in a bench are rooted, they should be potted in 2½-inch or 3-inch pots in the soil previously mentioned. Water thoroughly after potting and keep the plants shaded until they are established. Frequent syringing is beneficial at this time.

Each plant will bear one flower if not pinched, and more than one if pinched. The top of a young plant may be removed and rooted, but make sure at least two leaves remain on the parent plant. The removal of the top of the plant with several leaves is known as a hard pinch, and plants should not be hard pinched after August 1. The rolling off of just the tip of the stem is called a soft pinch. Like the hard pinch, the soft pinch promotes branching. Soft pinching may be practiced until about mid-August. Don't pinch plants that are not well-established.

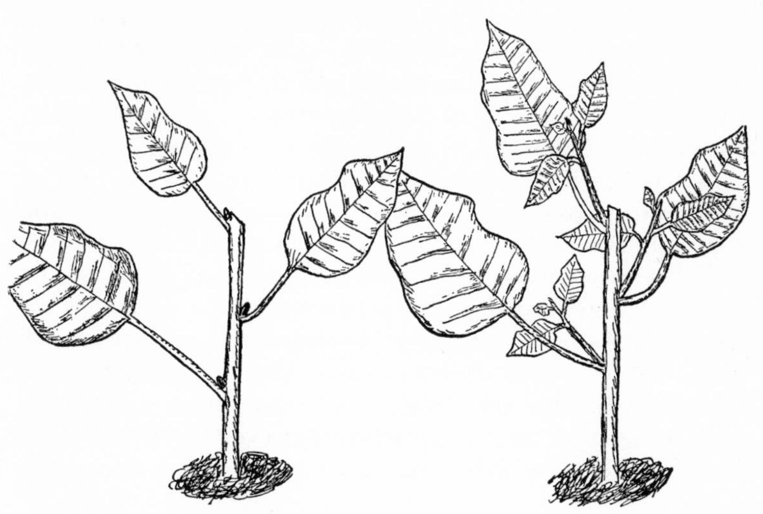

Left: a pinched plant. *Right:* the plant at a later date. Three branches developed.

The plants should be repotted as necessary. They may be grown singly in pots, or a number of plants out of 2½-inch or 3-inch pots may be planted in a pot. Placing two or more plants in an azalea pot is called panning; this is generally done in September, but may be done as late as early November. A 6-inch azalea pot is about the right size, but larger pots can be used. Three or four pinched or unpinched plants may be placed in a 6-inch pot. An 8-inch pot will hold about 6 plants. Select uniform plants for each pot and avoid breaking the ball of soil. Rooted cuttings made late in the summer may be panned directly. Some commercial growers plunge an empty 2½-inch pot in the center of the pot. Just before Christmas this pot is replaced with a fern from a 2½-inch pot. Pinched plants with two or three stems may be grown singly in 4- or

5-inch standard pots and smaller plants from late cuttings will flower in 3-inch pots.

Immediately after panning or repotting, water the plants. Throughout the growing period neither overwater nor underwater. Either practice will cause leaf drop. The plants should be grown at a night temperature of 60 to 62 degrees without drafts. It may be necessary to fertilize the plants once between the time of panning and November 15, when the color of the bracts should be showing. After the color appears, fertilize the plants every two or three weeks, using a complete fertilizer dissolved in water.

Throughout the season, watch for mealy bugs, scale, and root aphids and control them. Poinsettias may become infected with a virus disease which causes a mottling of the leaves. Plants showing symptoms of this mosaic disease should be burned. Occasionally poinsettias get a bacterial disease which results in watersoaked longitudinal streaks on the stem. In time the streaks crack open and a yellow ooze containing countless bacteria becomes evident. Plants with this disease should be burned.

CHAPTER 21

FLOWERING AND FOLIAGE PLANTS OF VARIOUS FAMILIES

In the previous chapters we considered interesting families of plants, each of which included a number of kinds that grow well in a 60-degree greenhouse. There are other noteworthy families with only one or two species in each that interest us. Because of the limited kinds in these families we shall list the genera alphabetically instead of grouping them in families. Among the plants grown chiefly for their flowers we will consider azalea, bougainvillea, browallia, gardenia, hydrangea, impatiens, kalanchoë, and strelitzia. Foliage plants of interest are draceana, fittonia, maranta, peperomia, pilea, and sansevieria.

Azaleas

Greenhouse azaleas are handsome evergreen plants that flower profusely in the winter and spring. There are many varieties, some bearing single flowers, others double ones. The flower color ranges from white through many shades of pink to red. Azaleas are in the genus *Rhododendron,* a member of the heath family, Ericaceae, which also includes heather, arbutus, mountain laurel, cranberry, and huckleberry.

To get a start purchase during the autumn plants which have the flower buds well formed. When you receive the plants, unpack them and soak the balls in water until they are wet through. Let each ball drain and then pot the plant in a 5- or 6-inch azalea pot. Azaleas should not be overpotted. If you know that the soil in your region is acid, mix one part of soil with one of peat moss and use this mixture. If the soil is not acid use only peat moss or humus from a pine forest. Azaleas thrive only in acid soil; in alkaline soil they are weak, flower poorly, and have yellow leaves. Rainwater is ideal for azaleas. If you use tap water that is alkaline, a wise precaution is to water the plants at two- or three-week intervals with a solution of one ounce of iron sulfate in two gallons of water.

To have azaleas in flower by Christmas obtain plants which have been raised on the West Coast. Such plants will have well developed flower buds by early fall, whereas those grown in the midwest will not have mature buds until later in the season. Certain varieties of West Coast azaleas will flower by Christmas if they are placed in a 60-degree house the first week of November.

Among the varieties which are suitable for early season forcing and their flower colors are Paul Schame, salmon-pink; Jersey Belle, coral salmon; Dorothy Gish, deep salmon; Alaska, white; Constance, cerise pink; Pink Ruffles, deep rose pink. Varieties suitable for later flowering are Jean Haerens, rosy carmine; Coral Bells, coral pink; Snow, white; Pink Pearl, salmon-rose; Salmon Perfection, salmon; and Niobe, white.

Flower buds of these azaleas do not develop when the temperature is 45 degrees. Hence, flowering can be delayed by keeping the plants at this temperature. You can then move them, a few at a time, from the cool place into the 60 degree greenhouse, thus obtaining a sequence of flowering. The cool spot used to retard flowering may be either a cool greenhouse or a cool, well-lighted basement room. The room must be lighted, otherwise the leaves will turn yellow and fall off. If there is not enough natural light, place a 150-watt lamp 2 feet above the plants and keep it turned on for twelve hours a day. In January and February, the plants flower six weeks after they are brought into the 60-degree house. During the brighter spring months, when the days are longer, only three weeks are required for flowering. These times for flowering are average ones; some varieties come into blossom in a shorter time than do others.

When the plants are in the 60-degree house and the flower buds are developing, remove new shoots that develop below the flower clusters. Keep them watered carefully. They must not be allowed to become dry, nor should they become waterlogged. Daily syringing promotes the development of fine flowers.

The plants can be grown for the next and subsequent years. Overhaul the plants after flowering, just as the new growths begin. After knocking a plant from its pot, remove some of the old peat and then pot in the same size pot or one slightly larger. Generally plants can be grown in the same size pot for two years. It is essential to pot firmly and to provide good drainage.

When the plants are established and actively growing, they benefit from fertilization with ammonium sulfate and iron sulfate prepared by adding 1 ounce of ammonium sulfate and 1 ounce of iron sulfate to 2 gallons of water. Water the plants with this solution every two or three weeks. The plants will also benefit from two applications of 4-12-4 fertilizer during the summer.

When the danger of frost is over in the spring, move the plants to a cold frame. They may either be removed from their pots and planted or they may be left in their pots, which should be plunged into peat moss. Shade the frame with lath shading until August 1, after which remove the shade and allow the plants to have full sunlight to check vegetative growth and promote the formation of flower buds. Keep the plants well watered throughout the summer and syringe them frequently.

If you have planted the azaleas, dig them up and pot them in early September. At this time the plunged ones should also be lifted. Then move them into the greenhouse and grow them for three weeks at a temperature of 55 degrees. During this period the flower buds will complete their development, after which the plants may be kept at a temperature of 45 degrees until it is time to force them. The first batch can be brought into the 60-degree house in early November and others at later dates.

Azaleas are propagated by grafting and from cuttings. The cuttings are made in May and rooted in a mixture of two parts sand and one of peat moss with bottom heat of 65 degrees. The cuttings should be shaded, and syringed frequently. They will begin to root in four or five weeks. The rooted cuttings are best moved into flats of peat. When the plants crowd each other, transplant them into other flats of peat, this time spacing them 4 inches by 4 inches. Young plants do better in flats than in pots because moisture is more uniform. From the second flat the plants are moved into pots. Young plants should be kept growing all of the time, by keeping them where the night temperature is 60 degrees. As the plants develop, pinch them at intervals to produce a bushy, compact plant and give them a complete acid fertilizer periodically.

Among the insect pests attacking azaleas are the red spider, thrip, mealy bug, leaf miner, and leafroller.

Bougainvillea

Bougainvillea (in the family Nyctaginaceae) is a showy plant that bears panicles of beautifully colored, leafy bracts in the center of which are the small flowers, generally white in color. Bougainvillea thrives best in a 60-degree greenhouse. However, we know a number of gardeners who have success with them in a 50-degree house. They are easily increased from stem cuttings made in the spring. The plants will be ready for 6-inch pots by fall and will flower during the coming winter or spring. Pot the plants in a mixture half loam and half leaf mold or peat moss. Prune annually when flowering is over by cutting back each new growth so that 3 or 4 inches remain on each branch. Cut off all thin and weak growths.

B. glabra and its many varieties make excellent pot plants when thus kept small, although they grow to a height of ten feet out-of-doors in warm climates.

Browallia

Of the six species of this South American genus of the potato family (Solanaceae), one species, *Browallia speciosa major,* is commonly grown in greenhouses. This species flowers during winter and early spring, giving blooms of a rich deep blue that have a white throat and are about 2 inches across. It is also suitable for outdoor bedding. Sow seeds in July for winter flowering plants. Barely cover them with soil. Transplant six seedlings to a 6-inch pot, in which the plants will flower, or pot the seedlings singly in 2½- or 3-inch pots and later shift them into larger ones. Browallia does well in a light soil of medium fertility, and with a night temperature of 60 degrees. The plants should be pinched about three times to encourage a bushy habit. Seeds may be sown in February for plants to set out in the garden. These plants can be moved back into the greenhouse in the fall.

Dracaena

Dracaenas, members of the lily family (Liliaceae), are grown for their ornamental foliage. The leaves are sword-shaped in some species, broader in others. A number of species have variegated leaves. They grow well in a greenhouse with a night temperature between 60 and 65 degrees and with plentiful moisture. During the brighter months of the year they should be furnished light shade. Dracaenas should not be overpotted. They grow well in a mixture of three-fourths loam and one-fourth peat or leaf mold.

A few species of dracaena may be started from seed and all may be propagated by air layerage or from cuttings. The top of the plant may be cut off and rooted. Cut the rest of the old stem into pieces about 2 inches long and embed them horizontally just below the surface of a medium of half sand and half peat. Or, if you prefer, embed the entire cane in this mixture without cutting it into segments. Shoots develop rapidly from the whole cane or the pieces if the temperature is kept at 80 degrees and the humidity is high. You should use a heated propagating case if you wish quick development. One or more shoots will develop from each cutting. Remove the shoots from the cane whether they have rooted or not and pot them in a mixture of three-fourths loam and one-fourth leaf mold or peat.

Some favorite species of dracaena are *Dracaena indivisa* (more correctly, *Cordyline indivisa*), *D. fragrans, D. godseffiana, D. goldieana,* and *D. sanderiana. Dracaena indivisa* has dark green leaves about 2 to 3 feet long. There are a number of named varieties of this species which have more distinctive foliage, among them Doucettii, with variegated leaves, Veitchii Superba, with a bright red midrib, and Atropurpurea, whose foliage is a deep reddish brown. *Dracaena fragrans* grows almost too rapidly for the small greenhouse; it has arching corn-like leaves about 2 feet long and 3 inches wide. *Dracaena godseffiana* has a branching habit and bears deep green leaves, about 4 inches long, which are irregularly spotted with yellow or white. It is indeed a decorative plant. *Dracaena goldieana* is another fine foliage plant with glossy green leaves conspicuously spotted and banded with white. The leaves are about 8 inches long and 4 inches wide. *Dracaena sanderiana* bears leaves about 8 inches long and 1 inch wide, and they are glossy green, broadly margined with white.

Fittonia

Fittonia, a member of the Acanthaceae family, is a compact plant of dwarf habit with beautifully netted leaves. *Fittonia argyroneura* is characterized by bright green leaves with conspicuous silver-white veins. *F. verschaffeltii* has deep green leaves with red veins. Fittonias are easily propagated from stem cuttings rooted in a medium of half sand and half peat. The plants grow well in soil which is rich in peat or leaf mold. A mixture of one part soil and one part leaf mold is good.

Gardenia

This beautiful evergreen shrub (in the family Rubiaceae) with glossy foliage is prized for its delightfully fragrant, waxen, white flowers. *Gardenia Veitchii* and such variations of *G. grandiflora* as Belmont, Hadley, and McLellan's 23 are favorites for growing in the 60-degree house. Gardenia was named for a South Carolina physician, Alexander Garden.

Gardenias are propagated by cuttings taken from November through March. Make cuttings, 3 to 5 inches long, from healthy plants and root them in sand or in a mixture of sand and peat. Treatment with Rootone or Hormodin hastens rooting. A bottom heat of 70 degrees and a close atmosphere are desirable.

The rooted cuttings are potted in 2½-inch pots in a mixture of equal parts of loam and peat moss. If the loam is alkaline, add a tablespoon of iron sulfate to each bushel of the mixture. When the roots fill the pots, shift the plants into 4-inch pots, using the same mixture. By August the plants should be ready for shifting into 6-inch pots. A high humidity, a night temperature of 60 degrees, and a uniform water supply promote good growth. Applications of iron sulfate at two- or three-week intervals are desirable if the soil tends to be alkaline or if the water is hard. Dissolve one ounce of iron sulfate in two gallons of water and water with this solution. In summer, occasional applications of 4-12-4 fertilizer promote good growth. During the bright months light shade is needed and the plants should be syringed frequently. Remove the shade gradually, beginning in September. During winter, monthly applications of ammonium sulfate (prepared by dissolving 1 ounce of ammonium sulfate in 2 gallons of water) and periodic applications of iron sulfate are beneficial.

Gardenia plants can be grown for several years. However, the largest flowers of the best quality are produced by one-year plants. In May one-year-old plants should be cut back to 24 to 30 inches, and repotted.

Gardenias can be cantankerous plants, often dropping their flower buds. Temperatures too high or too low, and an inadequate or excess supply of water may bring about flower drop. Mealy bugs and red spiders can be serious pests. Frequent syringings are helpful in controlling them.

Hydrangea

Hydrangea macrophylla, a member of the saxifrage family (Saxifragaceae), can be forced for early- or late-spring flowering. Certain varieties bear blue flowers; others have white, pink, or red blooms. Merveille and Strafford are good dark pink varieties; Rosabelle, a light pink. Regula and Engels White are good whites. Kunert, Gertrude Glahn, Helen Merritt, and Rosabelle are naturally rose or pink, but the flower color can be changed to blue by adding aluminum sulfate to the soil.

Hydrangea plants may be purchased in the fall. Pot them, using a soil consisting of two parts loam, one of leaf mold, and one of peat, plus a 4-inch pot of superphosphate per wheelbarrow of soil. After the plants are potted keep them in a cold frame until early November, when the plants should be placed in storage until late December. A dark place where the temperature is 40 to 45 degrees is ideal for storage. Perhaps you have a basement room at such a temperature or a frame which can be covered with boards, heavy cloth, or straw mats to exclude light. The temperature in the frame should never drop below 20 degrees; if it does the plants will be killed. The plants will do reasonably well if stored under the bench in a cool greenhouse, but the other storage methods are preferred. During the storage period clean up the leaves as they fall from the plants and never let the pots become dry. You can bring the plants into the greenhouse from late December on. Bringing them in at intervals gives a sequence of flowers. Plants brought in the last week of December should flower at Easter, those brought in during mid-January on Mother's Day. When the plants are in bloom, provide shade from strong sun.

Until growth begins, the greenhouse temperature should be 50 to 55 degrees. Then grow the plants at 60 degrees. Frequent syringing produces longer stems and better-quality flowers. When the pots are filled with roots an occasional application of fertilizer is beneficial. If the soil has good reserves of phosphorus and potassium, you need only fer-

The magenta-flowered hybrid Epiphyllum (Prof. Ebert) at the left is suitable for small pots. (Ladislaus Cutak photo) *Above:* succulents from several families are growing side by side in this bench.

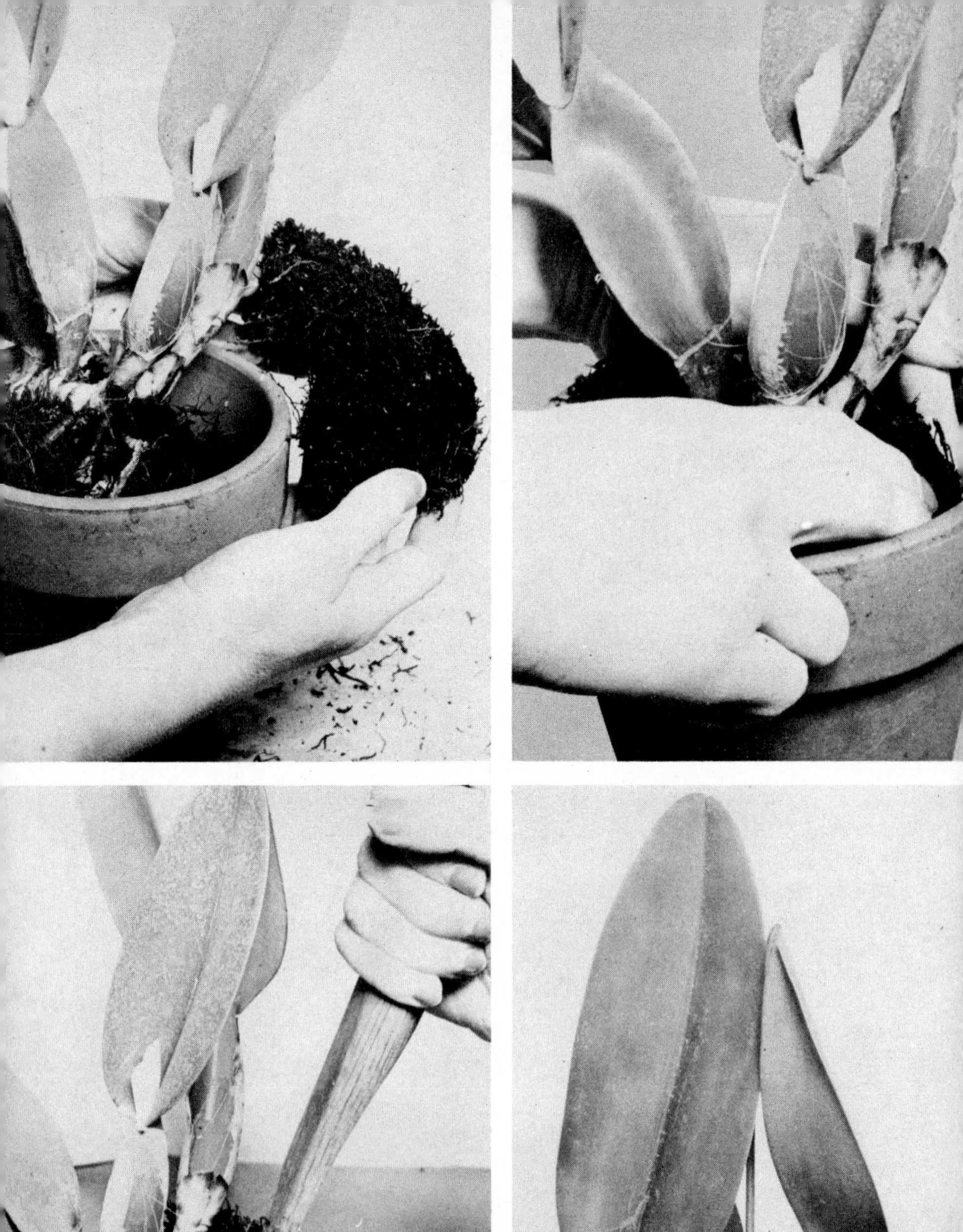
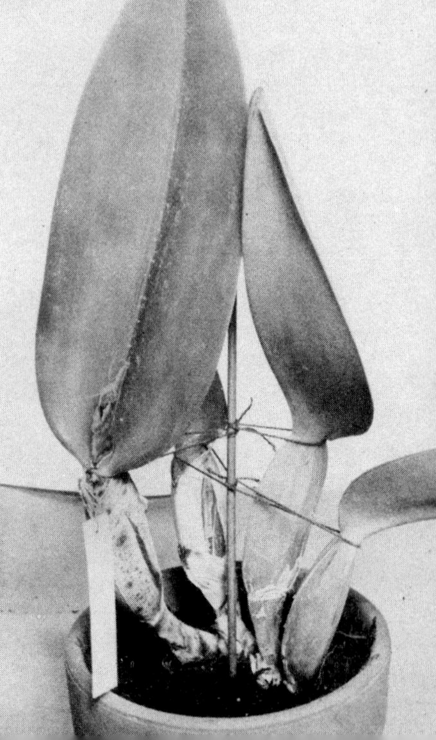
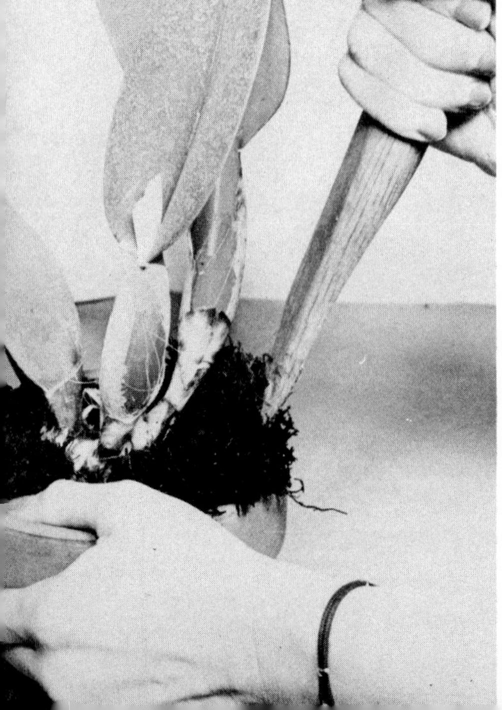

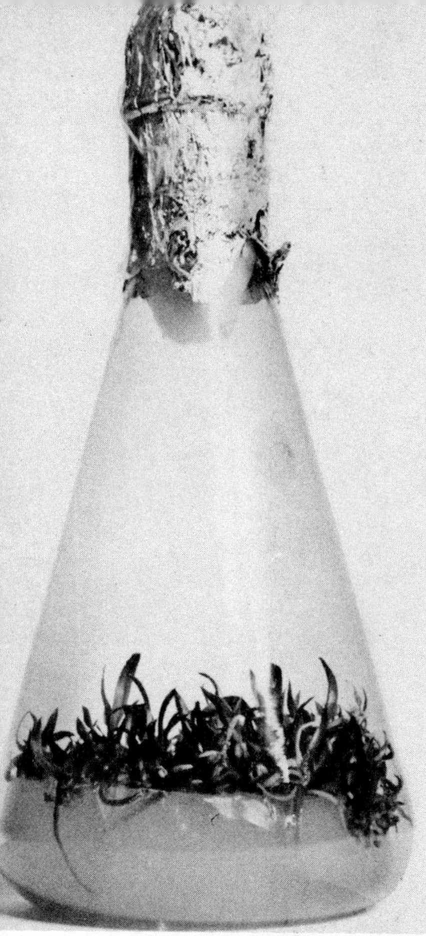

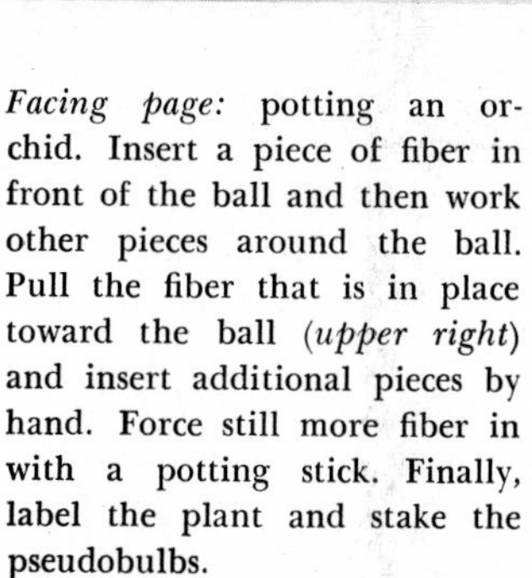

Facing page: potting an orchid. Insert a piece of fiber in front of the ball and then work other pieces around the ball. Pull the fiber that is in place toward the ball (*upper right*) and insert additional pieces by hand. Force still more fiber in with a potting stick. Finally, label the plant and stake the pseudobulbs.

This page: the seedlings in the flask are ready for potting. *Right:* the "sandwich" technique of potting seedlings. Lay seedlings on a piece of osmunda fiber, cover with another piece, and then insert into a pot. Repeat until the pot is full.

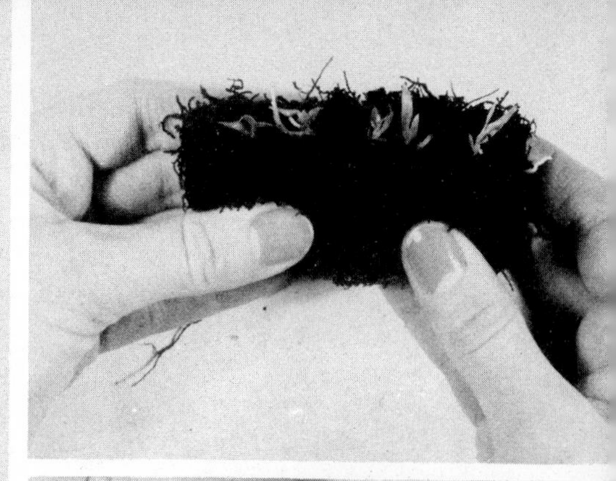

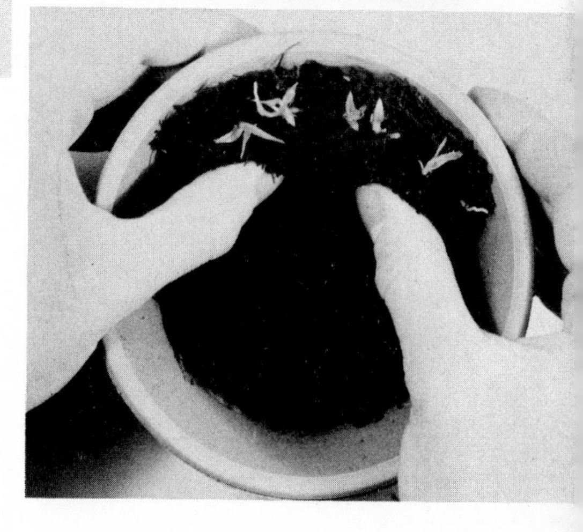

Interesting cacti for the greenhouse: *upper left, Astrophytum asterias,* from Mexico. *Upper right: Echinocereus chisoensis,* from Texas. *Lower left: Gymnocalycium mihanovichii,* from Mexico. *Lower right: Mammillaria microcarpa,* from Arizona. (Ladislaus Cutak photos)

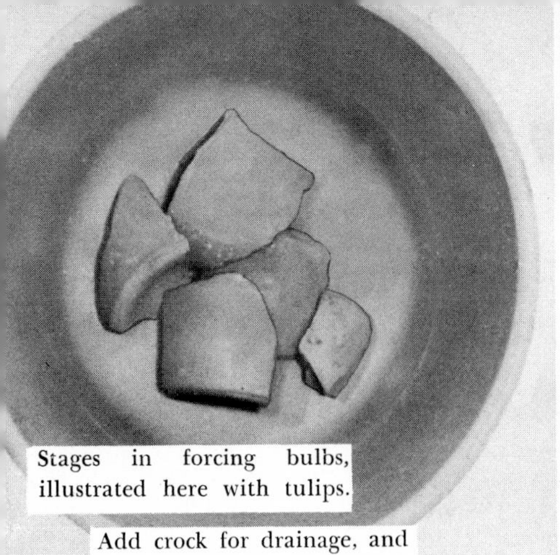

Stages in forcing bulbs, illustrated here with tulips.

Add crock for drainage, and then some soil.

Space the bulbs, fill with soil,

and firm.

Water thoroughly

Place pots in trench.

When storage period is over bring pots into greenhouse.

King Alfred daffodils.

These hyacinths were maintained in a trench outdoors, brought in, and then placed under a darkened bench where it was warm. The plants have just been removed from the dark and placed on the bench.

tilize with iron and nitrogen, both of which will produce a rich green color of the foliage. One ounce of ammonium sulfate dissolved in 2 gallons of water and applied at intervals will give the plants ample nitrogen. For iron, use a solution made by adding 1 ounce of iron sulfate to 2 gallons of water.

To obtain blue hydrangeas, add aluminum sulfate to the soil after the plants are growing actively and have good root action. Add a teaspoon of aluminum sulfate to each 6-inch pot and then water it into the soil. Repeat in about two weeks. Three to seven applications are necessary to give blue flowers. All pink and rose-colored varieties will bear blue flowers if given aluminum sulfate. Of course, white-flowered ones cannot be changed, because they produce no pigment, and therefore do not contain the chemical basis for color.

When the plants are through flowering, cut the flowering shoots back to two joints and repot. When danger of frost is over the plants can be moved outdoors. The pots may be plunged in sand or soil in a cold frame equipped with lath shading. Partial shade promotes vigorous growth. The plants should be well supplied with water and fertilized every two weeks, using ammonium sulfate and 4-12-4 fertilizer, alternately. Biweekly applications of iron sulfate may be needed to prevent yellowing. The plants can be pinched early in the summer, but not after July 10. Remove the lath shading on August 1 and thereafter grow the plants with full sun, which promotes the setting of flower buds. In September the plants may be repotted if necessary and transferred to a cold frame where the temperature does not drop below 20 degrees. In November place them in a cool, dark storage place. Bring them into the greenhouse at intervals, beginning in late December.

Hydrangeas are easily propagated from stem cuttings or by leafbud cuttings, rooted in sand or in a mixture of two parts sand to one of peat. Cuttings are made in February or March, using the blind wood (that which will not produce flowers) of older plants. Rooted cuttings are potted in 3-inch pots, then into 5- or 6-inch ones in May. The plants are grown with a temperature of 60 degrees. They should be pinched in May. The young plants are placed in a frame during summer and the same cultural conditions are followed as for older plants; that is, remove shade in August, place in cold frame in September and in storage in November. Plants started in February will flower in spring of the following year. Rooted cuttings are sold by some supply companies for spring delivery and are inexpensive.

Red spiders, thrips, and aphids are pests that attack hydrangeas.

Impatiens

Few, if any, plants are more bountiful in flowering than impatiens, also called Sultana. The plants are always in flower. The bright red or orange iridescent flowers contrast beautifully with the glossy deep green leaves. Impatiens grows well with light or dense shade. We grow them on the bench along with cattleya orchids, but some plants have scattered their seeds under the bench. Here plants developed without care and here they thrive. Impatiens are started from seeds or from cuttings. They grow well in a mixture of half loam and half peat moss.

Kalanchoë

This is a large genus of succulent plants of the family Crassulaceae. We will consider some species of kalanchoë in Chapter 22. Of the many species of kalanchoë, one, *K. blossfeldiana,* is an attractive flowering plant. This species bears many small crimson flowers that last a long time.

The plants may be propagated from leaf or stem cuttings taken in January, but the choicest plants are raised from seed. Sow seeds in the spring for flowering the following winter and spring. Move the seedlings into 2½-inch pots. When the young plants are ready for shifting move three of them into a 6-inch azalea pot, or pot them singly in 4-inch pots. A soil consisting of two parts of sandy loam and one of peat moss or leaf mold is suitable. Kalanchoës grow rapidly at a temperature of 60 degrees, but slowly at 50 degrees. The plants benefit from occasional feedings.

The normal flowering time is spring. However, you can have them in flower from October on by artificially shortening the days. Plants placed in a chamber made of black cloth from 5 P.M. to 7 A.M. each day from July 20 until September 20 will flower in October; those shaded in like manner from August 15 to October 1 will flower in December. Kalanchoës are perennial, but two-year-old plants are not so attractive as those one year old.

Mealy bugs and red spiders are the most serious pests. Don't use DDT on kalanchoës. It causes severe injury to the foliage and may kill the plants.

Maranta

Maranta, a member of the arrowroot family (Marantaceae), often called the "prayer" plant, is a tropical American genus of about twenty-three species. They grow well with a night temperature of 60 degrees, require shade during the entire year and plenty of water during their growing period. During winter the plants should be kept somewhat on the dry side. A soil made up of peat and loam in equal parts with some leaf mold and sand suits them. The pots should be well drained. Marantas are increased by dividing the crowns in the spring just before growth begins.

Two frequently grown species are *Maranta arundinacea variegata* and *M. leuconeura.* The former grows about a foot tall and has oblong green leaves variegated with yellow. The leaves of *M. leuconeura* are grayish-green, velvety, with large decorative purple spots. They are broadly elliptical and about 6 inches long. Other species sometimes grown are *M. splendida* and *M. bicolor.*

Peperomia

Peperomia, a member of the pepper family (Piperaceae), is an enormous genus of tropical plants grown for their beautiful foliage. Of the 500 species, two are very popular, *Peperomia sandersii* variety *argyreia* and *P. obtusifolia.* Peperomias thrive in a warm greenhouse with a minimum night temperature of 60 degrees, and with shade during the bright months. They grow well in a mixture of half loam and half peat moss with the addition of some well-rotted manure. During their active growing season, which usually begins in February, they require a good supply of water, but during their inactive period be careful neither to overwater nor to let them get completely dry. The plants can be quickly increased by leaf cuttings rooted in sand with a bottom temperature of about 75 degrees.

Peperomia sandersii var. *argyreia,* commonly called Watermelon Begonia, is one of the most beautiful species. This is a stemless plant with heart-shaped, fleshy leaves, and red petioles about 4 to 8 inches long. The leaves have attractive silver bands alternating with green stripes. *P. obtusifolia* bears thick green leaves on erect or semitrailing stems. A variegated variety of this species has cream-colored markings on the foliage.

Pilea

An attractive member of this genus is *Pilea cadierei,* the "aluminum" plant. It is dainty and graceful, and adds a striking note to a group of foliage plants. The oval variegated leaves have the appearance of being quilted and brushed with strokes of aluminum paint. They require a mixture of one part soil and one part peat or leaf mold. They must be kept carefully watered and not be allowed to become dry. A half-shaded location suits them nicely.

Sansevieria

These are bold plants of the lily family (Liliaceae) which have stiff marbled leaves. The plants are grown chiefly for their distinctive forms and attractive leaves. They produce conspicuous, slender-tubed flowers of white or greenish-white color, sometimes tinted with purple or pink. The flowers are fragrant, short-lived, and generally open in the evening. The genus is a tropical one containing more than fifty described varieties. Many species grow in tropical Africa, and others in India, Burma, and Ceylon. Some species are cultivated for their valuable fibers.

Sansevierias, commonly called Bowstring Hemp, Snake Plant, Leopard Lily, or Mother-in-Law's Tongue, grow well in an even mixture of loam, sand, and peat moss or leaf mold. They can survive prolonged periods of drought but make better growth when watered regularly. During the brighter months of the year they should be shaded. They grow well in the 60-degree house. Sansevierias are propagated by seed, rootstock divisions, or leaf cuttings. To increase a plant by leaf cuttings, cut a leaf into pieces 3 inches long and insert about half the length into sand. In a month or two, one or more young rooted plants will form at the base of each piece. The plant, plus the old leaf, may be potted, or the new plant may be severed from the parent segment and potted.

Among the choice species of *Sansevieria* are *S. trifasciata* (usually sold and called *S. zeylanica), S. ehrenbergii, S. aethiopica, S. arborescens,* and *S. hahnii. Sansevieria trifasciata* is a stemless plant bearing two to six erect, leathery leaves 3 to 4 feet long. The leaves have alternate bandings of silver and dark olive green. *S. ehrenbergii* produces a short stem which is completely hidden by the clasping leaves. The five to nine bluish-green leaves, with conspicuous white edges, spread out in a fanwise manner. *S. aethiopica* is a stemless plant with pointed bluish-green leaves about 18 inches long and 1 inch wide. *Sansevieria arborescens* has a stem that gets to be 4 feet high. The stem is covered with spreading, twisting, grass-green leaves. The leaves vary from 5 to 18 inches in length, and they are thick with a wavy white margin. *Sansevieria hahnii* has comparatively short leaves arranged in a rosette.

Strelitzia

Strelitzia, the bird-of-paradise, is in the banana family (Musaceae). It is a native of South Africa and is a good companion plant for orchids, begonias, African violets, and gloxinias. All of these plants grow well in a shaded 60-degree house.

Strelitzia is well worth growing. The foliage is attractive and the flowers, a mixture of orange and blue, are most exotic and striking. The flowering season is winter and spring.

The plants grow quite large, about 5 feet tall, so unless your greenhouse is large limit yourself to one or a few plants. You can purchase young plants from nurserymen or start them from seeds, planted singly in small pots plunged in peat. Those started from seed will flower in four or five years. As the plants grow repot them as necessary. By the time flowering size is reached the plants should be in 8- or 10-inch pots. Provide good drainage and use a mixture of half loam, one-fourth well decayed manure, and one-fourth peat. Periodic waterings with fertilizer are beneficial. The plants should be kept well watered. If grown in small pots and with insufficient water the plants become stunted and flower sparsely or not at all.

CHAPTER 22

CACTI AND OTHER SUCCULENTS

DESERTS ARE FASCINATING places with their blue skies, bright days, interesting animals, and strange plants. The plants are exposed to scorching sun interrupted only occasionally by heavy rains. Following a rain the plants plump up, grow, and flower. Many of the desert plants have extensive root systems and lack leaves or have small ones. After a rain, the extensive roots absorb water which is then stored in fleshy stems or fleshy leaves. The small leaf area cuts down evaporation, and results in a slow rate of foodmaking and therefore growth, enabling us to grow such plants for many years in small pots. Plants with fleshy stems or leaves or both are called *succulents*.

The strange and varied forms of the succulents, the rare beauty of some of their flowers, and their remarkable adaptations for desert life make them appealing plants. Building up a collection of these interesting plants has become almost a mania for some greenhouse gardeners. There are those who have designed desert landscapes of great charm in their greenhouses, even devoting the whole greenhouse to their collection. You may wish to make these plants your hobby and use your greenhouse only for them. Or perhaps you will want just a few. You can raise them in pots. Then if you want a more natural setting you can plunge the pots in sand or gravel so that the pots do not show. A few attractive rocks artfully spaced will add to the naturalness of the scene. If you wish, you can move the plants outdoors in the summer and have a desert arrangement in part of your garden. Of course, you can plant cacti and other succulents directly in a bench where they can remain year after year.

Deserts are not the only places we find succulents. Strangely enough, some succulents grow in tropical rain forests which are always humid and moist. Here they grow on trunks or branches of trees or on rocks, where they are shut off from a supply of ground water. Plants which grow perched on trunks or branches of trees are called *epiphytes*. They are rooted in small accumulations of debris. During a rain and shortly thereafter water is available, but soon the scant debris in which they are rooted dries out and the plants are subject to drought. In the interval between rains, however, the plants use the water stored in their fleshy stems or leaves. Among the cacti which are epiphytes are the orchid cactus, the Christmas cactus, and *Rhipsalis*.

Cacti are the most abundant succulents of our deserts and those of South America. But there are plants other than cacti which have the succulent habit, and in the deserts of India and Africa they are the dominant plants. We know that in the animal world unrelated animals have evolved mechanisms that enable them to carry on similar activities. Thus insects, birds, and bats can fly. Unrelated plants have evolved similar forms and structures which enable them to cope with desert conditions: thus we find plants of a succulent habit in the cactus, lily, amaryllis, crassula, milkweed, and spurge families. Let us consider some families which have members with succulent habits.

The cactus family—Cactaceae

You have only to visit a greenhouse of a cactus fancier to realize the great variety of cacti. Some, such as the Saguaro cactus, grow to great heights; others, the Peyote for example, to less than an inch. The stems of certain species are globular in shape; those of others are cylindrical, triangular, quadrangular, or flattened. The stems may be smooth, channeled, or tubercled. The flowers vary in color, time of opening, and in size. The night-blooming cereus has flowers a foot long, while those of the mistletoe cactus are only a quarter of an inch across. The spines are interesting, too. Some cacti are formidably armed; others lack spines. Even though cacti are diverse in shape, size, and spine pattern, they all have a number of features in common. None have expanded foliage leaves, and foodmaking is carried on by the green stems which also store water.

The flowers of all cacti are alike in many ways. With only one exception, the flowers are borne singly. The flowers of all cacti have many petals and many stamens; both the petals and stamens arise from the top of the ovary.

In our greenhouses we should not try to simulate exactly the environment of a desert. On the desert the day temperatures may exceed 100 degrees on many days, yet the plants will thrive better in a greenhouse if day temperatures are kept down to 70 degrees. A night temperature of 60 degrees is ideal for many. In their native homes cacti withstand the full glare of the sun, but in our greenhouses full sun during the summer might burn them. To avoid excessive temperatures in summer, light shade is needed.

We have learned that a soil with more humus than desert soils contain makes for better growth. Cacti thrive when potted or planted in a mixture of equal parts of sand, loam, and leaf mold. This mixture is sufficiently porous that stagnant water will not remain around the roots. The roots may be confined to small pots; 3- and 4-inch ones are ample for small plants. When potting, put pieces from a broken pot over the drainage hole and then a layer of gravel, followed by some charcoal or moss. Then pot the plants with the mixture suggested above, over which you may place a layer of fine gravel. You had better wear leather gloves when you handle the plants. Newly potted cacti are best watered from below, but subsequent waterings are done with a hose or can.

January to March is a good time to pot most cacti. Some kinds may need to be repotted annually, but others can go for several years without repotting. If the plants are thriving, don't be too anxious to repot them—let well enough alone.

Although cacti survive long periods of drought in their native homes, when grown in pots they may be injured if their roots remain dry for a long time during the growing season. In winter most cacti are dormant; during this season let the soil become nearly dry before watering again. A weekly watering is sufficient for most kinds. Overwatering during winter can be harmful, because it may bring about a soft watery rot that may be fatal. When spring comes, growth will start and then the plants should be watered more frequently. In the summer when the plants are actively growing, give them ample water and do not permit the roots to become dry.

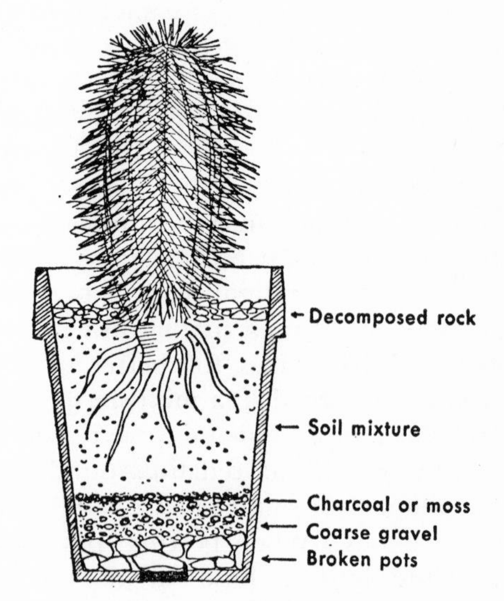

A correctly potted cactus plant. (From *Cactus and Succulents,* by Scott E. Haselton; Abbey Garden Press)

Cacti are increased by offsets, by stem cuttings, and by seeds. Some kinds produce offshoots which may be removed and placed on sand until they root, after which they are potted. Stem cuttings root quickly. If the plant is a branching type, break or cut off a branch at the socket. If the variety does not produce offsets or branches but only a single stem, you can cut off the upper 2 or 3 inches of the stem and root it. After the cuttings are made, allow the cut or broken surface to dry for a few days until a corky layer forms. Then insert the base of the cutting in sand with the base just a little below the surface. If the cutting is slender and floppy, fasten it to a wooden stake with rubber bands. Water the cuttings sparingly at first, just enough to keep them from shriveling. When the cuttings are rooted, move them into small pots.

Many fanciers of cacti start plants from seeds and are always hoping that some unusual form will appear among the offspring. Add drainage material to a pot; then fill the pot to within an inch of the top with sterilized sandy soil. Firm the soil and sow the seeds. Then cover the seeds with a quarter-inch layer of a mixture of sand and pea-sized gravel. Damping-off is the greatest hazard to success in raising cacti from seed. We recommend the use of sterilized soil and treatment of the seed with Semesan. After sowing, water with a fine spray. The pot should be covered with glass and paper until germination occurs; then remove them. The seedlings of most genera will appear in about ten days. When spines are evident on the seedlings, transplant them to flats. The plants may remain in the flats from one to several years, depending on the rapidity of growth. Eventually the plants are moved into pots.

Many fanciers of cacti produce novel forms by grafting. For example, a ball-shaped cactus may be grafted on the top of a cactus which has a straight columnar stem, or even several different kinds may be grafted to the top of a stem. You may wish to graft a Christmas cactus on the top of some high-stemmed variety so that the flowers may be displayed more attractively. Grafting of cacti is easily done and nearly always successful; even distantly related cacti can be grafted together. We call the part above the graft union the *scion,* and the part below the union the *stock.*

One of the simplest ways to graft cacti is to cut the stock off horizontally at the desired height, and similarly slice off the scion. Place the cut surface of the scion on that of the stock. Use a few cactus spines to hold the scion in place, and then

Grafting cacti. *a,* cut the grafting stock; *b,* trim the rough edges from the stock; *c,* cut off a scion from the desired plant and place it on the stock (*d*). Secure the scion to the stock with rubber bands anchored to a spine or extending under the pot (*e*). Sketch *f* shows how Christmas cactus is grafted to *Pereskia* stock. (From *Cactus and Succulents.*)

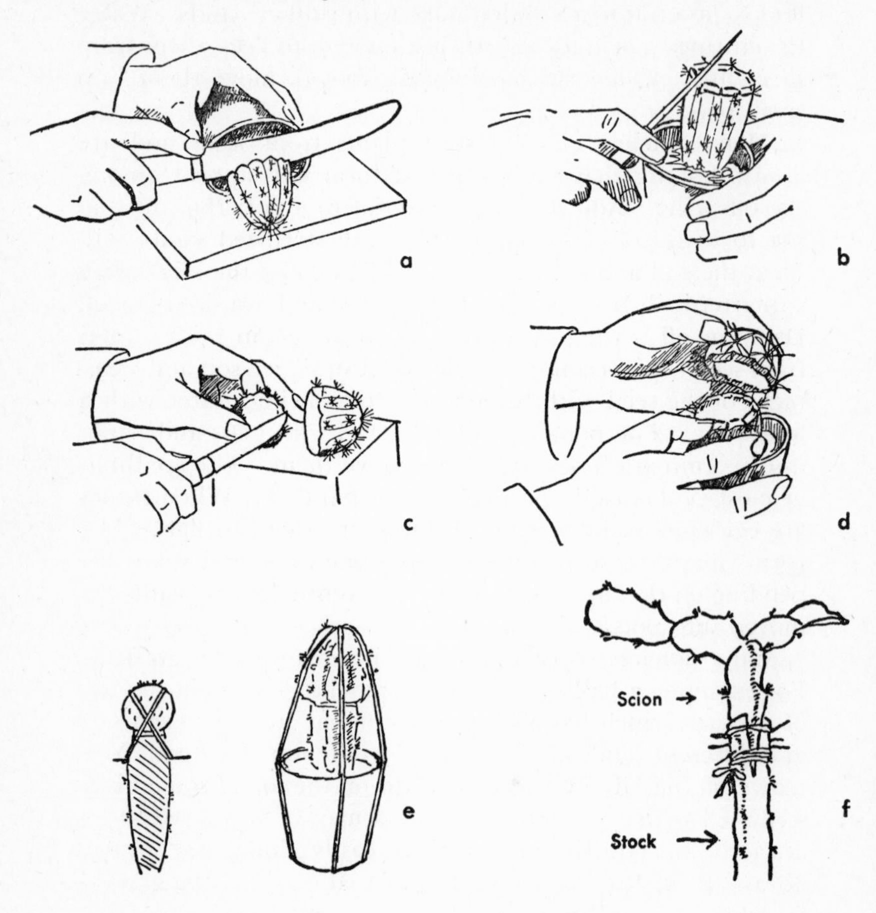

to keep the stock and scion firmly together stretch a rubber band over the top of the grafted plant and under the pot. Two rubber bands at right angles are necessary. You can use string if you prefer.

Another method is to cut a V-shaped piece out of the top of the stock and then bevel the lower surface of the scion to fit into the groove. The scion is held in place with spines and with string or rubber bands. This method is frequently used to graft scions of the rattail cactus onto a stock of *Selenicereus.* The grafted plant is quite attractive, with its upright stem of *Selenicereus* crowned at the top with pendant branches of the rattail cactus.

The pendant Christmas cactus makes a nice standard when it is grafted on to *Pereskia.* Cut off the top of the latter cactus and then make a slit about an inch deep. Into this slit insert a scion, one or two joints long, of the Christmas cactus. The basal part of the scion should be wedged shaped so that it will easily fit in the groove. Pin the scion in place with a couple of cactus spines and then shade the grafted plant until the union is complete. If you wish you can use *Opuntia* for the stock instead of the shrublike *Pereskia.*

Varieties of cacti

Because the cactus family is very large, including over a hundred genera and 1300 species, it is difficult to recommend varieties that you may want in your greenhouse. The more usual kinds may appeal to the beginner whereas the advanced grower may wish only the rare ones.

The space available for cacti will also influence your selection. Certain varieties are naturally dwarf; others grow to a considerable height. Among the kinds which do not get large are certain species of *Astrophytum, Chamaecereus, Echinocereus, Echinopsis, Gymnocalycium, Hematocactus, Lobivia, Lophaphora, Mammillaria, Notocactus, Opuntia,* and *Rebutia.*

The bishop's cap cactus, *Astrophytum myriostigma,* is about 2 inches high, has an attractive form, and bears yellow flowers. The peanut cactus, *Chamaecereus silvestrii,* also grows to a height of about 2 inches, is covered with white spines, and produces orange-scarlet flowers as large as the plant. The hedgehog cereus, *Echinocereus delaetii,* grows to a height of 8 inches, is covered with white hairs, and bears pink flowers. The Easter lily cactus, *Echinopsis hybrida,* is noted for its white flowers and deeply ridged globe shape. The chin cactus, *Gymnocalycium damsii,* is a globe-shaped cactus with pink flowers. The strawberry cactus, *Hematocactus setispinus,* grows to a height of 8 inches, but may produce yellow flowers with a conspicuous red throat when it is only 2 inches tall. A choice species of cob cactus is the scarlet-flowered *Lobivia cinnabarina.* The peyote, *Lophophora williamsii,* is a flattened globe, 3 inches or less in diameter, that produces pink flowers 1 inch across. There are many species of *Mammillaria,* the pincushion cactus, which make good greenhouse subjects, among them *M. bocasana, M. campotricha, M. carnea, M. elongata, M. fragilis, M. kewensis,* and *M. wildii.* Among the species of the ball cactus, *Notocactus,* that may appeal to you are *N. haselbergii* and *N. scopa.* The rabbit's-ear cactus, *Opuntia microdasya,* is suitable for the small greenhouse. *Rebutia minuscula* makes a globe about 2 inches in diameter and produces bright crimson flowers.

If you have plenty of space, you may wish to raise some large cacti, various species of *Aporocactus, Cephalocereus, Cleistocactus, Echinocactus, Lemaireocereus, Oreocereus, Selenicereus,* and *Trichinocereus.* The rattail cactus, *Aporocactus flagelliformis,* can be trained on a support, allowed to grow pendant, or grafted onto a straight stem of some other species; it is easy to grow and produces crimson flowers about 3 inches long. The old man cactus, *Cephalocereus senilis,* always attracts attention with its cylindrical stems covered with shaggy white hair. Scarlet bugler, *Cleistocactus baumannii,* grows to a height of 6 feet, has cylindrical stems about an inch and a half in diameter, and bears orange-scarlet flowers 3 inches long. One of the favorite barrel cacti is *Echinocactus grusonii.* This species is 4 feet high and 2 or 3 feet in diameter. The flowers are red and yellow.

The organ pipe cactus, *Lemaireocereus marginatus,* grows to a height of 25 feet and has ribbed, pipelike stems. Old man of the Andes, *Oreocereus celsianus,* grows to 3 feet and is covered with white hairs. Queen of the night, *Seleni-cereus macdonaldiae,* produces flowers about 14 inches across; the petals are white, the sepals reddish or yellowish. The white torch cactus, *Trichocereus spachianus,* grows to a height of 3 feet, has ribbed stems, and bears white flowers 6 inches across.

Epiphyllums. The epiphyllums come from tropical rain forests, where they grow as epiphytes. They are found with orchids and grow in large clusters on the branches of trees. From the debris which accumulates on the branches they absorb water and nutrients. Unlike other cacti, they require more shade during the bright months, a higher humidity, more frequent waterings, and they benefit from occasional syringings. The epiphyllums are more at home with orchids than with other cacti. They like a soil made up of four parts leaf mold, two of peat moss, two of well-rotted manure, two of gravel, and two of sharp sand. The epiphyllums should be potted somewhat loosely and the pots provided with good drainage by placing 1 inch of crock in the bottom of the pot. Water newly potted plants sparingly for a week or two until the roots are established. When epiphyllums are actively growing give them ample water. During their dormant season keep them on the dry side but don't let the roots become completely dry. They grow well and flower regularly when the night temperature is 60 degrees.

The epiphyllums are easily propagated from stem cuttings, and they can be grafted on to *Pereskia* or some other stock. You may wish to start them from seed. It takes about three years to get blooming plants. An interesting experience would be to cross epiphyllums.

Three choice species of epiphyllum are *E. strictum* (white orchid cactus), *E. ackermannii* (red orchid cactus), and *E. crenatum.* The flowers of the white orchid cactus are about 6 inches long, opening in late evening and closing before dawn. The red orchid cactus blossoms during the day.

The flowers are about 6 inches across and they are red with a greenish-yellow throat. *E. crenatum* is another attractive plant that flowers during the day. The flowers are delightfully fragrant and 6 to 10 inches long.

Many plants commonly called epiphyllums are in different genera, some being in the genus *Schlumbergera,* others in *Zygocactus. Schlumbergera gaertneri,* the easter cactus, is a good greenhouse plant. This species bears scarlet flowers about 3 inches long. The culture is the same as the true epiphyllums.

Botanically, the Christmas cactus, also called crab cactus, is *Zygocactus truncatus.* The flowers are beautifully translucent, about 3 inches across, and red in color. When grown with a night temperature of 63 to 65 degrees the plant flowers at about Christmas time. If grown at a night temperature of 55 degrees it may flower during the short days of winter or during the long days of spring. When grown with a night temperature of 70 to 75 degrees it does not flower.

In addition to the various species of *Epiphyllum, Schlumbergera,* and *Zygocactus* there are many hybrids now available, and some of these surpass the species.

Fig-marigold family—Aizoaceae

Included in this family are a number of plants which always attract attention, among them tiger's-jaw, stoneface, and living rocks. These are admirably adapted for life on rocky deserts, where the plants are hardly noticeable until they are in flower. Some members of the family bear only two thick succulent leaves, in which water is stored. In some species the leaves are partially buried, leaving only the upper surface to act as a light-gathering window. The brilliantly colored flowers are often quite large and superficially resemble daisies. The flowers have many petals and stamens.

The members of this family grow well in a 60-degree greenhouse when potted in a mixture of equal parts of loam, sand, and leaf mold. Like all desert plants, they should be grown with good drainage and the soil should not be waterlogged.

During the summer the plants require frequent waterings, but during the winter they should be kept on the dry side. Many of the fig-marigolds are slow growers and require only small pots. Members of this family are propagated by cuttings, by division, or from seed. Cuttings should be allowed to dry for a day or two before they are inserted into sand.

Among the genera of interest to greenhouse owners are *Conophytum* (cone-plants), *Faucaria* (tiger's-jaw), *Glottiphylum, Lithops* (stoneface), *Pleiospilos* (living rocks), and *Titanopsis*. The cone-plants form rounded clumps, and each growth consists of two leaves joined together.

The leaves of the tiger's-jaw occur in pairs, and the upturned edges bear long soft teeth, giving a fanciful resemblance to the open jaws of a tiger. The flowers are produced in the fall and are stemless, bright yellow, and about an inch across. *Glottiphylum* has bright green leaves that feel cool, and bears yellow flowers 3 inches across.

The stoneface (*Lithops*) resembles pebbles on the ground. The leaves are partially buried, with only their upper surfaces exposed to light. There are a number of species—*L. framesii, L. lactea,* and *L. Meyeri,* as well as others which differ in the color of the leaves and flowers.

Two favorite species of living rocks (also called split rocks) are *Pleiospilos bolusii* and *P. simulans*. Both species resemble stones, and both bear yellow flowers about 3 inches across.

The leaves of *Titanopsis schwantesii* form small rosettes. The tips of the fleshy leaves are covered with white tubercles. The flowers are about an inch across and are produced in the spring.

Lily family—Liliaceae

Several members of this family are adapted to desert life, among them *Aloe, Gasteria,* and *Haworthia*. They grow slowly and can be confined in small pots which are provided with good drainage. The soil mixture should be equal parts of sand, loam, and leaf mold. The succulents of the lily family require shade from April or May until early autumn. Water them freely in summer and moderately during winter. They may be increased from seed or more usually by offshoots or leaf cuttings. If you remove a leaf and lay it on sand, plantlets will develop which can be potted up.

Aloe. An interesting species is *Aloe variegata,* called tiger aloe by some and partridge-breasted aloe by others. When young, this plant has a compact form. The three-sided green leaves are banded with white and grow in a triangular rosette.

Gasteria. These plants are known as file aloes. They are dwarf plants with tongue-shaped leaves that form a dense basal rosette. *Gasteria acinacifolia* and *G. verrucosa* are favorite species. The first has dull gray leaves that are very fleshy and about 10 inches long and 2 inches wide. The flower cluster is up to 4 feet long, and has reddish flowers about 2 inches across. *Gasteria verrucosa* is characterized by the white warts on the grayish green leaves. The leaves are about 6 inches long and 3/4-inch wide. The flowers are pink, about an inch long, and are borne on a cluster that is 2 feet tall.

Haworthia. These are known as pearl aloes. Among the interesting species are *Haworthia cymbiformis, H. margaritifera,* and *H. arachnoides. H. cymbiformis* has pale, oblong, smooth leaves and produces a flower stalk about 1 foot tall. *H. margaritifera* has large pearly warts on the leaves and bears flowers on a cluster 2 feet high. *H. arachnoides* has three-sided leaves which are fringed. The flower cluster is about 1 1/2 feet high.

Milkweed family—Asclepiadaceae

Certain members of this family deserve a place in a collection of succulents, among them *Caralluma, Hoodia, Huernia,* and especially *Stapelia.* These odd plants superficially resemble cacti; they have thick fleshy stems and lack foliage. The milkweeds have unique flowers of intricate construction that are very different from those of cacti or any other family. The succulents of this family can be grown in small pots in an even mixture of sand, loam, and leaf mold. For best growth a night temperature of 60 to 65 degrees should be maintained. As with other succulents, they should be watered freely when they are actively growing and kept on the dry side during their dormant period, generally in winter. These succulents are easily propagated by breaking off sections of the stem and inserting them in moist sand.

Caralluma. All of the species of *Caralluma* are low-growing succulents with leafless, four-angled stems that have teeth on the ridges. The flowers are borne near the top of the stem and they are purple, brown, or yellow, depending on the species. They vary in size from the eight-inch flowers of *Caralluma sinaica* to the quarter-inch ones of *C. nebrownii.*

Hoodia. The branches of these cactus-like plants bear spine-tipped tubercles. There are a dozen or so species, of which *Hoodia gordonii* is most frequently seen in collections. The flowers of this species are pale purple with greenish-yellow stripes, and they are about 3 inches in diameter.

Huernia. These dwarf succulents produce odd bell-shaped flowers. The flowers of *Huernia penzigii* are black-purple in color; those of *H. primulina* are cream-yellow.

Stapelia. The showy and distinctive flowers of the stapelias make them the most spectacular of the milkweeds. Because their appearance leads one to liken them to a starfish, they are sometimes known as starfish flower. The unpleasant odor of the flowers at close hand has led to another common name, carrion flower. Stapelias have thick, fleshy, four-sided, green stems without leaves. The flowers are grotesquely marked and barred with dull red, purple, or yellow. The petals are fleshy, and near their base there is a two-rowed crown that may be curiously colored. The flowers are large, 3 inches in diameter in *Stapelia verrucosa* and 12 inches in *S. gigantea.* The flowers of the former have red spots against a yellow background. The yellow flowers of *S. gigantea* are barred with many crimson lines. Other species that you may want in your collection are *S. variegata, S. grandiflora, S. patula, S. revoluta,* and *S. verrucosa.*

Spurge or poinsettia family—Euphorbiaceae

The genus *Euphorbia* of this family includes a number of species which resemble cacti in several ways. Some of the succulent euphorbias are globular, others columnar, and still different ones are climbers. Some are very spiny. Unlike the cacti, however, all of the euphorbias have milky sap, which in some species is extremely poisonous. Cultural conditions suggested for cacti suit the euphorbias. They are propagated by stem cuttings. Allow the base of the cutting to callus somewhat before inserting it in sand.

One of the favorite succulents is the Medusa's head, *Euphorbia caput-medusae,* which has a globular main stem that bears many declining branches 1 to 2 inches thick. *Euphorbia pseudocactus* is gray-green in color and has upright three- to five-angled stems with spines along the ridges. Other species of interest to collectors are *E. cereiformis, E. meloformis, E. globosa, E. cooperi,* and *E. beaumierana.*

The Stonecrop family—Crassulaceae

This is a large family, including 900 species in twenty genera. The plants are noted mostly for their thick, fleshy leaves and interesting forms. However, certain kinds produce beautiful flowers. Members of the family prefer good light, a temperature of 55 to 60 degrees, and a dry atmosphere. A soil consisting of equal parts of sand, leaf mold, and loam is suitable for potting. The pots need not be large, but ample drainage must be provided. When the stonecrops are actively growing, the soil should be kept moist; when dormant, keep the plants on the dry side. The stonecrops are easily raised from seed and by leaf or stem cuttings.

Among the genera that appeal to fanciers of succulents are *Crassula, Echeveria,* and *Kalanchoë.* In addition you may want to try *Cotyledon, Sedum,* and *Sempervirens.*

Various species of crassula are grown for their distinctive forms and some for their flowers. All species are from the Old World, and mostly from Africa. Among the favorites for greenhouse culture are the scarlet paint brush (*Crassula falcata*), princess-pine (*C. lycopodioides*), and the necklace vine (*C. rupestris*). The scarlet paint brush may grow to a height of 8 feet but the other species are quite dwarf and may be grown in small pots.

You may know the echeverias by their common name of hen-and-chickens. They grow in symmetrical rosettes, bear attractive orange-red or coral flowers, and most species have bluish-white fleshy leaves that are broad and flat. The genus is a large one of more than sixty species. Among those available for greenhouse culture are *Echeveria elegans, E. gibbiflora, E. glauca, E. setosa, E. secunda,* and *E. weinbergii.*

There are more than one hundred species in the genus *Kalanchoë*. They have interesting foliage and produce an abundance of attractive flowers. We have already considered (page 280) *Kalanchoë blossfeldiana,* which is noted for its attractive flowers. One of the most common species is *K. pinnata,* which is known as the miracle leaf, air plant, and good luck leaf. Its main interest is its habit of producing small plants in the notches along the margin of the leaf. The plantlets appear at times when the leaf is on the plant, and will develop from a severed leaf. *Kalanchoë digremontiana* is another species which has this same capacity. The panda plant, *K. tomentosa,* is distinguished by its fleshy leaves arranged in a rosette. The leaves are covered with hairs; the hairs are white except for those near the tips of the leaves, which are rust-red or almost black in color. *Kalanchoë marmorata* is another interesting pot plant. It bears leaves about 6 inches long that are blotched with purple and creamy white or yellowish flowers nearly 3 inches long. *Kalanchoë flammea* is also of interest, bearing flowers that are yellow and orange-scarlet.

CHAPTER 23

BULBS FOR FORCING

BULBS ARE EASY to grow, and furnish a succession of blooms during winter and spring. Your efforts will be rewarded by beautiful flowers and pleasant fragrances.

Tulips, hyacinths, narcissi, irises, grape hyacinths, as well as others, may be forced in the greenhouse by starting bulbs in the fall. Order the bulbs early so that you will get a good selection of top-quality ones. Only the best grades of varieties especially suitable for greenhouse culture should be used; always remember that it takes as much work to flower an inferior bulb as one which produces flowers that you can be proud of.

It is best to plant the bulbs as soon as you receive them. If for some reason you cannot plant them promptly, store the tulip and narcissus bulbs at a temperature of 48 degrees and those of hyacinths at 70 degrees. Plant the bulbs in pots, or in flats (about 4 inches deep) if you are primarily interested in cut flowers. Standard 5- or 6-inch pots and 7- and 8-inch azalea pots can be used. In sizes above 6 inches, azalea pots are preferred because they are more stable and attractive than standard pots. Often a number of bulbs may be planted in a pot, spacing them about an inch or an inch and a half apart. A 7-inch pot will accommodate about six tulip bulbs or three or four narcissus bulbs. One hyacinth bulb is planted in a 5-inch pot or three in a 6- or 7-inch one.

Bulbs require good drainage, provided by placing several pieces of crock or pebbles in the bottom of the pot. A mixture of three parts loam to one of peat moss with the addition of superphosphate or bone meal is a good potting medium. Add soil to the pot. Then gently press the bases of the bulbs into the soil without turning them. Add more soil, firm it with your fingers, and then tap the pot on the bench to settle the soil. When the job is done correctly the soil level should be about half an inch below the rim and the noses of tulip and narcissus bulbs should be just protruding. The nose of a hyacinth bulb should be about half an inch below the soil surface. Place a label in each pot and water thoroughly.

It is best to plant only one variety in a pot. If bulbs of several varieties are planted together in a pot, growth and flowering will not be uniform.

After potting, labeling, and watering, the bulbs should be kept at a cool temperature, which favors root development and initiates the development of the shoot. The best storage temperature for tulips and narcissus is 48 degrees and for hyacinths 50 degrees. Lower temperatures are not harmful, but they slow development and necessitate a longer cool period. A cellar or storage room where the temperature is between 40 and 50 degrees is suitable for storing the potted bulbs. The bulbs should remain in storage until the roots are well developed and the shoot is 2 or 3 inches high. Do not let the pots become dry during storage. Water them at intervals.

An excellent substitute for a storage room is a trench outdoors. In an out-of-the-way place in the garden dig a trench 15 to 18 inches deep. Spread about 2 inches of cinders in the bottom to provide good drainage. Then place the pots in the trench, leaving about an inch between them to facilitate their later removal. Group together in first place those pots which will be first removed from the trench, those that come second in second place, and so on. Cover the pot with 2 inches of sand, which can be easily shaken off the shoots when the pots are removed. Fill the trench with soil and then add a 1-foot mulch of leaves, straw, or salt hay.

Bulbs can be removed from the trench and placed in the greenhouse when they have made good root growth and when the shoots are 2 to 3 inches high, generally in late December at the earliest for untreated bulbs. The bulbs will not be injured by a longer storage. Hence you can bring bulbs into the greenhouse at intervals from late December on for a sequence of blooms.

When the plants are brought into the greenhouse, you can keep them under the bench until growth begins, after which they should be placed on a well-lighted bench. Hardy bulbs can be flowered at a temperature of 50 degrees or at 60 degrees. In a 60-degree greenhouse, tulips and narcissi flower in about four weeks and hyacinths in three weeks. At a temperature of 50 degrees, blooming will take a week or two more. The best way to force hardy bulbs is to grow them at 50 degrees at first and then gradually increase the temperature to 60 degrees. Do not grow bulbs at temperatures above 70 degrees, which may cause buds to blast and flower tips to turn white. Keep the plants well watered during the forcing period.

Hardy bulbs should not be forced a second time. However, you can plant them outdoors. If you wish to save the bulbs for planting in your garden, keep the plants watered after they are through flowering. Then let the foliage dry off gradually. When the soil in the garden is workable, plant the bulbs. They will not flower the first season outdoors but will the next year.

So far, we have considered the general methods for forcing hardy bulbs. Let us next talk about the varieties that may be forced and special techniques that may be used.

Hyacinths

The common garden hyacinths (*Hyacinthus orientalis*) come in a variety of colors and can be brought into bloom during winter. They add delightful fragrance as well as beauty. Hyacinths are in the lily family (Liliaceae).

Hyacinth bulbs may be planted when received in the fall, or planting may be delayed until as late as January if the bulbs are stored in a dry place at a temperature of 65 to 70 degrees. Delayed planting is sometimes practiced to get quality blooms in early spring. Bulbs planted in the fall will flower from January on. Pot the bulb so that the nose is about half an inch below the surface of the soil. Store the pots in a trench or cool room. The plants can be brought into the greenhouse when the buds are visible and the bulbs are well rooted, at the earliest in late December or early January. Do not let the plants get frozen or chilled while digging or transporting them to the greenhouse. If they are chilled the flower spikes may appear cut off or fail to develop.

Plants which are brought into the greenhouse during December or early January should be kept in a dark place at 60 degrees until the shoots are 4 inches high. It is a simple matter to rig up a box of canvas, black cloth, or paper to give them darkness, which results in the elongation of the leaves and flower stalk.

Plants kept in darkness should be given light gradually until the normal green color has developed, after which they can stand full sun. Bulbs brought into the greenhouse during mid-January or later do not require darkness. They can be grown directly on the bench. A temperature of 60 degrees is ideal for hyacinths.

Some varieties of hyacinth, their descriptions, and the earliest dates at which they may be brought into the greenhouse are shown in the following table. Of course you can bring the plants in at later dates to get a sequence of flowers.

Variety	*Color*	*Earliest date to bring in*
Bismarck	Light blue	December 22
City of Haarlem	Golden yellow	January 15
Edelweiss	White	January 15
Gertrude	Rose pink	January 1
Grand Maitre	Dark porcelain	January 1
Jan Bos	Scarlet	December 22
King of the Blues	Dark blue	January 15
La Victoire	Red	January 1
L'Innocence	White	December 22
Marconi	Rose pink	January 5
Ostara	Clear blue	December 22
Pink Pearl	Pink	December 22
Queen of the Blues	Azure blue	January 18
Queen of the Pinks	Rosy pink	January 15

Narcissus

There are many species of narcissus which can be grown in the greenhouse. All are native to southwestern Europe. Narcissus is in the amaryllis family (Amaryllidaceae).

The daffodil or trumpet narcissus (*Narcissus pseudonarcissus*) is especially fine for greenhouse growing. The varieties of this species are yellow or cream in color, and the trumpet is as long as, or longer than, the petals. Among the choice varieties of this species are King Alfred, Aerolite, and Rembrandt.

King Alfred is hard to beat and is frequently grown by commercial florists. You can have flowers at Christmas if you plant precooled, #1, double-nosed bulbs in late September or early October. After potting, keep the bulbs in a trench or storage room until December 1, when the plants should be brought into the greenhouse and grown at 60 degrees.

Precooled bulbs need not be used for flowering in mid-January or later. If you wish King Alfred flowers in mid-January, plant #1 size, double-nosed, regular bulbs in the fall and move them into the greenhouse from the storage place about the middle of December. Of course, pots can be brought into the greenhouse at intervals for a succession of blooms.

At a temperature of 56 degrees, allow five to six weeks for flowering, at 60 degrees four weeks. However, King Alfreds should not be grown at 60 degrees until the bud is visible. During the dark days of winter it is advisable to keep the temperature above 53 degrees, otherwise the petals may curve inward.

The poet's narcissus (*Narcissus poeticus*) has white petals and a small trumpet with a dark red edge. *Actaea* is a favorite variety with its pure white corolla and small, yellow, fiery-red edged cap. This variety is potted in the fall, kept in a trench until at least February 1, then forced in the greenhouse.

The poetaz narcissi are hybrids between *Narcissus poeticus* and *Narcissus tazetta* (the paper white). Early Perfection, a white and yellow variety, and Laurens Coster, with its white petals and orange cup, are good varieties. Early Perfection may be brought in from the cool place after January 1, whereas Laurens Coster should remain until at least January 20.

Unlike the species of narcissus previously mentioned, the paper whites (*Narcissus tazetta*) do not require cool conditions for rooting. The bulbs of this group may be potted, flatted, or planted in a bench in the greenhouse during fall, and they will flower at Christmas or before. They will do well if kept continually in the greenhouse. However, root development is hastened if they are kept in a cool dark place for two weeks before being brought into the greenhouse. They grow well in dishes of pebbles kept wet with water. After the container is partially filled with pebbles, the bulbs are placed on them. Sufficient water is added so that the bases of the bulbs are just wetted. The ideal time to start the paper whites is from October 15 to November 15, but the plantings can be made from October 1 to March 1. You can get a succession of blooms by planting at about ten-day intervals. The Chinese sacred lily, really a narcissus, may be grown in the same manner as the paper whites.

Tulips

Tulips are in the lily family (Liliaceae). A number of species are native to Asia Minor, China, and Japan. The species have been crossed and the hybrids recrossed until now we have a great number of varieties of delightful form and beautiful color. Some varieties force well, others cannot be recommended. Certain ones can be brought into bloom early, others only later.

To obtain tulips in flower during January, precooled bulbs must be used. Precooled bulbs are those which have been stored at a temperature of 45 to 50 degrees before you receive them. They should be potted as soon as received and then placed in a storage room or trench. The following table shows some varieties of bulbs which respond to precooling and which can be brought into flower in January.

Variety	*Earliest date to bring in*	*Blooming*
Albino	December 5	January 5
Bartigon	December 26	February 5
Golden Harvest	December 15	January 15
Red Pitt	December 20	January 20
Rose Copeland	December 10	January 10
Utopia	December 27	January 27
Wm. Copeland	December 10	January 10
Wm. Pitt	December 20	January 20

For flowering from late January on, precooled bulbs need not be used. If regular bulbs are used, the dates for bringing in and for flowering are:

Variety	*Earliest date to bring in*	*Blooming*
Albino	December 14	January 21
Bartigon	January 15	February 1
Golden Harvest	December 21	February 1
Red Pitt	January 1	February 10
Rose Copeland	December 21	February 1
Utopia	January 7	February 17
Wm. Copeland	December 21	February 1
Wm. Pitt	December 31	February 10

These bulbs should be potted as soon as received. Water them and then place them in the storage room or the outdoor trench.

After the tulips are brought into the greenhouse, keep them watered. The foliage will be more attractive and the flowers of better color and texture if the plants are given a weekly watering with a solution of soluble fertilizer, made up according to the manufacturer's recommendations. Some growers like to use a fish fertilizer.

Other hardy bulbs for winter flowering

Tulips, narcissi, and hyacinths are the major bulbs which are forced. There are others, however, which are readily forced, among them cape cowslips, crocuses, grape hyacinths, ixias, and scillas. Not only do they make a beautiful display but add charm and interest.

Cape cowslip

Early in August is the ideal time to start the cape cowslip (*Lachenalia*), which is one of the most beautiful of pot-grown bulbs. The bulbs are potted in 5-inch pots just below the soil surface and about 1 inch apart. They grow well in a rich loam. They may be kept in a shaded cold frame until growth begins, after which they are grown in a greenhouse at 50 degrees. If a cold frame is not available they may be placed under the bench in a 50-degree house. When growth appears bring them into full light. *Lachenalia Nelsonii* is a rich golden yellow, and *Lachenalia tricolor* a striking red. If the plants are dried off gradually after flowering, the bulbs may be used again the next autumn. The bulbs should be allowed to remain in the dry soil until August, when they are repotted.

Crocus

Plant eight to ten crocus corms, about 1 inch deep, in the fall in a 6- or 8-inch pot. Keep them in the trench or cool cellar until February 1, by which time the plants will be well rooted and top growth started. Bring them into the greenhouse and grow them at a temperature of 50 degrees. They will bloom six or seven weeks after they are brought in.

Grape hyacinth

The grape hyacinth (*Muscari armeniacum*) makes excellent pot plants and cut flowers. The flowers of this species are quite large and deep blue. The bulbs are planted in the fall, kept in the cool trench until early January, and grown on in a greenhouse. If the greenhouse temperature is 60 degrees they will flower in about six weeks, if lower, in a longer time.

Ixia

Ixia, also called African Corn Lily, is a choice plant for greenhouse culture. The corms are potted or flatted in a sandy fibrous soil in September or October, five or six to a

5-inch pot. The pots or flats are placed in a trench outdoors, remaining there until December, when they may be brought into the greenhouse and grown at a temperature of 50-55 degrees. They flower in March and April. After they flower, allow the foliage to die down gradually. The corms may be saved and used again in the fall.

Scilla

Two species of *Scilla* make good greenhouse plants, *Scilla sibirica,* the Siberian squill, and *Scilla campanulata,* the Spanish bluebell or wood hyacinth. The variety, Spring Beauty, of the first species has large, brilliant blue flowers on graceful spikes 4 to 5 inches high. The following are favorite varieties of *Scilla campanulata:* Alba Maxima, with pure white flowers; Excelsior, with beautiful porcelain blue blooms; and Rose Queen, a lovely lilac-pink variety. The bulbs are potted in September or October, placed in a cool place such as an outdoor trench or cool cellar until February or March, by which time they will be well rooted. They are then grown in a 50-degree house.

CHAPTER 24

BULBS FOR CONTINUOUS GROWTH

SOME BULBS do not require storage in a trench or in a cool room for their development. Among the bulbs that may be grown continually in the greenhouse are anemone, freesia, gladiolus, iris, lily, lily of the valley, and ranunculus.

Anemone

Anemone coronaria makes a grand display from January through March. The tuberous roots are planted in a mixture of three parts soil to one of peat moss in September or October. They grow well in a cool greenhouse, one maintained at 50 degrees. After flowering, let the plants dry off. Then clean the tubers and store them in a cool place until planting time in the fall.

Freesia

Freesias produce graceful sprays of flowers during winter and early spring. The color range includes blue, yellow, rose, purple, red, white, and pink. The bulbs, really corms, should be planted in August in pots, flats, or directly in the bench. Use a mixture of three parts of loam and one of leaf mold or well-rotted manure. The corms are quite small; about fifteen can be planted in a 6-inch pot. A flat 4 by 12 by 25 inches will hold about one hundred corms. In the bench the corms should be planted about 3 inches apart each way. The tops of the corms should be about an inch below the surface of the soil. Go easy on watering until top growth begins, after which keep the soil moist, not wet. You can pot corms at intervals of three to four weeks for a succession of blooms. The plants grow well at a temperature between 50 and 55 degrees, and flower in about twelve to fourteen weeks. The stems are weak and require supports.

The corms can be saved and forced a second year, but the percentage which will flower may be reduced. If you wish to save the corms, keep the plants watered after the flowers are cut. When the foliage begins to wither, withhold water and let the foliage dry up, after which remove the corms and store them until August.

Freesias may be quickly grown from seeds sown in May. Soak the seeds for twenty-four hours and then sow them an eighth of an inch deep. The seeds germinate in about a month's time. Keep the seedlings growing in the seed flat or pan without disturbance until September. Then withhold water until the tops have died down completely. Remove the small corms and plant them in a flat or bench with a spacing of 2 by 2 inches. They will bear excellent flowers in January and February.

Gladiolus

For a beautiful display of gladiolus in May plant corms 2 inches deep in a bench during January; space them 2 inches apart in rows 8 inches apart. The plants grow well at a temperature of 50 degrees. If the soil is kept at a temperature of 65 to 70 degrees by means of electric heating cables under the soil, the plants will flower earlier, in late April.

Iris

A number of varieties of iris do well in the greenhouse, among them Wedgewood, a beautiful blue; Imperator, a deep blue; White Excelsior, a pure white; and Yellow Queen,

Right: grape hyacinths in flower during late February. *Below, left:* three large, double-nosed King Alfred daffodil bulbs are ready to be covered with soil. They will be watered and placed in the trench. *Right,* shoots of King Alfred daffodil bulbs just after the pots were removed from the trench on December 23; these bulbs are ready for forcing in the greenhouse.

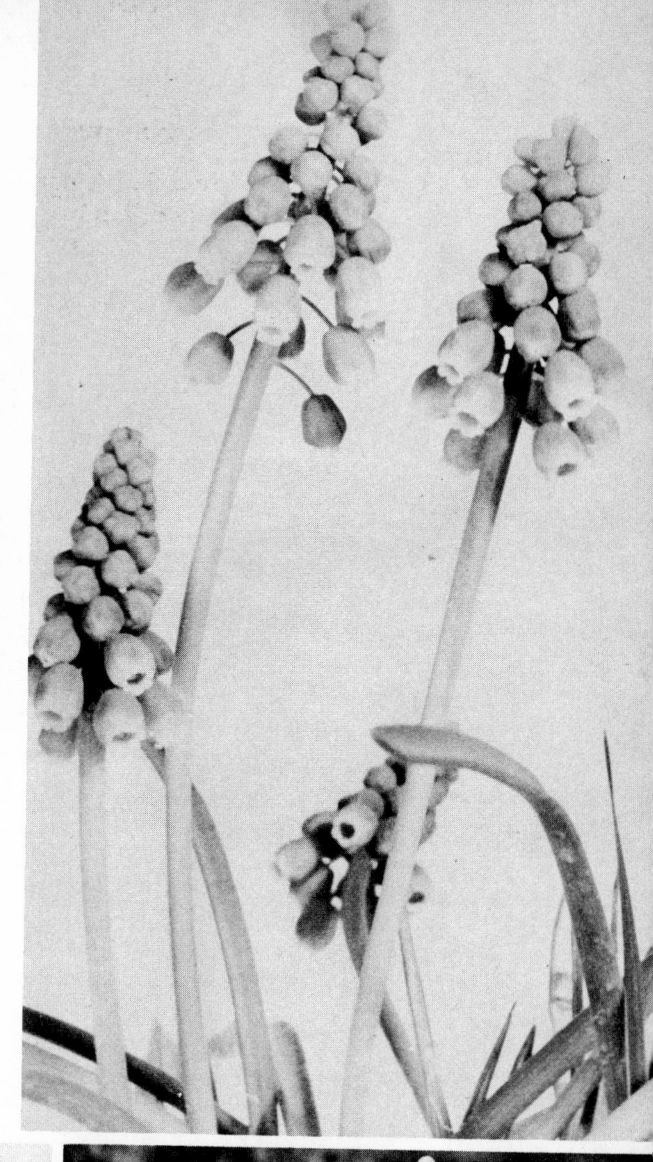

Anemone coronaria

Ranunculus asiaticus. (Bodger photos)

Lilium speciosum is easily grown.

The golden-banded lily, *Lilium auratum,* is probably the best-beloved of all lilies, gorgeously beautiful. (Romaine B. Ware photos)

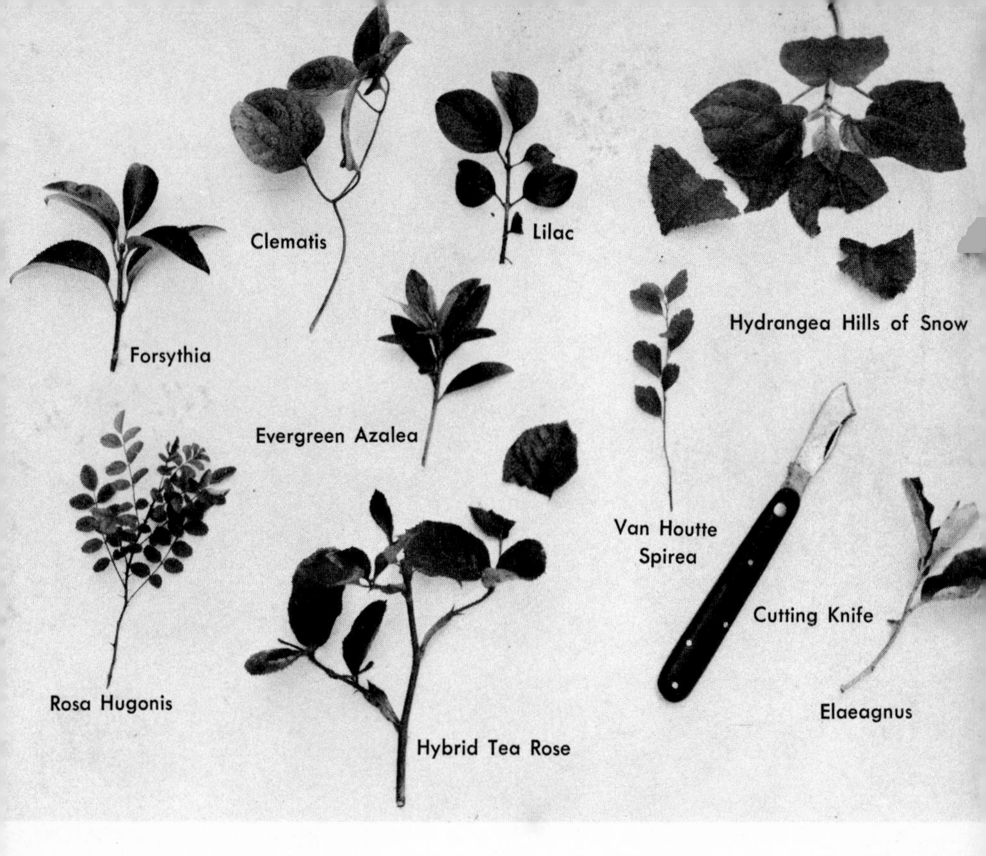

Above: many shrubs can be propagated from softwood cuttings made in June and July. These cuttings are ready to be inserted in sand. (Roche photo) *Below:* petunias (front flat) and snapdragons, transplanted to flats.

a splendid yellow. These varieties may be planted directly in a bench in the greenhouse in late October, November, or December and grown at a temperature of 50 to 55 degrees. They will flower in late winter or early spring.

Iris may also be grown in pots or flats which are stored at a low temperature in the same manner as tulips. With this method plant the bulbs in September or October. Space the bulbs 3 inches apart and plant them so that the nose of each bulb is 1 inch below the surface of the soil. Water thoroughly and then store the pots or flats in a cellar at 50 degrees or in a trench outside. The bulbs may be brought in at intervals from the middle of December on. At a temperature of 56 degrees the plants will flower six to eight weeks after they are brought in. They will flower nicely in a 50-degree greenhouse, but a longer time is required for blooming. Never let the pots or flats dry out. If the flats dry out once, you are not likely to get flowers.

If the largest Wedgewood iris bulbs (10 centimeters and up) are used, and if the bulbs are precooled, it is possible to have this iris flower for Christmas. The precooled bulbs are planted in 4-inch-deep flats in September or early October and then they are stored at a temperature of 50 degrees. The flats are brought into the greenhouse November 15 and grown at a temperature of 54 to 56 degrees. After they have been grown at this temperature for three weeks, the temperature may be increased to 58 degrees and later to 60 degrees to speed up growth. If grown above 60 degrees many of the plants will not flower.

Lilies

There are at least a hundred species of lilies from which you can select. All of them have magnificent, large flowers, and many are pleasingly fragrant. If you select varieties thoughtfully and plant the bulbs at intervals, you can have lilies in flower during all months.

Lilies do well in a porous soil enriched with superphosphate at a rate of a 4-inch potful per wheelbarrow. When planting use pots appropriate to the size of the bulbs. Large bulbs can be potted singly in 6-inch pots, or three bulbs may be planted in a 10-inch one. Bulbs in 6-inch pots should have an inch of soil below them, those in 10-inch pots about an inch of soil above them. After potting, water thoroughly and then keep the bulbs somewhat on the dry side until growth begins, when the plants can stand more frequent watering. If bench space is limited, the potted bulbs may be kept under a bench until growth begins, after which they should be given full sun. Lilies are spindly if they are grown with weak light and if they are crowded. After growth is well along, lilies benefit from weekly application of a dilute solution of fertilizer. A solution made up of 2 ounces of 8-8-8 soluble fertilizer dissolved in 10 gallons of water is suitable. Tall plants should be staked to keep the stem straight.

Lily bulbs can be grown in the greenhouse year after year. When flowering is through, keep the soil watered until the foliage dies down. Even when the shoots are gone, water the soil occasionally. Avoid letting the soil become dust dry. Repot the old bulbs at the usual time. Remove the old soil, but do not injure the living roots.

Lilies are readily propagated from offsets and from bulb scales. Offsets are separated from the parent bulb and planted. The stock can be increased rapidly by plucking off the scales of a bulb and planting the lower 1-inch portion of each in moist sand. In time a small bulb will develop at the base of each scale. Separate the bulb and plant it in soil.

Lilies can also be started from seeds. About two years are required to get blooming plants from seed. Seeds are sown in rows (2 inches apart) on a firmed mixture of equal parts of sand, loam, and leaf mold. Then they are covered with a half inch layer of screened sphagnum moss. The seeds of *Lilium regale, L. candidum,* and certain others germinate within a few weeks by sending up leaves. Seeds of *Lilium auratum, L. superbum, L. callosum,* and others germinate by producing a minute bulb below the soil surface. The tiny bulbs form leaves only after they have been exposed to a cool temperature. Generally, the small bulbs are ready for a cool treatment three months after the seeds are sown. Then the seed pans should be stored for three months in a place where the temperature is between 34 and 50 degrees. They are then returned to the greenhouse, where the bulbs will develop. When the plants become crowded, transplant them to fresh soil.

Aphids frequently attack lilies, but they may be controlled with a nicotine spray. Nicotine smoke should not be used, because it often burns the tips of the leaves. A virus disease, mosaic, causes the leaves to become mottled with irregular, elongated light-colored streaks. Control of aphids which spread this disease will help minimize the damage, as will selecting disease-free bulbs and discarding diseased plants. Botrytis blight, a fungus disease, appears as small reddish-brown circular spots on the foliage. This disease may be controlled with a Micronized Copper spray.

Varieties of lily

Lilium auratum. Golden-banded Lily. Queen of Lilies. This is a gorgeous lily, 3 to 5 feet tall, that grows well in pots in a greenhouse. The flowers are white, dotted crimson, with a golden band running through the center of each petal. They are deliciously fragrant. Use fresh bulbs, not cold-storage ones, which do not force well. If the bulbs are potted singly in 5-inch pots about the middle of May, the plants will flower in August or September.

Lilium candidum. Madonna Lily. The Madonna lily, an old favorite, grows to about 4 feet and has beautiful, white, waxy flowers about 3 inches long. Bulbs are potted in August or September, grown at 45 to 50 degrees until March, and then at 55 degrees. With this schedule, the plants flower in May.

Lilium gigantium. This is an immense lily that may grow up to 12 feet high. The flowers are fragrant, about 6 inches long, white with reddish purple stripes inside. The bulbs may be planted during any month, and the plants flower in about three months. Bulbs potted on August 1 will flower in October and November, those on September 1 in December and January, on October 1 in January and February, and so on. The plants grow well at a temperature between 60 and 70 degrees.

Lilium krameri. This beautiful lily with its white and pink flowers is potted in December, grown at 45 to 50 degrees until March 1 and then at 55 to 60 degrees. With this procedure the plants blossom in May.

Lilium longiflorum. White Trumpet Lily. Easter Lily. The Croft variety of this species is the favorite Easter lily. This variety is not too tall, has attractive foliage, and beautiful, well-shaped flowers. Pretreated bulbs as well as regular ones are available. Pretreated bulbs are those that have been stored at 31 to 40 degrees for five weeks. The pretreated bulbs may be difficult to get in lots of less than a hundred, whereas the regular ones may be purchased in small quantities. If the following schedule is followed, pretreated bulbs will flower in 120 days and regular ones in about 180 days. If you wish the Croft lilies to flower at Easter count backward the appropriate number of days and pot the bulbs at that time. If possible, try to use pretreated bulbs and get them from a company that caters to florists. The stock from such companies is generally reliable. If it is necessary to store the bulbs, keep them in moist peat at a temperature of 50 degrees. The bulbs are potted in 6-inch pots, then grown on at a temperature of 60 degrees, day and night. Six weeks before Easter measure the length of the flower buds. If the buds are an inch long continue growing the plants at 60 degrees. If the buds are longer than an inch decrease the temperature gradually. If the buds are not quite visible raise the temperature somewhat, but not over 75 degrees. At 75 degrees the plants will flower four weeks after the buds are first visible. The flower buds should be just turning down two weeks before Easter. If they are more advanced than this lower the temperature; if less advanced, increase it. Never grow above 75 degrees. The best-quality blooms of Croft lilies are secured when the plants are raised cool during the last week. Throughout the whole growing period use water at the temperature of the greenhouse. After the plants are 2 inches high, they should be watered weekly with a solution made up of 3 ounces of an 8-8-8 soluble fertilizer dissolved in 10 gallons of water. The fertilizer should be applied at night. Throughout the growing period the plants should be well spaced.

Lilium speciosum. Showy Lily. This delightfully fragrant and beautiful lily can be highly recommended for growing in pots in the greenhouse. Varieties *album* and *rubrum* are available. *Lilium speciosum* var. *album* has nearly white flowers, whereas those of variety *rubrum* are white or blush, spotted with carmine. Both grow to a height of about 4 feet. The plants grow well at a temperature of 55 degrees. Plants flower about five or six months after the bulbs are planted. For flowers at Christmas, bulbs should be potted in July. For later flowering the bulbs may be planted in August, September, October, November, or any other month. After receiving the bulbs you may wish to plant some and set aside others for later plantings. Those which are not planted promptly should be stored in moist peat at a temperature of 34 to 40 degrees. Incidentally, all lily bulbs should be stored in moist peat to keep them from drying out.

Lilium tenuifolium. Coral Lily. This lily grows to a height of 1 to 2 feet and bears many brilliant scarlet flowers about 2 inches in diameter. The bulbs should be potted in October, about five in a 6-inch pot, then placed outdoors in a cold frame. If the plants are brought into the greenhouse in February and grown at 55 degrees, they will bloom for Easter. They may be brought in later for flowering at later dates.

Lilium tigrinum. Tiger Lily. The orange-red or salmon-red, black-spotted flowers of this lily are always admired. Bulbs potted in June and grown at 55 degrees will flower in October, those planted in July, at Thanksgiving.

Lily of the valley

The lily of the valley, *Convallaria majalis,* with its dainty white scalloped bells, adds beauty and fragrance to the greenhouse and is a choice cut flower. The lily of the valley has a horizontal rootstock from which arises a small upright portion made up of a bud and many roots. These upright portions are called pips and are used for propagation. Use pips that have been stored at a temperature of about 28 degrees for three months. These pips can be obtained from supply houses. The pips may be grown in flats or pots, planting about twenty-five in a 7-inch pot. The potting medium may be sphagnum moss, peat, or sand. Sand is generally used. Plant the pips close together, with the crown of each about half an inch above the surface. Pack the sand firmly and then water thoroughly. Pips flower in 19-21 days if grown with a bottom temperature of 80 degrees and a top temperature of 75 degrees. A closed propagating case is a good place to grow them. For the first two weeks grow the plants in darkness and keep the atmosphere humid. Then increase the light gradually and give the plants more air. The temperatures indicated above are those used by the specialists. However, they will flower nicely even if grown at a lower temperature. The planted pips may be kept in the dark at 60 degrees until the leaves and spikes make good growth, after which the plants are gradually given light and the temperature increased to 70 degrees. Lilies of the valley may be had in bloom from January through May by successive plantings. Once the pips have been forced they are useless.

Ranunculus

The so-called Victoria hybrids of *Ranunculus asiaticus* are vigorous plants with large double flowers. The color range embraces pink, yellow, orange, scarlet, apricot, and others. The clawlike tubers should be planted about 2 inches deep in the fall, with the claws downward. Three or four tubers may be planted in a 6-inch pot. They grow well in a mixture of four parts sandy loam to one of leaf mold or well-rotted manure. They may be grown in a greenhouse at 45 to 50 degrees or in a cold frame until February, after which they are grown in the greenhouse at 50 degrees, flowering in March and April.

CHAPTER 25

GREENHOUSE AND OUTDOOR GARDEN

THE GREENHOUSE can be a wonderful adjunct to your outdoor garden, enabling you to beautify the yard and to raise a variety of delicious vegetables. To have early flowers and vegetables in the garden it is necessary to sow seeds in the greenhouse long before outdoor planting is possible. By starting flowers and vegetables in the greenhouse you can get earlier maturity outdoors, even allowing you to raise some plants which, if started outdoors, would be nipped by frost before they matured. The use of plants from the greenhouse enables one to make fuller use of outdoor garden space and eliminates the uncertainty that comes from the erratic germination of seeds under outdoor conditions. The young seedlings can be given better care and protection in the greenhouse than they can outdoors. Furthermore, it is a chore to weed stands of seedlings outdoors, whereas, if transplants are used, early weeds can be eliminated before the plants are set out. If you raise your own plants, you have more to say about what goes into your garden, because your choice is not limited by the standard varieties that are available at garden supply houses.

In nearly all communities flower and vegetable plants are in strong demand in late spring and sell for a good price. If you want your hobby to pay its way, you might consider raising plants for sale to gardeners. You can raise superior plants and better meet the desires of gardeners in your community.

Plans should be made before the first of the year. The kinds and numbers of each to raise may be based on your own likes and dislikes as well as those of prospective buyers. Certainly you should secure varieties that do well in the climate and soil of your area. For your own garden, you will probably want to plan for a sequence of flowers and vegetables throughout the summer. This succession may be achieved by starting some seeds in the greenhouse, others at appropriate times outdoors, and by the selection of early, midseason, and late varieties.

The time for sowing seeds of various flowers and vegetables varies from region to region and according to the date the product is wanted. If you want extreme earliness you must start the plants sooner than for flowers and vegetables later in the season. The amount of space available in the greenhouse during the spring months will also determine to some extent the time of sowing.

The following tables show the approximate dates for starting various annual flowers and vegetables in the greenhouse. These dates are based on having moderate-size plants ready for planting in the garden in late May. If you prefer large plants and have ample greenhouse space, sow the seeds two or three weeks earlier. If frosts occur in late May in your locality, the seeds may be started proportionately later. In localities with long growing seasons the seeds may be planted earlier than indicated in the tables.

TIME TO SOW SEEDS AND TO TRANSPLANT ANNUALS TO HAVE PLANTS READY TO SET IN THE GARDEN THE LAST WEEK IN MAY *

Plant	*Sow seed*	*Transplant to plant bands or to flat*
Ageratum	March, third week	April, third week
Amaranthus	April, third week	May, first week
Baby's breath	April, fourth week	May, second week
Bachelor's button	April, third week	May, first week
Balsam	April, third week	May, second week
Calendula	April, third week	May, first week
China Aster	April, third week	May, first week

* From *Cornell Extension Bulletin 579*

Plant	*Sow seed*	*Transplant to plant bands or to flat*
Chrysanthemum	April, third week	May, first week
Clarkia	April, fourth week	May, second week
Cockscomb	April, third week	May, first week
Cosmos	April, fourth week	May, second week
Dianthus	April, first week	April, fourth week
Gaillardia	April, third week	May, first week
Larkspur	April, first week	April, fourth week
Marigold	April, third week	May, first week
Mignonette	April, third week	May, first week
Morning-glory	April, third week	May, first week
Nicotiana	April, second week	May, first week
Petunia	March, first week	March, fourth week
Phlox	April, second week	April, fourth week
Salpiglossis	April, first week	April, third week
Schizanthus	April, third week	May, first week
Snapdragon	March, second week	April, first week
Verbena	March, third week	April, third week
Zinnia	April, fourth week	May, second week

Approximate Dates for Sowing Vegetable Seeds Under Glass and Ranges of Day Temperatures *

Vegetable	*Date of sowing*	*Approximate temperatures (day)*
Beets	March 1-15	60-65
Broccoli	February 20-28	60-65
Cabbage, early	February 20-28	60-65
Cauliflower	February 20-28	60-65
Celery	February 20-29	60-65
Eggplant	March 15-25	70-75
Endive	February 20-28	60-65
Kohlrabi	February 20-28	60-65
Leeks	February 20-28	60-65
Lettuce	February 20-28	60-65
Melons	April 15-25	70-75
Onions, sweet Spanish	February 1-10	60-65
Peppers	March 15-25	70-75
Squash	April 15-25	65-70
Tomatoes	March 15-25	65-70

* From *Cornell Extension Bulletin 448*

Seeds are generally sown in flats. Large seeds may be planted in furrows and covered with soil, sand, or sphaghum moss which has been forced through a 1/8-inch mesh screen, or with vermiculite. Very small seeds should be broadcast and left uncovered. Seeds of plants which are set back by transplanting (for example, cucumber, squash, melon) should be sown in pots, from which they can be moved to the garden. Sow three or four seeds to a 4-inch pot and later remove all but one seedling.

As with other plants, careful attention should be given to watering the seedlings. The ideal temperature for most indoor-grown seedlings is 55 to 60 degrees; if possible the temperature should not go above 70 degrees.

When the first true leaves are developed, the seedlings should be transplanted to pots, plant bands, or to other flats where they will be more widely spaced and have more room for development. If plant bands are used, they are first placed in the flat and then all filled at once. After the seedlings are transplanted, water them and keep them in a shady place until the plants have recovered from the shock of transplanting.

Do not let the plants become crowded and starved. It is important that ample supplies of water and nutrients be available at all times. Liquid feeding is desirable to keep the plants growing. If the plants become too large before it is time to set them in the garden, they can be transplanted a second time into pots or plant bands. Most seedlings of flowers should be pinched when the plants are 4 or 5 inches tall in order to develop bushy specimens.

A cold frame is a good intermediary between the greenhouse and the garden, enabling one to harden plants. One to three weeks before the plants are to be planted in the garden move them into the cold frame to inure them to outdoor conditions. Lift the sash during bright days to keep the frame from becoming too hot, but during the first period close the frame at night. Later, open the sash slightly at night and then gradually increase the ventilation. If you do not have a cold frame and if conditions permit, give the plants in the greenhouse more ventilation and a lower temperature for a week prior to planting outdoors. Also keep them somewhat on the dry side. These techniques result in hardier plants that are better able to withstand the shock of transplanting. For outdoor planting do not try to rush the season; wait until danger of freezing is over. Watch for such pests as red spiders, thrips, aphids, and slugs.

In preparation for moving plants out of flats, a practice known as *blocking* is desirable. Blocking consists of cutting the soil between the plants with a knife, as you would cut fudge, about a week or ten days before the plants are to be planted in the garden. Cutting back the roots stimulates the formation of a compact system of branch roots which holds a good ball of soil. Before transplanting, dampen the soil in the boxes in which the plants have been grown, and let it become uniformly moist. This will make it easier to lift each plant with a good ball of soil around its roots. If it is necessary to remove a lot of plants at a time and carry them some distance, wrap wet cloth or newspaper around them.

The soil in the garden should be moist and in good tilth. Make a hole large enough for the root system, set in place, draw in the soil, and firm it around the roots. Then water the plant with water or, better, with a starter solution. The starter solution is prepared by dissolving the appropriate amount of chemical fertilizer in water. Many chemical fertilizers are available under such trade names as Hyponex, Miracle Gro, Rapid-Gro, Take-Hold, Manna, and Bio-Gro. When using these preparations, follow the manufacturer's recommendations carefully.

You may wish to start some garden plants from cuttings. Cuttings of a number of plants may be made beginning in January and continuing until April—among them ageratum, fuchsia, geranium, heliotrope, lantana, and verbena.

Don't forget that the garden can be an adjunct to the greenhouse as well as the reverse. Before frost you may wish to take cuttings from geraniums, heliotropes, fuchsias, and others. Perhaps you will want to lift plants from the garden and pot them, or plant them in a bench in the greenhouse.

The following table shows the number of vegetable plants needed for a hundred-foot row and the spacing of the plants in the row.

NUMBER OF VEGETABLE PLANTS REQUIRED FOR 100 FEET OF ROW AND DISTANCE APART FOR ROWS AND PLANTS

		Distance apart		
		Rows		
Crop	*Plants needed for 100 feet of row*	*Horse or machine cultivated*	*Hand cultivated*	*Plants in the row*
Broccoli	50-75	2½-3 feet	2-2½ feet	14-24 inches
Brussels sprouts	50-75	2½-3 feet	2-2½ feet	14-24 inches
Cabbage	50-75	2½-3 feet	2-2½ feet	14-24 inches
Cauliflower	50-75	2½-3 feet	2-2½ feet	14-24 inches
Celeriac	200-250	2½-3 feet	1½-2 feet	4-6 inches
Celery	200-250	2½-3 feet	1½-2 feet	4-6 inches
Eggplant	50	3 feet	2-2½ feet	36 inches
Lettuce, head	100	2½-3 feet	1-1½ feet	12-15 inches
Onion, plants	400	2-2½ feet	1-1½ feet	2-3 inches
Pepper	50-70	3-4 feet	2-3 feet	18-24 inches
Tomato	35-50	3-4 feet	2-3 feet	18-36 inches

Perennials

Perennials are started from seeds, cuttings, or by dividing plants. Seeds of many perennials may be sown in flats or pots in the greenhouse during February and March. The seedlings are transplanted to flats, pots, or plant bands, and then, when the weather is settled, they are planted in the garden. During the first summer they will make sturdy growth, and during the second season they will produce excellent flowers.

If you prefer you can sow the seeds of many perennials in a cold frame during July. After the soil in the frame has been finely worked and is in good tilth, sow the seeds sparsely in rows. Then cover them with soil. Keep the seed bed watered, weeded, and shaded. Give the young plants protection during the winter. The following spring they can be moved into the garden, where many will flower during the summer.

Most perennials can be propagated from cuttings rooted in sand in the greenhouse. The best time to make cuttings of various perennials is given below. Unless indicated otherwise, stem cuttings are used.

Plant	*Make cuttings in*
Achillea millefolium	July and August
Anchusa italica	February and March (root cuttings)
Anemone japonica	March and April (root cuttings)
Asters	May
Campanulas	June and July
Chrysanthemum	May
Coreopsis grandiflora	May
Delphinium	June and July
Dicentra spectabilis	September
Eupatorium aromaticum	June and July
Gypsophila paniculata	June and July
Helenium autumnale	May
Heuchera sanguinea	May
Papaver orientale	March (root cuttings)
Phlox paniculata	May

Of course, practically all large perennials can be divided. This is best done in the spring.

Propagating trees and shrubs

Many deciduous shrubs may be propagated from cuttings made in June and July when the new wood is neither too soft nor too hard. The stems are in the proper stage if they snap clean when broken. The cuttings are made about 3 to 6 inches long from the new growth. We used to think that it was necessary to cut the shoots at a node, but we now know that cuttings root well if cut about half an inch below a node as well as if cut just below the node. Remove the lower leaf or leaves, but allow the terminal ones to remain. Keep the newly made cuttings from wilting by wrapping them in moss or moist cloth. Insert the cuttings in a flat or propagating bench containing sand or an even mixture of sand and peat moss. With a knife, make a slit in the rooting medium and insert the cuttings. Firm with the hand and then water thoroughly. The cuttings should be shaded by stretching cloth 3 or 4 feet above them. Keep the atmosphere moist and syringe the cuttings several times each day. When the cuttings have rooted, pot them in 2½-inch pots. If the climate in your region is mild, the young plants may be planted outdoors later in the season. However, in most regions, they should be carried over the first winter in a cool greenhouse or in a cold frame and planted outdoors in the spring.

Among the many plants that can be propagated from cuttings made in June and July, so-called softwood cuttings, are kerria, viburnum, abelia, azalea, deutzia, forsythia, hydrangea, rose, spirea, lilac, caragana, kolkwitzia, weigela.

Cuttings of conifers are best made in November. Make the cuttings 4 to 6 inches long, remove the foliage from the lower portion of the stem, and treat the cuttings with a rooting powder. Then insert the basal end of each cutting in sand. A bottom temperature of 65 degrees speeds rooting. As with softwood cuttings, provide shade, a moist atmosphere, and syringe the cuttings. Yew, chamaecyparis, juniper, and thuya root quite rapidly, sometimes in three weeks. Others, such as firs, spruces, hemlocks, and pines, root more slowly, requiring two or three months or even longer. Many conifers lose part of their needles during the rooting period. These dead needles should be removed. The rooted cuttings are potted and grown for the first season in pots in a greenhouse or cold frame.

Such broad-leaved evergreens as aucuba, box, daphne, euonymous, vinca, and holly can be propagated by making cuttings in late August or September. The cuttings are planted in the greenhouse in sand or in a mixture of sand and peat moss.

CHAPTER 26

VEGETABLES

Greenhouse-grown vegetables are tastier than those purchased at the store. They can be harvested at the peak of their color and flavor, and they can be prepared before any of their high quality is lost. Some hobbyists raise only vegetables, but many raise some vegetables along with their flowers—a few tomato plants and perhaps some lettuce, onions, and radishes, raised in pots, flats, or in a bench.

You can plan your operations so that there will be a supply of vegetables throughout the year. Or you can raise vegetables only during the summer when the greenhouse may be empty of flowering plants and when the cost of heating will be slight. Cucumbers and tomatoes are excellent summer crops.

Your own likes and dislikes will influence your selection of vegetables. If chives, cress, mustard, and other hard-to-obtain greens appeal to you, by all means raise a few. Vegetables which mature quickly and give a high yield in a limited space are most suitable for the small greenhouse. Lettuce, onions, beets, carrots, parsley, and radishes require comparatively little space and some of them can be intercropped with young flowering plants. On the other hand, a considerable area of peas, beans, sweet corn, melons, spinach, and potatoes would be required for just one meal, and these are not well suited to a small greenhouse.

Vegetables grow well in loam enriched with well-rotted manure. Good light is essential, as is an even supply of water. Don't let the growth become hard from lack of water. Periodic applications of fertilizer make for rapid growth and succulence in many vegetables. The ideal temperature varies with the vegetable; some kinds prefer a night temperature of 50 degrees, others 60 degrees, and a few 65 degrees.

The greenhouse is of great value in starting vegetable plants to be set out in the garden. For a discussion of this topic see Chapter 25.

Vegetables for the 50-degree greenhouse

A great many vegetables can be grown in a greenhouse maintained at a night temperature of 50 degrees—among them asparagus, beet, carrot, cauliflower, celery, chard, chive, cress, lettuce, mustard, parsley, pea, radish, rhubarb, and spinach. Beets, carrots, and radishes at times may be planted between the rows of slow-growing plants, to make more effective use of your greenhouse space.

Beets

For fresh beets in late winter and early spring, seeds are sown about the middle of January directly in the bench 1 inch apart in rows 8 inches apart. When the roots begin to make globes, thin the plants so that they are 3 inches apart. Of course, the removed plants can be used as greens. Beets do well in rich soil and with an ample supply of water. An early variety, such as Improved Early Egyptian, is good for forcing.

Carrots

Seeds of carrots may be sown in January for a crop in the spring. The seeds are best sown in rows 6 inches apart. Later, thin the plants so that they are 2 inches apart in the rows. A light sandy soil favors the formation of straight roots. Early Nantes is a good variety.

Cauliflower

Cauliflower will grow well and produce choice heads in a humid greenhouse maintained at a night temperature of 45 to 50 degrees with a 10-degree rise on bright days. Plants grown from seeds sown in the middle of September will mature in late December or January. Sow the seeds in a pot or flat. The seedlings may be transplanted 15 inches apart in a bench, or they may be moved into 3-inch pots and later planted in the bench. The bench should be filled to a depth of six to eight inches with a loam soil enriched with well-rotted manure. Cauliflower should be furnished an even supply of water. When the cauliflower head is about the size of an egg, it should be covered to protect it from bright light, which will turn the head brown. The head may be covered by lifting the surrounding leaves up and tying them above the head. Be careful not to injure the leaves, and do not tie them together too tightly. They are still needed for food manufacture. Snowball is an excellent variety that produces compact, uniform, solid white heads.

Lettuce

If you have bench space available for two or three months you might want to use it for lettuce, a satisfactory and easily grown vegetable for the 50-degree house. If you want a continuous supply of lettuce, plant seeds about the middle of August and at monthly intervals thereafter. You can sow them in pots, or directly in the bench. For sowing in the bench sow two or three seeds at 8-inch intervals in rows 8 inches apart. When the seedlings are up, remove the surplus plants, leaving one at each spot. You can start radishes in the space between the young lettuce plants, for they will mature before the lettuce covers the area.

If you prefer, the seeds may be broadcast in a pot of soil. From the seed pot the plants may be planted 8 by 8 inches in the bench, or if bench space is not available at the time, you can move them into flats with a spacing of 2 by 2 inches. When the plants in the flat begin to crowd each other, plant them in the bench, or move them on into 2½-inch or 3-inch pots. If there is room between the rows of lettuce plants previously benched, you can plunge the pots in this space temporarily and later plant them in another part of the bench. Frequent transplantings do not make for better plants but provide more effective use of bench space.

The soil should be well enriched with manure. Throughout the whole growing period the plants should be kept actively growing. Never let the soil become dry. It is best to water early in the day so that the leaves will not be wet during the night. Provide good ventilation and control aphids and cabbage worms—two of the more usual pests of lettuce.

There are many varieties of head lettuce and of leaf lettuce that grow well in a greenhouse. Among the good head lettuce varieties are White Boston, May King, and Boston Market. Grand Rapids Forcing and Salad Bowl are good leaf varieties, and Matchless is a choice Romaine or Cos lettuce.

Mustard

The leaves of such varieties of mustard as Tendergreen, Florida Broadleaf, and Improved Ostrich are useful in salads or can be boiled like spinach. The plants mature in a month or two. A spacing of 6 inches in rows a foot apart is ample for most varieties.

Parsley

These plants are attractive as well as useful for garnishing and flavoring. A half-dozen plants growing in pots or in a bench will generally be ample. For use in winter and early spring, seeds are sown in the fall either in a bench or in a pot. The seeds germinate slowly. Plants are best spaced 4 inches apart in rows 6 or 8 inches apart. Plants from the garden may be moved into the greenhouse in the autumn. When harvesting, it is better to remove a few leaves from several plants rather than many from one plant. In seed catalogs you will find both flat- and curled-leaved varieties listed. Both are suitable for greenhouse culture.

Radishes

Radishes are easy to grow. Because they mature in about a month, they are suitable for intercropping between slower-growing plants. For a succession, sow seeds at two-week or four-week intervals from October on. Seeds are sown in rows

4 inches apart. Sow at the rate of about twenty seeds per foot of row and later thin, leaving eight plants to a foot. A light sandy soil, 5 to 6 inches deep, is suitable for radishes, as is a night temperature of 45 degrees. The soil should be kept moist but not wet.

The globe varieties are preferred for growing in the greenhouse—among them Early Scarlet, Globe Select, Crimson Giant, Cardinal Globe, and Colonial Forcing.

Peas

Peas grow well in a 50-degree house. It takes a large area to provide enough for many meals. Little Marvel is a good dwarf variety for greenhouse culture. You can raise peas in pots, or in the bench in rows 12 inches apart.

Rhubarb

Rhubarb forced in a greenhouse is more tender and tasty than that grown outdoors. In the fall, dig up rhubarb plants from the garden and move them into a cold frame or unheated garage. Cover the crowns with soil or mulch to keep them from drying out. In December or later, move them into the greenhouse. Rhubarb should be forced in darkness. A convenient place is under a bench. With canvas or heavy brown paper, curtain off an area under the bench. Scatter a thin layer of well-rotted manure on the soil. Place the plants on this, packing them close together. Fill the spaces between the roots with soil to the level of the crowns and then water thoroughly. It may be necessary to add more soil. If you prefer, you can plant the crowns in boxes of soil. Two to four weeks later some stalks can be harvested. After the last leaves have been harvested, you can divide the roots and plant them outdoors. These divisions should be grown outdoors for two years before they are forced again.

Vegetables suitable for growing in a 60-degree greenhouse

Bean, cucumber, eggplant, onion, pepper, and tomato grow well in a greenhouse maintained at 60 degrees during the night. If you have plenty of space you may want to grow them all. Of the group, onions, cucumbers, and tomatoes are favorites for greenhouse culture.

Cucumbers

Cucumbers require a greenhouse that does not go below 60 degrees at night, and will do their best in one maintained at 65 degrees, with a rise of 10 degrees during the day, even more when the days are bright. If you want to raise cucumbers as an early summer crop in the greenhouse, plant two to four seeds in each pot or plant band about March 1, and later thin, leaving one vigorous seedling to each pot. Plant in a bench about April 1, spacing them about 2 feet apart each way. A suitable soil is loam, enriched with well-rotted cow manure and a sprinkling of bone meal. Cucumbers require an abundance of water, especially when they are in fruit. Never let the soil become dry.

The plants should be trained to stakes or to vertical strings, either of which should be anchored to horizontal wires strung above the rows and fastened to the greenhouse roof. The lateral branches should be cut back, leaving one to three female flowers on each branch. Flowers must be pollinated if cucumbers are to develop. Perhaps bees will enter the greenhouse and do the work for you, but rather than count on this it is better to hand pollinate the flowers. With a brush, transfer pollen from the anthers of the male flowers to the stigmas of the female ones. The male flowers occur in clusters and the female flowers generally occur singly, or occasionally in groups of two or more. The ovary of the female flower is evident back of the petals, and after pollination it rapidly enlarges and develops into the "cucumber."

Onions

If green onions are a favorite of yours, sow seeds at monthly intervals from fall on. A fall sowing will produce green onions early in the spring. One good variety is White Lisbon, which produces tender, long white onions. Onions grow best with a night temperature of 60 degrees. Seeds are sown half an inch deep and about an inch apart, in rows 6 inches apart. A sandy but rich soil is desirable.

Tomatoes

For tomatoes in spring and early summer, sow seeds in January. For a supply of tomatoes from September until January, sow seeds in June. Seeds are best sown in flats in rows 2 inches apart. After sowing, cover the flat with glass, paper, or burlap until the seeds germinate; then remove the cover. When the seedlings are large enough to handle, transplant them into flats, spacing the plants 2 by 2 inches. The plants may be transplanted from the flats directly to a ground bed or to a bench, or they can be moved into 4-inch pots. If you wish just a few plants, you may grow them satisfactorily in 8- or 10-inch pots, or wooden boxes of about equivalent volume, transplanting them from the 4-inch pots. A soil made up of three parts loam, one of peat, and one of well-rotted manure is excellent. Plants in benches or ground beds should be spaced about 2 by 2 feet or 1½ by 3 feet. It is best to have the soil 8 to 10 inches deep.

In greenhouse culture, plants are grown erect and usually with only one main stem. Remove the side shoots from the axils of the leaves as soon as they develop. Each plant may be supported with a perpendicular string. The string is anchored to a wire at the base of the plant and extends vertically to an overhead wire. As the plant grows, twist the vine around the supporting string. A wooden stake can also be used for support.

Tomatoes should be grown with a night temperature of 60 to 65 degrees and with a day temperature about 10 degrees higher—and even higher when the days are bright.

Tomatoes require an ample supply of moisture. Lack of moisture stunts growth and may cause the flowers to fall off. The plants benefit from overhead syringings on bright days. A complete fertilizer should be applied at intervals. When the foliage shows a paling of color, it is time to fertilize.

Flowers must either be pollinated or treated with a fruit-setting hormone if tomatoes are to develop. You can facilitate pollination by jarring the plants at intervals, or you can use a camel's hair brush to transfer pollen from the pollen sacs to the stigmas of the flowers. Hormones have been discovered to take the place of pollen, and the resulting fruit is seedless. Apply the hormone according to the manufacturer's directions.

Varieties which have been developed especially for greenhouse culture should be selected. Among the varieties that force well are Livingston's Globe Strain A, Livingston's Globe Wilt Resistant No. 3, Michigan State Forcing, and Waltham Forcing.

INDEX